DEATH, SOCIETY,
AND HUMAN EXPERIENCE

DEATH, SOCIETY, AND HUMAN EXPERIENCE

ROBERT J. KASTENBAUM, Ph.D.

Superintendent, Cushing Hospital for the Aged,
Framingham, Massachusetts

SECOND EDITION

The C. V. Mosby Company

ST. LOUIS • TORONTO • LONDON   1981

MOSBY
1906 **75** 1981
YEARS
A TRADITION OF PUBLISHING EXCELLENCE

Editor: Charles K. Hirsch
Manuscript editor: Judi Jamison-Perkins
Design: Gail Hudson
Production: Betty Duncan

SECOND EDITION

The C. V. Mosby Company
11830 Westline Industrial Drive, St. Louis, Missouri 63141

Library of Congress Cataloging in Publication Data

Kastenbaum, Robert.
　Death, society, and human experience.

　Bibliography: p.
　Includes index.
　1. Death—Psychological aspects.　I. Title.
BF789.D4K36　1981　　306　　81-2860
ISBN 0-8016-2640-4　　　　AACR2

C/VH/VH　9　8　7　6　5　4　3　2　1　　02/B/249

For **Velvet**—
a good cat

❖ PREFACE

❖ The physician looks away and begins to speak in an overcontrolled, disembodied tone of voice. . . . A telephone rings unexpectedly and late—much too late—at night. . . . We are invited to the funeral tomorrow of a person we were talking with just the other day. . . .

In such ways does death intrude itself into our lives and thoughts. To be sure, death has never truly been absent either from our personal lives or from the human community in general. But we live in a society in which it is possible to be jolted and astonished by reminders of mortality. People who are otherwise worldly and mature often find themselves unprepared to cope with the intrusion of death into their own sphere of experience. And some people insist there is no point in bringing up this "morbid subject" in advance. The assumption is that our only choices are to ignore death until "our number is up" or to simmer in the juices of anxious depression instead of enjoying life while we have it.

Obviously, neither this book nor anybody interested in picking it up fully shares the assumption that we prepare best for death by not preparing at all. But this book does not address itself solely to musings about mortality. Attention is also directed to the interplay of life and death throughout all levels of our society. How much there is to learn about the structure and themes of society in general by exploring the way we come to terms with mortality! The interplay between the individual and the *death system* richly deserves the keenest sensitivity that any of us can bring to this challenge. This book is concerned, then, not exclusively with the individual or society, but with the individual *in* society. It is deeply concerned with the quality of life—how else to understand whatever is within our power to understand about death?

May I say a few words to the student or instructor who uses this book in association with a course. As a matter of fact, these words apply whether this book is used or is set aside in favor of another. It is extremely difficult to maintain psychological and intellectual balance in a course focusing on death. You start to read or lecture in an objective, open frame of mind, but suddenly you have become engrossed in very personal thoughts and feelings. Or you try to concentrate on the intimate, subjective side of death orientations and find yourself overgeneralizing from your experiences to conclusions about life and death writ large. It is possible to insist that in this course we will focus only on the "gut level," and it is possible to insist that we will instead focus on logical analysis and firm research findings. For what my experiences and suggestions might be worth, I would encourage an approach in which both emotional and intellectual, both individual and socially oriented, both experiential and scholarly facets of the educational process are welcomed.

A book or a course in "death education" can make its most significant contribution if it helps us to integrate our total selves rather than leads us to either "emotional trips" on the one hand or aloof intellectual analysis on the other. There is no better area in which to bring our thoughts, skills, and feelings together.

Tolerance, patience, true *listening*—these are among the qualities that can serve us well in exploring the area of death, society, and human experience. Both instructor and student may stumble occasionally or be momentarily assailed by feelings that might seem to be "irrelevant" or uncontrolled. We have so many self-discoveries to make in this realm (and easier to make when in the company of good-willed, sensitive people) that the ability to tolerate, appreciate, and learn from our occasional "hang-ups" or "missteps" is a precious one. It is also helpful to remember that death concerns may be very close to the person sitting next to you in class, even if today the topic appears to be chiefly an "academic" one to you. A person with serious thoughts of self-destruction, another person either anticipating or mourning the death of a loved one, somebody else whose own life is threatened by illness—people in situations such as these are likely to bring a different set of sensitivities and needs to the situation. Furthermore, tomorrow it may be somebody else (you or I) who feels a more intense involvement with the subject. Instructors will recognize that their responsibilities include but also transcend the responsibilities for offering any type of course. But there is also a basic human responsibility for the students as well that reflection and sensitive attention will gradually reveal. Perhaps it is enough to say that a death education course is not the ideal place for either the instructor or the student who conceives of the learning process as the transfer of "points" from lecture or text to the notebooks and examinations of the student, and nothing more.

This book is also intended for the person of any age who is willing to be his or her own instructor and student combined. The same orientation suggested above applies to this person as well. Be kind and tolerant to yourself. Accept the existence of whatever thoughts and feelings are touched off in you—but, after a pause, reflect on them and see if you can integrate them with the observations offered in this book and the suggested readings. So much the better if you can enter into dialogue with a friend or relation! Sharing of emerging thoughts and feelings not only will help you to articulate and sort them out but also will likely help you to discover new facets of your relationship with the other person.

In the first edition I tried to make sense out of the multitudinous observations and opinions that arose from a decade of renewed death awareness. It was obvious that this phenomenon had its faddish aspects, but it has become increasingly obvious that there are enduring and consequential aspects as well. The closet marked *Death* has been opened, and it is not likely to be locked again.

The author of this second edition is no longer a professor of psychology free to dispense opinion to any and all takers, but the director of a hospital that cares for approximately 500 aged men and women. This was a sought responsibility. I felt the need for a return to substantial contact with people embedded in critical "real life" (and "real death") situations. How, if at all, this different perspective might have affected the revision will perhaps be easier for the reader than for me to determine.

Although the interval between editions has been fairly short, a number of important developments have appeared. The *hospice* has moved resolutely from concept to actuality. It has been my pleasure to add more information on the hospice movement, but it has also been my responsibility to insert some cautions and questions. New studies on *bereavement* have suggested that more attention be given both to its psychophysiological aspects and to individual coping styles. *Innovative and follow-up research* on various death-related topics has continued to appear, and some of the most illuminating investigations have been included throughout the book. Our death system has continued to change so rapidly that I have provided a *mini-history of the death-awareness movement*, bringing it right up-to-date.

"Life after life" has become such a provocative topic in the past few years that at times it has commanded more attention than terminal care, bereavement, suicide, and other basic problems. I welcomed the surfacing of interest in this fascinating topic, although enthusiasms have run far ahead of critical thinking. A new chapter has been devoted to this topic. I have placed the current interest in *near-death phenomena* within the all-but-forgotten historical context and included material on case histories suggestive of *reincarnation* as well. This chapter is intended as an evaluation of what has been done up to this point and a guide to what the future might bring forth.

Throughout the book I have added various other materials that I thought might increase its usefulness. The suicide chapter, for example, includes a *risk-taking self-assessment questionnaire* that you might want to take yourself and share with others. *Case history material* has been added in several places, such as a transcript from ongoing research on parents' perceptions of their children's knowledge of death. The concept of *denial*, so often invoked in death-related situations, has not often been examined critically. I have tried to clarify this concept and also to add and to "touch up" in various other places to take advantage of this opportunity for second thoughts.

The *death system* concept have been found useful by many teachers and researchers. I have freshened it up a bit with new examples drawn from a variety of sources in our own and other cultures.

There are more changes as well, but why deprive those who know the first edition from discovering these themselves? For those who come to the second edition first, I have found no occasion to revise the concluding paragraph of the preface:

I am more grateful than I can say to all those I have learned from in various ways. I cannot utter the ritualistic appreciative words for the person who typed this manuscript, although I think I did a pretty good job of it. But I can and must say that those who author books of this nature in the future definitely should have a live-in consultant with the knowledge and acumen of Bunny Kastenbaum. In fairness, however, I cannot encourage any hopes that she will be available to provide such services to any but this fortunate writer.

Robert J. Kastenbaum

For their comments, suggestions, and criticisms I wish to thank Mary Elizabeth Allen-Minzer, OTR, M.S., University of Wisconsin Center for Health Sciences, and Samuel Z. Glaser, Ph.D., Hofstra University, New York, who reviewed this second edition.

❖ CONTENTS

DEATH, SOCIETY, AND HUMAN EXPERIENCE

CHAPTER 1

❖ INTRODUCTION

❖ A man is falling out of the sky. For just one instant more, he is a living person, a super-executive whose success one might envy. But in the next instant there will be no life in this body, nor will the body itself resemble a human being.

What will society find interesting about this death—and why?

❖ Is she alive? Is she dead? Or some place between life and death? The attractive young woman has been in a deep coma for weeks. She is not aware of the interpersonal, medical, and legal conflict that swirls around her. Anonymous while alive and flourishing, this "sleeping beauty," as one journalist has called her, is now a page-one celebrity.

What is really happening inside and outside this person? Why has society responded in this particular way to her plight? How is such a situation to be understood? And what ought to be done?

❖ The young man has family and friends: Or at least he thinks he has family and friends. His relationship with them has not been the same in recent months, not since it was discovered that he is suffering from leukemia. He now feels as though an invisible but all too effective forcefield separates him from most of the people who had been important

in his life. This disturbance within his intimate social network troubles him even more on a day-by-day basis than the medical problem itself.

Why do so many of us have difficulty relating to a person who has a life-threatening disease? What if anything might be done to improve this situation?

❖ The bed: not her own. The room: somebody else's. The smell of the place: certainly not home. Nothing of home is here. The other people? They do not really know her. The showy rhododendron in the lobby receives more affectionate care. What a place to be. What a place to die.

How is the final phase of life experienced by an aged and dying person? Is the present typical style of death one that should be perpetuated or are there better alternatives to be developed?

❖ The nurse finds herself hospitalized for a vascular condition that is somewhat unusual for her age. She will probably be on her feet again soon, but there is a definite threat to life here that must be controlled. The physician has no way of knowing that this is the third time this woman has become physically ill on the anniversary date of a significant and traumatic event in her personal life.

It is possible that the timing of our deaths or of the crises that threaten our lives could have some relationship to very personal *meanings*? Are we also to believe that people have the ability either to will themselves safely through a crisis or conversely to induce their own death without actually committing suicide?

❖ So quiet is the apartment that the ticking of the kitchen clock dominates the scene. The table is set. The nice dishes. Cloth napkins. Although there is food on the plate before her and she really should be hungry, the woman is hardly eating at all. There is no food on the other plate. There is no person in the other chair.

Do we truly leave the past behind us when a loved one dies? Or do we find ways to keep the lost one alive in our thoughts and feelings? What is the "healthy" way to function after a death? How long should it take for a survivor to "get back to normal"? How well does our society understand and support the bereaved?

❖ "Grandma's been sleeping a long time. A whole, whole month. But she's going to come back soon."

"No, she won't, stupid! Grandma is dead!"

"I *know* that, and don't call me stupid. I just mean that when she gets all through being dead, *then* she'll come back."

"Don't you know anything? *Dead* means she won't ever come back. She never gets through being dead."

(Very quietly, to herself and her doll), "Don't cry. A brother doesn't know *everything*. Grandma will come back when she's through being dead . . . won't she, Taffy?"

How do ideas of death develop from childhood onward? What are children capable of understanding at a particular time in their lives? How can parents, teachers, and others be help-

ful to them in interpreting death-related phenomena?

❖ Two young people have discovered each other at a party. Mutual fascination is rapidly growing.

"Say, Randy, what do you do between parties?"

"Do?"

"You know, work, go to school, whatever."

"I work for my Dad."

"Doing what?"

"Well, Dad, he's sort of a funeral director. . . . Sue? Sue?"

"Oh, that's perfectly all right, Randy. I mean, somebody's got to do that, I guess. But, listen, Randy, it's nothing personal, you know, but I just couldn't, I mean . . ."

What is the social status of people who are closely associated with dying, death, or the dead? How do we treat them? What do we expect from them? Furthermore, why would anybody choose a death-related occupation? Are they mostly very dedicated people, weirdos, or what?

❖ "I appreciate your telling me about this, Mrs. Lynch. I will make sure Danny gets his homework done and that he gets his classroom work back to where it should be."

"It is not just Danny's schoolwork that concerns me, Mrs. Arnold. I don't know quite how to say this, but he doesn't seem to be, well, he's not really the same boy lately. He seems to have trouble concentrating, and he will do things that are just not like him at all. Could there be anything happening lately that . . ."

"You mean at home? No, nothing wrong that I can see. We are all doing . . . as well as can be expected. Everything is under control."

"I don't mean to pry, Mrs. Arnold, or to,

um, but do you suppose that Danny could be reacting to, um . . . ."

"Reacting to what?"

"Mr. Arnold, his father."

"That? No certainly not. He took it very well. A real trooper. We have all pulled together. I'm very proud of Danny, you know. I'm proud of my little man. Anyhow, that was more than a year ago, and he never even talks about it."

How are children affected by the death of a parent—both immediately and over a longer span of time? Does the death of a significant person influence us somehow throughout our lives? Is it better to talk about our losses or to keep the problems to ourselves?

❖ "I felt so-o good. Really peaceful with myself and everything. Maybe this is death, I was thinking, but then what have I been afraid of all this time? If this is what it is, then I could (smiling) stay dead forever! But that figure, that person, that one-man light show I was telling you about: he just wouldn't let me stay dead. I don't know whether he said anything or not, but he blocked my way and made it clear I had to go back. And I didn't want to get back into that body and get back into that life. I was just getting to enjoy myself!"

Reports of near-death experiences have been appearing with increased frequency during the past few years. Have these experiences demonstrated human survival after or through death? And what do they tell us about the times we live in?

These have been a few glimpses of the ways in which our lives interpenetrate with death. We will encounter these situations again and give them more sustained attention. Many specific death-related phenomena are explored on these pages, but the actual variety of such phenomena in our lives is so great that one could

not realistically hope to catalogue, let alone analyze and explain, all such experiences that might await us in our lives. We can, however, address ourselves to many situations and issues. And we can hone our abilities to comprehend the unexpected, unpredictable confrontations with death to which none are immune.

Do we study death in hopes of relieving some of the anxiety and dread that this topic can induce in us? Not a bad idea, although success is not guaranteed.

Or do we study death with the aim of becoming more effective in helping others when they are in peril or in sorrow? Again, a reasonable idea.

Perhaps we study death with a resolve to change the world in some way, unsatisfied with the length or quality of life today. Perhaps we study with the intention of reading the future—how *is* the world changing, and how will these changes affect life and death, whether or not we have the power to influence the outcome?

Yet again, we might study death because like Mt. Everest, it is there, a universal phenomenon, a mighty challenge to both heart and intellect. How could we persuade ourselves that we know life if we maintain a state of ignorance or nonrecognition concerning death? An incisive study of death might provide fresh perspective on our general assumptions, values, and actions.

Clearly, there can be more than one reason to study death. Perhaps your own reason has not even been guessed at here; perhaps it is not quite clear to you at this time. No matter. Curiosity about death and its place in our lives hardly requires justification. Humankind has been curious about death for a long time. Given the choice, we might as well orient this curiosity in a promising direction. Think along with some of the best thinkers. Look at the facts along with some of the best scientists. Explore images and feelings with some of the most sensitive and creative poets, artists, musicians.

One book will not do the job for us: not this book, not any one book, not all the books we might read. Just as death is interwoven with our personal and cultural experiences on many levels, so our inquiries must be varied. And it is doubtful that the persistent mind will ever be fully satisfied. The view of death that you develop now with this book, with a teacher, perhaps, with some friends to talk things over with—this view will endure until it is time to be re-viewed and revised. We change. The world changes. Today's mode of understanding may not stand us in quite so good a stead tomorrow.

This book, then, does not promise a simple package of answers that can be applied to any death-relevant phenomena at any time. It does offer the services of a guide and companion. The book itself has had the advantage of guidance from the best available resources of library and laboratory and from many good people whose experiences and wisdom it has been my privilege to share.

Shall we begin?

CHAPTER 2

❖ DEATH HAPPENS

"While taking my noon walk today, I had more morbid thoughts. What *is* it about death that bothers me so much? Probably the hours."[1]

Woody Allen is not the only person to have asked this question, although few have provided so quick and concise an answer. But another question demands prior consideration: What is death? There is more than one way to define this key term. Each definition carries with it a different set of meanings and potentials for action. This chapter focuses upon one type of definition.

We often think of death as an *event*, something that happens. As a happening, it can be associated with a specific time and place (e.g., early this morning in City Hospital). This view of death seems straightforward enough. In practice, however, the concept of death as event lends itself to a variety of meanings and uses. Consider the following examples.

IN MEDICAL SETTINGS

❖ The surgical team worked together brilliantly. Although it was a very high-risk procedure, there was a definite sense of optimism in the operating room. But the patient's debilitated condition could not withstand the stress and . . . .

And the patient was subsequently pronounced dead, in the recovery room. Given any latitude at all, hospitals typically prefer to delay the pronouncement of death until the patient has been removed from the operating room. It makes for bad morale, perhaps, and bad statistics to show a high death rate in the surgical arena itself. The death event occurs a little while after the operation, in a different room, when this can be arranged; for example, by terminating what appears to be a losing battle soon enough to have the patient moved elsewhere or by postponing the pronouncement while there is still some ambiguity as to whether life has completely ceased.

The nurse's face is almost as white as her uniform. She is near exhaustion from constant and demanding work throughout her shift. Her emotional energy has been drained by responsibility for the care of a terminally ill patient to whom she had become attached over the past weeks. The patient has been sinking rapidly this afternoon, yet the nurse has other sick people to look after as well and also has not forgotten that her husband is counting on her to be fresh and vivacious tonight when they entertain some old friends. Only 15 minutes left on her shift now as she passes the failing patient's room. The nurse mutters to herself, "Oh, Lord! Please don't let him die on me."

In a situation such as this there is not much likelihood that the patient will be moved to another *place*. The death event will happen *here*, on the ward where this nurse works. The timing of the event is uncertain, however. The uncertainty itself creates tension among staff members and among any of the patient's family who might also be on the scene. Whether the death event is considered to occur on or off her own shift is a matter of some concern to the nurse. She herself is not authorized to pronounce a patient dead; officially, the death event is not certified until that judgment is made by a physician.

❖ The old woman is feeling more chipper today. When she entered this hospital, one of the few devoted exclusively to care of the sick aged, she was in low estate both physically and mentally. Good medical and nursing care have helped her to feel stronger and more comfortable. But there is another reason as well for her rise in spirits. When she first realized that she was coming to a hospital for the aged, it was as though a great heavy door had clanged down behind her. Life was over. She had come to the death place. Now she has had some chance to become acquainted with the hospital and observes that, as a matter of fact, there is life as well as death here. She herself has been transferred from the intensive-care unit to a more residential-type ward. There is even a kitchen she is free to use when she feels a little better.

In our society a geriatric facility is often seen as the place to which old people come to die. From an insider's viewpoint, however, the death event may be understood as limited usually to certain areas within the general facility. Death takes place there, not here. It is comforting to know that the death event obeys certain spatial patterns; because it happens most often in a specialized area, this means that one can breathe a little freer so long as one is functioning in another area. The old woman can think about getting on with life again; the death threat has been limited to that far unit a long way down the corridor and off to the right.

IN GENERAL SETTINGS

❖ "It was a perfect apartment. Just what we had been looking for. But when the landlord told me that the last occupant had . . . well, I just didn't feel good about it anymore. Well, what do you think? Would you want to move into a place where a person had just died? It gives me the shivers!"

When death is regarded as an event that occurs in a particular place, it can take on a power to influence our attitudes toward that place. Even among intelligent and educated people there may arise the distressing feeling that a place somehow belongs to death or is contaminated by it.

❖ The guide spoke in a hushed and sober tone. "Yes, this is the place. Here, in this very room, one of the bloodiest deeds in our nation's history. . . ." The tourists listened intently. Two young adolescents in the grouped nudged each other and giggled for no apparent reason.

The place where death happened can be an attraction instead of a threat. If death happened a long time ago, this seems to reduce the peril. And if it happened in an interesting way or to important people, then the attraction aspect is highlighted.

❖ "Naw, I wasn't scared. I volunteered because somebody had to do that job, and it might as well be me. Anyway, how I figure it is that if your time has come, it's come, and there's nothing you can do about it. And if your time hasn't come, then you're going to get through it OK, know what I mean?"

The interpretation of death as an event makes it easier to take a fatalistic view of one's own survival chances. Death will happen when it is going to happen.

COMMENT

The preceding examples, and others that could be given, illustrate some of the functions and implications of the tendency to regard death as an event. Note that specifying a particular time and place for the death event can have the anxiety-lowering benefit of keeping other times and places free of this threat and contamination. This does mean, however, that we pay for this apparent decontamination by loading certain times and places with more than their share of death saturation.

Note also that people in various occupations may have rather different conceptions of death. The nurse providing care for a terminally ill person, for example, senses death as an event edging closer in time. The funeral director becomes an important figure *after* the death event. Within restricted limits, the physician has some control over the specification of the death event: Should it be recorded as of this moment? When the body was discovered half an hour ago? Before that? While medical personnel generally specify the death event within a limited time-space framework, broader classifications may be used elsewhere. Did this soldier die in battle, behind the lines, or off duty? Is it possible to determine the precise hour and place of death, or must this be guessed at? A soldier's widow or child might find it even more difficult to accept and adjust to the death if the particular circumstances remain indeterminate. The military official who releases the information may have some decisions to make regarding how specifically to locate the death event in time and space, given the ambiguities of the information available to him.

By contrast, the minister may be less concerned than the medical personnel who are responsible for terminal care with death as an event. And any of us as individuals may give either much or little attention to the when and where of a death compared to some of its other dimensions and meanings.

ACTIVE OR PASSIVE EVENT

In thinking about *any* kind of event, we are likely to express some impression of its active or passive character. Did this happening happen to us? Or did we make it happen? The work of J. B. Rotter[2] and other social psychologists has called attention in recent years to this aspect of our relationship to life events. Our relationship to the death event often implies either a passive or active characterization as well.

"Death strikes!" is the type of expression that endows the event with a force of its own. By implication, death has attacked its victim, moved aggressively. It is not only an event but an intrusive event. With just a little imagination, we can see death as more than an event: it is an act of malignant intention, aimed at us by outside forces.

The death event can also be seen as having an internal source and a more passive quality: "He passed away to his final reward." The individual himself is in motion. When characterized this way, the death event does not arouse the image of an external act of aggression or of a targeted victim. Instead, we are inclined to think of the death event as the culmination of a process that somehow belongs to the individual himself. Other combinations of internal and external and passive and aggressive features in the death event can also be observed. The person who raises his hand against himself in a suicidal act, for example, may make death happen through an internal, that is, self-motivated, and aggressive route.

There are also circumstances in which we speak of the death event as though it were an interaction: "He met his death on the lonely, windswept highlands." Life and death meet each other halfway. It is neither invasion nor internal cessation, but an event in which the person interacts with his or her environment for the last time.

If we are going to think of death as an event, we are also going to have some thoughts and feelings about the specific characteristics of this event as well as its time-place framework. These thoughts and feelings will require our attention in many contexts. Theoretically, perhaps, we should have the same orientation toward all death events; what the events have in common should outweigh any of the differences among them. Yet in practice, many of us do think, feel, and respond differently, depending upon the time, place, and actual or supposed character of the death event. Additionally, the significance of the death event can differ appreciably from one culture to another and at different periods within the same culture.

SOME FUNCTIONS OF THE DEATH EVENT

The termination of a human life is an event that can evoke a deep response from survivors and witnesses. But this is not invariably the case. Death events can be deliberately invented, for example, to serve other functions. An evening in front of the television set can provide as many incidents of this sort as one is likely to require. In a typical "antihero" detective series, for example, the leading character proceeds from violence to violence en route to bringing a wrongdoer to justice. One homicide between each station break is a conservative estimate. "Bang!" Another body falls. We have witnessed the death event. Why do we not weep, cringe, or respond with any depth of feeling? It is not simply because we are watching a dramatic presentation rather than real life. The same viewer who is totally unmoved by a death event on a routine crime-fighting program might be touched by the death of Shakespeare's Falstaff or by some other vignette in theater, cinema, or television.

One of the likely reasons for our nonresponse is the recognition, which even children quickly learn, that these death events do not matter much in themselves. The deaths serve to advance the plot. The action takes a slightly different turn, keeps moving right along, another character is exited. Seldom do the camera and the pacing give the viewer the opportunity to develop a sense of loss or any strong constellation of thoughts and feelings around the deceased. The action presses forward; the death events themselves have little intrinsic meaning.

By contrast, a death event can take on meanings of a general and enduring nature well beyond its particularities. "The Victorian Age," for example, might be said to have ended with the death of the queen, as had "The Elizabethan Age." While the cultural life-style associated with each of these formidable monarchs did not come to a full and immediate halt with their deaths, it was obvious that things would not continue to be the same. The death of powerful and charismatic individuals has often signaled the end of one epoch of life and the start of another for others in society. Waiting for the death of the powerful leader is often a time of particular tension, and his or her actual demise the signal for intense struggle on the political if not the physical level.

Other death events have impacts that are more localized but still powerful for those affected by them. Has your world been the same since that moment when death took Babe Ruth? Franklin D. Roosevelt? Marilyn Monroe? Mahatma Gandhi? Charles de Gaulle? John F. Kennedy? J. Edgar Hoover? Jack Benny? Duke Ellington? Each of these deaths, for some people, represented the end of an epoch. The event cleaved something significant of what had been from what will be. Within smaller interpersonal networks, the death of a person well known to just a few people can have similar psychological effects. The media may never have heard of a particular person, but the lives of a few people changed forever at the moment he or she died.

Emphasis upon death as an event also sharpens the focus of our attention. Certain questions are likely to come to mind. Was the person free of pain or in agony? With loved ones or abandoned? Conscious until the last or comatose? Were there last words? If so, what were they? In our society today the clinical aspects of the death event seem to be especially prominent. The questions take a more religious or theological direction within some cultural contexts. Did this person die at peace with God? Was the departing soul free to leave in grace, or at the last breathings did the spirit remain sullied by the sins of a lifetime? Public health and medicolegal concerns also cluster around the death event. Precisely what was the cause of death? Distinguish between primary and secondary causes. Distinguish between the most immediate modality of the death event and the background condition from which it emerged. Was the death event a natural occurrence or one in which aggression, neglect, or mismanagement can be detected?

Add one other general concern common in our society today: What should we *do* when the death event seems near at hand? Many people, including technically skilled health personnel, feel uncomfortable in doing nothing, yet have no really appropriate behaviors to fall back on. Waiting for the death event to occur can be a frustrating and anxious experience for those who feel best when they are engaged in efficient actions and exercising close control over the situation.

SUMMARY

Death often is interpreted as an *event*. This implies that death happens at a particular time in a particular place. Our responses to the time-space dimensions of the death event include the tendency to contain death within a limited, specifiable framework so that we can feel relatively free of death at other times and in other places. Other types of response are also illustrated. The death event is seen variously as *active*, *passive*, or *interactive*. It also can serve more than one *function in society*. Examples given include the bland utilization of death as a device to move the plot along in melodramas, but also the profound reorganization of individual and social fabrics of time, as when the death event of a prominent person signals the end of an epoch. Furthermore, emphasis upon death as an event tends to focus attention on details of the final scene. Clinical, religious, and medicolegal concerns often center around *the last moment* (e.g., questions of pain control, spiritual estate, official cause of death). All of these matters can be seen in better perspective as we continue to explore the meanings that have been given to this familiar word, death.

REFERENCES

1. Allen, Woody. *Without feathers*. New York: Random House, Inc., 1975.
2. Rotter, J. B. Generalized expectancies for internal versus external control of reinforcement. *Psychological Monographs*, 1966, *80* (1, Whole No. 609).

CHAPTER 3

❖ DEATH IS

Death is an *event?* Something that happens? If so, then what happens *after* death? In our thought and language we sometimes slip unawares from one concept of death to another. Death is the word we use to describe the event that signals the termination of life. But death is also the word we use for the state of being—or nonbeing—that follows the termination of life. These two interpretations of death suggest radically different relationships to time.

The soloist in Bach's haunting Cantata No. 53 sings

Schlage doch, geunschte Stunde,
brich doch an gewunschter Tag!

Strike, oh strike, awaited hour,
approach thou happy day!

The hour that is awaited eventually will be shown upon the face of an ordinary clock. It belongs to public, shared mortal time. The hour and day of death will be entered into the community's vital statistics. What the devout singer anticipates, however, is entry into a new realm of being in which the time changes of terrestrial life no longer apply. The survivors continue to measure their own lives by clock and calendar. They may also remember that she had been dead for six months, five years, whatever. But this conventional manner of marking time actually has no bearing upon the situation of the deceased. She will have entered into heaven. Time will have ceased for her. It matters not whether one moment or a thousand earth years have passed since the awaited hour struck. The death event simultaneously cleaved her from the community's shared time framework and introduced her to eternity.

This of course is just one interpretation of death as a *state.* Whether or not we share this particular view, it is useful to distinguish clearly between event-oriented and state-oriented interpretations. Even supposedly scientific or learned discussions sometimes suffer by unannounced shifts back and forth. "Death is what comes after death" can be the perplexing assumption when event and state are not distinguished. In this chapter, then, we explore selected aspects of death as a state.

INTERPRETATIONS OF THE DEATH STATE

What death *is* varies considerably from culture to culture and from individual to individual. In what follows here we will be concerned mostly with the basic ideas themselves. How these ideas on the nature of death function in the lives of particular individuals and societies will be suggested at appropriate points later in this book.

Death is: enfeebled life

Young children often think of death as a diminished, rather deprived variation on life. As Maria Nagy learned in her pioneering study,[1] the preschool child is likely to envision the dead person as one who thinks and feels but not very well. A number of little boys and girls have informed me that the people who "live" in the cemetery feel good only once in a while; mostly, they are tired, sad, and don't have much to do.

This view of death as decrement is an ancient one. The little child of today who temporarily holds this interpretation is in a sense carrying forward the belief system common in Mesopotamia thousands of years ago. The deceased person is gradually submerged into the underworld. There he is transformed into a "grisly being" that retains no capacity for value or pleasure.[2] The mightiest ruler and the fairest maiden lose all power and beauty. The dead are equal in their abysmally low estate.

Hebrews of the Old Testament period confronted the gloomy prospect of dwelling in *Sheol*, mere remnants and wretched shadows of what they once had been. This death state held special terror because it signaled isolation from the protective custody of *Yahweh*. God was literally the creator and judge of life. He had no dominion over death. The despairing soul was consigned to a dark realm into which the illuminating and warming presence of God did not reach.[3]

Interpreted in this manner, the death state was more to be feared than the death event; certainly, such a vision of continued existence could bring little if any comfort to the living. Throughout much of the ancient world, this decremental model of the death state prevailed. Neither the achievements of a productive life nor the belief in the culture's reigning theological system were likely to insulate one from the dread of a death state comprised of perpetual enfeeblement and misery. It is worth bearing in mind that this model of the death state was not as yet much affected by moral pressures. Abandonment, depletion, and suffering were the lot of all, or almost all, mortals, the virtuous person as well as the wicked.

Death is: life as usual

Passage from the life familiar on earth has sometimes been interpreted as a transition to, well, more of the same! This idea may seem odd to people in our society today. The death event so obviously wrenches one of us away from the group. Surely, if there is some form of continuation, it must be rather special and different from what has gone on before. Even the decremental model recognized a profound change, if not a desirable one.

Yet a number of tribal societies have pictured the death state as one that has much in common with life as usual. Continuation after the death event is by no means identical with immortality. The individual faces challenges and crises just as before, although their sources might be different. It is even possible for the dead person to be destroyed again. In reviewing what was known about the customs of various Borneo tribes around the turn of this century, for example, Robert Hertz[4] declares that for the Dayak "the soul does not enter the celestial city in order to enjoy an eternal rest there: immortality no more belongs to the inhabitants of the other world than it does to those of this. The soul stays in heaven for a period of seven generations, but each time it has reached the end of one existence it must die in order to be reborn."[4,p.60] The soul returns to earth after its seventh death and there enters a mushroom or fruit near the village. This returned soul invades the body of the woman who chances to eat the mushroom or fruit, and soon is reborn. Should a buffalo, deer, or monkey find this delicacy first, however, the soul will be reborn in animal form—in this case, the saga of this particular being comes to its final termination.

The cyclical model of the death state (to be discussed below) is mingled in this instance with the view of death as a continuation of life's hazardous journey. Cyclical interpretations of death have been rather common. What is distinctive about the belief described here is the accompanying assumption that one goes on through the death state with essentially the same personality, motives, and needs that characterized life before death. Yes, the death event makes a difference. No, it does not mean the person necessarily has become better or worse, more ennobled or more miserable. Although different in some particular respects, death tends to be life as usual.

Death is: perpetual development

Suppose that the universe itself is not completely determined or shaped. All that is really is en route to making something else of itself. And what you and I make of our lives is part of this universal process. What might be the death state in such a universe? For answers to this question we do not turn to the ancient people of Mesopotamia or tribesmen maintaining their traditional customs against the encroachment of contemporary technological society. Instead we consult with prophets and philosophers of evolution, individual thinkers who either anticipated or built upon Darwin's discoveries in fashioning a different view of life and its place in the universe.

The British philosopher Samuel Alexander[5] offered a grand vision of the in-process universe. The "beginning" was a bare time-space manifold from which other levels of existence have emerged and continue to emerge. Life itself was one of the emergent qualities, and mind a quality that has since emerged from life. It is not only life and mind that bud out of space-time, but the entire universe is in process of "flowering into deity." God is still being created. In this thoroughgoing evolutionary framework, we might well expect further transformations in the relationship between life and death. Lloyd Morgan[6] and C. S. Pierce[7] are among the other post-Darwin thinkers who constructed world views in which the idea of *continued development* was prominent for both individual and universe.

For a vivid depiction of development through the death state itself we step back *before* Darwin. Gustav Theodor Fechner was a remarkable person—scientist, humorist, philosopher. Although he is famous today as one of the founders of experimental psychology, this achievement was only a spinoff from his more fundamental interests in the relationship between the realm of the psyche and the realm of the physical world. (Psychology retains the term he gave it, "psychophysical methods," but not the breadth of his interests.) It was in his still little-known book of 1836 that Fechner proposed a perpetual development model of the death state.[8] He began by likening the death event to birth: transition to a freer mode of existence in which tremendous new possibilities for spiritual growth can be found. Titled *The Little Book of Life After Death*, it might as appropriately be read as *The Little Book of Life Through Death*.

The role of both the individual and society are celebrated in this philosophical construction. The so-called living and the so-called dead can interact on a spiritual level to advance universal development. Precisely what the death state is or means to the individual depends on the stage of spiritual development that had been attained up to the moment of the death event:

This is the great justice of creation, that every one makes for himself the conditions of his future life. Deeds will not be requited to the man through exterior rewards or punishments; there is no heaven and no hell in the usual sense . . . after it has passed through the great transition, death, it unfolds itself according to the unalterable law of nature upon earth; steadily advancing step by step, and quietly approaching and entering into a higher existence. And, according as the man has been good or bad, has behaved nobly or basely, was industrious or idle, will find himself possessed of an organism, strong or weak, healthy or sick, beautiful or hateful, in the world to come, and his free activity in this world will determine his relation to other souls, his destiny, his capacity and talents for further progress in that world.[8,pp.17-18]

The death state, then, varies from person to person. Theoretically at least, a "Spiritual Development Quotient," similar to intellectual, moral, or maturational scales that are applied in psychology today, might be established to rate each of us at any point up to and including our death event. The death state not only varies among people, but it is not a fixed, motionless state. It is in the nature of the evolutionary universe for change to occur, and emphasis is placed upon a perpetual process of change for the better. By "better," Fechner and some others intend a condition of higher consciousness. In this crucial sense, then, the death state provides everyone with at least the opportunity to become more alive than ever.

Death is: waiting

What happens after the death event? We wait. In our own society, this tends to be a triphasic conception: (1) beginning with a sleeplike or suspended animation period that is (2) terminated by the dramatic Day of Judgment, after which (3) the soul proceeds to its ultimate destination or condition. In the familiar phase, "the sleeper awakens," receives judgment and takes his "place" either for "eternity" or "for all time" (concepts that are not identical but that generally are treated as though functionally equivalent).

These phases may be emphasized differently by particular individuals and societies. Some Christians, for example, associate chiefly to the taking-a-good-long-rest phase. Others focus attention upon the critical moment of judgment. Still others, contemplate that ultimate phase when sorrows and anxieties will have passed away, the just rewarded, and everlasting radiance and peace prevail. By contrast, descriptions of custom and belief in ancient Egypt[9] lead one to suppose that the act of judgment occurred more promptly after the death event. Emphasis was more upon the judgment and final state periods that the waiting phase.

This general conception of the death state has been characterized as *waiting* to emphasize its time-related characteristics. A tension exists between the death event itself and the end state. The dead may seem to be at rest but, for those with particular religious views, it is a restful waiting. Furthermore, the sense of waiting cannot be contained on just one side of the grave. The aged and the critically ill at times may be regarded as waiting for death. From a broader perspective, all the living, regardless of their present health status, are only putting in time until they too move through the event into the state of death. The waiting is not over until all souls have perished and awakened for judgment and final disposition. Not everybody shares this view of death and its relationship to deity, of course. But it embodies a sense of time-oriented process between the moment of life's cessation and a final outcome that influences and is influenced by our total pattern of life.

Death is: cycling and recycling

One of the most traditional and popular conceptions of the death state is also one of the most radical. Death comes and goes, wending in and out of life. Like the decremental model mentioned earlier, the cyclical interpretation often is expressed by children: after a person has been dead for a while, he will probably get up again. Adults also have regarded the death state as a temporary condition that alternates with life or that represents a transition stage between one form of life and another. It has, for example, been seen as one position on a constantly revolving wheel, the great wheel of life and death. Many examples of this view are given in Philip Kapleau's interesting little book, *The Wheel of Death*.[10] He points out that the wheel itself is one of the basic symbols of Buddhism. Another important symbol is that of flame passing from lamp to candle. This is meant to indicate a rebirth that continues an ongoing process rather than the simple transference of a substance. Kapleau also reminds us of the *phoenix*, "a mythical bird of great beauty who lived for five hundred years in the desert. It immolated itself on a funeral pyre and then rose from its own ashes in the freshness of youth, living another cycle of years."[10,p.viii] The phoenix represents both death and regeneration.

Kapleau argues that the cyclical view of life and death is more rational than many people in our own society are willing to grant.

The assertion that nothing precedes birth or follows death is largely taken for granted in the West, but however widely believed, it is still absurd from a Buddhist viewpoint. Such as assertion rests on the blind assumption—in its own way an act of faith— that life, of all things in the universe, operates in a vacuum. It asks us to believe that this one phenomenon, the invigoration of supposedly inert matter, springs out of nowhere and just as miraculously disappears without a trace. Most people who hold such views consider themselves "rational," and yet in this question of life and death they deny the conservation of energy, one of the essential laws of physics.[10,p.xvii]

Anthropological observations indicate that the recycling of life through the death state is an article of faith for many peoples. One excellent guide to this area is *Wisdom of the Serpent* by Joseph L. Henderson and Maud Oakes.[11] This book is replete with examples drawn from the world's mythology. We learn, for example,

how people living at great distances from each other have somehow arrived at similar interpretations of cyclical phenomena, how life-and-death cycles readily become seen as a natural part of the rhythms of nature. The serpent in the title of their book is just one of many symbols of rebirth from the death state (although usually given a different interpretation when it wriggles into the Garden of Eden). Another classical examination was conducted late in the nineteenth century by Sir James George Frazer, most accessible now in revised and abridged form as *The New Golden Bough*.[12] Both sources indicate how gods and natural phenomena, as well as human lives, are seen to pass from one manifestation to another. Indeed, it would be difficult to find a more common or universal theme than the cycling and recycling of life through death.

The name chosen for a newborn often reflects the recycling view of the death state. The LoDagaa of West Africa, for example, believe that a male child who dies quite young will return to his mother's womb to be reborn. The name and family position of the deceased child is bestowed upon the baby boy who next appears on the scene.[13] Philip Aries[14] tells us that in French medieval art, the soul often was depicted "as a little child who was naked and usually sexless. . . . The dying man breathes the child out through his mouth in a symbolic representation of the soul's departure."[14,p.36] And by the way, whom were you named after . . . and why?

Death is: the endpoint of biological process

The death event takes time, perhaps a little, perhaps more than a little. Theoretically, when the death event itself has terminated, that is, when life has ceased, then the death state prevails. But the distinction is not easy to make either in theory or in practice. Does the death state begin when the heart stops? When breath fails? When the individual does not respond to external stimulation? These are among the tests that have been applied. For years, however, careful medical observers have been aware that such tests can be in error.[15,16]

The development of new techniques for determining the absence of life has altered the dimensions of the problem but not solved it. Much of the discussion today centers around electrical activity of the brain. Some specialists propose that a person be regarded as dead when a flat EEG recording has been obtained for a 24-hour period; others believe that a shorter time period is sufficient. Whatever the technical disagreements about the precise measurement and duration involved, there is a current trend toward accepting brain death as the critical factor in certifying death. This approach achieved particular influence when it was incorporated as a key component in the recommendations of a committee of the Harvard Medical School under the chairmanship of Henry K. Beecher.[17]

Consider the opening paragraph of this committee's report:

Our primary purpose is to define irreversible coma as a new criterion for death. There are two reasons why there is need for a definition: (1) Improvements in resuscitative and supportive measures have led to increased efforts to save those who are desperately injured. Sometimes these efforts have only partial success so that the result is an individual whose heart continues to beat but whose brain is irreversibly damaged. The burden is great on patients who suffer permanent loss of intellect, on their families, on the hospitals, and on those in need of hospital beds already occupied by these comatose patients. (2) Obsolete criteria for the definition of death can lead to controversy in obtaining organs for transplantation."[17,p.55]

This statement makes it clear that medical thinking about the death state is changing. Could this possibly mean that the death state itself is changing? Is the death state whatever a physician or committee of physicians agrees to call it at a particular point in time? And as technology and social need continue to change, will the death state be revised again, and again? Furthermore, what does it mean if criteria for the definition of death can become obsolete? Do we have a firm, unqualified biomedical definition of death hidden away someplace, or is this to be one more condition that must be interpreted relatively, not absolutely?

We will have several further occasions to explore the boundaries between death as event and death as state in the course of this book. For the moment we will simply acknowledge that the person who wishes to maintain that death is the endpoint of biological process has not so much of a definitive answer at his command as he does a set of complex questions that challenges our facts, logic, and values.

Death is: no state at all

Perhaps we are deceiving ourselves, ensnared in habits of thought and language, when we imagine death to be any kind of state at all. Dying is something. There are bodily changes, feelings, behaviors, processes. The death event is something: the (at least potentially) observable cessation of life processes. But death as a state? Death is nothing. It is absence of life, absence of process, absence of qualities. Whatever we attribute to the death state has the effect of reification, that is, converting a convenient abstraction into an actual phenomenon.

This approach to the definition of death has some obvious disadvantages. Most of us are accustomed to thinking of death as something. Even those who do not believe in any form of afterlife and pride themselves on tough-minded objectivity often speak of death as though it were some kind of state. Indeed, it is very difficult to unthink and unspeak death as a state. We know little about *nothing*; our minds do not know what to do with themselves unless there is at least a little something to work with. Call death a void or a great emptiness. Does that really preserve the idea of death as a non-state, or does it instead allow us slyly to construct images that can stand in the place of nothing? Perhaps there are not many people who care for the definition of death as nonstate, and fewer still who would exercise the necessary mental rigor to stick faithfully to this view. Nevertheless, this survey of approaches to the death state would not have been complete without including the possibility that the best way to conceptualize death is not to conceptualize it at all.

A FEW IMPLICATIONS

What we think death *is* can have an important influence on our thoughts, feelings, and actions. A person may refuse to approach or touch a corpse, even though it is that of an individual much beloved to him or her. Many of our ancestors in the world of the Old Testament revered their aged and attempted to bring comfort to them. But who would want to be contaminated by contact with a body that was beyond the pale of life and by so doing dip one's own hand into the dark and dismal stream of *Sheol?* The notion of the death state as somehow representing an outcast status for the soul, with resultant power to harm the living, is not necessarily limited to people of ancient times and distant lands. There are both religious rituals and individual behavior patterns on the current scene that have as their purpose the avoidance of contact with the alien and contaminating aura of the dead human body.

By contrast, if death is waiting, and waiting is mostly a restful sleep, then the terminally ill person can say along with the late Stewart Alsop that "as the sleepy man needs to sleep, so the dying man needs to die."[18] Yet the prospect of waiting will be anything but tranquil for the person who is attuned to the moment of judgment instead of the interlude between death event and final state. Two people, good Christians both, and both stricken with the same life-threatening ailment, might differ in their specific anticipations of death and therefore in their here-and-now mood and behavior.

Still again, a person who shares the vision of a universe in process might confront the terminal phase of life with more than acceptance. Like Fechner, such a person might see in the death state an unprecedented opportunity for spiritual development. Why then not move enthusiastically into this realm?

These are but a few of the implications that can be drawn from the varying conceptions of death as a state. Certainly, if we wish to understand how people confront their own death and the death of others, some attention must be given to their core conceptions of what death *is*.

SUMMARY

Death often is interpreted as a *state* as well as an event. But the particular kind of state that we have in mind when we think of death varies considerably from person to person and from culture to culture. Several views of the death state have been considered here. Death has been seen as a more enfeebled form of life, a decremental model known both to ancient Mesopotamians and young children today. Some have regarded death as essentially the continuation of life as usual, with both individual personality and the hazards of existence persisting. This was illustrated by the beliefs and customs of certain tribespeople in Borneo. Imaginative, evolution-oriented thinkers such as Morgan, Alexander, and Fechner have proposed the concept of a universe that is still being created and in which the human spirit is capable of perpetual development. On this view, the death state offers but another medium through which both the individual and humanity in general can achieve self-actualization.

For many people in our own society, the

death state comprises three stages: (1) sleep or suspension; (2) the enactment of divine judgment; and (3) final disposition of the soul. *Waiting* is one of the primary characteristics of this interpretation of the death state. The dead, in effect, are in eternity's waiting room until that instant when all souls are to be judged and given their ultimate place. Another conception, very popular over the centuries and still common in our own times, is that of death as part of a series of cycles, the great wheel of life and death. Although associated strongly with Buddhism, the cyclical view of the death state appears in many other societies as well.

It is also common to regard death as the endpoint of biological process. This conception seems clear and straightforward in its broad outline but becomes more complex and controversial when examined in detail. There is much activity on the current scene intended to establish a firm demarcation between death as event and death as state, largely because of new developments in medical technology and therapeutics. Perhaps the simplest and for that reason most difficult conception to comprehend, however, is death as a nonstate. Death is *nothing;* to say anything at all that attributes actual qualities, dimensions, or properties to this nonstate would be a self-deceptive falsification.

A few implications of these various approaches to the death state (or nonstate) were touched upon; more will be encountered in subsequent chapters.

REFERENCES

1. Nagy, M. The child's theories concerning death. In H. Feifelo (Ed.), *The meaning of death.* New York: McGraw-Hill Book Co., 1959. (Reprinted from *Journal of Genetic Psychology,* 1948, *73,* 3-27.)
2. Brandon, S. G. F. *The judgment of the dead.* New York: Charles Scribner's Sons, 1967.
3. Bultmann, R. *Life and death.* London: A. & C. Black, Ltd., 1965.
4. Hertz, R. *Death and right hand.* Glencoe, Ill.: The Free Press, 1960.
5. Alexander, S. *Space, time, and deity* (2 vols.). London: Macmillan & Co., 1920.
6. Morgan, L. *Emergent evolution.* London: Williams & Norgate, Ltd., 1923.
7. Pierce, C. S. *Chance, love, and logic.* New York: Harcourt, Brace, & Co., 1923.
8. Fechner, G. T. *The little book of life after death* (1836). Boston: Little, Brown & Co., 1904.
9. Gardiner, A. *The attitude of ancient Egyptians to death and the dead.* Cambridge, England: Cambridge University Press, 1935.
10. Kapleau, P. *The wheel of death.* New York: Harper & Row, Publishers, 1971.
11. Henderson, J. L., & Oakes, M. *Wisdom of the serpent: the myths of death, rebirth, resurrection.* New York: Macmillan, Inc., 1971.
12. Frazer, Sir James. *The new golden bough* (Rev. ed.). New York: Doubleday & Co., Inc., 1959.
13. Goody, J. *Death, property, and the ancestors.* Palo Alto, Calif.: Stanford University Press, 1962.
14. Aries, P. *Centuries of childhood.* New York: Alfred A. Knopf, Inc., 1962.
15. Shrock, N. M. On the signs that distinguish real from apparent death. *Transylvanian Journal of Medicine,* 1835, *13,* 210-220.
16. Ducachet, H. W. On the signs of death, and the manner of distinguishing real from apparent death. *American Medical Record,* 1822, pp. 39-53.
17. Beecher, H. K. A definition of irreversible coma: report of the "ad hoc" committee of the Harvard medical school to examine the definition of brain death. In D. R. Cutler (Ed.), *Updating life and death.* Boston: Beacon Press, 1968.
18. Alsop, S. *Stay of execution.* Philadelphia: J. B. Lippincott Co., 1973.

CHAPTER 4

❖ DEATH IS LIKE

Sometimes we try to comprehend a strange phenomenon by comparing it to one that is more familiar. This happens frequently when we think and speak of death. Not entirely persuaded by our own grasp of this concept, or attempting to convey what we mean to others, we may call upon analogy. It is really a two-way process: we liken death to something else, or we liken something else to death. Exploring some of our death analogies will further expand our appreciation of the varied mental pathways by which we approach and retreat from this topic and lead us as well into certain problem areas that deserve sustained attention in their own right.

CONDITIONS THAT RESEMBLE DEATH
Inorganic and unresponsive

Developmental psychologists have learned that young children tend to think of certain natural phenomena as being somehow alive or animate.[1,2] Clouds float across the sky because that is how they enjoy themselves. The sun rises through its own power to make sure that we know it is morning. Adults through the centuries have also been impressed by the active quality of some natural phenomena, such as fire, lightning, and the flooding river, and have based core analogies and metaphors around them.

Similarly, one can also be impressed by the *lack* of activity in the world. This kind of perception sometimes leads to a sense of comforting stability. Look upon those everlasting mountains. They were here in the days of our ancestors and will continue to tower above our children's children. At other times, however, the inert, unresponsive character of some features in the physical environment elicits a sense of deadness. "Stone cold dead in the marketplace" goes one old phrase. The parallel with the stiff form of a cadaver is obvious enough. "Stone cold" reinforces the deadness of the dead.

"I am a rock!" declared the popular Paul Simon–Art Garfunkel duo. As the song reminds us, "a rock feels no pain." The hard, unyielding surface contrasts greatly with human flesh and spirit that can be wounded so easily. The person who is suffering or who is overcome with a sense of vulnerability may seem to envy the durability and unresponsiveness of the rock. For a living person to liken himself to stone suggests a fascinating compromise: "I live, but to do so I must not experience life."

Stone as a representation of death is also familiar to us through a succession of mythological unfortunates who were instantly transformed from flesh and blood into insensate rock by unfortunate incident or unwise action—a glimpse of Medusa's terrifying visage, that backward glance upon leaving Hades. . . .

The subsequent discovery of human bodies actually hardened into stone as a result of the historic volcanic eruption that destroyed Pompeii blends into this view. And it was not long ago that our own newspapers and other media were filled with reports of Watergate defendants who were trying to "stonewall it." Keeping up an unyielding appearance in the midst of stress is another variation on the theme.

The apparently inert, unresponsive, enduring features we see in some aspects of our physical environment serve as a ready representation of death to be used as a support for thought, an emphasis in language, or even a partial identification when we are troubled.

But we live in an invented as well as a natural world. The machine provides us with another readily accessible analogy. The motor has died. Perhaps a dead battery is at fault. Whatever the specific cause, this piece of apparatus no longer works. We age, and we see our machines wear out. We see death, and we see machines abandoned and scrapped. The family that lived close to the rhythms of earth had fire and stone to inspire representations of life and death. We have added the mechanical and electronic apparatus, from the windmill to the computer and beyond.

Take one situation in particular. Stand at the bedside of a critically ill person whose life is being sustained only through connections with a whole battery of contrivances. Interpret, if you can, the kind of process that is going on. Is it a person living? Or a set of machines functioning? Or again, can it best be understood as an interwoven bioelectromechanical process in which the human and nonhuman components have merged to form a special system of their own? While you are considering the situation, it ends. But *what* has ended? Do we say the the machines failed or the body? The point here is that today the machine is more than a casual analogy to human life. It is very easy for medical personnel to look upon the termi-

nation of human life as a sort of mechanical failure, for machines of various type have been integrally involved in diagnosis and treatment, and the personnel have learned in their own training much that is conducive to a mechanical analogy.

Perhaps we have here something more than analogy. When we liken death to the hard, cold unresponsiveness of a stone we usually recognize that we are dealing in an evocative figure of speech. But the distinction between analogy and solid fact is often blurred in current treatment of the terminally ill. Failure of the machine can be seen as failure of the machine that is the person as well. Unless alternative conceptions of the human person and of the death state are in evidence, the scene as the end of life approaches may come increasingly under the domination of a mechanical analogy that is not even clearly recognized as analogy.

Sleep and altered states of consciousness

Sleep has long served as another natural analogue to death. The ancient Greeks pictured sleep *(Hypnos)* as twin brother to death *(Thanatos)*. Herman Feifel reminds us that "many of our religious prayers entwine the ideas of sleep and death. Orthodox Jews, for example, on arising from sleep in the morning thank God for having restored them to life again."[3, p. 120]

Apart from its direction religious significations, sleep sometimes is used as a more gentle, less threatening way of speaking about the death state. However, when children are told that a deceased person is only sleeping, it is appropriate to question what message is intended and what message is coming across. Does the parent intend to soften the impact of death somewhat or essentially to deny that death has occurred at all? The young child is not likely to have a firm grip on the distinction between sleep and death. The analogy, no matter how intended, may register as reality. "Go to sleep!" a child is told late in the evening. Early in the day, this same child may have been told by the same parent that Grandmother is asleep or that death is a long sleep. In these circumstances, we should not be surprised if the child has some difficulty in falling or remaining asleep. Indeed, many children do have nightmares in which death-related themes are prominent.[4] Furthermore, adults as well as children may experience insomnia as a symptom of disturbance when death has intruded in their lives. While working in a geriatric hospital, for example, experience taught me to expect insomnia and other nocturnal disturbances on a ward where a patient had died unexpectedly. An aged man or woman might speak matter-of-factly about the death and seem not to have been personally affected to any appreciable degree but that night awaken in terror and confusion, seeking the company of a living face and comforting word.

Whether used appropriately or inappropriately, however, sleep remains one of the most universal, easily conveyed analogues of death. Myth and fairy tale abound in examples of characters who, believed dead, are actually in a deep, possibly enchanted sleep. Snow White and Sleeping Beauty are among the examples best known to our children.

Altered states of consciousness occurring in sleep or resembling sleep have also been taken as analogies to death. A person may dream he is dead or actually experience while lying in a not quite conscious state the sense of being frozen, immobilized, powerless to act. Drug- and alcohol-induced states of mind sometimes are likened to death, either as a joyful or a terrifying "trip." Certain medical procedures have produced experiences described as deathlike by the survivors, sometimes by the onlookers as well. Insulin coma therapy is one such example. This form of treatment for severely disturbed psychiatric patients profoundly alters the individual's mental, emotional, and physical condition. The experience has been described as terrifying by many who have gone through it and there is, in fact, risk of actual death involved medically. This treatment modality is seldom used today.

Normal sleep is not identical with the various other altered states of consciousness that occur as a result of disease, trauma, drugs, alcohol, or other special influences. The coma of the seriously ill person, for example, is not likely to represent the same psychobiological state as what we usually know as sleep, but the distinction is sometimes neglected. The temporary loss of consciousness in some epileptic seizures has at times been interpreted as a deathlike state (e.g., Freud's commentary on the meaning of Dostoevski's seizures).[5] It remains prudent, however, to keep the different types of altered states of consciousness distinguished from each other and from normal sleep. This is good practice if we wish to select the most appropriate analogy for death, as well as to keep our facts straight. For example, we might want to liken death to either a normal or a drugged sleep, to a stormy seizure, or to a low ebbing that may eventually recycle its way back to the waking state. As you can see, it is possible to relate the choice of death analogy to a more general conception of death as state or event.

BEINGS THAT RESEMBLE OR REPRESENT DEATH

In the human mind, death has often taken on the shape and characteristics of a living creature. It may be a mythological being, a known animal, or a creature that appears in human form. Death beings are found in folklore, plays, poems, music, and motion pictures and in our own waking and sleeping fantasies. Let us take a partial and selective inventory of death as a being.

Fabulous beings

Why is that man tied to the mast of his ship? Ulysses knows the peril that confronts him. Enormous birdlike creatures with the heads of women menace him and his crew. Some are perched on a rock, trying to lure them hither with sweet song; others are circling near the vessel. Well before the classical period of Greek achievement, Homer had spoken of these evil creatures who bring a violent death.[6] Vases, urns, and other treasures from the Corinthians, Etruscans, and their neighbors depict this scene. The hybrid bird-person has been a major figure in art and mythology for many centuries; in some contexts it has also been seen as the incarnation of agonizing death. Not all winged or flying beings are associated with death, or with violent death in particular, but such imagery is very common. In post-Homeric Greek times, *sirens* were distinguished from *harpies*. Both were rather nasty creatures, but while sirens brought death, harpies had the special knack of obliterating memory. Death, then, might come with or without loss of memory, and this distinction, at least during one moment in human history, has been represented by two different creatures.

The winged hybrid at other times was depicted as a soul-bird. This was a representation of the spirit leaving the body at time of death, suggesting resurrection. Later in history the bird-persons are joined by a variety of fish-persons, many of whom are also associated with death. The hybrid death beings usually are portrayed as females. Some historians hold that among ancient peoples there was a tendency for peaceful death to be represented in masculine terms, while painful and violent death came through female agencies. Perhaps it is best to suspend judgment on this point until the symbolic currents in ancient cultures have been thoroughly reexamined by feminist scholars. It is clear, in any event, that females dominate in the various flying and swimming figures that swarmed about in those days.

One particularly interesting change occurred in the character of these soaring death beings between the archaic and classical period in Greece. Some of these creatures became transformed into *Muses*. The Muses, as we know, hover about creative souls to inspire their efforts. But Muses also had the function of singing at funerals and guiding departed souls to their new journey through the underworld rather than to mutilation and destruction. For those who entertained hopes of immortality, the Muses were also the indispensable guides.[7]

Orpheus was a being fabulous for his powers rather than his appearance. He appeared as a human, whether or not he is best regarded as ordinary mortal or god. A master musician, Orpheus represented power over death. He could not only liberate Eurydice from Hades through his song but could also bring rocks and trees to life. Orpheus belongs with those personified symbols of resurrection that the human mind has created over the centuries, such as the *phoenix* mentioned in the preceding chapter.

The human *skeleton* obviously differs both from winged hybrids and the magical musician. Palpably, the skeleton represents the physical remains of an actual deceased person. But the skeleton has also enjoyed a long career as a fabulous, animate being. Examples can be found from scattered sources in the ancient world. The skeleton's heyday, however, came in medieval Europe. It appears in numerous works of art, most frequently around the fifteenth century. We see it, for example, bearing a scythe on its shoulder and confronting a young man with the world behind them and hell underneath—this on the title page of one of many books of the time called *Ars Moriendi*

(The Art of Dying).* It is also a prominent figure in van Eyck's rendering of *The Last Judgement,* its appearance in this instance well described by Kathi Meyer-Baer as "a Satan-skeleton."[8,p.294]

The animate skeleton did not simply pose for pictures. It danced! One whirl with this dancer was all that a mortal needed. Colloquial terms in the fourteenth and fifteenth centuries that referred to performing or taking part in the Dance of Death also meant to die. These were centuries of virulent and lethal disease, the foremost being outbreaks of the bubonic plague, or (black death). Images of the Dance of Death flourished during this period.

> In all versions of the Dance of Death the skeleton is the leader and is intended to represent death. The figures are shown either in a series of single scenes, where death confronts representatives of different ways of life and different age-groups, or the skeleton leads a kind of procession or pageant, a procession which sometimes takes the form of a round . . . there is sometimes an open grave before the dying person.[8,p.299]

Death is a quiet, almost sedate dancer; such is its power that extreme movements are not required.

We have not entirely misplaced this representative of death today. It dangles from many a door on Halloween, and the image of skull and crossbones remains familiar on bottles containing poisonous substances, highway safety brochures, and old Erroll Flynn pirate films. More lavishly, the skeleton represents death conspicuously on the Mexican Day of the Dead,[9] often in the form of skull-shaped hunks of sugar or candy.

---

*The Ars Moriendi tradition is well described by Nancy Lee Beaty in *The Craft of Dying* (New Haven: Yale University Press, 1970). The most significant literary work in this tradition is Jeremy Taylor's *The Art of Holy Dying,* first published in 1651 (New York: Arno Press Reprint, 1977).

These are but a few of the shapes resembling and representing death that have formed themselves in the human mind.

In person

"Man be my metaphor!" declared the poet Dylan Thomas. The human form has in fact been a significant metaphor in the realm of death. Picturing death as a person seems to come readily to many children.[10] Furthermore, children's games throughout the centuries often have involved the participation of a death-resembling character.[11] More will be said about the child's personification of death in a later chapter. Here we focus upon the death personifications of adults in our own society.

My first study on this topic asked 240 mostly young adults the following questions: "If Death were a person, what sort of a person would Death be? Think of this question until an image of death-as-a-human-being forms in your mind. Then describe Death physically, what Death would *look* like. . . . Now, what would Death *be* like? What kind of personality would Death have?[12,p.155] If age and sex of death were not specified spontaneously, the respondent was then asked to do so. Another 421 people were asked to respond to a multiple-choice format in a follow-up study: "1. In stories, plays and movies, death is sometimes treated as though a human being. If you were writing a story in which one character would represent Death, would you represent Death as (a) a young man, (b) an old man, (c) a young woman, (d) an old woman? If other, please specify. 2. Would death be (a) a cold, remote sort of person, (b) a gentle, well-meaning sort of person, (c) a grim, terrifying sort of person?"[12]

Four types of personification were offered with some frequency by the participants in the open-ended study.

The *macabre* personification vividly depicted ugly, menacing, vicious, repulsive characteristics. "I see Death as something I don't want to see at all," replied one undergraduate. "He or she—I guess it's a He, but I'm not sure—has jagged, sharp features. Everything about how he looks looks sharp and threatening, his bony fingers with something like claws on the end of all of them, even a sharp nose, long, sharp teeth, and eyes that seem as though they can tear and penetrate right into you. Yet all this sharpness is almost covered over by . . . hair, bloody, matted hair." A young nurse had difficulty in personifying death at first and then said, "I can imagine him, Death, being nearby. It makes me feel trembly and weak, so I don't want to take a good look at him. No look at him could be good, anyhow, if you know what I mean. I feel his presence more than actually see him. I think he would be strong, unbelievably strong and powerful. It would make your heart sink if you really had to look at him. But if he wanted you, there wouldn't be anything you could do about it."

Macabre personifications sometimes included signs of physical deterioration as well as sheer unattractiveness. It was fairly common for the respondents to express personal emotional reactions to their own creations; for example, "When I look at this person—don't think it isn't possible—a shivering and nausea overwhelms me."[12,p.156] The macabre personification often was seen to be an old person and almost always as a terrifying being who is the sworn enemy of life. The relationship between age and type of personification is not so simple, however, as the next image reveals.

The *gentle comforter* could hardly be more different. Although usually pictured as an aged person, there was little physical and no psychological resemblance to Mr. Macabre. The gentle comforter was the personification of serenity and welcome. People who gave this kind of personification generally were those who found the task easiest and most pleasant to do. A typical example is this one from a registered nurse:

A fairly old man with long white hair and a long beard. A man who would resemble a biblical figure with a long robe which is clean but shabby. He would have very strong features and despite his age would appear to have strength. His eyes would be very penetrating and his hands would be large.

Death would be calm, soothing, and comforting. His voice would be of an alluring nature and, although kind, would hold the tone of the mysterious. Therefore, in general, he would be kind and understanding and yet be very firm and sure of his actions and attitudes.[12,p.157]

Although often seen as an aged person, the gentle comforter could also be seen as a younger individual, most often a male. Respondents were not always clear as to whether this was a male or female being, and the importance of this distinction varied from one participant to the next. In general, this personification seems to represent a powerful force quietly employed in a kindly way.

The *gay deceiver* is an image of death usually seen as a young and appealing or fascinating individual. This personification can be either male or female, often with sexual allure. The gay deceiver tends to be an elegant, knowing, worldly-wise person who can either provide one with or guide one to tempting adventure. But "one could not trust him. He would be e elusive in his manners, hypocritical, a liar, persuasive. Death would first gain your confidence. Then, you would learn who he really is, and it would be too late."[12,p.160]

One young woman described Death in the following manner:

She is beautiful, but in a strange way. Dark eyes and long dark hair, but her skin is pale. She is slender, and she is sophisticated looking. . . . I imagine her beckoning me to come with her. She will take me to a new circle of people and places, a lot fancier, more exotic than what I have in my own life. I feel sort of flattered that she would want my company, and I sort of want to go with her, to discover what I may have been missing. . . . But I am scared, too. How will this evening end?

The gay deceiver is unique for its mixture of allure, excitement, and danger. Death remains the outcome, but at least the getting there seems interesting.

The *automaton* is relatively undistinguished in appearance. In fact, the physical hallmark of this personification is that you might pass him by in the street or in almost any situation and not really notice him. The automaton tends to be dressed somewhat conservatively. There are no obvious mannerisms. If there is any distinctive quality, it is a sort of matter-of-fact blandness or a vacant kind of facial expression. One woman, for example, characterized him as

having no feeling of emotion about his job—either positive or negative. He simply does his job. He doesn't think about what he is doing, and there is no way to reason with him. There is no way to stop him or change his mind. When you look into his eyes you do not see a person. You see only death.[12,p.159]

Essentially the automaton appears in human guise but lacks human qualities. He does not lure, comfort, or terrify; he is merely an unresponsive employee or representative who is just doing his job.

On the multiple-choice version of this task, respondents were most likely to see death as "a gentle, well-meaning sort of person"; the "grim, terrifying" image was the least frequently cited. Death usually was personified as a relatively old person. Among all the types of people sampled (college students, nurses, student nurses, geriatric personnel, and funeral directors), masculine personifications were given more frequently than feminine. It should be obvious that these samples do not represent the total population structure of our society and that much more extensive study is needed.

Some possible meanings of representing death as person or as fabulous being will be explored later in this chapter and in other contexts during the course of this book.

CONDITIONS THAT DEATH RESEMBLES

Now we turn the tables and consider some of the phenomena that suggest the use of death as analogy. In other words, while the expression "stone cold dead" is one way of finding in nature a condition that can be likened to deadness, we now emphasize phenomena that we try to understand or describe through comparisons with death. This difference in direction of emphasis will become clearer as we proceed.

Between people we may observe spirited, intensive, and varied interactions. They are having a "lively" time together. We observe the other extreme as well: people sharing time and space but nothing else. "That was an awfully dead party," we might say on the way home, just as actors might remark to each other when the final curtain drops, "Whew! What a dead house (audience) tonight!" Emphasis instead might be on a particular individual instead of a group: "He has no life in him, just going through the motions."

Expressions of this kind voice our recognition that people alive in the usual sense of the term vary in their degree of animation or zest. He is alive but not lively. It is not surprising that we characterize sluggish, unenthusiastic actions as lifeless. By inviting a comparison with the ultimate or technically correct case of lifelessness, we gain perspective on other degrees of animation. We relax our usual assumption that an organism must be either dead or alive, knowing that we are not really confusing ourselves or anybody else in this use of language. Indeed, comparing routine or listless actions to the state of death is almost forced upon us by the lack of other readily accepted words and concepts in this area. Neither our culture's otherwise rich store of language and concepts nor such disciplines as psychology and psychiatry have yet given us truly effective ways of acknowledging variations in the *quality* of life. It is easier in our culture to communicate about length of life than quality. And so the use of universal anchoring points comes to the rescue. Likening dim, drab behavior to death gets the idea across, but one might also use the familiar state of sleep as the anchoring point; for example, "He's sleepwalking," instead of "He's dead on his feet," without necessarily meaning in either case that he is suffering from actual fatigue.

There are other ways in which deadness serves as an instructive way of acknowledging or comprehending certain aspects of life, as we shall now see.

Social death

You are there, part of a situation. But nobody is paying attention to you. Nobody addresses remarks to you or looks you in the eye. You might as well not be there at all.

Social death must be defined situationally. In particular, it is a situation in which there is absence of those behaviors we would expect to be directed toward a living person, and the presence of behaviors we would expect when dealing with a deceased or nonexistent person.[12,13] Social death is read by observing how others treat and fail to treat the person with whom we are concerned. The individual himself may be animated enough and potentially responsive. As a matter of fact, the individual may be desperately seeking recognition, attention, interaction. The concept of social death recognizes that a significant aspect of being a person is being a person in the eyes of others. In other words, this concept calls attention to the basic status of being a person in society. We may appreciate more keenly how contingent and even precarious being a person in society can be when we are alert to the possibility of a living human being treated as though dead or nonexistent.

Here are some of the ways in which social death can be seen:

1. A person has violated one of the taboos of his group. As a consequence, he or she is "cut dead." This could be the West Point cadet who is given the silent treatment—a stressful, painful emotional experience by all accounts. This could be the son or daughter who married somebody of the "wrong" religion or crossed racial lines against parental wishes. This could be the corporate official who let a piece of confidential information leak out. This could be the tattletale who informed on another student . . . and so on. When an individual is cut dead by the group, it is usually easy to observe a pattern of specific behaviors on which to base this judgment. A capable outside observer will have little difficulty in identifying the person who is avoided, not included, and talked around.

The possibility that this socially annihilated person might later be restored to authentic status in the group is important to keep in mind. However, this does not change the fact that, for the moment at least, this person is being given every sign from others that he or she simply is not there.

2. A person has violated so serious a taboo that he or she is ritualistically expelled and killed. In the examples that have already been given, the group treats the person as though dead without necessarily taking formal action. It resembles an interpersonal reflex ("This is what we naturally do when somebody lets us down or undermines us"). Some groups, however, have a more elaborate and official way of reading a member out. In a sense, excommunication from the church is such an example: the individual is still alive, but not longer one of us. The law may strip a person of some or all privileges of citizenship. This can include branding an individual as an undesirable alien and sending him "back where he belongs." It can also take the form of denying the person opportunity to vote, run for public office, hold

certain kinds of jobs, and so on. This perhaps should be regarded as partial social death: "You can stay around and even be acknowledged in certain respects, but from now on you are a subperson." For a more striking example, we might witness a bone-pointing ceremony. The tribal community officially certifies one of its errant members as dead. This public ritual does not harm a hair on the offender's head but has the effect of terminating his life as a group member. Property that once belonged to this person may be redistributed, and the name itself retired or assigned to somebody else after it has been decontaminated.[14]

In the ritualistic social death procedures, the victim at least knows clearly what is happening and why; furthermore, others who might be inclined to violate taboos in the future are given a powerful reminder of the fate they should expect. In more informal social death procedures, such as those of our own society, a person perhaps runs more risk of being cut dead without quite understanding the peril.

3. There is an intrinsic change in the individual that results in loss of live person status. One important example in our own society applies potentially to all of us. Despite recent progress and advocacies, growing old in the United States still represents a decrement in social value.[15,16] There tends to be a further diminution when an individual enters a nursing home, geriatric hospital, or other such age-segregated facility. The old person may or may not still mean something to a few people in the community. But for society at large, the ailing old person has moved to a sort of buffer zone between life and death. The individual has broken no taboos and committed no crimes, unless it be an implicit sin against a youth-glorifying culture to grow old. Even the old person living independently in the community often can be observed as victim of the socially dead treatment: for example, being passed over while

trying to get the attention of a store clerk or being placed at the bottom of the medical and educational priorities. The old person who becomes accustomed to being invisible has in effect acknowledged the status of social death.

Effective, if largely informal, exclusionary actions also operate against some people because they have developed feared or unpopular diseases. "Don't talk to him, sit next to him, or invite him into your house, he has _____" (fill in the name of your favorite loathsome condition, even one that is not contagious). People with disfiguring scars or physical infirmities also may be treated as though not one of the group. A person whose face has been severely burned in an accident may discover that his or her life has changed more radically than the injury itself would warrant—the eyes of others are averted, and people tend to keep a greater distance. Aversive behavior in the presence of a corpse, or even in the area where a corpse had been or might be, is common in our society. A living person may also encounter this kind of treatment for a variety of reasons.

4. The terminally ill or dying person may be treated as though already dead. Clinical and research examples will be presented later. The main point for now is that an elaborate pattern of aversive and person-denying behavior can be generated around a living individual whose demise is, correctly or incorrectly, anticipated. Particulars often include minimal eye contact, if any; reluctance to touch; making decisions for the individual as though that person no longer had preferences or any possibility for exercising options; and talking to others in the presence of the person as though he were not really there.

If we stand at a distance and observe the pattern of interactions in the environment, we might conclude that whatever is there in that bed surely is not a living person. People don't treat other people that way. It must be that the person in that bed is deceased, or that what is living is not really a person. In either case, the person is socially dead.

There is another type of situation that differs from all the above chiefly in its future prospects rather than in what actually is taking place at the moment. To become socially dead assumes that one once was an authentic living member of the group. Some people, however, have yet to be accepted as full members of the group. The age or circumstances that determine acceptance of a child as a true part of the family or society have varied from culture to culture and time to time. An infant may be considered alive but not as a person—an issue that takes on particular tension in our own society today, if we substitute *fetus* for infant. The adult who enters a new society may be accepted promptly, after a while, or never at all. Even the individual who has come into adulthood within a particular society may never be vested with certain of the marks that signify full membership. These phenomena are mentioned because the treatment accorded people in such circumstances can resemble social death to some degree. They differ conceptually, however, because the person, no matter how vibrant a human being, has not yet been granted full social status and therefore cannot be put to social death as such.

Phenomenological death

Concentrate now on what is taking place *inside* the person. Regardless of society's attitudes and actions, is the individual alive to himself? There are at least two ways in which a condition of *phenomenological death* can manifest itself.

1. Part of the person may die in the mind of the surviving self. The specifics of this kind of internal death range from the relatively trivial to the profoundly disturbing. It is not limited to a particular kind of person or a particular age level, although good research would probably

indicate that certain kinds of partial phenomenological death are more common with some people and at some ages than others. We will just take a few examples here.

A young woman undergoes life-saving surgery that results in the loss of her capacity to bear children. She has lost the potential for motherhood, whether or not she ever would actually have become a mother. In her own mind, one part of her total self has in effect died prior to birth. There is much else about her own self that remains alive to her, but there is also now the mental and emotional challenge of working through the loss of one of her potential dimensions.

A young man is physically fit by most standards. But he has sustained an injury in athletic competition that is just disabling enough to end his career. He is, let us suppose, a pitcher suffering from a dead arm, or a running back whose bad knees limit maneuverability and make him excessively vulnerable to additional injuries. This person has lost a part of his total functioning that already existed in a palpable and public way. He was an accomplished athlete both in his mind and in the minds of others. Now he has to remake his identity minus this valued dimension—not easy to do, while still mourning privately for the athlete who has died.

Another woman retained her capacity for motherhood and, in fact, still devotes much of her energies to raising a large family. In fulfilling one valued side of her personality, however, she has so neglected some of her personal talents and aspirations that she sometimes has a sense of partial self-murder. Only a couple of her closest friends realize that she is deeply troubled by this. Although she knows that she could now create the opportunity to return to these interests, she fears such an attempt would only confirm her suspicion that part of her has perished from neglect.

Two old men are depressed, each for more than one reason. But for one person, it is the loss of his role as giver and protector that he just can't seem to get over. Forced retirement from his job was later followed by other setbacks that endangered his financial independence. What he misses most of all is the ability to show his affection (and power) by giving to others. Having recently discovered that he can't even afford to buy the birthday gift he had in mind for his favorite grandchild, the old man can no longer see himself or present himself to others as a delight-giving sugar daddy. The other old man is agitated as well as depressed because he can't move. He can't just pick up and go. Through much of his life, he would simply take off when a scene became unpleasant, overdemanding, unrewarding. Infirmities he has acquired with age now prevent this kind of mobility. It is not the physical limitation itself that disturbs him so; rather, it is the fact that immobility has laid low that part of him that knew how to solve problems by drifting away from them. He is still alive and not so badly off, but his wandering spirit has been snuffed out from any chance of expression.

The essence of phenomenological death in this first sense, then, is that there is a surviving self that recognizes the loss of one or more components of the total self. The person is alive enough to know that part of him has died. The individual may in fact speak and think with death language. But whether or not this occurs, the psychologically attuned observer can see strong parallels with the state of mourning for the death of another person.

2. The total self may take on a deadened tone. The person does not experience life as freshly or intensely as in the past. Pleasures do not really please. Even pains may have become heavy, tedious burdens rather than sharp, sensitizing pangs.

Feeling dead to one's self is a quality of ex-periencing that can shade into depersonalization: "I have no body," or "This body is not mine." Some psychotic people present themselves as though dead, either in the sense that they have actually died or through the impression that they do not relate to their own body and biography as though it were that of a living person. This may be accompanied by a depersonalized attitude toward other people as well. The person may be mute, very slow moving, and giving to striking and maintaining a rigid posture for protracted periods of time. The self we expect to be associated with the body seems to be receiving and transmitting few messages.

It is important to distinguish, however, between the outside observer's impression that the person has a markedly reduced level of self-experiencing and what might actually be felt by the individual. Caution in this regard is always a sound policy. There have been many instances, for example, in which a catatonic person has recovered from this condition and brought back sharp recall both of his or her own internal state and of environmental happenings. The methodological difficulties in trying to determine whether a person is or only seems to be phenomenologically dead are considerable. Yet there is little question but that each of us experiences our own self as more or less sensitive and lively at different times and in different circumstances, and that there are indeed valleys of phenomenological deadness as well as the peak experiences charted by Maslow.[17]

The sense of inner deadness or a movement toward fading out sometimes is experienced in conjunction with the use of drugs or alcohol. It can also occur with other alterations in bodily state. However, there is reason to believe that the experience can be essentially psychogenic as well. Profound despair sometimes finds expression in a phenomenological state that is virtually beyond all feeling, a benumbing or depletion.

To Ache is human—not polite—
The Film upon the eye
Mortality's old Custom—
Just locking up—to die[18,p.117]

These lines from Emily Dickinson[18] capture the sense of inwardness and withdrawal that can anticipate demise of the body by minutes—or by years. Whatever the cause, the circumstances, or the outcome, we must recognize a state of mind in which the person becomes as death to himself.

A FEW IMPLICATIONS
"If I die before I wake"

Here we will touch on a few of the many implications that derive from our tendency to use death as analogy or metaphor. For example, look again at the sleep-death comparison. The familiar bedtime prayer beseeches God to take the soul "if I die before I wake." This prayer serves more than one purpose. It is a reminder or confession of mortality and a confirmation of trust and dependence upon deity, to cite just two of the more obvious meanings. But the prayer also strengthens the emotional connection between sleep and death. Conscious control and awareness are surrendered in both instances. Does faith in God comfort the person who is approaching "the long sleep"? Or does fear of death invade one's thoughts and feelings as one lies abed, trying to slip off into a normal night's repose? Both possibilities deserve consideration. Likening sleep and death to each other, and then raising the possibility of death *during* sleep, are ways of thinking that are fairly common in in our society.

Neither society nor the individual keeps the distinction between sleep and death as figure of speech clearly set apart from the notion of death *as* sleep or sleep *as* death. Where does analogy end and reality begin? Does the fact that we are accustomed to awakening after sleep reinforce the belief in awakening after death? Is some blurring of the distinction between analogy and reality partially responsible for certain self-destructive behaviors (e.g., the person who overdoses with sleeping pills because if death results, this will just be a long, a better sleep?). Because most of our days do fade into night and sleep, the comparison between sleep and death is of particular interest.

Eminent scientists have sometimes taken the sleep-death comparison very seriously. Elie Metchnikoff, one of the great turn-of-the-century bioscientists, considered it likely that we have instincts for both sleep and death based on the likelihood that each represents a state of "intoxication" growing out of physical exhaustion.[19,20] He was sufficiently impressed with the analogy between sleep and death (although recognizing that we knew little about either subject from a scientific standpoint) that he proposed the existence of a death instinct. Metchnikoff's serious attention to the sleep-death analogy helped to reinforce the continued perception of these states as closely allied. It was also important because Metchnikoff appears to have been the first person in modern times to employ the term *thanatology*, introduced the term *gerontology* (study of aging), and wielded considerable influence because of his own research contributions.

As it turned out, Metchnikoff and his contemporaries drew some conclusions that do not stand up because of the limited research then available on the nature of sleep. A significant new wave of research over the past two decades has made it clear that sleep is by no means a simple "resting state" and cannot be reduced to a notion such as self-intoxication.[21] A scientist today is not likely to press the comparison between the complexities of human sleep and the still essentially unknown "state" of death. (Sigmund Freud's version of death instinct theory, not hinged on a supposed parallel with sleep, has run into conceptual problems of its own.[22,23] Today it is something of an indulgence to regard sleep and death as identical states. There may be moods in which we prefer to see these states as similar if not identical, but a solid body of sleep research makes it difficult to take the comparison seriously in a strictly factual sense.

From earth-demon to automaton

Why do we sometimes represent death in the form of a person or fabulous being? Let us consider, very briefly, two approaches to this question, approaches that differ more in their emphases and data sources than in their basic contentions. Edgar Herzog, a German historian and psychologist influenced much by the work of C. G. Jung, shows that early in the history of our race, humans associated the earth itself with death (even though earth is also our abode and source of sustenance for life). Death was seen by ancient peoples as *Hider,* a sort of being that takes people away from us and keeps them where they cannot be found. Soon this was joined by the image of an earth-demon: "gigantic but formless . . . with gaping jaws."[24] As centuries went by, we formed an increasing variety of personified images in which actual as well as fabulous animals were seen as embodiments or representatives of death. These images often had direct implications for a culture's practical relationships with death. Herzog cites a number of peoples who yielded corpses to wild dogs or wolves. Quoting Sven Heden, he tells us, for example, that "In Lhasa (Tibet) and other towns and temples special dogs are kept, and they destroy the dead bodies with astounding appetite. In many temples the corpse-eating dogs are regarded as holy, and a man acquires merit by allowing his dead body to be eaten by them."[24,p.47]

Holy dogs, wolves, birds, and other creatures have figured in both the actual body disposal practices and the theology and religious art of many cultures, performing a variety of death-related functions. Herzog's interpretation of these phenomena is part of a complex theory involving the psychology of symbols that cannot be pursued here. He views the gradual evolution of death imagery, especially the personification trend, as evidence of humankind's increasing ability to develop a sense of selfhood and to find objectifications for what would otherwise be experienced only as vague and nameless threats. Inner experiences and half-shaped thoughts find expression in ways that the whole community can share and understand.

Some of my own research on this topic has been described earlier in this chapter. The accompanying theoretical orientation has much in common with that of Herzog, although not linked specifically with Jungian psychology. Essentially it is proposed that:

1. The tendency to see the world in so-called objective terms has become an increasingly dominant force in all realms of thought with the emergence of modern science and technology.

2. While in the past centuries we humans tended to overproject our own internal states into the cosmos, the reverse process is now at work. Having at least partially convinced ourselves that the universe is (at best) neutral and that objectivity is the most justified orientation, *we now apply to ourselves the aloof, only-the-facts-please* model that we have made of the universe.

3. This phenomenon shows up in the willingness to see death as objective and objective only. Important, up-to-date people in white laboratory frocks or white medical jackets seem able to regard death as a biomechanical event; so should we!

4. Consequently, our surging emotions and shifting thoughts about personally revelant death have lost some of their pathways for expression. Subjectivity is a kind of weakness,

and we are led to believe that in communicating with each other about death the cool, objective model is most appropriate.

5. While people with certain kinds of personality structure find the objective-only approach to their liking, others are left to their own devices in finding ways to represent and cope with the subjective side of death. Death personifications may have gone semiunderground, then, but they still have an important role to perform, even if not so readily available for us to share with each other. The death personification remains one way to counterbalance the emphasis upon the neutral, distant, objective approach.

Three possible implications of this change over time (a long way from the hider and earth-demon of early pretechnological society!) can be seen in the available care data: (1) The *automaton* personification seems to represent an attempt of some people to come to terms with a mechanical, computerized, soulless-universe context of death. Interpreting death as a feelingless apparatus in human guise does not necessarily make a person feel comfortable, but it does at least perform the classical function of a personification: set the inner perception, need, or anxiety into a more palpable and controllable form. The automaton may be the newest of the death personifications that come forth with any frequency today, although earlier versions were not completely unknown. What we do with the automaton after we have created it as our contemporary version of death remains to be seen. (2) Since the study cited here,[12] we have discovered an increasing proportion of personifications in which death is seen as female. (Male personifications still are clearly the most frequent.) One naturally wonders if this shift represents still another way in which our relationship to death, in this case through personification, changes along with the general cultural climate. What is women's liberation

doing to death, and vice versa? This is again a question that remains to be answered. (3) Preliminary evidence suggests that people with high manifest death anxiety have more difficulty than others in coming up with images of personified death. Their minds seem to go blank or reach for the most stereotyped of culturally available images.

Aliveness and pain

Phenomenological death is a state that people sometimes appear to visit upon themselves, either intentionally or subintentionally. Edwin Shneidman[25] introduced the distinction between intentional and subintentional actions to clarify the motivation in acts of self-destruction. The distinction is not necessarily limited to suicidal behavior, however. An individual may reduce the sense of personal aliveness either by direct, deliberate actions or by indirect, accomplicelike behavior. The pain of a life gone wrong may seem too much to bear. Subdue the pain with drink or drugs, find some technique for reducing level of conscious experience! The resulting condition of more or less partial and more or less temporary deadness is the price one pays for pain reduction. It may not be the only price, of course. Inattentiveness and reduced coping ability are likely to accompany psychological deadness, and these make the person more vulnerable to a variety of life-threatening forces.

But the opposite relation between pain and aliveness can also be observed:

Mrs. A. was a 62-year-old Puerto Rican who constantly refused to take any medicine, even when in great pain. Her rationale was similar to other Puerto Rican patients [with far advanced cancer] I met. Doctors don't know as much as they think they do about the person's body. Each body has a soul, and if the doctor cannot see the soul, then he cannot see the body. "I know, I know that my family does not want that I suffer . . . but suffering is part of life

. . . and without it you are not a man. No medicine can help with any pain . . . or, sometimes it could help putting all your body asleep . . . like a baby . . . and then it takes away my pain . . . but it also takes away all that I feel and see. If I could feel the pain I also can feel my body . . . and then I know that I am still alive."

As a warning signal, pain acquires a symptomatic significance for most of the [cancer] patients. It may be welcomed, as we saw with Mrs. A., for whom pain is an indication of life. In some cases the absence of pain would signify total or partial death. Pain then becomes a symbol of life.[26]

One person, perhaps in good physical health, sets about to reduce his or her sense of aliveness in an effort to avoid emotional pain; another person, perhaps in extremely poor health, accepts intense physical pain as a link to life itself. These differences in our relationship to phenomenological aliveness–deadness are but two of the variations that must be acknowledged as we continue our explorations into the human encounter with death.

SUMMARY

When we speak or act as though something resembles death or as though death resembles something else, we are giving indirect definitions of death. Inorganic and unresponsive forces of nature, such as mute stones and enduring mountains, have been seen as possessing attributes of death, just as more active forces, such as clouds and rivers, have been regarded as though animate. In recent years there has been an increasing tendency to compare death to the failure or running down of a machine.

Some altered states of consciousness, notably sleep, have been likened to death. Serious questions may be raised as to whether a particular person is thinking of sleep–death relationship as figure of speech only or really believes that the two states are fundamentally similar.

Throughout history there has been a ten-

dency to represent death as though it were a being of some type: a known animal, a mythological creature, a being in human form. A wide range of personifications have been employed, from the ancient *hider* and *earth-demon*, through the *sirens* and the *skeleton*, to the contemporary *gentle comforter, macabre, gay deceiver*, and *automaton* images.

Certain individual and interaction states also bear parallels to death. The concept of *social death* involves the absence of those behaviors that the group usually directs toward living members and the presence of behaviors usually reserved for the dead or nonpresent. A person is socially dead, then, when his or her continued existence is no longer acknowledged.

Phenomenological death, by contrast, refers to a reduction or complete phasing out *within* the individual himself. This can take two general forms: part of the person dying to himself and a deadening of the total self. Both types are exemplified.

A few selective implications of these likenings unto death are given.

REFERENCES

1. Klingberg, G. The distinction between living and not living among 7–10 year-old children with some remarks concerning the so-called animism controversy. *Journal of Genetic Psychology*, 1957, *105*, 227-238.
2. Safier, G. A study in relationships between the life and death concepts in children. *Journal of Genetic Psychology*, 1964, *105*, 283-294.
3. Feifel, H. Attitudes toward death in some normal and mentally ill populations. In H. Feifel (Ed.), *The meaning of death*. New York: McGraw-Hill Book Co., 1959.
4. Mack, J. E. *Nightmares and human conflict*. Boston: Little, Brown & Co., 1970.
5. Freud, S. Dostoevsky and parricide. *Collected psychological papers of Sigmund Freud* (Vol. 21). London: The Hogarth Press, Ltd., 1961.
6. Homer. *Odyssey*.
7. Plato. *Phaido*.
8. Meyer-Baer, K. *Music of the spheres and the dance of death*. Princeton, N.J.: Princeton University Press, 1970.
9. Green, J. S. The days of the dead in Oaxaca, Mexico. *Omega*, 1972, *3*, 245-262.

10. Nagy, M. H. The child's theories concerning death. *Journal of Genetic Psychology*, 1948, *73*, 3-27.

11. Opie, I., & Opie, P. *Children's games in street and playground*. Oxford, England: Oxford University Press, 1969.

12. Kastenbaum, R., & Aisenberg, R. B. *The psychology of death*. New York: Springer Publishing Co., Inc., 1972.

13. Kastenbaum, R. Psychological death. In L. Pearson (Ed.), *Death and dying*. Cleveland: Case Western Reserve University Press, 1969.

14. Cannon, W. B. Voodoo death. *American Anthropologist*, 1942, *44*, 169-173.

15. Glaser, B. G. The social loss of aged dying patients. *The Gerontologist*, 1966, *6*, 119-121.

16. Butler, R. *Why survive?* New York: Harper & Row, Publishers, 1975.

17. Maslow, A. H. *Religion, values, and peak-experiences*. Columbus, Ohio: Ohio State University Press, 1964.

18. Dickinson, E. *Final harvest: Emily Dickinson's poems*. Boston: Little, Brown & Co., 1961.

19. Metchnikoff, E. *The nature of man*. New York: Arno Press, 1977. (Originally published in 1903.)

20. Metchnikoff, E. *The prolongation of life*. New York: Arno Press, 1977. (Originally published in 1908.)

21. Hartmann, E. L. *The functions of sleep*. New Haven, Conn.: Yale University Press, 1973.

22. Levin, A. J. The fiction of the death instinct. *Psychiatric Quarterly*, 1941, *25*, 257-281.

23. Wilbur, G. B. Some problems presented by Freud's life–death instinct theory. *American Image*, 1941, *2*, 134-196.

24. Herzog, E. *Psyche and death*. New York: G. P. Putnam's Sons, 1967.

25. Shneidman, E. S. Orientation toward death. In R. W. White (Ed.), *The study of lives*. New York: Atherton Press, 1967.

26. Baider, L. Private experience and public expectations on the cancer ward. *Omega*, 1975, *6*, 373-382.

CHAPTER 5

❖ DEATH MEANS

We have been exploring death as event, state, and analogy. But this has left almost untouched a crucial aspect of our relationship to death: what is *means* to us. Whether or not we have a clear idea of what death *is*, we are likely to have a complex set of feelings and attitudes. This chapter opens our inquiry into the meanings that death has taken on for both the individual and society, an inquiry that will continue to be pursued in various ways throughout the book.

What is meant here by "meaning?" We are in the realm of meaning if we substitute the question: What *difference* does death really make to us? Some behave as though death makes little or no difference. Others, at the other extreme, make every significant life decision under the spell of personal death interpretations. Death at least seems to mean either much or little to us, a difference that itself invites curiosity. The degree of importance we attach to death is not the whole story, however. There are also appreciable differences in the particular kind of meaning death has for us. You and I might both consider death as a topic second to none in significance but for entirely different reasons.

A few selected meanings of death will now be considered.

THE GREAT LEVELER

Human equality has seldom existed as a concrete fact in society, especially in the civilizations familiar to us through traditional history and in our own lives. We have been sorting each other out by class, by caste, by sex, by race, by geography—by just about any imaginable criterion. Some societies have consisted primarily of the high and mighty and the lowly. In other societies there have been a variety of life stations in between the extremes. People usually have known their pace, like it or not.

Within this context, death sometimes has taken on an ironic or revolutionary aspect. Bear in mind the image of people frozen throughout life into a particular place in the social hierarchy or trying desperately to raise themselves above their assigned station. And then scan such a poem as the following, written by Peter Patrix (1585–1672) just a few days prior to his death by execution:

> I dreamt that, buried in my fellow clay,
> Close by a common beggar's side I lay.
> And, as so mean a neighbour shock'd my pride,
> Thus, like a corpse of quality, I cried,
> "Away! thou scoundrel! Henceforth touch me not;
> More manners learn, and at a distance rot!"
> "*Thou* scoundrel!" in a louder tone, cried he,
> "Proud lump of dirt! I scorn thy word and thee.
> We're equal now, I'll not an inch resign;
> This is my dunghill, as the next is thine."[1,p.292]

Those who had either been granted or achieved a relatively high station in life did not always find the grace and (dark) humor to accept the leveling effect of death. Indeed, much better known than the verse quoted above is the following passage from Shakespeare's *King Richard II*. The embittered, cynical, power-lusting hero expresses himself in a memorable speech:

Let us talk of graves, of worms, and epitaphs;
Make dust our paper, and with rainy eyes
Write sorrow on the bosom of the earth.
Let us choose executors, and talk of wills:
And yet not so,—for what can we bequeath,
Save our deposed bodies to the ground?

Our lands, our lives, and all are Bolingbroke's,
And nothing can we call our own but death,
And that small model of the barren earth,
Which serves as paste and cover to our bones.

For God's sake, let us sit upon the ground,
And tell sad stories of the death of kings:

How some have been depos'd; some slain in war;
Some haunted by the ghosts they have depos'd;
Some poison'd by their wives; some sleeping
    kill'd;
All murder'd: for within the hollow crown
That rounds the mortal temples of a king,
Keeps Death his court; and there the antick sits,
Mocking his state, and grinning at his pomp;
Allowing him a breath, a little scene,
To monarchize, be fear'd, and kill with looks;
Infusing him with self and vain conceit—
As if this flesh, which walls about his life,
Were brass impregnable; and, humor'd thus,
Comes at the last, and with a little pin
Bores through his castle wall, and—farewell king!
                                    [act 3, scene 2]

The power and democratic spirit of death can best be conveyed when it is the highest and the mightiest who are brought low. The true monarch is death, who mocks and plays with the most powerful of mortals, "allowing him a breath, a little scene." How incredibly little it takes to level those who have been raised above all others, how useless are pretensions and defenses when, personified, death "comes at the last, and with a little pin bores through his castle wall."

The leveling power of death has subtle and labyrinthian implications. If the most powerful monarch falls at death's whim, what hopes dare ordinary mortals maintain? Yet, for those of us who are not monarchs or celebrities, what a delightful revenge upon those who are! "You'll get yours!" the downtrodden mutter with grim satisfaction and just a touch of glee. The death of monarchs and of all proud or exploiting people can be interpreted as an exceptional bringing down, as compared to the demise of humbler individuals from whom death has less to repossess.

Some of the elite, as the King Richard II of Shakespeare, if not necessarily the historical Richard, themselves contributed to this recognition of death as the great equalizer. Work of art commissioned during medieval times often displayed this theme. Gallant young knights and beauteous maidens are greeted on their journeys by Death the skeleton,[2] and human skulls stare sightlessly from tables, shelves, and unexpected places as scholars ponder their books or marriage rites are performed. In such ways did the elite encourage remainders that pride and triumph have drastic limits indeed.

As winds of social change and revolution swept through Europe, it is not too farfetched to credit (or blame) death the leveler with a distinctive role. What emboldened the common person to resist the established order? How dare he reach beyond his assigned station in life and dream of overturning the powerful? Explanations can be given at many levels: political, economic, technological, and so on. But there should be a place in our explanations for the image of death cutting down with his scythe the mighty as well as the ordinary mortal. "Death to the tyrant!" was the cry in many a popular uprising, culminating, perhaps, in the French Revolution. Even if the daily facts of life for centuries had confirmed the dominance of a few people over the many, experience had also confirmed the fact that death claimed all. The democracy of the dead ("We're equal now, I'll not an inch resign; This is my dunghill, as the next is thine") indicated that rank and privilege disappeared on the other side of the grave; why could it not then be abolished or at least modified on this side of the grave as well? Furthermore, since it was death who erased differences among people, it was only fitting to call upon this force to achieve equality or a new balance in life. War, murder, execution, assassination—all the modalities of death-bringing to which we have given names—were given an extra measure of justification. It was as though the person or mob that slays the oppressor were doing death's own work of leveling.

In recent years in our own society we have suffered assassinations, attempted assassinations, and cult murders by people whose mental stability was open to serious question. Each such assault requires its own explanation if indeed an explanation can be found. But the fantasy of bringing down a powerful and celebrated person and thereby acquiring fame for oneself appears to be one of the more common themes. Somebody has risen above the rest of us; such distinction is not to be tolerated. The assassin steps forward with a twisted sense of destiny, a self-appointed agent for death the leveler.

THE GREAT VALIDATOR

Upon discovering one major theme in human life, one is well advised to seek its opposite as well. Death has been regarded as a powerful force that levels any distinction among people. But death also has been regarded as the final validation of an individual's worth or distinction. These two meanings do not simply exist side by side. It is probable that the leveling and validating significations of death closely interact on both the individual and societal levels.

Consider funeral practices. Consider, in par-

ticular, the relationship between the splendor of the final arrangements and the status of the deceased. (There is much more than this dimension to be understood, as we will see in later explorations of funeral practices.) Funeral directors in the United States have been severely criticized on occasion for encouraging lavish and costly arrangements. A critic may portray the funeral director as a sort of ghoulish salesperson, skillfully persuading the mourning survivors to spend much more than is necessary. As a merchandiser, he or she is said to utilize the theme of status. Cleverly, the funeral director conveys the impression that this simple and inexpensive casket would not be good enough for a person so distinguished or so beloved as the deceased. Similarly, the other funeral arrangements should also be in keeping with the deceased's status. The deceased's relatives risk being exposed as heartless, insensitive, or miserly if they are not willing to authorize the proper level of expenditure for the proper type of funeral.

Naturally enough, funeral directors resent this criticism. One kind of reply often made is that only a few unscrupulous individuals employ this sharp practice on the public, the handful of bad eggs one might find in any business or profession. More relevant to our present purpose is another way that funeral directors respond to this criticism. One midwestern funeral director said it for many others:

I do what you want me to do. You come in here and say you want simple arrangements, and that is exactly what I will provide. You know what you want, and I am here to meet your needs. Makes it easier for me, in fact, if you have already thought it all through. But maybe you come in here not in the clearest frame of mind. Or you just haven't had the experience, you don't know what the alternatives are, what kind of choices can be made. I will try to guide you. I will not make up your mind for you. If I led you to make the wrong kind of decisions, then this would become part of my reputation sooner or later. I can't afford that and I can't live with that. I live here in this city, too. I want to look people in the face just as I do right now, and see some respect in return . . . couldn't expect that if I took advantage of people at such a tragic time in their lives. Many of my clients come to me through word of mouth. I know them already, or they know somebody I know. I am not going to be a success year after year if I lead people astray.

But let me tell you why I sell some of the more expensive items—it's because the people themselves want it that way! I have my theories why, but I'm not a psychologist. I just know that some people take funeral arrangements very seriously; they are not satisfied until they feel they are getting the best funeral for their loved one that they can afford. Listen, there are times that I just don't bring up some options that exist because I think they might really overspend, in terms of their own economic situation. If everybody wanted bare-minimum funerals, that is what we would be providing. When you see a big, a magnificent funeral, you are seeing what the family felt it truly must have.

Both the funeral director and his critics agree on the seeming relationship between the grandeur of the final rituals and social status. An impressive funeral seems to speak well for the deceased. It lends, in effect, a last stamp of approval or validation. The participant and on-looker recognize once again the quality of the deceased's life through the unstinting homage that is being paid. A funeral that does not measure up to the expected standards threatens to have the opposite impact; it is as through the individual's life has been downvalued because the final rites of passage are so threadbare.

This sentiment, although certainly observable in our own society today, has also surfaced repeatedly throughout history. The heroine in a Greek tragedy risks her own death by advocating the proper burial of her outcast brother.[3] Decisions are made as to whether or not a deceased person of some distinction deserves burial in sacred soil. If the person is not honored and accepted in this manner, then how distin-

guished was he or she, after all? The cowboy implores: "Bury me not on the lone prairie."

Funeral rituals are not equivalent with death itself, but, as one of society's last opportunities to relate publicly to the deceased, they do provide the opportunity to bestow a rank or classification. This social judgment is often interpreted as either the validation or invalidation of what previous status the individual had held. Is the whole city plunged into mourning? Do people come from miles around to honor the memory of the deceased? Is the ceremony and the final disposition of the body carried out on the highest level known to the society? All this tends to confirm worth. Many a person of distinction has imagined his or her funeral, and some have anxiously attempted to arrange for just such an impressive validation.

But where is Mozart's grave? The man who has come to be regarded as one of the greatest musicians ever produced by the human race received the poorest level of ritual and burial known to Vienna—one unaccompanied hearse clattering to the pauper's field where no marker would distinguish his grave from any other. This is an instance in which invalidation of a human life by a rejecting mode of passage to death was subsequently reversed by the court of world opinion. A monument now stands on the guessed-at site of Mozart's grave.

From the standpoint of the survivors, a low-status type of final ritual and body disposal can also threaten their own sense of worth. "If Father's death seems to mean so little, then Father could not have meant much to society— and I am, after all, his child." To some extent, it is in the self-interest of the survivors to validate the worth of the deceased through whatever means are acknowledged to be appropriate within a particular society. Our own worth is validated by the final validation given to a loved one.

We have focused upon funeral arrangements as an index of the way in which society can use death to measure the value of one of its deceased members. This is not the only type of example that could be given. We will see later, for example, that treatment of the dying person, experiences on the deathbed itself, and social consequences of death also can reflect the value placed upon the person when alive.

DEATH UNITES/SEPARATES
Unites

Death can be seen as the opportunity to join or rejoin others or as an act of separation from all hope of companionship. Whichever meaning dominates for a particular individual or society, there is a common denominator: death radically alters our relationships with others.

Occasionally death has been seen as a route for unification of friends and foe. Differences that kept us apart during life now are resolved. Alexander Pope wrote in the seventeenth century:

My expiring breath
Smiles o'er the tombs of foes made kin by death.

And, again:

The grave united, where even the great find rest
And blended lie the oppressor and oppressed.

Two centuries later another British writer imagined his own death. This young soldier, Wilfred Owen, was in fact soon to be killed as World War I drew to a close. The theme of unity through death here is made to carry a fervent antiwar statement. The poem begins:

It seemed that out of battle I escaped
Down some profound dull tunnel, long since
   scooped
Through granites which titanic wars had groined.
Yet also there encumbered sleepers groaned,
Too fast in thought or death to be bestirred.
Then, as I probed them, one sprang up, and
   stared
With piteous recognition in fixed eyes.
Lifting distressful hands as if to bless.

And no guns thumped, or down the flues made
   moan.
"Strange friend," I said, "Here is no cause to
   mourn."

The brotherhood of death—much different in spirit from the bringing-down, the leveling-of-the-mighty theme—is emphasized as the former enemies together look back on life.

"Strange friend," I said, "Here is no cause to
   mourn."
"None," said the other, "Save the undone years,
The hopelessness. Whatever hope is yours,
Was my life also: I went hunting wild
After the wildest beauty in the world,
For by my glee might many men have laughed,
And of my weeping something had been left,
Which must die now. I mean the truth untold,
The pity of war, the pity war distilled. . . ."

After additional passages the poem concludes:

I am the enemy you killed, my friend.
I knew you in this dark; for so you frowned
Yesterday through me as you jabbed and killed.
I parried; but my hands were loath and cold.
Let us sleep now.[4]

Owen's poem was revised at the conclusion of still another war. In one of his major works, the contemporary British composer Benjamin Britten called on these lines to conclude his *War Requiem*.* A German baritone and a British tenor, representing two of the nations that had fought bitterly against each other in World War II as in World War I, ended with the duet, "I am the enemy you killed, my friend." This statement signified a renewed commitment to develop a sense of unity in life as well as death for many of the performers and listeners on its premier in Coventry Cathedral.

Death may be seen as uniting the individual with God, especially when deity is conceived

---

*The complete text accompanies the authoritative recording of this work on London album OSA-1255.

as personally concerned about the human spirit ("Nearer My God to Thee"). The despairing or dying person who sees death as unity with the divine may reach out rather than shrink away from terminus. An end to pain and suffering is promised, but even more, a union with God. With such prospects in mind, the individual may not be content merely to await death but actually may yearn for it. This sentiment has gained expression in many hymns and carols. These pieces from *The Original Sacred Harp* (1844)[5] are typical:

"Northfield"
How long, dear Savior, O how long
    Shall this bright hour delay?
Fly swift around, ye wheels of time,
    And bring the promised day.

"Sardis"
Come on, my fellow pilgrims, come
And let us all be hast'ning home.
We soon shall land on yet blest shore,
Where pain and sorrow are no more;
There we our Jesus shall adore,
    Forever blest
No period then our joys shall know,
Secure from ev'ry mortal foe;
No sickness there, no want nor pain
Shall e'er disturb our rest again,
When with Immanueal we reign,
    Forever blest.

We see in "Northfield" that mortal life on earth merely delays the promised hour, while in "Sardis" it is made clear that joys will endure without end when one has joined the Lord. (The emphasis here, by the way, is to be "Secure from ev'ry mortal foe" rather than to develop a new sense of relatedness to others.) This theme of unification with God through death, no matter how it is expressed, tends to create a problem for the survivors. At the least, one is taxed to develop an understanding of death's double meaning: everlasting joy for the deceased but pain of separation and loss for the survivors.

A late seventeenth-century gravestone in Watertown, Massachusetts, informs us:

HERE LYES THE BODY OF
DEACON JOHN STONE WHOSE
LIFE WAS MUCH DESIRED &
WHOSE DEATH IS MUCH
LAMENTED AGED ABOUT 55
YEARS HE WENT REJOYCING
OUT OF THIS WORLD IN-
TO THE OTHER THE 26 DAY
OF MARCH 1691

Children especially may find it difficult to reconcile the lamenting with the rejoicing.

A more somber, even threatening implication of the meeting-one's-maker theme is expressed by gravestone messages such as the one carved into the marker of Miss Polly Coombes in Bellingham, Massachusetts, in 1795:

READER ATTEND: THIS STATE
    WILL SOON BE THINE.
BE THOU IN YOUTHFUL HEALTH
OR IN DECLINE;
PREPARE TO MEET THY GOD.

The prospect of arriving at a secure, home-like heaven could be tempered, then, by doubts as to whether or not one was prepared to meet the judgment of God. And what would happen if God found the individual lacking? Would this mean rejection? And would rejection mean abandonment? Those sturdy in their faith might think only of the promised affinity with God, but those less sure of themselves might feel squeamish or even terrified at the prospect. It makes a great deal of difference, in other words, whether salvation is interpreted as a sure thing or as a contingency whose outcome one will not know until that final moment.

There is still another sense in which death has been regarded as the opportunity for union or reunion. The individual may look forward to being again with specific people dear during life. An old woman dreams that she has become a little girl once more and is being welcomed by her father. A child wrestles privately with thoughts of suicide so that he can join the big brother he misses so much. The only person in the family who survived death in a concentration camp does not actually consider herself a believer in any form of afterlife, yet she often feels overcome by an intuition that some day they will all be reunited, needing only her death to accomplish this.

Anthropologists have long known that rituals oriented around death can serve a unifying function for society. This is a different sphere of meaning from what has been described up to now. Emphasis is not so much on the meeting-again that one might expect in the "next life" or a hoped-for "gathering unto the bosom of the Lord." Attention is focused instead on the ways in which ceremonies associated with death can maintain and strengthen the forces that bind people together during their earthly existence. Consider, for example, what Judith Ann Vollbrecht (1978)[9] learned in her recent study of an Ashanti village in Ghana. She lived for a year and a half in Donyina, a village whose people have become increasingly exposed to the influence of the politics, economics, and technology of modern life as well as to Christianity. Vollbrecht started with the premise that "For a society to remain stable it must provide moments that emphasize what all its members have in common. These moments are experienced chiefly through ritual celebrations that renew in the whole group of feeling for the underlying values on which its social structure is based, the shared humanness and concerns which make them what they are as distinct from other groups."[9,p.3] She discovered that the traditional rituals that provided such a sense of sharing and renewal of values had been seriously undermined by external pressure and interaction as well as by the competitive Christian theology. What did the people of

Donyina have left to remind themselves of who they were and why they belonged together? According to Vollbrecht, "only the rituals surrounding deaths, burials and funerals are now shared by the village as a group. These rituals have *gained importance* [italics added] for the villagers as the principal remaining occasion for maintaining their experience of communitas."[9,p.122] Death—or, more specifically, the rituals surrounding death—now performs a critical role in holding a people together on a symbolic and emotional level. It is probable that similar observations could be made in many other cultural and ethnic groups whose traditional ways of life have been diminished by contact with social forces external to themselves. (The role of burial and funeral practices is also discussed elsewhere in this book—e.g., Chapters 6, 8, and 14.)

Separates

Although some of us may cherish the prospect of reunion with loved ones through death, the more obvious consequences is *separation*. A familiar face is not to be seen again. Somebody important in our lives has left us. Death often has been interpreted essentially as a leaving, a departure, or a journey. This gives another twist to the idea of death as a happening (Chapter 2). If we are objective bystanders, we might focus on the death event as it involves the affected person only, our concern being mode, time, and place of death. In our own personal lives, however, we tend to register the death event differently, more in relationship to our own needs and circumstances. The death event really means that moment we become aware that a person has become lost to us.

"I felt like part of me had been pulled apart. Like I wasn't a whole person any more. And then I went numb. Like I was in shock, with loss of blood, just like I had lost an arm or a leg or worse." This is the way a young woman described the impact of news that her husband had been killed in action in Viet Nam. He had been alive to his loved ones until the message came, although actually dead for an indeterminate time. The moment that his wife was made aware of their final separation is when the death event occurred for her. The moment we as survivors feel the shock and anguish of separation, then, may be the most socially significant moment of death.

The sense of separation can anticipate actual death and can also linger long afterward. Parents may live for years in apprehension that one of their children will be taken away by a lethal disease. Should this actually happen, then for years later, perhaps the rest of their own lives, they may continue to feel a deep sense of loss and separation. Some families undergo the extreme stress of facing the probable death of their living children while still suffering over the loss of one or more who have already died.

The family were still grieving Ann's death when Roy began to exhibit symptoms of the same disease. His mother first noted the early signs, as she said she would. The doctors confirmed her worst fears. Having lost one child the parents faced the situation once more. Because of his learning difficulties, Roy was transferred to a special school which he found stressful. Later he went to a training school. As the dementia slowly increased he had to remain at home. Roy could not settle, walking aimlessly from room to room, hand-clapping, grimacing, gradually losing remaining skills. He made only odd noises, hardly knew his parents and could find only fleeting contentment listening to records. He became incontinent and had to be fed. Eventually he was hospitalized for a short time before he died.

Adam has a similar form of the same illness. The parents detected the early symptoms some months before Roy died. "We know it all now—we shall be left with nothing—no children—nothing."[6,p.66]

Realization that all their children are likely to die young burdens parents with an almost unbearable sense of loss. The children also experience the sorrow of separation from each other even if they do not fully understand the concept of death:

He had lost one sibling and was facing the experience a second time. His sister, in the latter stages of her illness, seemed unaware and unresponsive. Yet her little brother seemed to evoke some faint recognition. She appeared to smile with her eyes— a last window into the darkness. He said: "I don't mind if you don't talk to me. It's lonely without you. I can talk to you." He prattled on about his rabbit, his cars, and his wish to have a party on his birthday. . . ."[6,p.69]

This dying and unresponsive girl was by no means dead to her little brother. He loved and needed her. He would keep the conversation and relationship going for both of them as long as she was physically present and perhaps afterward as well. The difficulty in understanding death, coupled with the strong need to continue the relationship, can lead children—and not only children—to behave at times as though final separation had not really taken place. There is not much doubt that separation is one of the most universal meanings of death for those who are left to continue their own lives on earth. Separation itself can have a variety of meanings, some of which will be explored later. For the moment it is enough to bear in mind that separation is one of the most significant meanings of death to many of us, whether we are focusing on the anticipated loss of a loved person, the absence and emptiness experienced since the person actually died, or that painful phase in which we feel the wrenching away of one life from another, the acute crisis of separation.

We have been looking at separation from the standpoint of the survivors. But the departure from all relationships that one has known can also be a source of concern to the people who anticipates his or her own death. As we will see later in this book, many people with a life-threatening illness express a fear of being abandoned in their last hours. Furthermore, many of those who have studied or tried to be of help to the terminally ill also emphasize the importance of *being with* the dying person even when there is nothing specific that one can "do." It seems probable, although not yet clearly proven, that there is a link between the dying person's concern about separation and the need for human companionship right through the last moment. To know that somebody is there and will be there can be a great comfort. For those who interpret death basically as separation, there is perhaps no substitute for the reassurance of interpersonal contact through the entire terminal process.

THE ULTIMATE PROBLEM—OR THE ULTIMATE SOLUTION

Life could be interpreted as a continuing series of problems, some of which yield themselves to our effort and some of which defy solution. Likewise, death is sometimes regarded as either the ultimate problem or the ultimate solution. In fact, we humans are complex enough to consider death as *both* ultimate problem and ultimate solution in some circumstances.

Let us begin with the theme of death as solution. In the aftermath of the French Revolution, a jest made the rounds. "Come and see the wonderful new machine—a miracle! One treatment by the good Dr. Guillotine and never again a headache!" Indeed, Dr. Guillotine had intended the device that bears his name as solution to the problem of painful, lingering forms of execution, a mercifully quick dispatch. From a political standpoint, the guillotine was favored to solve other problems. Public execution in general has an ancient, many-cultured tradition of problem solving. To be sure, it has usually been society's problem that execution has been expected to solve,

rather than the individual's. Putting an undesirable person to death has seemed the surest, most conclusive way of removing a threat or annoyance.

The ultimate solution has been endorsed and applied on a mass as well as an individual basis. History reveals many an example of one group of people slaughtering another to achieve what, at the moment at least, seemed to be an important objective. Those who differed from the local majority on some point of theological doctrine or religious practice were thereby condemning themselves to brutal and violent death. The Spanish Inquisition is probably the best known, but certainly not the only illustration. Ironically, the Inquisition sometimes operated as though it were doing a favor by torturing and killing a suspected dissident because this treatment could help the victim purge himself of heretical sentiments.

Ethnic and nationalistic interests have also dictated death as the solution on a mass scale. Perhaps it is unfair to single out particular examples from the past. This could perpetuate or rekindle old hostility and invite criticism of certain religious, ethnic, or national cultures. Nevertheless, I have been astounded time and again to learn how many people with reasonably good education had no glimmer at all, for example, of the Turkish massacre of Armenians or of the blood that flowed when the present nations of India and Pakistan were in process of forming their separate identities. It is also striking that there are people today who do not know of or who simply do not believe the mass murders carried out by Hitler's Germany. The role of the state was never more explicit. "The final solution of the Jewish problem" was a familiar phrase; death to men, women, and children was the reality.

But the state has not enjoyed exclusive privilege. Death is a problem-solving strategy that individuals also apply to other individuals. Reference has already been made to assassination.

The agent of destruction may be a self-ap-pointed judge-executioner-hero convinced that the act of destruction solves a major problem to society at large. Often, however, there is reason to believe that it is the assassin's own unrecognized personal problems that the mur-der is intended to solve.

Self-destruction is still another familiar way of attempting to solve problems. The problem may be one's sense of failure or the terrible an-ger one can not bring oneself to express. Other solutions have not seemed to work: perhaps the ultimate solution is required.

Counterpoised against this theme is the con-viction that death, far from being the final so-lution, is humankind's worst enemy and most profound problem. In fact, this theme provides one of the most ancient links that connect peo-ple of the present with all of history. We might consult historical scholarship such as Zandee's *Death as an Enemy According to Ancient Egyptian Conceptions*.[7] Or we might consult current high-priority efforts to prevent or cure cancer. Some specific approaches that have been taken in the effort to overcome death as ultimate problem will be considered else-where. Of particular interest here are some of the reasons why the death problem has been considered so critical to individual and society.

The death of individuals can threaten the continued existence of the total society. This threat is not based simply on the increased vul-nerability of society when an especially power-ful leader perishes or when an unusually large number of people die within a short period of time. The threat can instead take the form of generalized apprehension that the forces of dis-solution, chaos, and malevolence are about to triumph over the forces that enable people to remain together. Nature itself may be seen as conspiring to annihilate society, or the society may believe that the gods have become seri-ously displeased with how the people have been behaving. That a virile, admired young

person has died may disturb us because it un-dermines our assumptions, as well as for more personal reasons. If the cause of death is not clearly known, or even if it is, we might fear that the evil influences at work in the universe are gaining dominance. It is helpful in these circumstances if the society can identify partic-ular wrongdoers (such as a neighboring tribe), and take actions that demonstrate its continu-ing power (such as killing one of their young men in return). In other circumstances we might propitiate the gods in advance by offer-ing the life of one of our kinspeople in ex-change, say, for a bountiful harvest. The death of an individual, then, can either signify a ma-jor problem for the survival of society in gen-eral or serve as a means of facilitating survival.

Death is a fundamental problem because it ends our opportunity to achieve. Obviously, the importance of this theme is relative to the emphasis placed on achievement in our own lives or in society in general. "Need to achieve" is a familiar term in personality theory and research.[8] Psychologists recognize that this need is of much consequence not only to many people in the United States but also to those in other industrialized nations. This often is con-sidered to derive from the so-called Protestant ethic in which prolonged hard work and mak-ing something of ourselves offers a kind of sal-vation. Although this cannot be an all-encom-passing or completely satisfying explanation, it does suggest that our relationship to death is closely linked with our basic aims in life. If we are what we achieve, then death threatens to blow the whistle on us before we have become what we should be. "But I can't die yet—I have so much to do!"

Death is the ultimate problem because it erases us as experiencing beings. We do not think. We do not feel. We are insensible to the further course of time and event. For people who hold this view of death and for whom the inner life is of great significance, it is difficult to imagine a fate worse than death. All other considerations become secondary or even nonexistent. Death is far and away the greatest of calamities, for it closes down the theater of inner experience.

Death is the ultimate problem because it defies understanding. Never mind what little we think we know about death. What is death *really?* On both an abstract philosophical and a person level, death is perhaps the most difficult challenge to human understanding. This view may not be especially common. It is not likely to trouble people who are not troubled by thought problems in general or who have a preestablished answer that they find acceptable without critical scrutiny. But people with a strong need to think their way through problems, or at least to think they have thought their way through problems, may find death a challenge that dwarfs their understanding. It is the ultimate problem because it is the one that neither science nor logic can unravel.

THE ULTIMATE MEANINGLESS EVENT

Some events in life seem to have less meaning than others. It is also possible to regard the ending of life—death-as-event—as devoid of meaning. This interpretation should be distinguished from the conception that the *state* of death is identical with nonbeing. Maurice Maeterlinck (1936) did not leave blank the pages of his book entitled *Before the Great Silence*.[10] It is possible to think of death as nothing, and yet to have much to feel and express about our relationship to the void. Enormous emotional and intellectual tension can be generated in a dialectical process between a person's hopes and strivings on the one hand, and the prospect of a void that swallows everything without a trace. Much of human culture (the arts most obviously, but also many other fields of endeavor) bear witness to resourcefulness and creativity in the face of this confrontation.

The interpretation of death as meaningless

should also be distinguished from death as inexplicable. To say, "I don't know what death is, not really" is one thing. To conclude—or even to suspect—that death *has* no meaning or *means* no meaning is quite another matter.

What do we intend, then, by the suggestion that death is sometimes interpreted as a meaningless event? This refers to situations in which death appears to occur without context. It is (or seems to be) just an isolated or random event that comes along "without rhyme or reason." What we take as "meaning" in general involves a network of propositions or interrelationships. A comment may strike us as meaningless in one conversation, but relevant in another. A daub of color might appear as a meaningless splotch in one picture, but an enhancement in another. When a particular death, or death in general, seems to us to be without rationale, without context, then we are likely to interpret it as meaningless.

Many of us have grown up in the belief that death is *supposed* to be supremely meaningful, in one way or another. When the facts of experience appear to contradict this view, then there may be an inclination to swing to the diametrically opposite position: death is the epitome of nonmeaning. Random, senseless death is the ultimately meaningless event.

Two very different studies may help to clarify further the general point that is being made here. The typical detective novel has been a "who-done-it" that requires a corpse to provide raison d'étre for the plotwork. Kathlyn Ann Fritz (1975)[11] has examined representative British and American novels published during two decades, the 1930s and the 1960s. Most relevant here are the decades rather than the national differences in the attitudes embodied by these novels. In the 1930s the usual fictional homicide was presented as a rare event that interrupted the set ways of middle- or upperclass life. The murderer and the detective both had special characteristics, and there were often complex interrelationships among all the people involved. Thirty years later, however, murder seemed to be "almost as much out of control in the novels as in life, with some killers evading detection or penalty."[11,p.198] Death had become more rampant in society as well as literature since the 1930s. It was as though anybody could be killed, and anybody could kill, and none of it made much sense. Murder, as one form of death, had lost much of its place as a special event that would yield special meanings to those equipped to trace their way through clues false and true.

By contrast, aborigines in Australia's Northern Territory have held on to their conceptions of death meanings throughout the twentieth century despite continuing interactions with technological culture. Janice C. Reid (1978)[12] found in her recent fieldwork that ideas about the cause of serious illness and death were much the same as those recorded by anthropologists half a century earlier (and which probably had been dominant for many years before that). Essentially, the belief is that illness and death are the punishments to be expected when one transgresses against significant sanctions of social and religious law. Sorcerers and/or spirits serve as the agents who enforce the laws. The people who hold onto this typically "primitive" view of illness and death include many who are educated in Western ways and who do, in fact, make use of modern health services. One cannot cite ignorance, lack of intelligence, or defiance of "new ways" as explanation for this persistence. What, then? It is most probable that the aborigines continue to maintain their previous belief structure because it works! Reid observes that the transgression–punishment theory is not only logically consistent within itself (like the better modern medical theories), but has the advantage of providing "ultimate explanations for illness and death (that is, it explains why a certain person should be afflicted in a certain way

at a given time) . . . "[11,p.137] In other words, the aborigine finds that the "why" of death question is better answered by a time-honored "theoretical model" of the individual in the universe, rather than by modern medical science. To put it another way, the terminally ill aborigine is less likely to ask, "Why me?" than his or her counterpart in the general population. This prospect of death can be seen within a context that gives it meaning.

We will be coming on this question from another direction when we consider the *death system* in the following two chapters and elsewhere in this book.

A FEW IMPLICATIONS

Through the preceding chapters we have seen that people may have different ideas and events in mind when using the word *death*. This impression can only have been strengthened by the present examination of selected death meanings.

Perhaps the most obvious implication is that we would be wise not to assume that our own conceptions and meanings are shared by everyone we encounter. Even people who are much a part of our daily lives might have different interpretations and emphases. Most often we do not know what other views are held because death is not considered a fit topic for conversation. Lacking specific knowledge of the other person's orientation, it seems natural enough to assume that one's thoughts are his or hers as well. Those who have had experience in exposing their own thoughts and encouraging others to do the same will have already learned that this assumption is difficult to maintain.

The notion that everyone thinks about death as we do sometimes carries over to situations that are beyond our own daily experience. We may assume that a dying person who is a "good Christian" either is or should be pleased with the prospect of being gathered unto the Lord and rejoining loved ones. This assumption, however, may have little correspondence with the individual's own thoughts and feelings. If we insist upon believing that he or she must be thinking the way we think we would in the same situation, then we are apt to behave in an insensitive and inappropriate manner.

Perhaps, instead, we look on death as the ultimate catastrophe. It has no redeeming features whatsoever. In the wake of death the survivors can only feel desolate and traumatized and behave accordingly. We might then be puzzled, shocked, even angered by certain types of behavior on the part of survivors. It may not have crossed our minds that these deviations from what we think we would do under the same circumstances make good sense when understood within somebody else's frame of reference. We might brand someone else as a hypocrite when that person is faithfully carrying out obligations that come from a view of death that does not coincide with our own.

Placing a nurse's cap on one's head or allowing a stethoscope to bulge proudly from a white jacket does not necessarily change this mental orientation. Education in the health fields these days covers a broad span of knowledge and techniques, all subject to constant reexamination and revision. But until recently few provisions had been made to prepare future nurses, physicians, and other personnel for coping with death-related problems. Despite first-rate technical skill, then, the health-care provider may bring a set of unexamined, perhaps even inarticulate assumptions to the bedside of terminally ill patients and to their interactions with family members. Some care givers do not realize that each and every patient might have conceptions of death different from their own—and be entitled to hold these conceptions. Under these circumstances a wide variety of miscommunications, noncommunications, and unfortunate behaviors can result.

Notice that we do not have to assume any *special* anxieties, hang-ups, or misconceptions on the part of health personnel. Even less do we have to assume any inclination to use their position of power vis-à-vis the patient inappropriately. All that we need to question is whether or not the process of selecting and educating health professionals overcomes the *ordinary* anxieties and misconceptions that people in our society generally experience concerning death-related problems. Some critics have pressed further than this, claiming that physicians have even more hang-ups about death than people in general. This is a topic that will engage our attention later. But we do not have to go this far to light up the question marks in our eyes. Do technical education and the acquisition of health-care skills automatically result in a flexible and sophisticated perspective on the meanings of death? If not, should some serious attention perhaps be given to this matter?

When there are cultural gaps between ourselves and another group of people, there is even more likelihood of our misunderstanding their death-related behavior. We are more apt to arrive at conclusions based on anecdotal information that is incomplete, unrepresentative, outdated, or otherwise not thoroughly dependable. It is tempting to read their thoughts and behavior in ways that are most convenient for us. The assumption that Oriental people really do not become as upset about death as we do because "life is cheap over there" is one example that has had many political and military implications. Whenever we recognize that an assumption about somebody else's death meaning nicely fits our own predispositions and actions concerning them, then we might wonder if we truly understand their views or have indulged instead in a self-serving rationalization.

Perhaps the most general implication here is one that many sensitive people have learned for themselves since the current death-awareness movement has come into existence: we are a lot more likely to understand the meanings of death to another person if we give that person a full opportunity to express these to us. This occurs more readily, of course, if we have the ability and willness to listen.

SUMMARY

What difference does death make to us, what does it really mean?

Death can be seen as *the great leveler*. It is the powerful, relentless force that brings down the high and mighty as well as the lowliest of mortals. This interpretation of death warns those who set themselves above others to keep their pride and ambition within limits. It also establishes a mental and emotional context within which antiestablishment movements can flourish.

A contrasting theme is death as *the great validator*. This view emphasizes the ways in which death can confirm and support the status or distinction of an individual. Examples from the realm of funeral practice were emphasized. Some people behave as though the type of funeral arrangements carried out bear significantly on the status of the deceased and his or her survivors. Whether expressed in funeral practices or in other death-relevant behaviors, this theme makes death important as a final opportunity to "grade" the kind of life that has been lived.

The observation that death radically alters our relationship with other people has gained expression in a pair of contrasting themes. Some people emphasize the theme of *union* or *reunion* through death. The unification theme can center rather philosophically on friend and foe making a final peace or on the anticipation of dwelling with God. Perhaps the most common meaning, however, is the desire to be rejoined with specific people in one's own life who have gone before. Rituals associated with deaths and funerals can also serve the function of supporting the unity of society in general in the here-and-now.

The *separation* theme also recognizes the relationship-transfiguring aspect of death. Separation is experienced as an acute, wrenching-away crisis at the moment one becomes aware of a loved one's departure but may also be a cause of suffering both in advance of the death and afterward. One example given was that of the doomed family in which all the children faced death through illness that is beyond current medical expertise.

Another pair of related death meanings is death as the *ultimate solution* and the *ultimate problem*. Annihilation of individuals or groups of people is one characteristic "solution" that various societies have embraced. There is much large-scale precedent, then, for the individual who seeks to resolve a problem by taking a life, including his or her own. The conviction that death is the ultimate problem rather than the solution expresses itself in some of our individual and social priorities. Common invocations of this theme include the following sentiments: death of certain individuals can threaten the continued existence of society as a whole; death ends our opportunity to achieve; death erases the capacity for inner experience; death defies intellectual understanding.

The possibility that death is *meaningless* was also raised. Death (in particular or in general) is likely to apparently lack meaning when there is no context of rationale available. The need to attach *some* kind of meaning to death may underlie many individual and social behaviors, as will continue to be seen throughout this book.

All these diverse meanings have at least one implication in common: the desirability of suspending our own personal convictions long enough to learn what other people truly think and feel about death.

REFERENCES

1. Patrix, P. In F. P. Weber, *Aspects of death and correlated aspects of life in art, epigram and poetry*. London: H. K. Lewis & Co., Ltd., 1922.
2. Gottleib, C. Modern art and death. In H. Feifel (Ed.), *The meaning of death*. New York: McGraw-Hill Book Co., 1959.
3. Sophocles. *Antigone*. In L. Cooper (Ed.), *Fifteen*

Greek plays. New York: Oxford University Press, 1943.

4. Owen, W. Strange meeting. In E. Blunden (Ed.), *The poems of Wilfred Owen*. New York: New Directions Publishing Corp., 1959.

5. *The original sacred harp* (Denson Revision). Bremen, Ga.: Sacred Harp Publishing Co., 1971. (Originally published, 1855.)

6. Atkin, M. The "doomed family"—observations on the lives of parents and children facing repeated child mortality. In L. Burton (Ed.), *Care of the child facing death*. London & Boston: Routledge & Kegan Paul, 1974.

7. Zandee, J. *Death as an enemy according to ancient Egyptian conceptions*. Leiden, Netherlands: Leiden University Press, 1960.

8. McClelland, D., Atkinson, J. W., Clark, R. A., & Lowell, E. L. *The achievement motive*. New York: Halstead Press, 1975.

9. Vollbrecht, J. A. *Structure and function of communitas in an Ashanti village: the role of funerals*. Dissertation, University of Pennsylvania, 1978.

10. Maeterlinck, M. *Before the great silence*. New York: F. A. Stokes, 1936/New York: Arno Press (reprint), 1977.

11. Fritz, K. A. *Patterns and perceptions of homicide in detective novels*. Dissertation, Yale University, 1975.

12. Reid, J. C. *Sorcery and healing: the meaning of illness and death to an Australian aboriginal community*. Dissertation, Stanford University, 1978.

CHAPTER 6

❖ THE INDIVIDUAL IN THE DEATH SYSTEM
Two perspectives

Each of us has a life and death of our own. This establishes one fundamental perspective.

Everybody else has his or her own life and death as well. This establishes another fundamental perspective.

A serious exploration of death will respect both perspectives and respect the differences between them. Your personal orientation toward death and mine cannot truly be interchanged, added together, or otherwise made indistinguishable. No matter how much we might have in common, two different selves are the central characters in each framework. There are two basic individual perspectives to consider, then, one's own death, and the death of the other person.

Still another perspective demands our consideration as well. Although it is the individual who dies, each individual is member of a society. We have already seen that death ideas and meanings are expressed through society as well as the individual. To ignore the systematic orientations toward death on a sociocultural level would be to misunderstand and falsely isolate the individual from his context. It would also neglect many of the most crucial influences upon the individual's relationship to death, both mentally and physically.

This chapter introduces the two individual perspectives. In the next chapter the *death*

system itself will be introduced as such. The separate attention given now to each perspective taken separately is not meant to fragment our thinking. On the contrary, it is by making the effort to distinguish these frameworks and appreciate each in its own right that we will find ourselves more competent in understanding the individual *in* the death system.

YOUR OWN DEATH

You are your own best source of information regarding your personal orientation toward death. What follows here are a few thoughts and questions intended to help you become better acquainted with your personal orientation.

First, perhaps, we should face the problem of being asked to consider personal thoughts and feelings at all. Usually we expect a book or an academic course to educate us about phenomena outside ourselves. Even if the course is about what is *inside* us (e.g., anatomy and physiology), we expect to be studying somebody else's bones and nerve endings. There is really no substitute, however, for incorporating our personal framework into the study of death. We are mortals all, and each of us a separate mortal. If we include ourselves out, then we are implying a very special relationship to life and death, perhaps even the extreme position of denying that we need to maintain any personal perspective. You might, then, find it interesting to monitor your own feelings and thoughts as personally oriented questions are presented, both here and in later sections. Notice what questions make you smile, what questions make you wince, what questions touch off sparks or liberate a flow of ideas, images, feelings, what questions leave you drawing at least a momentary blank, and so on. Notice when you feel satisfied that you have come up with the answer that is correct for you, at least at this moment in your life, and notice when you have not quite been able to persuade yourself.

Early memories

Begin with an exercise in memory. Think back to your *first* experience with death. (An even earlier memory might come back to you at another time, but search for the earliest that you can bring to your mind right now.) This

---

YOUR EARLIEST DEATH-RELATED MEMORY

1. This is my memory: _____

   _____

   _____

   _____

   _____

   _____

   _____

   _____

   _____

   _____

   _____

   _____

2. I was about age _____ at the time.

3. The experience, *when it happened*, could best be described by words such as: (choose 3 or 4 adjectives) _____ _____ _____ _____

4. The experience, *as it comes back to me now*, can best be described by words such as: _____ _____ _____ _____

5. The *memory itself* is ☐ Very clear ☐ Fairly clear ☐ Vague to me.

6. Until today, I have thought about this experience: ☐ Often ☐ More than once ☐ Once ☐ Not at all

7. The *effect* this experience has had on me is probably: ☐ Very influential ☐ Somewhat influential ☐ No influence at all

memory might involve *any* kind of relationship with death. As this memory filters into conscious awareness, capture it in words. It is suggested that you write down this memory while it is still fresh to you. Using the form provided in this chapter will enable you to keep a record of this memory for yourself, as you might well want to consult it later. You will be most faithful to this memory if you allow yourself freedom of expression, using the words that best

---

YOUR FIRST REALIZATION OF PERSONAL MORTALITY*

1. This was the *situation* (time, place, what was happening, who you were with, etc.): _____
_____
_____
_____
_____
_____
_____

2. These were *my thoughts and feelings*, as best as I can recall them: _____
_____
_____
_____
_____
_____
_____

3. I *shared* these thoughts and feelings with: _____
_____

4. The *reply or response* I received when sharing my realization of mortality: _____
_____
_____
_____

---

*Perhaps you have not yet come to a full realization of your personal mortality. If this is the case, then try to imagine the type of situation in which this realization might develop for you.

seem to describe the experience as you now recall it and not fussing too much about grammar.

You will have noticed a few items in the boxed material requesting specific information about the memory. Complete these items.

Now, while you still have your early experiences in mind, think of one situation in particular—the situation in which you first realized that you were certain to die some day. Some people are able to report a specific moment in their lives when this realization emerged. Perhaps you can do the same, after a little thought. But if you cannot pinpoint your *first* recognition of personal mortality, then recall *any* situation in your past life when this awareness was clearly on your mind. Give yourself enough time to let the memories drift back. Again, it is suggested you make use of the guide provided in this book (boxed material), and make a record of this memory for your own continued use.

Reflections

Reflect a moment now. Did you find both personal experiences coming readily to mind? Or did one or both memories prove elusive? When you did recapture these scenes, were they clear and vivid or dim and out of focus? The ease with which your own death-related experiences are available to you is an important aspect of your total relationship to mortality. These two memory exercises will not fully explore this question, of course. But they provide a beginning in your taking stock of what you already have learned, experienced, and thought about death and what use you might wish to put this background.

Perhaps, for example, you blocked on one or all of these questions. For some reason you drew a blank, or the memories eventually came forth only in a grudging manner, fragmentary, vague, not quite sharp. This could mean that the task itself aroused anxiety within you. Scanning your past for death-relevant experiences might have been so discomforting an experience that your mind was not about to be cooperative, even though you started the search willingly enough. Another possibility is that something about the memories themselves resisted the retrieval. The person you are today could manage the challenge of calling forth past death experiences; but the memories are embedded in life-points to which disturbing feelings are still attached.

Stay with the first possibility a little longer. If personal death anxiety is relatively high for you these days, then you might find yourself turning off still other stimuli that have implications for your own life. It might not be a problem for you to learn about the way in which other people relate to death. You are ready to be a good student of dying, death, and related phenomena so long as you keep a safe distance from what you are studying. But whenever the topic comes close to your own feelings, you might draw back. This drawing back can take a perceptual form: the words are spoken or written, but somehow do not register on you. It can also be conceptual: information is registered, but it is walled off from any implications for your own life—into the notebook it goes and there it remains! And it can also be more purely emotional: exposure to death experiences with personal implications may hurt you, make you feel upset. All of these drawing-back responses can occur more or less together as well.

Some of this anxiety may wear off as you gradually open yourself to the topic. You will read more about death; you will share your ideas with others. Perhaps you will discover that some of your anxiety was generated by concerns based on incomplete or misleading information. Yet it might also be that the discomforting experiences stirred up by personally relevant death material will prove more persistent. What is to be done if this is the situation in which you find yourself? You might simply close the book. You could withdraw from the class, if you are taking one in conjunction with this book. You could engage in other retreat maneuvers, at least temporarily. It is not necessarily a sign of "weakness" to do so. There are times in our lives when we are not ready to take on certain problems or adventures, and forcing the issue is not always the best strategy. Or you might instead approach somebody in whom you have much confidence and respect to find other ways of coming to terms with your present discomfort with the subject of death. Whatever choice you make, it may prove to your advantage simply to recognize that, for one reason or another, you do have some personal concerns that are making it difficult to include your own frame of reference as part of the more general quest for understanding death, society, and human experience.

Awareness of our own anxiety level about death and related topics can spare others as well as ourselves some unfortunate consequences. Particularly unfortunate are those situations in which a person who is unable to cope with his or her death problems becomes a decision maker or control agent for others. Hysterical behavior on the part of a parent, for example, or rigid, uncommunicative behavior on the part of a physician can have negative outcomes for those who must rely on them. Whatever your current ability to cope with death-related problems on a personal level, it is unlikely that you could—or should—delegate all responsibility to others. But if anxiety is running high at a particular time in your life, it may be a service to yourself and others if you do not *seek out* situations in which death-related decisions must be made or death-related actions performed.

But isn't there still another possible explanation for difficulty that might be experienced in trying to retrieve death-related memories— that is, that there are no memories to retrieve?

Theoretically, a person might have been around life as long as you have been and just not had any experiences related to death. Few people move from early childhood to the adult years without encountering death in some form. But the possibility that you might be one of these exceptions cannot be dismissed. More often, a person may not classify certain experiences as being death relevant. In such a case, there is not so much an emotional blocking as a frame of reference in which death means only a very specific and limited range of phenomena. The *range* of phenomena you regard as death related is part of your perspective, as is the *accessibility* of personal death experiences to conscious awareness.

The age at which you first came to a clear realization of your own mortality is another personal characteristic that should be taken into account. Perhaps you still do not really hold the view that your life will end in death. The "really" in the preceding sentence is meant to suggest the kind of realization that requires cooperation from the emotional and so-called deeper layers of our personalities as well as intellectual acknowledgement. But perhaps you have been carrying this realization around for many years now. In trying to understand your general orientation toward life, it would be valuable to know what contribution has been made by your personal developmental history of death concepts and attitudes.

At this point we will not delve into every aspect of the two memory questions. Some of the implications will be taken up in appropriate places later; others go beyond the scope of this book. But you are now starting to make your own death-relevant experiences accessible to yourself. This is perhaps the most important aspect of the total learning experience. You will become increasingly able to frame your own questions and perhaps find your own answers while continuing to explore death in its more general aspects as well. More ready access to your own thoughts, feelings, and experiences, whatever they might be, will help you discover what it is you really want to know about your relationship to death and what, if anything, you might wish to change.

THE OTHER PERSON'S DEATH

We shift perspective now. Focus is still on the individual, but it is somebody else, anybody else, everybody else. This is the name we read in the death notices, the body in the hearse that passes by, the patient we see coming out of the physician's office before we take our turn, his face ashen and tense. There may be much in common between the other person's life and death and our own, but the unbridgeable fact that we are two different people provides a frame of reference that he cannot have for himself. A full and sympathetic case history approach can yield the impression that we know what the other person is thinking and feeling. We can *construct* a more or less adequate picture of his relationship to death as we think he himself sees it. This is valuable but should not be mistaken for the perspective and feeling quality that only the person inside can have. The same distinction remains, of course, when the positions are reversed and we are the other person ourselves.

Let us sample a few of the ways in which we can learn about the other person. Each method has its advantages and disadvantages. All involve some form of observation or data collection, analysis of the observations, and interpretation. These processes may be carried out in an organized, scientific manner or as an integral part of daily life among the many observations, judgments, and decisions we make without necessarily paying much attention to the process as such. It would be simpler just to consider the results of our learning experiences—agreed! But neglect of process and methodology would leave us poorly prepared to evaluate, compare, and integrate the variety of conclusions that are reported, or that we reach on our own. We would be in the position of having to accept or reject conclusions based on how "authoritative" we take the source to be (and, possibly, how we feel about authorities in general and whether or not we happen to like the particular results that are reported). Furthermore, without some attention to method we are apt to forget that all information has to come from somewhere and has to come through use of specific observational and analytical techniques.

Some people yawn at method. Describe a technique or flash a chart and they drift off immediately into the sleep of the blessed. Others maintain that there is no way—no way!—to study death scientifically. Interestingly, the yawners and the scoffers often are the same people who bristle with ideas of their own on the subject. They "know." But where did their ideas come from? What are their limits? How can they be evaluated? These questions are not to be asked! Obviously, I am suggesting that openness to experience is useful when we are interested in the other person's death as well as when the focus is on ourselves.

Living with a person who is facing death

Before considering scientific approaches to understanding the other person's death, let us remind ourselves that many of us have had or will have the experience of living with a person who faces the certainty or unusually high risk of death. For some people this is a continuing, everyday situation. Perhaps somebody in your family is engaged in a high-risk occupation, one in which a life-threatening confrontation could occur at almost any time. The "widow's watch," a small tower that sits atop seaside houses, is a vestige from previous generations in which the families of sea-faring men knew that every departure could be the last one. A police officer or fire fighter might carry out more or less routine duties most of the time, but an emergency situation might suddenly place this person in great jeopardy. Today we tend to think of death as a possible outcome of serious illness or chronic and progressive disability. It is worth remembering, however, that there are still many families who live with the knowledge that one or more of their members are at unusual risk even though in good health. This sphere of concern for the person facing death has been relatively neglected both by "thanatologists" (a name sometimes given to or taken up by those who study death-related phenomena scientifically) and by those who study the dynamics of family life in general. It is likely that there are some important similarities along with many important differences between the family in which one member is clearly afflicted with a terminal illness and the family in which a healthy individual functions within a framework of unusually high life jeopardy. The sea still claims its victims, for example, despite the many advances in technology and safety through the years. How do crew members of a small fishing vessel think and feel about death as they set out, knowing that they may encounter severe storms or other emergency conditions? How well are their thoughts and feelings understood by those who remain at home? Does death have the same meaning in these family constellations as it does for families in which nobody is in particular life jeopardy?

The most commonly reported type of living-with-death experience today, however, involves terminal illness. The situation is frequently a complex and ambiguous one, since, for example, it is often not clear precisely when and if a person is dying (Chapter 11). There have by now been many personal accounts offered by those who have lived intimately with the terminally ill. Books that share such experiences include *Death Be Not Proud* (Gunter, 1965)[1]; *Death of a Man* (Wertenbaker, 1957)[2]; *Eric* (Lund, 1974)[3]; *Ending* (Wolitzger, 1975)[4]; *Gramp* (Jury & Jury, 1976)[5]; and *Rachel*

(Smith, 1975).[6] Briefer accounts also continue to appear in both the popular media and the professional literature. Many of these contributions can educate our feelings in a way that is seldom accomplished by more scientific reports. This is in part because the person sharing such an experience is not bound to the objectivistic tone expected in scientific and clinical reports. The accounts can be more expressive and "natural." But there is also likely to be a different emphasis in the aims of the report. Scientists in all fields seek dependable generalizations, the laws or principles that apply to a whole class of phenomena. En route to developing these generalizations, the scientist is apt to compile a vast amount of descriptive information on many cases or instances. Most particular instances are seen as important only as they contribute to the accumulation of a stockpile of information that will make it possible to classify, predict, explain, and control phenomena in general. This is a long way from what happens within the intimate circle of human concern in daily life. The focus here is on the individual. General principles and the experiences of others may be of interest only if they can provide some help in understanding and comforting the particular person whose situation has compelled our attention. It is not surprising that individuality shines forth more clearly in reports concerning death-of-the-other when the communication is of a personal rather than scientific nature.

If we ourselves have lived in close relationship to a terminally ill person, this singular experience may have exerted a strong influence on our general thoughts and feelings about death. The same may be true to a lesser extent if we read only one account written by somebody who has been in that position. We may learn much from this access to another person's experiences, but also may come away so much under the influence of this one experience that we are inclined to generalize our reaction to other situations that are actually just as unique but very different.

Suppose, for example, that we had either experienced what a young woman went through after the birth of her first child, or read about it in her own words. Wende Kernan Bowie (1977) prepared a journal reporting on Michael's short life.[7] She herself was a healthy person who had enjoyed a happy pregnancy, was joined by her husband in Lamaze training, and was admitted to "our community's excellent teaching hospital" for delivery of the child. "As my husband left my . . . hospital room that bright afternoon, I said to him, "Lee, we have a son! We have a son!" I was happy; I was exhausted; and I couldn't possibly sleep; I wanted to call just one more person to tell them our child was finally born! I wanted to tell the world."

This proved to be the end rather than the beginning of the new mother's happiness. An intern informed her that night that Michael had required a plasma transfusion along with draining of some of his blood to bring down an excessive count of red blood cells. He was downstairs, being observed in a special nursery but would be brought up to the regular nursery by midnight. Mrs. Bowie waited through the night and the early-morning hours to see her baby or at least to hear further news about him. Neither of these things happened. The next day she heard a group of physicians reviewing her case outside her room in low voices. This made her angry and increased her anxiety for Michael. ("I thought they were concealing facts from me.")

Finally, the doctors stood at the foot of my bed. One of them told me that my blood pressure was too high. I said, "Of course my blood pressure is too high, I'm worried about my baby!" Honestly, I was thinking, what happens to me is so very unimportant; of course I have high blood pressure! I've not slept a wink for waiting all night and worrying and hoping. The doctor replied curtly that he certainly knew more about my condition than I did and asked me to bare my knee so that he could check my reflexes. My reflexes were fine. The doctor turned on his heel and without another word to me, left the room, followed by the others. I was once again left alone with my thoughts, which were becoming progressively more ominous. There was not a word about Michael.

Further information about Michael's condition came in bits and pieces, none of it accompanied by any apparent sensitivity to the feelings of the parents. Mrs. Bowie herself was approached by a student nurse with some pills (no explanation of the pills and their purpose offered). When she inquired, the reply was that they were Valium and phenobarbital and would really "knock her out." It took another unpleasant go-around between the parents and a physician reluctant to explain or discuss his prescription, and then Mrs. Bowie, drugged and in a wheelchair, was taken to see her baby for the first time. The scene was discomforting, a neon-lit room dominated by medical equipment. All visitors had to scrub down and wear sterile gowns, further adding to a sense of alienation. Michael himself, was "adorable." She was allowed to feed him with a bottle of formula but felt too intimidated to ask the questions that came to her mind. When she returned to her room, "the flood of maternal feelings overcame me. The sense of separation from Michael was unbearable. I felt a strong need to be near him. It was agony, and I was very frightened that this separation would interfere with my future relationship with this baby for whom I was responsible."

As the day-to-day situation unfolded, more problems with Michael's condition were either discovered or reported, and the treatment of both parents by the health-care establishment continued to come across as authoritarian, aloof, and unsympathetic. It became increasingly clear that the medical staff was having a difficult time in establishing a definitive diag-

nosis and that this was their major preoccupation. The parents, meanwhile, were experiencing great anxiety and Mrs. Bowie, in particular,
a desperate need to be near her firstborn. She
finally worked up the courage to ask her pedia-
trician if she could breast-feed Michael (the
baby had been kept in the hospital but she had
been discharged). Consent was given, although
with mixed feelings by the medical staff, and,
with quite some difficulty but much emotional
satisfaction, she did have several opportunities
to feed him successfully. Even one of the
breast-feeding opportunities turned into a
scene of tension and humiliation when two pe-
diatric cardiologists decided to observe. Michael was sleeping at the time and hard to
arouse.

The female cardiologist broke in: "Now, when you
feed this baby, I want to see no fooling around; he
must get right down to the business of eating and
waste no time outside of his isolette. . . ." Michael
remained asleep. Finally, when it became clear that
he just wasn't interested in his breakfast that day,
the cardiologist asked, "Have you ever breast fed a
baby before?" I felt defensive and surprised at the
question. "No," I responded truthfully, "this is my
first baby." She walked out of the room briskly,
leaving me, breasts still bare, sitting in an armchair.
As she left she threw over her shoulder, "Well, we
shall just have to get someone down here who knows
what they're doing."

This undermining of Mrs. Bowie's competence as a mother was one more part of what
she progressively felt as enforced alienation
from her baby. Later in the process there was
a miscommunication from the hospital that
caused acute—and unnecessary—alarm on the
part of the parents. And, still later, there was
a serious error by a technician that resulted in
the injection of the wrong substance into Michael's heart. Paradoxically, when one of the
physicians immediately admitted and explained
the error, the parents felt a sense of relief in
the discovery that here at last a member of the

medical staff whom they could trust. This doctor turned out to be their only dependable
source of information about the plans that the
staff had for Michael. The staff in general continued to resist efforts on the part of both parents for information on Michael's condition (although both parents were well educated and
could understand medical findings, especially
with a little help).

The remaining time left to Michael was
eventful both in terms of medical events and
their impact on the parents, although there is
not space to give the details here. Hope flick-
ered at times, and, in at least one further instance, an arbitrary decision had been made
when a resident on duty not very familiar with
the history of Michael's situation had him taken
off the respirator, with very unfortunate results. Near the end:

Michael was white. He lay limp on his pillow with
his eyes opening and closing slowly. Lee (Mr.
Bowie) said that he was cold to the touch. I took one
look and covered my eyes—he was so obviously
dying. No one spoke to us and no one looked up
when we entered the nursery. All we could hear
were the machines bubbling and sighing—and Michael lay white on his bed. . . . It was very quiet.
We left the hospital. We didn't know what to do
with ourselves, not wanting to go home for the inevitable phone call. Finally we went home and the
resident called to tell us that Michael had died ten
minutes after we left. We were shaking inside.

There is much that could be said about this
experience with the death of the other person.
We must limit ourselves to just a few observations here. The unexpected complications and
eventual death of Michael would have been difficult for the parents to bear under any circumstances. Their anguish was heightened, however, by attitudes and behaviors on the part of
the health-care establishment that came across
as insensitive, unsympathetic, and heavy-
handed. Michael's life and death could not easily be separated, then, from a generally alien-

ating social and physical context. The account was "biased" in that Mrs. Bowie reports on her own personal experiences (although she does also make reasonable speculations on why some of the others behaved as they did). A more rounded account would require access to the experiences and viewpoints of the various physicians, nurses, and technicians who were involved in Michael's care. It is the impact of the experience on Mrs. Bowie herself, however, that matters chiefly here, the young woman who was to lose her first born to death. Suppose that this was and remained an individual's only experience with the death-of-the-other. How strongly this experience might influence the individual's view of death in general!

It is important to remind ourselves, then, that one life and death is not necessarily like another. There are limits to generalization. Nancy Harjan (1978) lost her Michael at age 16 after five months of struggle with acute leukemia. As a young child he had shown symptoms consistent with chronic leukemia, a condition that is easier to control; but now it became evident that he had a particularly intractable form of acute leukemia.[8] In a fundamental sense the outcome was the same: this Michael also died. The course of his life while death was in prospect, however, was vastly different. We would expect major differences, of course, since Michael Harjan was a full-fledged personality with all the psychological resources of a normal adolescent. Nevertheless, he *might* have become a medically captive, socially abandoned person. Fortunately, this was not the case. There was, for example, a friendship with "Little Nancy" (he also had another good friend, "Big Nancy") that deepened and became especially sustaining throughout this process. During a month of hospitalization, every day,

from the start of visiting hours at 10:00 a.m. until 8:30 in the evening, Little Nancy was at Michael's bedside. She nursed him, read to him, played cards and games with him, and encouraged him to keep

going. And, indeed he did; his own courage and morale were equally amazing. Michael and Nancy became an inspiration to all of us and won the respect and love of the doctors and nurses as well.[8,p.81]

Michael made a remarkable recovery, but was in trouble again a couple of months later. He was in and out of the hospital. When he was able to be home for a day, he took Little Nancy on a motorcycle ride and showed her how to operate it herself. When he had to return to the hospital, the staff had enough affection and respect for the two of them, that Little Nancy was allowed to stay with him all night. Other friends and relatives were also on the scene. The apprehension that death might not be far away was shared by many of these people, but it did not drive them off. Instead, Michael had constant companionship from the people who were important to him (and to each other). When Michael's companions were not at his bedside during the last few days they often would visit each other around a coffee table near his hospital room. Michael's mother had the direct-presence support of the other involved people when she saw him for the last time. "Sheila (a friend) and the nurses were in the hall telling us that Michael had just passed away and that he'd gone very peacefully. I went in to say good-bye to Michael and remember thinking to myself how beautiful he looked, that his dead body was neither frightening nor repulsive. I thought to myself, *death isn't so bad*" [italics in the original].[8,p.81]

During all this time the family took security and comfort in the fact that the physician responsible for Michael's care remained available to them, answered their questions, and seemed genuinely sensitive to his personal welfare. Both this physician and the staff members of the hospital proved willing to stretch the rules on occasion to help Michael live out the kind of life he preferred and to accommodate those who were close to him.

Never did the doctors or nurses make us feel that we were in the way. Thus, Michael was allowed to have a death of dignity and love. I remember being struck by the feeling that Michael's hospital room was charged with tremendous energy. It was as if intense love were being passed from person to person and between Michael and each one of us. It was truly awesome and I cannot imagine his death happening otherwise. It seemed so natural.[8,p.83]

These have been samplings from only two experiences with the death-of-the-other-person. You can see how exposure to either one of the experiences could lead to strong but very different constellations of thought and feeling about death. Talking with a variety of people who have been close to another person when death was in prospect or reading a variety of accounts can help us to transcend the limited number of experiences we may have had directly in our own lives and thereby enable us to develop a broader perspective. These personal accounts cannot provide some of the vital information that well-designed research can yield, but they are important to the education of our feelings and the search for clues to better care of terminally ill people and those close to them.

Self-report

Asking the other person to provide personal information is perhaps the most obvious technique when we turn to formal research methodology. It is used for many topics in psychology and related fields and frequently employed in death-related studies. The self-report technique may be open-ended, fixed choice, or some combination of both. The earliest death memory inquiry presented earlier in this chapter asks one major question that the respondents answer in their own words, supplemented by several fixed-choice items.

Let us look at a few fresh examples of this kind of technique and what kind of information it can provide. The first edition of this book took as an extended example a study by David Lester (1974) and his colleagues that made use of his own well-known death-anxiety questionnaire.[9] Included among the 57 items on the questionnaire are such as: "I would avoid death at all costs." "I am disturbed by the physical degeneration involved in a slow death." "I would avoid a friend who is dying." The particular study reviewed was conducted with students and faculty associated with a school of nursing. Among other findings, this study indicated that the respondents often did answer quite differently depending on whether the items centered around their own death or the death of other people. Students who are having their first exposure to death and dying in the clinical situation tend to report relatively high anxiety related to their own dying and death. As their experience in the situation increases, however, and as they receive more academic background, this type of fear appears to diminish while concern about dying and death of other people either remains about the same or increases. There was one interesting exception to the general finding that more knowledge is associated with lower self-related death fears. Faculty members expressed rather low levels of death concern in general, but "dying of self" was not only by far the highest of their concerns but reversed the trend toward less fear with increased academic preparation. Lester and his colleagues suggest that "the greater mean age of faculty members and a resulting chronological nearness to an age at which their own death is more likely to occur may account for the increased subscale score."[9,p.52]

Self-report measures such as the Lester Scale have their limitations (including, but not limited to the respondent's ability to misrepresent his or her own state of mind if inclined to do so). Nevertheless, they can be useful in accumulating a mass of information against which specific questions and situations can be viewed, and in testing out the value of distinctions such as the death-of-self vs death-of-others orientation.

A series of interrelated studies by Jerome Tobacyk and Dan Eckstein (1980) takes us a little further along the road to understanding the implications of self-reported death concern.[10] College students were asked to complete two questionnaires related to their personality styles. One of the questionnaires attempts to assess the level of "trait anxiety," essentially, the amount of perturbation or anxiety we carry with us from situation to situation, our "normal load of anxiety." The other questionnaire attempts to assess preference for either approaching or avoiding threatening stimuli in general. In addition, the undergraduates were given two different measures related to their death orientations. One was a straightforward 30-item death-concern questionnaire. The other was a slightly more complex procedure known as the Threat Index that has been found particularly useful in the past few years (e.g., Krieger, Epting, & Leitner, 1974[11]; Rainey & Epting, 1977[12]). In the particular form used by Tobacyk and Eckstein, this procedure asks the respondent to rate "self" and then "your own death" on each of 40 dimensions. A person might place these two terms on the same spot on any particular dimension, place them as far apart as possible from each other, or in any in-between position. A Threat Index score is computed by counting the number of "splits," that is, instances in which "self" and "your own death" are placed at great distance from each other. The more splits, then the more systematic reorganization of one's thoughts would be necessary to bring self and own death together, therefore, the greater the death threat. This is the logic behind the procedure and its basic methodology.

The pattern of findings included several worth mentioning here. The college student with relatively high trait-anxiety scores also tended to have approach rather than avoidance styles toward threatening stimuli in general, and to score higher on both the death-concern and Threat Index scales. Relatively high death concern, then, appeared to be related to more general aspects of the individual's psychological functioning. Those who reported more death concern or had higher death-threat scores might be described as somewhat more vulnerable, open, or undefended. And yet death concern could not be viewed as identical with responses to death threat. Those students who enrolled in a thanatology course showed greater conscious *concern* about death than those who did not enroll in this course, but they had lower scores on the death-threat procedure. In other words, while in general both instruments tap the individual's orientation toward death, it is one thing to have a general awareness and concern and another to perceive death as a more personal threat to one's self. Interestingly, response to the death-threat instrument also decreased more on a retest for those who had taken as compared with those who did not take the thanatology course. Students whose trait-anxiety levels were relatively low at the outset of the course showed even more decrease in the death-threat index at the end. This suggests that a high level of general anxiety may include high concern about the threat along with many other fears that burden the individual. People with more moderate levels of general anxiety may have "picked up" alarm reactions toward death that are not as consistent with their overall approach to life, and may therefore find it easier to reduce their vulnerability to threat of death when given an opportunity to explore the subject in a systematic way.

Many other studies on a self-report nature are being carried out with a variety of specific objectives in mind. Useful as such studies can be when properly designed and interpreted, they are not in themselves sufficient to bring all the facts to light. Several other general types of approach remain to be illustrated.

Naturalistic observation

We might observe what people actually do in death-related situations. This approach can be relatively unstructured; for example, quietly becoming part of the group at a funeral or wake. Or it can be tightly structured, with particular observational tasks and goals preestablished. The observer who himself becomes a part of the situation, especially for a prolonged period of time, is often called a participant-observer (PO). David Reynolds, for example, became a PO when he entered a mental hospital as though he were a suicidal patient to learn what takes place from an insider's perspective (Reynolds & Farberow, 1973[13]; see also Chapter 15). More recently, he used the same approach to study suicidality and related behaviors in psychiatric aftercare facilities (Reynolds & Farberow, 1978[14]).

Robert W. Buckingham and colleagues seem to have gone even further in their PO study of life among the terminally ill. A 31-year-old medical anthropologist in good health, Buckingham assumed the role of a patient with terminal pancreatic carcinoma. While several hospital officials necessarily were aware of the plan, gave their permission, and worked out some safeguards, for the most part Buckingham was treated as though he were in fact a terminally ill patient.[15] It was a rigorous experience for "M" (code name of the researcher during the course of his study):

To simulate features of his assumed medical history M submitted to supraclavicular incision, indicative of cervical lymph node biopsy, and ultraviolet irradiation to produce erythema over the epigastrium and spine, suggestive of radiation therapy to the pancreas. M reviewed medical charts and maintained close contact with patients dying with carcinoma of the pancreas. He was thus able to observe and imitate suitable behaviour. Puncture sites from intravenous infusion needles on the hands and arms, a 10-kg weight loss induced by a 6-month diet, patchy beard alopecia related to the stress of preparation, and abstinence of several days from washing or shaving completed the picture.[15,pp.1211-1212]

His risks and stresses continued throughout the course of the study. Some of Buckingham's observations will be reported in a later chapter. The point for now is that at times research may come very close indeed to "the action," and not limit itself to devising and handing out questionnaires.

Whatever the particular technique used, a key feature of naturalistic observation is the attempt to learn what takes place in the situation just the way it is usually to be found. Here is an example in which naturalistic observation was coupled with self-report. Every time a person crosses the street in busy city traffic there is some risk of accident. This risk can either be minimized or increased by the individual's behavior. Crossing the street, then, is one logical situation in which to make observations—the behavior is right out in the open for anybody to see and record.

The place was an active intersection in Detroit with bustling pedestrian and vehicular traffic. The investigators, Robert Kastenbaum and Laura Briscoe (1975), were interested in the problem of life-threatening behavior.[16] In particular, they wondered which of two possibilities was the more powerful in determining behavior: (1) Each of us has a certain characteristic level of lethality (Shneidman, 1973)[17] or life-riskingness that we take with us from situation to situation; (2) each *situation* has a characteristic "pull" that evokes either little or much life-threatening behavior. If the first alternative proved to be the more significant, then we should emphasize what the individual brings to the situation. The second alternative invites more attention to the environmental impact on the individual. In addition to this problem, the investigators were interested in the degree of correspondence between what people actually do (when naturalistically observed) and what they say about themselves (self-report technique).

First, the investigators simply observed people crossing the street. From these observations a set of categories was developed. Each of the five types of street crossing was defined by specific behaviors that could easily be seen. This can be illustrated through the extreme categories, type A considered as the one with minimal life-threatening characteristic and type E as the most dangerous.

The *type* A pedestrian:

Stood on the curb until the light changed in his or her favor

Glanced briefly at the oncoming traffic in the nearest lanes

Immediately entered the crosswalk

Moved across at a moderate-to-brisk pace

Checked out traffic from the opposite-direction lanes before reaching the half-way point

Exhibited no erratic or dilatory behaviors

The *type* E pedestrian:

Stepped out from some location other than the corner (e.g., middle of the block)

From between parked cars

With the traffic light against him or her

And without looking in either direction

This small study involved 25 people who were observed to fall into each of the five categories through observations made during the daylight hours. All 125 street crossers were asked to answer a few questions after they had reached the other side of the street; only one potential interviewee refused the request, and was replaced by the next person whose street-crossing maneuver placed him in the same category. The street crossers ranged in age from 17 to 55 years, many of them college students. There were 55 women and 70 men. (An incidental finding of this study was that a higher proportion of the women were more self-protective or less risk-taking in their behavior.)

The relationship between what the observer saw and what the individual reported about himself turned out to be highly systematic. People who had crossed the street carefully according to the observer's record reported themselves to have been more aware of the fact that they had, indeed, just crossed the street! Furthermore, they considered their crossing to have been more safety oriented than did the more risk-taking pedestrians. Next, all were asked several questions about the degree of risk taking in which they engage when they are in other situations. Those who had taken more risks in crossing the street reported themselves to be riskier when behind the wheel of a car. Nineteen of the type A crossers stated that they were the safest kind of motorist, compared to only one of the type E. The participants were then asked a more general question: "How much of the time do you consider your life to be in danger, in jeopardy?" Type A pedestrians felt that they were in jeopardy, on the average, 2.1% of the time during a typical week; type E pedestrians thought they were in jeopardy 16.1% of the time—about eight times more!

The same pattern emerged when the street crossers were asked, "Have you ever attempted or contemplated suicide?" Affirmative answers were given by 8% of the type A pedestrians, by 32% of the type Es. The pattern continued when the participants were asked, "Have you ever been involved in an automobile accident when you were the driver?" Five of the safest crossers answered yes, but *all* 23 of the type E crossers who operated automobiles reported at least one accident! Furthermore, *none* of the type A crossers reported more than one accident, while 19 of the 23 driving type Es reported multiple mishaps, for a group total of 61, compared with a group total of only 5 for the type As.

TABLE 1. Sense of frustration in life*

Level of frustration	Type A	Type B	Type C	Type D	Type E
Almost always	0	0	0	16	16
Usually	0	0	12	20	32
Often	4	16	40	32	32
Occasionally	24	40	36	32	16
Seldom	72	44	12	0	4

*Expressed as the percentage of participants of each type reporting corresponding frustration level.

TABLE 2. Marital status

Marital status	Type A	Type B	Type C	Type D	Type E
Married	14	11	8	6	3
Single	10	8	9	16	19
Divorced	1	2	4	1	1
Separated	0	2	3	2	1
Widowed	0	2	1	0	1

Findings of this kind suggested, first, that simple naturalistic observation can be closely related to the individual's own perception of his behavior and to his behavior in other situations. Additionally, these particular data indicated that people tend to bring a certain level of life-threatening or -safeguarding behavior with them from situation to situation.

One question entered the realm of inner feeling: "As you go through life, how much of the time do you have a sense of frustration? Think about a typical week, for example." Results are shown in Table 1. The safe pedestrians reported much lower levels of characteristic frustration than did the risk takers; only 1 of 50 people of the D and E types reported freedom from frustration. Another question explored interpersonal relationships by inquiring into marital status. Results are shown in Table 2. It is evident that more of the safer pedestrians were married than the risk takers.

This was a death-related study in which no actual deaths were involved. But the pattern of behavior observed and the pattern of behavior and mood reported indicate that some of the people crossing that busy intersection were alertly protecting their continued survival while others were either being careless or actually seeking a sudden and violent ending. Not too much should be made of this one particular study. However, it does at least suggest that there is a point to the naturalistic observation technique within the domain of life-and-death–related behavior. Seeing a person dart out from between parked cars in the middle of the block while the light is against him is a fair basis for concern. This person is more likely than others to be frustrated, risk-taking in a variety of situations, beset by suicidal thoughts, and without the solidarity of a marriage relationship: a guess, in any one instance, but an informed guess.

Other methods

Here are some further ways by which we can attempt to understand the other person's relationship to death. Detailed examples will be presented in other sections of this book.

The *in-depth clinical study* became an established technique through the efforts of the pioneering psychoanalysts. People with clinical skills today continue to develop in-depth understanding through one-to-one relationships. Usually these are diagnostic or therapeutic relationships. This means that insights into the individual's inner thoughts and feelings about death (and other topics) often have come from contact with troubled people. The insights can be extremely valuable but some caution is needed in generalizing to the total population. Furthermore, there are other sources of bias evident. Some kinds of people are more likely to be seen in a clinical relationship than others. A person of lower-class background, for example, is more apt to be treated through drug therapy or environmental manipulations than through one-to-one psychotherapy. The richness of the in-depth clinical study also tends to involve the particular personality of the psychologist, psychiatrist, or other therapist. It can be difficult to disentangle the client's thoughts and behaviors from the very special situation that has been created through interaction with the therapist. Additionally, this very richness of material can be difficult to sort out and dimensionalize. More than one interpretation of what the individual really meant, or why he did what he did, is usually possible. Occasionally we find the in-depth clinical study being made specifically for research instead of therapeutic purposes. The data may be easier to work with because of the built-in research orientation. However, the very complexity and intimacy that gives the in-depth case approach its distinction also present substantial problems if one is interested in clear-cut, generalizable conclusions.

There are a number of variations on the in-depth study. One of these has become known as the *psychological autopsy*. This is a team-study approach that centers around the death of a particular person. In its first formulation, the psychological autopsy was used in an attempt to determine the true cause of a death in which suicide was a possible interpretation. Edwin Shneidman, Norman Farberow, and their colleagues worked with a variety of experts from such fields as law, police science, medicine, and the coroner's office.[18] Was this an accidental death, a suicide, or what? Although the psychological autopsy has a rather specific applied goal in this usage, it also has served to generate new insights and findings of a broader nature.

Another version of the psychological autopsy was developed a few years later with a broader purpose in mind from the beginning. Avery D. Weisman and Robert Kastenbaum worked with a team of nurses, social workers, physicians, ministers, and other health-related personnel in attempting to reconstruct the life and death of an aged patient.[19] Specific cause of death, although investigated, was only one of the problems being considered. Subsequently, the psychological autopsy method has been reshaped to a variety of other applications. In whatever form we find it, the psychological autopsy is usually a research-oriented effort combining the talents of many people, with the hope of filtering useful knowledge back to the care-giving system.

There is another class of information-gathering strategies that might be described as the *indirect inference* type. Precisely how the information is gathered is secondary to the fact that only scientists who know what they are looking for can ferret out the implications. These strategies include *projective testing*. Instead of asking directly what a person thinks about death, for example, we might ask him or her to draw a picture, respond to an especially designed stimulus card, or free associate. The variety of indirect approaches is large and ever increasing. Some of these approaches bypass or supplement verbal report. A *psychophysiological* approach, for example, can help the researcher read the body's response to death situations with some independence from the individual's verbal report. The psychogalvanic skin response is one such measure that has been used in this area.[20] *Performance-type tasks* can also be used to assess a person's relationship to death. A high level of death anxiety might reveal itself as interference in perceptual tasks or problem-solving situations.

One approach that has proved of great value in most of the sciences has been used but rarely in death-related research. The *experimental* method features the introduction of planned change or intervention. Behavior is not simply observed. Something is done to *change* the situation in a carefully controlled way, and the effects of this change are then studied. It is understandable that responsible investigators have been reluctant to use the experimental method in the area of death. Nevertheless, there may be circumstances in which this method can be applied on an ethical basis. Complete neglect of the experimental method would impose a major limitation on the knowledge-gaining enterprise.

There is an apparent contradiction between what has just been said and the fact that medical experimentation has been going on for years. Some of this experimentation has had significant implications for dying and death. The ethical and pragmatic basis for medical experimentation has been receiving closer scrutiny in recent years, and this will probably continue to be the case. But at the moment we are concerned more about the psychological and social aspects of the individual's relationship to death, and in this sphere very little of an experimental character has been ventured.

Are there still other ways in which to understand the death of the other person? Have you read a compelling biography? A sensitive novel? A poem that captures something of the human relationship to death that no scientific study can touch? An incisive philosophical analysis in which the contribution is lucid and imaginative thought rather than new empirical observations? There are many pathways to understanding how our fellow humans perceive, interpret, and ultimately confront the mortality we all hold in common. You may prefer one pathway; I may prefer another. But there is no reason for either of us to forego the discoveries that all the approaches have to offer.

SUMMARY

Two individual perspectives on death can be distinguished: *one's own death* and *the death of the other person*. Each of us lives within our personal life-and-death framework with its unique focus and quality. And each of us can attempt to understand the situation of fellow humans for whom we in turn are the other person.

An introduction to monitoring and understanding our own personal orientations toward death is made. Two *death-related memory exercises* are given, along with a few comments. It is suggested that you take advantage of such exercises as they continue to appear throughout the book. They will be helpful in making your own frame of reference more accessible to you and in relating your personal perspective to more general considerations.

Several approaches to understanding the death of the other person were outlined. *Living with a person who is facing death* can be a powerful experience; there is also much to be learned from listening to or reading accounts from those who have had such experiences. Two contrasting examples are given. A variety of research methodologies have also been applied to understanding how other people relate to death. The *self-report* technique was illustrated by two studies of death fears, one involving nurses, the other college students. The *naturalistic observation* method has not yet been used extensively in this area, but examples were given to the *participant-observer* method and of a study of risk-taking behavior in crossing a busy intersection. The results of these studies are of interest in their own right but also illustrate the varied approaches that can lead to improved knowledge.

Discussed in less detail were several other approaches: the *in-depth clinical study*, the *psychological autopsy*, and *indirect-inference* strategies. The latter include *projective testing*, *psychophysiological measures*, and *performance-type tasks*. The *experimental* method—in which planned change is introduced into the situation—has been sparingly used in the psychosocial sphere and has much potential value, but is controversial for ethical reasons (as is the participant-observer method previously mentioned).

While the emphasis has been on learning about the individual's relationship to death through empirical observations, a well-rounded approach will take advantage of the insights that can be found in philosophy, literature, and the arts as well.

These introductions to individual perspectives on death must now be placed within their real-life context: the network of relationships, symbols, practices, and traditions known as society.

REFERENCES

1. Gunther, J. *Death be not proud.* New York: Harper & Row, Publishers, 1965.
2. Wertenbaker, L. T. *Death of a man.* New York: Random House, Inc., 1957.
3. Lund, D. *Eric.* Philadelphia: J. B. Lippincott Co., 1974.
4. Wolitzger, H. *Ending.* New York: Macmillan, Inc., 1975.
5. Jury, M., & Jury, D. *Gramp.* New York: Grossman Publishers (Viking Press), 1976.
6. Smith, A. A. *Rachel.* New York: Morehouse-Barlow, 1975.
7. Bowie, W. K. Story of a first-born. *Omega,* 1977, *8,* 1-18.
8. Harjan, N. One family's experience with death. In C. A. Garfield (Ed.), *Psychosocial care of the dying patient.* New York: McGraw-Hill Book Co., 1978, pp. 78-85.
9. Lester, D., Getty, C., & Kneisl, C. R. Attitudes of nursing students and nursing faculty toward death. *Nursing Research,* 1974, *23,* 50-53.
10. Tobacyk, J., & Eckstein, D. Death threat and death concerns in the college student. *Omega,* 1980, *11,* 139-155.
11. Krieger, S., Epting, F., & Leitner, L. Personal constructs, threat and attitudes toward death. *Omega,* 1974, *5,* 299-310.
12. Rainey, L., & Epting, F. Death threat constructions in the student and the prudent. *Omega,* 1977, *8,* 19-28.
13. Reynolds, D. K., & Farberow, N. L. The suicidal patient—an inside view. *Omega,* 1973, *4,* 229-242.
14. Reynolds, D. K., & Farberow, N. L. *Endangered hope.* Berkeley, Calif.: University of California Press, 1978.
15. Buckingham, R. W., Lack, S. A., Mount, B. M., MacLean, L. D., & Collins, J. T. Living with the dying: use of the technique of participant observation. *Canadian Medical Association Journal,* 1976, *115,* 1211-1215.
16. Kastenbaum, R., & Briscoe, L. The street corner: a laboratory for the study of life-threatening behavior. *Omega,* 1975, *6,* 33-44.
17. Shneidman, E. S. *Deaths of man.* New York: Quadrangle/The New York Times Book Co., 1973.
18. Shneidman, E. S., Farberow, N. L., & Litman, R. E. The suicide prevention center. In N. L. Farberow & E. S. Shneidman (Eds.), *The cry for help.* New York: McGraw Hill Book Co., 1961.
19. Weisman, A. D., & Kastenbaum, R. The psychological autopsy: a study of the terminal phase of life. *Community Mental Journal Monograph* (Vol. 4). New York: Behavioral Publications, Inc., 1968.
20. Alexander, I. E., Colley, R. S., & Adlerstein, A. M. Is death a matter of indifference? *Journal of Psychology,* 1957, *43,* 277-283.

CHAPTER 7

❖ A LARGER PERSPECTIVE
The death system

Personal death is unique for each individual. What will be said in this chapter does not change or challenge that fact. Individual frameworks for relating to life and death will remain intact and respected. But we begin here the task of understanding death from a more than individual standpoint. The existence of something that might be called a *death system* has been assumed from the beginning of this book. Now this system will be made more explicit.

BASIC CHARACTERISTICS
A working definition

The death system has been defined as a "socio-physical network by which the relationship to mortality is mediated and expressed."[1,p.310] *Network* is the key word in this sentence. It suggests that our relationship to death is far from simple. We must look for patterns. It is not enough to limit ourselves to any one idea or fact, no matter how significant. The rest of this definition will become clearer as we touch on the components and functions of a death system. Examples will be drawn from the past as well as the present, and from other cultures in addition to our own because all societies know death and all have developed systematic relationships to mortality.

The people

People are part of every death system, whether we are examining a small band of nomads or a huge technological society. In a society so complex and specialized as ours, some individuals are *defined* by their roles in the death system. The funeral director is an obvious example. The individual who takes up this responsibility becomes a permanent and conspicuous person-component of the American death system. By *permanent*, I mean that he or she maintains this role day after day. It is not implied that the profession and business of directing funerals always has been and always will be with us. There was a time when we did not have professional funeral directors, and the possibility that this profession might be transformed or absorbed into a new constellation of death-related behaviors in the future cannot be ruled out.

Let us now add some examples of other people who have a continuing relationship with death in our society. The agent who sells us *life* insurance is very much into the facts and statistics of death. Not only do most policies center around their *death* benefits, but the premiums that are charged depend on the insurance company's calculation of mortality risk. While life insurance is a business and, to some extent, an art and science, it also involves judgments and actions that are decidedly psychological. Should the agent come right out and discuss death with a prospective policyholder? Or is it better to keep death in the shadows and emphasize instead life and other aspects of the policy? How insurance agents present their services and wares and how potential clients respond are components of the death system.

The insurance agent's role is more extensive than what has already been acknowledged. This is also one of the persons whose services are called on after a death has occurred. Furthermore, the enormous financial interchange in the insurance business, much of it predicated around the fact of death, influences our society in many ways. The premium we pay to guarantee death benefits is part of a complex network of investments. This comes down to some people becoming richer, some buildings being razed to the ground and others being erected, new jobs being created and existing jobs being phased out, and so on. People associated with the insurance industry have a major role both in our culture's death system and in its economic status.

The florist is also part of the death system. Historically, a significant fraction of the florist's sales have been associated with "floral tributes" to the deceased or their survivors. The lawyer is still another person who is likely to participate in the death system, although this is only one sphere of income-generating activity for the legal profession. Take for just one example the lawyer's role in drawing up wills. This is one of the relatively few situations in which a healthy adult is likely to sit down and discuss personal death–related issues with a person of professional background. The lawyer often is on the scene after a death as well, helping to interpret and implement the provisions that have been made for distribution of the deceased's estate. In these ways and many others, the lawyer plays a role in our death system.

There are many other people whose association with the death system may not come so readily to mind. Think, for example, of that big truck you saw pull up behind a supermarket the other day. It was filled with pet food, case after case. Every can in every case contains some type of meat product, and all that meat, of course, comes from animals that were themselves once alive. The truck driver, the person who shelves the cans, the assistant store manager who makes sure they are priced correctly, the clerk at the checkout register—all are but a few of the people who participate in the death system through their processing of pet food. If we wanted to be more complete on this matter, then we would have to include those who select, those who slaughter, and those who prepare a variety of living animals to become food for pets. The people in the canning factory would be included, as would the accountants, the executives, and the advertising agency. The cat who meows so convincingly for his favorite brand on television is also part of the death system.

This way of looking at people and death may seem peculiar, even outrageous. But it is a simple fact that our nation does boast major pet food industries and that death is programmed right into them. In similar fashion, one might turn from industry to industry and from occupation to occupation. What jobs have close bearing on death? It is not our intention to compile an exhaustive list here, even if that could be done. Perhaps enough has been said to make the point that there are people in our death system, and more people representing a greater variety of life-styles than we might have thought at first. We have not even mentioned the health-related professions in this context, nor the minister, the priest, and the rabbi, all of whom have important roles in the death system. And it would not do to leave out the scientists who are busily designing lethal weapons, the legislators who vote the budget appropriations for their production, and the armed service personnel who take the new devices into custody. You might find it interesting to expand the list of death-related occupations based on your own thoughts and observations.

A distinction should be made between people whose basic position in society associates them with the death system and those who are recruited as occasion demands. It is difficult to determine how many people comprise the first group. But it is clear that the second group potentially includes all of us. At any moment we might become drawn actively into the death system, and through a variety of paths. A friend unexpectedly reveals to us that she has a terminal illness. We are caught in an automobile accident in which somebody dies. A funeral procession interrupts our cruise along the highway. Or perhaps it is the insurance agent asking gently if we have made adequate provisions for the education of our children, should we no longer be there. The points of entry are numerous indeed.

The places

Certain places in our culture have become identified with death. The cemetery? Certainly. The funeral home? Again, affirmative. Beyond such very obvious places, there are others whose associations with death are more variable, subtle, or dependent on the particular ideas and experiences we carry around with us. The hospital—*any* hospital—is a death place in the minds of some people. For most people, including hospital staff themselves, it is only certain places within the facility that have such a meaning. What makes this ward a death place may be the statistically evident pattern that has expressed itself over time: this is where the most seriously ill patients in this hospital usually come. Or it may be more occasional and circumstantial: a patient died unexpectedly on a floor that usually has low expectation of mortality and now, for a while at least, this resonates as a death place.

Historical battlefields may be thought of as death places for decades or even for centuries. The Tower of London is celebrated for many reasons, including famous royal murders said to have taken place there. The Ford Theater in the District of Columbia is remembered as the place where Lincoln was assassinated. Alongside these generally acknowledged death places can be set areas that have taken on death-related meanings for smaller groups of people. A pathway in the woods may be spoken of in hushed tones by the schoolchildren who discovered a human corpse while on a nature walk. Many a city in the United States today has a nursing home or two located near a mortuary establishment, the whole constellation suggesting a death's row in the minds of some passersby and residents.

Anyplace can become a death place, at least temporarily, but other places are conspicuous for a prolonged period of time because of their death-related associations.

Times

Death also has its times or occasions. Memorial Day, for example, is a regularly occurring time set aside by our society to honor those who have fallen in defense of our nation. Both the original purpose of Memorial Day and the way its meaning has changed in recent years (just another day off for workers and an opportunity for holiday sales by merchants) raise questions about the ways in which our society comes to terms with death. In some tribal cultures, one or more days are devoted to communal mourning and ritual to honor all who have died during the preceding year.[2] This comprises one of the tribal community's most significant group interactions. The Days of the Dead in Mexico are likely to startle the unprepared visitor who associates death observances with the somber and restrained.[3] Many societies have established times or occasions in which death is meant to hold sway over everybody's thoughts and feelings. Both the similarities and the differences from society to society invite close study.

Times devoted to death in our own society do not begin and end with Memorial Day. Prayers for the dead are offered on regular occasions, for example, by Jewish and by Japanese Americans who are keeping the faith, while Catholics regularly celebrate mass. Good Friday is an occasion dominated by observances of the death of Christ. December 29 is a date that some native Americans observe in honor of the Sioux annihilated by the Seventh Cavalry at Wounded Knee, South Dakota. The deaths of martyred individuals and groups in various parts of the world have been perpetuated in memory, often by observations on the anniversary of their demise.

These examples have all been drawn from death times that are embedded either in the general culture or in a subculture. But it is also possible for a single individual to acknowledge a death time that has deep personal significance even if it is not shared by others. This can take the form of what some psychiatrists call an anniversary reaction.[4] A year (or 2 years, 5 years, etc.) from the death of a loved one, the survivor may suddenly fall ill, behave erratically, or suffer an accident.

Our society has even more general expectations about time and death than what has been said up to this point. People often speak as though there are certain times appropriate for death and other times that are wrong. Later in this book we will consider the implicit distinctions that are made between "timely" and "untimely" death.

Objects

Death has its objects and things as well as its people, places, and times. The hearse and the death certificate are among the conspicuous objects in our own death system. Obituaries and death notices comprise a separate section within the daily newspaper. Handguns have become closely associated with sudden death. The noose, the gallows, the electric chair, the bottle with skull and crossbones on the label, are also among our more obvious things of death, as are tombstones, shrouds, and a variety of other paraphernalia. Germs or "bad germs" in particular may be associated with death; yet so may be the unexpected telegram. The little spraying device that "kills bugs dead" is an object in our death system; the same may be said of the nuclear devices that we aim at potential enemies and that they aim at us.

Objects whose intended uses have little to do with death may produce lethal effects through accidents or violent misuse. A British friend confirmed my guess as we were passing through her homeland that, yes, that was indeed a nuclear reactor plant off to our right. "It is our only nuclear plant," she added, "and, fortunately, it doesn't work!" The recent increase of known problems with nuclear energy plants is a salient example of objects created for constructive purposes but which have come to arouse death-related thoughts and feelings in society. Critics of the automobile and of cigarettes have long spoken of both types of objects as instruments of death. Alcoholic beverages and many pharmacological substances have also been viewed as death-related although they are neither intended nor marketed for such a purpose. Again, there is no intention here to compile an extensive catalogue, but simply to suggest something of the scope and variety of components in our death system, whether people, places, times, or objects.

Symbols

Language and other symbols play a major role in our culture's death system. The black armband tells a story. The black border around the card we receive in the mail also signifies death and mourning. The funeral director provides black or other dark-hued limousines, not red and yellow, for the funeral procession, and garbs himself also in the established dark hues of mourning. Not all societies symbolize death with dark colors, but one soon learns to recognize those particular colors and other symbolisms meant to convey a death-related message in a given society or subculture.

The choice of music, if music is chosen at all, also tells us something about a culture's orientation toward death. Slow, solemn music intoned on an organ suggests a different orientation than a simple folk song with guitar accompaniment, and different again from a brass band moving down the street playing "When the Saints Go Marching In." A particular kind of music may seem either perfectly fitting or outrageous to us when brought into a death-related situation, indicating that we do have a sense of the "appropriate," even if we cannot always put it into words.

In some neighborhoods, closing the shutters on all the windows has been a traditional signal of a death within, although this practice is fading. Administration of the priestly ritual for the sick is a highly symbolic interaction that is sometimes related to the prospect of death (although it is technically not regarded by the Catholic Church as "last rites" despite this common attribution given to the ceremony). Many of our public and private responses to death have significant symbolic components.

The words we use and those we refrain from using also reveal much about the nature of our culture's death system. Many observers have noted, for example, that we tend to prefer almost any term to such direct, straight forward words as "death" and "died." People pass on, expire, or go to their great reward. The occasional use of a synonym may not be important, but when we observe a consistent pattern of substituting other words for those most apt and direct, we might well wonder about the functions served by these evasions. I remember

being puzzled about the frequent oral and written references to patients having been transferred to "Allen Street" when I served briefly as a consultant to one of the nation's most prestigious hospitals. Inquiry revealed that this was a local euphemism for a morgue. Both the morgue and Allen Street itself had been out of existence for years, but staff in this modern, state-of-the-art hospital remained more comfortable in communicating by this quasi-secret code rather than by using direct and honest language.

We also use words to explain death or at least to integrate death into our total world view. Turning from society to society, we might ask: *Who* has the words that explain death? Is it the holy man? The ruler? The scholar? The physician? The poet? Is there general agreement, or is society divided on death explanations and meanings? Under what circumstances does society seem most in need of words and other symbols for death? Under what circumstances do the traditional explanations and symbols appear to falter? These are just a few of the questions that might launch useful inquiry into the role of symbols in a death system.

FUNCTIONS OF THE DEATH SYSTEM

What functions are served by the death system? Although it has already been defined in general as a sociophysical network by which the relationship to mortality is mediated and expressed, the system can also be analyzed in terms of a set of more specific functions.

Warnings and predictions

"The day of judgment is at hand!"—or is it? Warnings and predictions of death take many forms. The barefoot, wild-eyed individual carrying an end-of-the-world poster was until recently a favorite cliché of the cartoonist. I have not seen quite so many depictions lately; perhaps awareness of mega death threats is no longer regarded as a sign of bizarre thought. Certainly, there have been times in various cultural settings in which prophets of catastrophe have been taken quite seriously and other times in which they have been ignored. Our own society has been warned of impending disaster repeatedly over the years. If we limit attention to the most "respectable" sources, it is still easy to develop an impressive list of alarms that have sounded since, say, the end of World War II. One of the most conspicuous was the prospect that the "cold war" between the United States and the Soviet Union might suddenly explode into nuclear holocaust. Many families considered and some actually built or purchased bomb shelters. A new civil defense emphasis established itself, and some of its remnants and spinoffs remain with us today. Note that the development of a civil defense response system is itself one more example of people, places, and objects coming into the orbit of the death system, and of all having impacts of various kinds on the economy.

Californians repeatedly have been warned they are literally standing on the edge of disaster, especially if they inhabit areas directly threatened by the San Andreas fault. The warnings and predictions in this case come from respected scientists who support their conclusions with detailed descriptions and explanations. (Some of these earth scientists themselves live and work in California "earthquake country.") Additional warnings have come directly from "Mother Earth" herself, who has sent several substantial tremors through the area in recent years.

Ecological disasters of various types have been predicted. One of the oldest such prophecies still being advanced is the supposed danger of a new ice age, in which either frigid climate gradually will make its way from the polar caps to more temperate zones, or in which the globe will tilt and capsize in a sudden shift of ice and snow. One of the newer threats identified in the ecological sphere is that posed by aerosol spray cans, thought by some scientists to endanger the atmospheric conditions vital to continued human survival. Water and air pollution are other sources of threat for which the alarm has often sounded in our times.

People have long kept their eyes on the weather. Both federal and local agencies provide predictions and warnings of storms and other conditions that could threaten life. "Small-craft warning" and "tornado watch" are familiar phrases in some parts of the nation. We expect to be advised of possible floods, blizzards, avalanche conditions, and so on. The government has added other prediction and warning services within fairly recent times, as, for example, an obligatory statement on every pack of cigarettes. A number of consumer advocacy organizations regularly provide warnings, some of which involve the possibility of life-threatening illness or injury related to commercial products. We are certainly an alarm-ringing society, even if attention is restricted to only the most acceptable or authoritative sources.

Some of the warnings and predictions emphasize the prospect of universal catastrophe— not just the destruction of large numbers of people, but of most if not all of the human race. While many have advanced opinions about the impact of these statements on the individual's thoughts and feelings, few studies have been conducted to sample attitudes more directly. Overpopulation, pollution, and thermonuclear warfare are the most often cited candidates for bringing about "Doomsday" (e.g., Taylor, 1970[5]; Ehrlich & Ehrlich, 1972[6]). V. A. Braithwaite and H. G. Law,[7] a pair of Australian psychologists, delved into this question with the cooperation of 170 psychology students at the University of Queensland. They did not find strong evidence for the existence of a general "doomsday consciousness." Many of the young men and women did express concern about population and pollution problems, along with a sense of responsibility. These were areas of threat in which the alert and resourceful individual might be able to do something effective. "The bomb," however, was more widely regarded as a threat that the individual could do little if anything to alter. There were also findings suggestive of a general sense of powerlessness. The individual's attention to "doomsday" issues seemed to be held in check because it was felt that there was not very much that could be done to neutralize or ward off the major threats of megadeath. More studies of this kind are needed to explore the relationships between perception of a socially transmitted death warning or prediction and the individual's response to it.

Our death system also provides warnings and predictions to specific individuals as well as to larger units of society. The physician is a major component of this system. What do that x-ray film and those laboratory reports mean? How serious is my condition? Many others can also warn and predict: the mechanic who declares our car is an accident waiting to happen unless we fix those brakes and replace those worn tires, the inspector who points out fire hazards in our home, and so on.

Societies can be compared with respect to the warning and prediction components of their death systems. Who issues the warnings? What kind of warnings are taken most seriously? What kind of warnings are neglected? How accurate are the predictions? In our own society some warnings and predictions are generated by specialists making use of sophisticated techniques. Less obvious perhaps is the fact that we do not always pay heed to these warnings. People remain right in the pathway of devastating storms; others perish in fires that could have been prevented or succumb to physical ills that could have been cured or controlled. There is much to discover about the way warnings are given and utilized. This and

other functions of the death system will be taken up again in other contexts.

Preventing death

All death systems have techniques intended to prevent death. These are not identical with warnings and predictions. A natural disaster, virulent epidemic, or catastrophic war may be predicted as retribution for a society's sinful ways. The warning may be in the nature of a pledge: "I'll get you sooner or later!" Knowing that one has deadly enemies is not intended in this case as comforting information but rather to induce terror and dismay.

For the prevention of death in our own society, we tend to think first of the physician and allied health professions and sciences. The control of contagious diseases that once took a high toll, especially among the very young and the very old, has been a major accomplishment this century, although still not as complete as it might be. Major efforts are currently being made to prevent other causes of death, such as cancer and heart disease, and continuing progress can be noted.

The treatment of acute and emergent conditions that threaten life has attracted particular interest. Specialists and advanced equipment are rushed to the bedside of a person suffering from a condition that almost surely would have been fatal in the past. Surgery on the most vital and delicate organs of the body has become increasingly sophisticated and successful. The number of chemical treatments continues to expand, while the battery of life-sustaining machines and devices also continues to enlarge. Successes with the newer medical technologies lead to expectations and demands for more of the kind. More cures, please, and faster! There seems to be a social dynamic in which hard-won medical victories foster rising expectations. This at times leads to situations in which the climate of expectation far exceeds what is actually within the province of even the most advanced medical arts and sciences. This suggests a neglected aspect of one of the most frequent types of observation made of people who have life-threatening illnesses (and of those who are close to them). Many contemporary observers report *denial* to be a pervasive and characteristic response to death-threat in the United States. Denial of death or of death-threat takes many forms and is described in many contexts throughout this book. Notice, however, that advances in medicine and related fields during the twentieth century have provided an increasingly strong rationale in support of the denial attitude. This is not to say that firm denial of death is truly justified by the actual medical achievements. What it does suggest is that those of us who find denial to be a comforting way of dealing with death can draw more support for this attitude from the preventive arm of our society's death system than people have been able to do in the past. We can simply identify ourselves with the more optimistic extremes of the health-care establishment and assume that we have or soon will have death on the run.

In many ways the United States is a culture with a strong investment in the preservation of life. This has been displayed most vividly in efforts to eradicate menaces to public health, such as virulent contagious disease, and in all-out intervention efforts during acute life-threatening disorders. We seem to enjoy the idea of "making war" on disease. Although the prevention function of our death system has high priority, our system is also curiously selective and at times even contradictory in its prevention/intervention efforts. Whether or not a particular individual will benefit from the general emphasis on prevention depends on a variety of personal and social factors. Whatever makes a person of high social value in general tends to make him or her a more favored candidate for death-prevention efforts. "If you are going to have a heart attack, make sure you are wearing a good suit and are in the right part of town—also, try to be young and white!" Cynical advice of this type unfortunately retains its core of truth even today.

We will also have to pay attention to the *balance* between preventive and other functions of the death system. Is it possible, for example, that we have become too prevention oriented? Questions of this type will be easier to explore after we have completed this general introduction to the death system.

Care of the dying

A staff member in one of the world's most sophisticated medical research centers recently was describing her work to me in quite a professional manner. Tears of sorrow and frustration intruded themselves, however, as she tried to express what happens when a decision is made to shift from "cure" to "comfort" care.

❖ "Sometimes the point comes when the doctors decide that's it. There's nothing more we can do—or should do—all the cards have been played, and there's just no way we can really hope to arrest the illness. The brakes screech! We all have to come to a full and sudden stop. We may have been doing everything in the world to keep this person alive for months and now we have to stop all that and change everything immediately. It's hard to change what we do, but a lot harder to change how we feel about the patient and ourselves, about what we're doing. I don't think human thoughts and feelings were made for such sudden stops and starts!

The distinction between attempting to prevent death and providing care to a dying person is not always this drastic. In some situations it is possible for the same philosophy, attitudes, and set of behaviors to encompass both prevention and comfort giving. This is itself one of the questions to be raised in analyzing a particular death system: How great is the distinction between prevention and comforting efforts, and why?

This is linked to another question of more direct clinical significance: How can various health professionals, the family, and the life-threatened person himself achieve a continuing harmony if some of the people involved are persisting in the objective of death prevention, while others now believe that comfort and relief should take clear precedence over curative efforts? Should prevention of death continue to be the overriding goal until the very end, or are there circumstances in which the emphasis should shift to comfort and the relief of symptoms? Advocates of both positions can be found in the ranks of all those associated with terminal care. There are physicians who take quite literally the never-say-die orientation: so long as life has any chance at all, it is the physician's responsibility to do all within his or her power to support this chance. Even the physician who might admit privately that a particular patient has almost no chance of pulling through can feel obliged to continue these efforts for what might be learned of possible benefit to others in the future. But other physicians more readily accommodate their efforts to the signs of impending and inexorable death. This attitude sometimes comes across as old-fashioned, an approach more in keeping with earlier medical practices when the physician was inclined to see himself as Nature's junior assistant. Other staff members may also be divided on the cure/comfort approach for a variety of reasons, ranging from individual personality and vulnerability to economic and "cost-benefit" considerations.

It may seem aloof and heartless to look at care of the dying from the perspective of the total death system rather than the individuals intimately involved, but when we do so, we discover many questions that we must eventually answer if we wish to do justice to the relationship between individual and society. These include the following:

1. How much distinction does a particular society make between prevention of death and care of the dying?

   A more specific question here: Is the direction sharper, greater in research/teaching hospitals?

2. How many and what kinds of changes take place in the social status of a person when he or she is described as "dying"?

   Specific question: Do health-care providers then spend more or less time with him? How about family?

3. Under what circumstances is the passage from one status to the other made? And how do nonmedical factors influence the definition of a person as "dying"?

   Specific question: Will a physician with a high death anxiety shift over from cure to comfort care earlier or later than a physician with less personal death anxiety?

4. How much attention is given to care of the dying as compared with other functions of the death system?

   Specific question: Will a society that invests much in prevention be more inclined to turn away from the dying person because this represents an instance of failure, as compared with a society that has less expectation of warding off death through medical care?

5. What do the care-giving practices in terminal illness tell us about a society's general philosophy and values?

   Specific question: Is there a parallel between the rise and fall of value placed on the individual within a society and the incorporation of the dying person into a close interpersonal support network?

It may be frustrating to raise questions such as these and not move on immediately to their direct examination. But in the long run we can deal more resourcefully with the specifics after establishing a framework for the total problem.

Disposal of the dead

Disposal of the dead is perhaps a harsh-sounding phrase, but it is a task all societies must perform. At the very minimum there is a need to dispose of the physical remains. Seldom, however, is a society content with the minimum. Usually the specific actions involved in body disposal are but one component of a larger process. This process tells us something about the person who has died and perhaps even more about what that particular society makes of death. Let us take a few brief examples from our society.

❖ A minister dies unexpectedly. His wife and children are stunned, then grief-stricken. Forced to think of funeral arrangements, they find themselves in perfect agreement. He had been a family-oriented person. In his private life he preferred the simple, the intimate, the natural. These same characteristics should be carried over to the funeral: no ostentation. Only the family and a few special friends should be involved; in this way they can most appropriately share their grief and support each other.

But the church congregation cannot abide this plan. A small, simple, private commemoration would fail to symbolize the deceased's significant place in the community— it would, in effect, diminish the status of the congregation itself. The congregation would also be deprived of this opportunity to express its concern for this spiritual leader. No, it just wouldn't be right to let this death pass without a conspicuous public ceremony.

This might appear to be an inopportune time for conflict between family and congregation,

but that is what happened. The power of the many prevailed in this instance. The disposal of this man's body and the accompanying ritual became essentially a public event. It was a "beautiful" funeral, with participation from community leaders as well as members of the congregation.

How did the family feel? They reacted as though not only the husband–father had been taken away from them, but his death as well. What they experienced deeply as private loss and grief had become a public exhibit. And yet the community felt that it had strong rights and needs, too. Just as much of this man's life had been devoted to the public sphere, so should his death be shared. This is one of many examples that could be given of the contest between private and public "ownership" of the deceased. Some death systems emphasize one side, some the other, but the private/public dialectic seems to exist in all.

❖ Two young men are pushing a stretcher through the corridors of a large modern hospital. The action is planned to take as little time as possible and attract little or no notice. Soon they have reached the service elevator and the door closes behind them.

The casual observer will have noticed only an empty stretcher. A more sophisticated observer will know or guess that this is a false-bottomed stretcher designed expressly for disguised transportation of the dead. A society whose health-care establishment goes out of its way to devise a cloak of invisibility around the dead is telling us something about its fundamental attitudes toward the meaning of life. Do we think of the dead as fearful, disgusting, or dirty? Such an attitude is not difficult to read from some of the prevailing practical arrangements made for body disposal in our society.

❖ The old man has died. Family converge from everywhere. A funeral commands serious attention in this strongly ethnic, large, extended family network. Proper disposal of the body is important but so is the opportunity for reunion of relatives who have not seen each other for some time. There is a problem, however. Representatives of the oldest generation, including the widow, expect a strictly conventional observation of the death. All the time-honored rituals must be observed; anything less would be a sin and a disgrace. The younger generations, however, are more Americanized. Some find the arrangements for an elaborate, Old World/ethnic funeral not at all to their liking. The old way seems drawn out, too rigid, too formal, too consuming of time and money. The funeral director and several of the less polarized family members find themselves in the middle. The death of a respected and beloved person threatens to bring a bitter intergenerational conflict to the surface.

These examples reveal several of the problems that can be associated with disposal of the dead: the conflict between public and private functions of this process, negative attitudes toward the corpse, and the precipitation of intergenerational and other conflicts in the ranks of the survivors. In addition to such problems, we can also ask more structural questions about the place of body-disposal practices in a society's total death system. How much energy and expense, for example, is devoted to all the actions associated with body disposal as compared to the priority given to warnings and predictions or to death-preventing efforts? How much control is exercised by the government and by religious authority and how much is in the hands of the most immediately involved individuals themselves? How does the mode of disposal relate to the culture's beliefs about the ultimate value and destiny of the individual?

Within our own society there remain several subgroups whose life-styles are appreciably dif-

ferent. Kathleen Bryer's (1978) observations of "the Amish way of death" provides an illuminating contrast to what has already been described here.[8] There are approximately 80,000 Amish people in the United States, descendents of Swiss Anabaptists who were persecuted by other groups until granted refuge and religious liberty by William Penn in 1727. The Amish maintain a family-oriented society that emphasizes religious values, a simple agrarian life-style, separation from the non-Amish world, and a strong doctrine of mutual assistance. Marital separation and divorce are not sanctioned, nor is institutionalization (e.g., of the infirm or mentally ill) an accepted practice. Everybody lives together and looks after each other. Those who are familiar with Amish people also know that they function "at the same unhurried pace as . . . their forefathers, using horses instead of automobiles, windmills instead of electricity, and facing death with the same religious tenets and steadfast faith of their fathers."[8, p.256]

The Amish way of life and its attitude toward death is clearly expressed in behavior associated with body disposal. The deceased is dressed in white garments by family members.

It is only at her death that an Amish woman wears a white dress with the cape and apron which were put away by her for the occasion of her death. This is an example of the lifelong preparation for the facing of death, as sanctioned by Amish society. The wearing of all white clothes signifies the high ceremonial emphasis on the death event as the final rite of passage into a new and better life.[8, p.254]

The funeral is very much a home-oriented event. A large room is cleared for the simple wooden coffin and the hundreds of friends, neighbors, and relatives who will soon fill it. The funeral service is held in the house or barn, following a ritual the Amish have been using for many generations. The grave itself is dug by neighbors on the preceding day and all watch in silent prayer as the coffin is placed and the grave filled with earth. Other families have charge of arrangements for feeding the mourners. During the entire time period between the death event and the completion of the funeral, all the proceedings make it clear that a human being has, in fact, died. The coffin is in the center of the room; there are no adornments or distractions from the core fact of death.

The problems and conflicts described around body-disposal practices for our society at large do not characterize the Amish. Their way of life does indeed seem to involve a different way of death. This is expressed all through life (e.g., the old woman who carefully washes, starches, and irons her own funeral clothing so it will be ready when the time comes), so the individual and social responses touched off by a death in the family do not challenge the values that bind them together. A death may occasion grief and lead to various hardships for an Amish family, like any other, but many of the doubts, tensions, and conflicts that have become commonplace in the larger death system seem to be absent for these people who have maintained a life-style of their own.

Social consolidation after death

Death does not merely subtract one individual from society. It can also challenge society's ability to hold itself together, to assert its vitality and viability after death's raid. In small societies, the impact of *every* death is evident as a challenge to the well-being of the entire group. In a mass society, this challenge usually becomes obvious only when a "special" death occurs.

The assassinations of John F. Kennedy, Martin Luther King, and Robert Kennedy are examples of the "special death" in our own times. Each of these men was highly visible nationally, part of whatever consciousness a huge and diverse country is able to share. Each man also represented some form of power and some pos-

sible direction in which the nation might move; additionally, each man meant something on a more personal and emotional level to millions of others.

The manner of their deaths intensified the impact. Sudden, unexpected death of a significant person leaves us vulnerable, at least for the moment. The assassinations came too quickly to allow the development of a protective shield for our feelings. A core of vulnerability was more likely to be recognized than in the case of expected deaths for which both cultural and personal defenses could be employed. Each death was not only sudden, but violent. The scene became disorganized, confused. That powerful man had been alive and healthy one moment and was fatally stricken the next. There were invasive injuries, blood. . . .

Had death come suddenly, but by so-called natural causes, we might have been less alarmed. The impact of violence, blood, and disorganization added to the force with which each death struck society. And this was not all. Each death was *intentional*. Malice had taken charismatic leaders away from us. The chain reaction of fears and alarms that followed has not entirely disappeared today. Were there conspiracies at work to annihilate certain people in power? If so, who might be next? And why? Whom can we trust after all? If it was *not* a conspiracy, then must we believe that so significant an effect can be laid on the actions of a few obscure individuals obsessed with personal needs and fantasies? Are the most powerful people among us so vulnerable? And, if they are, what protection against capricious death do any of us more ordinary people have? Either way, society was confronted with both the fact and the continued prospect of sudden, violent, and hostile attack. It was not just the individual's personal sense of safety that was challenged. A parallel process was set in motion from society's standpoint. Do we have the collective strength to survive the malignant forces that attack us? This challenge and doubt arises often when "nice, safe routine" is shattered by the impact of a "special death."

One major function of the death system, then, is to meet the challenges posed to individual and group by loss of a member. The challenge may be obvious and of broad scope, as in the sudden and hostile demise of a powerful leader. It can also be more subtle and involve just a few people.

❖ A married couple had tried for years to produce a child. They sought medical, then psychological and religious counseling. Having a child was very important to their view of what it meant to be an adult and a contributing member of society. Both were exuberant when the woman conceived and subsequently brought forth an apparently healthy infant. One morning the baby was found dead in its crib. The infant's death was little noticed by society in general. Nevertheless, it constituted a serious challenge to the forces that bind people together. A devout couple, they wondered, "How could God do this to us?" This brought religious faith—an important component of the forces that linked this man and woman—into question. Their attitudes toward each other were also challenged, jeopardizing the previously stable marriage. Friends and relatives also took sides in the issue, and a larger network of interactions threatened to become unraveled. Even though the deceased was an infant who had just begun to function as part of family and society, the death disrupted many long-standing and intimate relationships.

For contrast, we can turn again to the Amish. Consistent with their general orientations toward life and death, the Amish provide direct and long-term support to those whose lives have been disrupted by the death of a loved one. Practical as well as emotional support is provided, depending on the circumstances of the bereaved. It is not a case of many people coming by to express sympathy for a short period of time and subsequently disappearing; instead, vital functions in the home may be taken over for months by relatives or friends until the family can get back on its feet, and those who have had bereavement experiences of their own provide a type of empathy that is found authentic and valuable by the newly bereaved. Social consolidation after death is one more function of the death system that is closely related to the group's characteristic way of interpreting and coping with life.

Making sense of death

Our efforts to explain death to each other represent another important function of the death system. Some explanations are handed down from generation to generation in the form of philosophical statements, poetic expressions, and commentaries on holy scriptures. There are also famous last words and scenes that have been attributed to heroes, leaders, and other celebrated people of the past—at times erroneously. Other explanations are handed down more informally, the little sayings that are passed along in a particular subculture or family or through successive cohorts in the military service or schools of nursing or medicine.

We do not intend to use the term *explanation* in a precise sense here. Sometimes it is not quite an explanation that we are seeking or receive. Rather, a need is felt to make sense of death. Laconic statements such as "Nobody lives forever!" and "When your number's up, your number's up!" hardly qualify as explanations. Yet much of the routine interchange of words on death is of this general style. Perhaps such statements are of some comfort to the person who makes them, as a way of bridging what might otherwise be a tense and awkward silence. Perhaps hearing any words on the subject has some value to the recipient. There has been little actual research on the perceived value of everyday "death philosophies." However, people often seem to feel a little better when they can either speak or hear words at times of crisis and vulnerability. Apart from what the words mean or how adequately they address themselves to the problem at hand, it can be anxiety reducing just to hear the human voice intoning our language.

Consider the alternative: *Not* to have words spoken might confirm the fear that death truly is unspeakable. It would also be an admission that death is unthinkable. Neither as individuals nor as a society can we shape thought and word on this topic. This conclusion would probably make us feel more helpless and alienated than ever. When we can at least go through the motions of exchanging words in a death situation, then we are indicating an ability to function under stress. We are at least trying to make sense of death, and this activity itself helps keep us together.

At other times, however, we are not searching for just any words about death. We are looking for the most cogent and powerful understanding possible. The kind of explanation we seek cannot be separated, of course, from the particular death-related questions we have in mind. These questions may be personal and highly specific, or they may relate to the meaning of life and the universe on the broadest level at which we can conceive. In comparing individuals or societies in their death explanations, we cannot ignore differences in the questions that seem most vital to each. Would the same explanation satisfy a person deeply rooted in an oriental tradition and one with equally strong roots in the Western world? Would a young child and an adult have the same questions and accept the same answers?

It is possible that some cultures have a greater need for the "answer" to death than

others. Examining the same culture over a period of time, we might also conclude that there are periods during which there is considerably more need expressed to make sense of death. Discovering the reasons for these differences would help to illuminate what is taking place in our own culture at the moment and perhaps predict where we are heading.

And where do people turn for the answers? In our own culture today, do we turn to the physician because, as the high-prestige person who both tries to prevent death and then provides the official certification, he should know what it's all about, if anybody does? Or do we rely on organized religion whose roots, some historians believe, can be found in the universal human need to receive comfort in the face of death? Or again, do we turn to specific people in our own lives whom we respect and credit with exceptional strength or wisdom? Does the old person know more about death because he or she has lived so long? Does the dying person have special knowledge because of proximity? Should we ask the scientist because of his or her training in rigorous inquiry? Or the newspaper columnist who dispenses advice on almost every imaginable topic five days a week? Where a culture turns for the answers and what evidence or authority it requires is still another dimension of the death system.

This is a timely occasion to monitor your own needs for explanation. As a particular person within a particular death system, what questions are of greatest concern or interest to you? Please give your attention to the boxed material. Think about these items for a few minutes, and then express the thoughts that occur to you. It is suggested you do this in writing, both to nudge yourself a little more to make your questions explicit and to preserve a record that you can look back on at a later time.

Perhaps you have raised questions to which answers might reasonably be expected. Some people, for example, want to know what it feels like to die, or how a person could want to kill himself. Although questions of this kind cannot be answered definitively, there is a growing body of information to consult. These two illustrative questions are in fact taken up later in this book, along with a number of other inquiries that require empirical observations.

But perhaps your questions were more philosophical. You may have found yourself concerned with matters that are difficult if not impossible to study through clinical or scientific methodology. Or your questions may have been of a type that do not ask for facts so much as for ethical or moral guidelines. This would be the case with many questions that begin, "What *should* . . . ." A common question of this sort is "What should a young child be told about death?" This question involves both eth-

---

YOUR QUESTIONS ABOUT DEATH

The question about death that I would most like to have answered is:

_____

_____

_____

_____

This question is particularly important to me because: _____

_____

_____

_____

_____

I have had this question in mind about _____ days/months/years *(circle one)*

I expect to find a good answer: ☐ Yes

☐ Probably ☐ Probably not ☐ No

The best answer will probably come from:

☐ Religion ☐ Psychology ☐ Science

☐ Medicine ☐ Experiences of other people

☐ Personal experiences ☐ Other (specify)

_____

Another question about death that I would like to have answered is:

_____

_____

_____

_____

This question is particularly important to me because: _____

_____

_____

_____

_____

I have had this question in mind about _____ days/months/years *(circle one)*

I expect to find a good answer: ☐ Yes

☐ Probably ☐ Probably not ☐ No

The best answer will probably come from:

☐ Religion ☐ Psychology ☐ Science

☐ Medicine ☐ Experiences of other people

☐ Personal experiences ☐ Other (specify)

ical and factual considerations. Quite another question is "What should a person live for, if everything ends with death?"

If a person is going to raise philosophical questions at all, death is a prime stimulus for such inquiries and reflections. Decide for yourself which is the more curious: an attitude of wonder and reflection about what death means for life and vice versa, or a mind that has no questions to ask.

Killing

All death systems have another major function that has not yet been made explicit: *killing*. Death is brought about in many ways. Capital punishment is an obvious example. It is practiced by many but not by all cultures, with widely varying criteria for the conditions under which a person should be put to death. Ordinarily, only a few people have their lives ended through this mode. However, capital punishment conveys a mighty theme even when it is responsible for few deaths: this same society that on many occasions functions to protect and prolong life will on certain occasions take life away. Even if there were no other examples to cite, we would have to conclude that death—killing—has been established as one of society's functions.

But there are in fact many other examples to cite. Reference has already been made to the people who participate in the pet food industry. This component of the death system broadens out even further when we include those who raise, slaughter, process, and consume "meat-bearing" animals. Even the casual fisherman kills ("drowning worms," as they say), whether or not he lands an edible fish for the family table. Any culture that is not thoroughly vegetarian is involved to some extent with killing for food. Living creatures may be killed for other reasons as well. The quest for fur and feathers has brought several species to the edge of extinction. Hunting may be pursued as

an exercise in skill, an opportunity to be outdoors and "away," a proof of one's "manhood," or a variety of other reasons apart from providing a good meal.

Warfare has brought death to millions over the centuries. But we do not have to leave the twentieth century to obtain more evidence of war's lethal effect than one would care to find.[9] The death system includes more than the actual conduct of war, the salvo or bomb drop that kills. It also includes all the preparations that are made for war—major financial investments, reorganization of lives, changing the nature of a community, developing new products and processes, tightening security, and restricting privacy and individual liberties. Everything that contributes to being poised for war may be counted as part of the death system.

Capital punishment, the killing of animals for food or other reasons, and warfare have in common a systematic quality. These activities are carried out in an organized way. They are not a matter of haphazard individual actions. Take capital punishment, for example. Historically, this form of manifesting the power of the ruling authority has often been expressed through executions open to the public (still a practice in some nations today). The systematization of killing by the state can be seen in the careful specification of the relationship between the crime and the precise mode of execution. This can be illustrated by following verdict passed upon an Englishman in the thirteenth century:

Hugh (Hugh Dispenser the Younger), . . . you are found as a thief, and therefore shall be hanged; and are found as a traitor, and therefore shall be drawn and quartered; and for that you have been outlawed by the king, and . . . returned to the court without warrant, you shall be beheaded and for that you abetted and procured discord between the king and queen, and others of the realm, you shall be embowelled, and your bowels burnt. Withdraw, traitor, tyrant and so go take your judgment, attainted wicked traitor (cited by Jankofsky, 1979).[10]

This example of "overkill" was not a random outburst, but part of a pattern established to convey moral and political messages. If the purpose of the official action was simply to punish or to remove an undesirable from the population, it would not have been necessary to match the precise style of the condemned individual's fate with his crime and his place in society. But public execution was also a way through which the death system could dramatically convey messages and strengthen the hand of those in power. A respected individual who had merely done wrong or who was a member of the aristocracy might simply have his head severed. As a special privilege, notes Jankofsky, the head of the executed might not be placed on a spike on one of the city gates. Capital punishment could either heap disgrace on the condemned or be content with taking his life and not his reputation.

Public execution, like all other phenomena in a culture's death system, has many dimensions and points of contact with other phenomena. Klaus Jankofsky's analysis of public execution in medieval England, for example, also calls attention to the different ways in which individuals met their fate. Large crowds would turn out not just to witness the spectacle of execution, but also to see how a fellow mortal would bear himself on the verge of certain death, "the desire to see for oneself how the riddle of death was about to be solved by those on the threshold."[10,p.54]

Killing by the death system (or, to put it the other way around, the social system turned killer) can take more subtle and indirect forms—forms that actually result in more deaths than capital punishment. Certain kinds of people routinely are denied access to nutritional and health resources that would enable them to enjoy a full lifespan. Whether or not the term *kill* is used, the outcome of systematic deprivation may be premature death. Glaring inadequacies in safety precautions in many areas of society regularly take a toll of lives. Once we step out of the narrow bounds of those deaths that can be directly linked with society's actions, there is room for controversy. It is hard to avoid the conclusion, however, that the effect of our social policy and action sometimes can be seen in the premature death of its own citizens.

Death systems can be compared with respect to how many and what kinds of people they kill, as well as who and how many they protect or rescue. Comparison can also be made at many other points. We might ask, for example, how much consensus exists within a particular society as to who should die, when, and how. In our own society we can find an impressive variety of views at the same time. To take just one illustration, certain groups in the United States, and in a number of other nations, are devoting themselves to the preservation of endangered species. This effort has included some personal risk taking (as by those seeking a moratorium against whaling), as well as the development of persuasive materials (films, books, television documentaries) to gather support for preservation of endangered species. Regardless of what degree of success these efforts yield, their existence requires us to acknowledge that our death system is complex enough to include more than one orientation toward killing. As a society, we are both killers and protectors of life in its many forms, and the general principles that underlie our sometimes contradictory-seeming behavior have yet to be made explicit.

Attitudes and behaviors related to killing can show up in many ways. For a cultural contrast, consider some aspects of funeral practices in Madagascar. The Merina people, an ethnic group of Southeast Asian origin, are dominant in the Madagascar population. The massive megalithic tombs on this island have attracted considerable attention. Some contemporary anthropologists are particularly interested in the way that the Merina belief system keeps the dead functional within their social and political organization. While we cannot expect to understand the significance of their funerary practices without extended attention to the Merina's total way of life, one facet can at least be mentioned here. Funerals are major events that involve the participation of many individuals. At a certain point in the funeral preparations, a bull is teased by the men. In quite a dangerous game, the bull is incited to rush around and around at them. Later a ceremony is enacted and the bull is killed. The relationship between the funeral and killing goes beyond this. If the "wrong" bull was selected, or it is killed at the wrong time or in the wrong way, then there may be fatal results. Members of the village may die because of this misstep in managing the rituals. According to the folklore, people have died immediately afterward when the killing did not go right for some reason. Maurice Bloch (1971) reports that there is general anxiety at funerals and other ceremonies at which bulls or cattle are killed.

The astrologer may be wrong on a number of points and any mistake is said to have fatal results. The informants did not suggest that this was due to any supernatural agents. The causation is much vaguer. It seems that killing such a large living thing as a bull is dangerous as its death might be contagious. Once death, in any form, has been introduced, only the greatest precautions can control it. [11,p.184]

Teasing, challenging, and then killing bulls appears to be an activity that is dear to the Merinas despite or because of the risks it entails. The fact that killing bulls and risking one's own death should be an integral part of the funeral process may be surprising to us, but the Merinas might be equally astonished by some of our interweavings of killing within our own death system.

SEX DISCRIMINATION AFTER DEATH: AN EXAMPLE OF THE DEATH SYSTEM AT WORK

No one example can do justice to the structure and function of the death system. A simple and focused example, however, may help us at least catch a glimmer of the systematics of death at work in our own society.

Does death alter or confirm existing values?

Sex discrimination can be taken as a significant example of a systematic process that operates in our society. Men have generally been treated by society as though more competent and valuable than women. Discrimination tends to follow women throughout their lives. This raises the question: Does discrimination also follow women through death?

The question can also be formulated at a slightly more abstract level: Does society use death as an occasion for reevaluating and revising its previous judgments? Or does society instead use death as an occasion for consolidating and confirming its previous judgments? In the first edition of this book we reported a little study conducted by two colleagues and myself. Since that time, two independent follow-up studies have been conducted and will be mentioned later. Our prediction in the original study was that death would be treated as an occasion for confirming the relatively low value of women. This hypothesis was limited to one sphere: the public recognition of death shortly after the event.

Death notices and obituaries

Most newspapers in the United States devote a section to reports of recent deaths. Concentrating on metropolitan newspapers, we typically see a distinction between the death notice (DN) and the obituary (OBT). The DN is a short stereotyped passage printed in small type. The listings are as uniform as a row of tiny grave plots and would have us believe that people die alphabetically. The OBT is more variable in length, almost always larger than the DN, and somewhat more flexible in content and style. It is usually printed in the newspaper's regular type size, with an individual headline for each OBT, either giving the deceased's name or some more specific information about position in the community or mode of death. A major distinction between DN and OBT is one of priority and value. Thousands of people receive DNs in a major newspaper throughout the year (an honor for which a charge is usually made), but relatively few are singled out for an OBT. This makes the DN/OBT differential a natural place to look for possible sex bias.

Patterns of sex bias in two major newspapers

All DNs and OBTs that appeared in the same month's publication run of two major metropolitan newspapers were examined.[12] *The Boston Globe* announced 1988 deaths through the DN method, but printed only 201 OBTs, while *The New York Times* published 1774 DNs and only 286 OBTs. For both newspapers the proportion of males and females listed as deceased (DNs) was approximately equal. One would have expected, then, an equal distribution of OBTs if sex discrimination halted at death. The precise expectations would have been 102 female and 99 male OBTs in the *Globe*. The actual distribution proved to be 38 female and 163 male OBTs. Instead of the balance slightly favoring the females (51%/49% expected), it proved to be 81%/19% in the reverse direction. A similar pattern was found in the *Times*. Once again there were approximately four male OBTs for every female OBT, although the sexes were almost equally distributed in the DN listings.

It was interesting to analyze the imbalance on a daily basis. If there were no bias operating, one would expect more female obituaries to show up on 15 or 16 days of the 31-day

month selected for study, and more male obituaries on the other 15 or 16 days. The actual finding much exceeded the predicted bias. Male obituaries dominated *every* day in the *Times*, and on 30 days in the *Globe* (the only exception was a day on which an equal number of male and female OBTs appeared). Continued bias against females also showed up in the length of the OBTs. Both newspapers gave more space, on the average, for male OBTs. One other finding sets the cap on this question. Only 66 people of the 3762 total reported deceased were given OBTs that included their photographs. What were the probabilities of a deceased man and a deceased woman receiving the special distinction of an OBT with a photograph? For both newspapers the differences were on the magnitude of 10; a man was 10 times more likely to receive this kind of attention on his death than was a woman. Should anyone care to take this statistical difference as a serious index of the prevailing attitudes of society (we do not recommend this!), the conclusion would be that 10 times as many men are really valuable, interesting, or important.

Bernard Spilka and his colleagues (1979) subsequently examined OBTs and DNs in two newspapers in a different part of the nation (Denver) over a full year.[13] These investigators, using a somewhat different mode of analysis, found a pattern of sex discrimination favoring men for length of obituaries and presence or absence of photographs, but the difference in proportion of OBTs was not as great as in the Boston/New York newspaper sampling and did not reach statistical significance. Among other things, this study indicated that a trend toward sex discrimination in OBTs is not limited to newspapers in one section of the nation, but that there seem to be regional variations as well that require further study. Newspapers from Ghana and Nigeria were analyzed by P. Eze Onu (1978).[14] His exploratory study also found a bias toward males over females in mortuary messages.

Sex discrimination and the death system

The results of these three little studies suggest that society has a tendency to confirm, continue, or consolidate its previous evaluations of a person on the occasion of his or her death. This is true at least when sex discrimination is at issue and our source of information is the public media. We do not routinely take advantage of this very special event—death—to rethink our values. The results might be quite different if we were examining some theme other than sex discrimination or looking at other types of information. The data presently available, however, suggest that the death system labors under the weight of society's traditional biases: the response to death must be interpreted within the context of a society's prevailing values and prejudices in general.

You will have noticed that this study involved some of the *people* in the death system, notably the recently deceased themselves, the funeral director who submits DNs on behalf of the family, and those newspaper staff members who select and prepare OBTs. It involves at least one *object*, the newspaper itself. The *place* of death is a little complicated. The DNs often, but not always, indicated where and when *(time)* services were to be held for the deceased. Place of death, however, often could not be determined from either DN or OBT. Experiences that go beyond these studies suggest that the place mentioned for death in either newspaper reports or the death certificate itself can be subject to systematic error. And the fact that the newspapers placed the death reports in segregated areas of their publications also tells us something about our society's preferences in this regard. (There are instructive exceptions to the segregate-the-deceased orientation of most American newspapers; some newspapers that serve tightly knit ethnic readerships include news of the dead as part of their overall coverage, perhaps reflecting a more accepting, integrative attitude toward life and death in general.)

Time was involved in the haste with which the reports are prepared and published. To be newsworthy, the deaths must be very recent. Death may be "forever," but the news value fades quickly. Time was also included as the "brief" or "lingering" illness usually cited when reference was made to the terminal phase of life. Use of *symbols* included the basic fact that all these deaths were acknowledged publicly through the written word. The newly deceased person was thus duly entered into the ranks of the departed, whatever else might or might not have been said about him or her. Mention was often made of symbolic rituals, such as church services or ceremonies planned by an organization to which the deceased belonged. In the more extensive OBTs, details were selected with the apparent intention of symbolizing the general nature of the person's life.

The DN and OBT do not usually contribute much to the *prediction* and *warning* functions of the death system except in the very general sense of reminding us, issue after issue, that death continues to strike among us. Occasional death reports do serve warning purposes, as for example when a faulty home heating system is held responsible for the death of a family by fire. Similarly, the DN and OBT do not ordinarily help *prevent* death, nor would this be expected. It would not be out of the question for OBTs—or even for slightly expanded DNs—to play a role in the *caring* and *explaining* functions. To offer just one illustration: if even a minority of death reports included information and, where appropriate, expressions of appreciation for those who were especially helpful during the terminal phase, this might have an alerting and stimulating effect on the care given to others. What we choose to emphasize and what to neglect in death reports reflect the way our culture operates through its death system. The death reports are integral elements in our society's way of *disposing of the dead* and in facilitating *social consolidation* after death.

SUMMARY

Individuals die; society goes on. This chapter prepares the way for a larger perspective to supplement the more personal views that it is natural for each of us to develop as individuals. The concept of the *death system* is introduced. All societies have a death system, and all may be analyzed with respect to their components and functions.

The components of a death system include its *people*, some of whom may be identified with it so firmly that all other aspects of their lives seem to be secondary. Other people have significant but less absorbing or visible roles, while everybody is a potential participant. A death system also has *times*, *places*, *objects*, and *symbols* available for its use. Visiting a military cemetery on Memorial Day and depositing a wreath on a grave would be one action pattern that includes person, time, place, object, and symbol.

The functions of a death system include *warnings* and *predictions*. *Preventing* death by timely safeguards or effective interventions in the midst of a life-threatening situation is another major function of a death system. But, since people do perish in all societies, some form of *care for the dying* is also part of the system. Ambiguities and conflicts in distinguishing between the preventive and the caring functions were cited as a problem of growing concern today. *Disposal of the dead* is another necessary function, including social as well as physical processes. The loss and challenge of death require *social consolidation*. People must find a way of regaining the confidence and cohesion to continue with life. *Mak-

ing sense of death* is not the least challenging function of the death system either. The reader was invited to express his or her own most salient questions that seek explanation.

Killing is a function of the death system that seems to stand apart from the others. Although death systems devote much attention to preservation of life, the opposite course of action also must be acknowledged. Attention is given especially to those actions that bring about death in organized, regulated, or predictable ways.

One detailed research example is given in which the operation of the death system is observed. It is found that sex-discrimination patterns that remain dominant in our society are continued and confirmed immediately after death as well.

Further dynamics of the death system—in today's United States and in other times and places—will be explored in later chapters as we attempt to see death from both social and individual perspectives.

REFERENCES

1. Kastenbaum, R. On the future of death: some images and options. *Omega*, 1972, *3*, 306-318.
2. Habenstein, R. W., & Lamers, W. M. *Funeral customs the world over*. Milwaukee: Bulfin, 1963.
3. Green, J. S. The days of the dead in Oaxaca, Mexico. *Omega*, 1972, *3*, 245-262.
4. Hilgard, J. R. Depressive and psychotic states as anniversaries to sibling death in childhood. *International Psychiatry Clinics*, 1969, *5*, 197-211.
5. Taylor, G. R. *The doomsday book*. London: Panther, 1970.
6. Ehrlich, P. R., & Ehrlich, A. H. *Population, resources, environment*. San Francisco: W. H. Freeman, 1972.
7. Braithwaite, V. A., & Law, H. G. The structure of attitudes to doomsday issues. *Australian Psychologist*, 1977, *12*, 167-174.
8. Bryer, K. B. The Amish way of death: a study of family support systems. *American Psychologist*, 1979, *34*, 255-261.
9. Elliot, G. *Twentieth century book of the dead*. New York: Charles Scribner's Sons, 1972.
10. Jankofsky, K. P. Public execution in England in the

late middle ages: the indignity and dignity of death. *Omega,* 1979, *10,* 43-58.

11. Bloch, M. *Placing the dead.* London & New York: Seminar Press, 1971.

12. Kastenbaum, R., Peyton, S., & Kastenbaum, B. Sex discrimination after death. *Omega,* 1977, *7,* 351-359.

13. Spilka, B., Lacey, G., & Gelb, B. Sex discrimination after death: a replication, extension and a difference. *Omega,* 1979, *10,* 227-233.

14. Onu, P. E. Sex discrimination after death: a study of mortuary advertisements in African newspapers. Unpublished paper, Simon Fraser University, Burnaby, B. C., 1978.

CHAPTER 8

❖ DISASTER AND THE DEATH SYSTEM

During recent years the American public has thronged to the movies to witness one wave of "disaster" films after another. Jet disasters have become almost a film genre of their own, but they have also kept company with fire, flood, earthquake, ship, and other assorted catastrophes. What has generally escaped attention is that actual disasters—real people threatened or killed—have also increased appreciably during this time. Coincidence or more than coincidence, both series of phenomena are part of our society's death system. Although there are a variety of agencies and individuals among us who have learned much about disaster and its place in our lives, as a total society it is questionable whether we have adequately registered this knowledge. Even the death-awareness movement has passed over disaster, expending most of its attention on the situation of the dying person and supportive family and staff. This is just one more example—but an important one—of our society's selectivity in attention to death.

This chapter examines the place of disaster in the death system. By disaster we mean life-threatening events that befall many people within a relatively short period of time. This includes both so-called natural disasters and accidental or man-made disasters—a distinction that is not always easy to maintain in practice.

WARNING, PREDICTING, PREVENTING
Inviting disaster

It seems reasonable to assume that almost everybody would prefer to avoid disaster. We would not want to find ourselves in the path of a tidal wave, trapped in a fire, or swept up by a hurricane. Therefore, we might consider our society's death system to be functioning well when it provides warnings and predictions that enable us to prevent or minimize such disasters. Yet one of the first facts to face is that we often ignore the relevant information. This observation has been made repeatedly; it can be found in many of the technical reports cited in the Harshbarger-Moran (1974) bibliography,[1] and there is no indication that this situation has changed appreciably over the past half-dozen years. It is not valid to assume that knowledge of impending or possible disaster is sufficient to trigger serious concern or effective behavior even when this is clearly communicated.

Consider this statement by a federal expert on disaster control. Richard E. Sanderson (1974) confirms that the number and severity of major disasters has increased in recent years. He then declares that:

The current increase in major disasters is likely to increase. Why? The fact of the matter is that our nation is becoming increasingly vulnerable. In the first place, our population is concentrated where disasters are most likely to occur—coastlines and river basins. Over 50% of our population, more than 100 million people, now live within 50 miles of our coastlines. The west coast is vulnerable to fires, floods, earthquakes, and landslides. The gulf and east coasts are vulnerable to tropical storms, hurricanes, and tornadoes. The midwest and south are vulnerable to tornadoes and floods. In many instances, land development and construction is taking place without consideration of natural disaster risks. Population growth and industrialization bring greater exposure to other types of disasters—such as the Texas City explosion and fire.[2,p.91]

The shift of our population to disaster-vulnerable coastal areas has continued since Sanderson's statement. One does not see any counterbalancing trend to reduce disaster vulnerability on the part of major governmental or industrial agencies, nor any general increase in public concern (although temporary and local flurries of alarm have been expressed after specific catastrophes, such as the battering of New England coastal areas during the "Great Blizzard of 1978").

If life protection (death prevention) were our society's primary goal, then population expansion might be discouraged in areas subject to the most frequent and severe disasters. Land development and industrial projects would be examined carefully for their possible contribution to mass disaster. But this has not been our society's pattern. The risk is taken, knowingly or not, by those who opt to reside in the popular but more hazardous areas. Many of us would strenuously resist governmental pressure to change our life-style or reduce our options to minimize risk. Notice what has *not* happened in those areas where the projected effects of an earthquake would be especially severe. San Francisco and Los Angeles are as bustling as ever. Yet in the San Francisco Bay area alone, a strong quake, figured at 8.3 on the Richter Scale, might be expected to kill more than 10,000 people and injure four times as many if it occurred on a late afternoon, with

perhaps another 100,000 lives in extreme jeopardy if the dams gave way (National Oceanic and Atmospheric Administration study, cited by Sanderson[2]). This is of particular interest because scientists believe they have well established the basis and likelihood of a major quake in this area and because memories of a historical earthquake still live in San Francisco. It is difficult to shrug off these warnings as empty talk or wild speculation. One begins to think of some form of *denial* as being operative throughout our society. Denial is a familiar concept when considering the response of individuals to terminal illness (their own or that of others). We may have been missing the larger point that denial, in some sense of this term, is quite prevalent in other life-threatening situations as well. In other words, the death-awareness movement may have permitted itself to narrow down so much on dynamics involving terminal illness that it has arrived at the assumption that certain processes and responses are especially characteristic of individuals facing personal crises when, in fact, this may represent a special case of more prevalent dynamics in our culture's death system. Perceptions and attitudes regarding terminal illness cannot be entirely separated from orientation toward large-scale disaster, for both occur within the same society. The death systems approach encourages us to identify and learn from such interactions; it must also be said that this approach has seldom been applied as yet.

Should people desert the San Francisco Bay area and other hazardous places? Should control be exercised over population buildup in some areas? It is doubtful that many of us would care to argue in favor of such alternatives. Preventing death from disaster is only one of our society's goals and, in competition with many other goals, is often consigned to a low priority. We can be in possession of sound warning and prediction over a long period of time and yet, for other reasons, decide not to act on this information.

Those who are interested in a careful analysis of the situation will want to distinguish between *awareness* of possible catastrophe and the *response* to this awareness. Again, there is a parallel with terminal illness. A person who appears to be unaffected by a terminal prognosis may possibly have closed off from consciousness the awareness/registration of this information, or may instead have taken the information in clearly enough but decided not to let it affect his or her overt behavior. It would be useful to explore both social and individual responses to the threat of death—to what extent do we shut off information we would rather not hear, and to what extent do we accept this information but choose to take certain risks in the service of other values and interests? In both the threat-of-disaster and individual-confronting-death sitautions, it is often difficult to distinguish between level of awareness or receptivity to the warnings and predictions on the one hand, and a decision-making process that acknowledges the facts but does not give them a central place in behavioral response on the other.

Notice also that the discrepancy between warning and response maintains a tension within our society. Here are a relatively few people taking the responsibility to warn of and predict disaster, and there is the larger society with its attention or values elsewhere. "You're getting to be a nuisance, a worrywart, and a bore!" we tell some of our people in the death system. They reply, "You are living in a fool's paradise. . . . Think ahead, consider the worst!"

Many failures of the warning and prediction process have been reported in specific disasters. It is one thing to know that we live in an area subject to certain kinds of threat. But it is something else to hear direct, immediate warnings and still act as though nothing were amiss.

Reviewing many disaster reports, Martha Wolfenstein (1977) found that a sense of *personal immunity* is one common reason for a person to remain in disaster's path.[3] Interestingly, this view often would become completely reversed after disaster struck. "However widespread the damage, the first impression of the disaster victim is that he alone was hit."[3,p.19]

Another psychological factor came to her attention. She found that people in a variety of disasters—storm, fire, flood—often interpret these events as *punishment*. Even the warnings and predictions can be enough to arouse the feeling that one may not only be hurt but be hurt on purpose because of misdeeds and failings. A person who makes this kind of interpretation may have a difficult time in taking the warning for what it is, as it now carries more of an emotion-laden meaning rather than being just an objective statement of danger ahead.

Inconvenience may be a simpler and more rational-appearing reason for ignoring warnings and predictions, but it can be just as powerful. Wolfenstein refers to the unwillingness to evacuate homes when threatened with floods or hurricanes. "The certain inconvenience of evacuation outweighs the greater, but less certain, hazard of being overtaken by the disaster."[3,p.19]

These personal responses to disaster may diminish the value of life-protecting processes generated by society. But society itself also has ways of contradicting its own death-preventing objectives. Wolfenstein suggests that one of these is:

a strong repudiation of anxious, worrisome or fearful tendencies. Children are taught from an early age not to be "scaredy-cats." The "over-protective" mother who hovers apprehensively over her child is a very negative figure from the American point of view. This contrasts with certain other cultures, for instance the Eastern European Jewish or the pre-Soviet Russian, in which incessant maternal anxiety about threats to health and the fragility of life pervaded the family atmosphere. For Americans, such anxiousness is not only futile and unnecessary, it is incompatible with a positive image of oneself. It is essential to one's self-esteem to feel: everything is OK with me.[3,p.21]

The keep-cool, stay-under-control spirit in our society might work against us when death threatens. By refusing to admit to vulnerability, we make ourselves all the more vulnerable.

Disaster and the ordinary

A variety of other needs, motives, and practices in society can also defeat the warning-predicting-preventing core of the death system. Consider a pair of fires in Boston. Starting in 1866, John S. Damrell, the city's fire chief, repeatedly warned of the danger faced by this growing metropolis. He made specific predictions of the kind of major fire that was likely to occur, and offered specific suggestions for preventive and interventive solutions. His requests to the city's officials became increasingly urgent over the months and years. Damrell specified what would be needed to obtain an adequate supply of water and made other suggestions intended to reduce the vulnerability of the city's buildings to flame. The officials chose not to respond. But one day fire was suddenly on everybody's mind. The great city of Chicago had just been swept by flames that burned out of control for almost 30 hours. Boston now went so far as to send Chief Damrell to inspect the scene. Much of what he learned about the Chicago disaster was in keeping with the specific warnings he had been making to his own city. He returned with even more urgent suggestions for a steam engine firehouse in the heart of the city, for improved methods of handling hoses in an emergency, for renovations on the roofs of public buildings to slow down the advance of a conflagration, and so on. These proposals had gone nowhere in particular in the city's politically dominated bureaucracy when, on November 9, 1872, Boston's flourishing commercial district went up in

flames. The fire had been anticipated in detail, as were the severe handicaps that would be faced in trying to bring it under control without the safeguards and improvements that had been repeatedly urged. Eleven firemen lost their lives, 17 were severely injured. The number of civilian dead and injured was never completely determined.

In its centennial analysis of this fire, *The Boston Globe* blamed the disaster on "old-style politics."[4] The officials were said to have been preoccupied with their own power and patronage games, not really much interested in spending even a little money in upgrading city services or in stepping on powerful toes by requiring safety regulations and their enforcement. There is no reason for questioning the newspaper's analysis as such. But it is naive to attribute this orientation exclusively to "politics," and, at that, to imply a fundamental difference between the "old-style" and what continues to be practiced today.

Seventy years after the great Boston fire, an artificial palm frond became ignited in a popular nightclub in the same city. Within 13 minutes 400 people were dead. Hundreds more suffered severe burns and inhalation of noxious fumes; of these, another 100 eventually died. In retrospect, it can be seen that all of these deaths might have been prevented. Ten of the 12 exits were locked or blocked, and one depended on a revolving door that quickly became jammed. Highly flammable materials were abundant throughout the nightclub; none had been treated with chemicals to retard fire; these materials also released lethal fumes when burned. Furthermore, aid was not sought until the situation was far out of hand. The patrons of the Coconut Grove did not express alarm at first. "If anything . . . the crowd was amused. They made light of the discomfiture of waiters, who squirted water on the tiny blaze."[5] When a state of alarm developed, it quickly turned to panic and the panic to catastrophe.

The profit motive played a major role in this

disaster. Renovation of this structure from garage to nightclub had been made with little attention to safety. Patrons were jammed into every available space for the same reason. Doors were blocked to prevent gate-crashers and thieves from entering. The indifference to fire danger was shared with Coconut Grove by officials of the same city that presumably had learned its lesson in 1872. But the contribution of economic motives cannot be limited exclusively to practice of "old-style-politics." It can be seen as readily in the business as in the governmentul realm. And repetition of a disaster is not in itself any assurance that it will not yet happen again and again, as exemplified by a recent nightclub fire in Kentucky, in which many of the same, sad, ordinary but lethal social dynamics already described for both Boston fires were again in evidence.

This brings us to so simple and slender a point that it does not seem able to bear the weight of mass injury, death, and destruction. *The failure of the warning-predicting-preventing system is often associated with the most common and ordinary attitudes and practices of our society.* The effects of a disaster are powerful. It is natural to look for explanations that are also powerful and somehow rather special. Usually, however, the critical factors prove to be those familiar practices that characterize much of our society's functioning. Employees might sneak away from work for a few minutes, for example, and thereby cut into profits. It just makes sense, then, to keep the stairway exits locked during the workday. This familiar practice in New York City "sweatshops" deprived the employees of the Triangle Shirt Waist Company of any opportunity for escape when fire engulfed them on the top three floors of their 10-story loft building. Within a few minutes, 147 women and young girls perished by leaping from windows, by being trampled in the useless rush to the exits, or directly from the flames. This disaster of March 25, 1911, is still remembered by some because of the number of lives lost. It was not the only preventable loss of human life in commercial firetraps during those years. Examples could be added of other times, places, and types of disaster in which existing practices were either responsible for the catastrophe in the first place or contributed much to the high death toll. If we look only for Big Explanations, then we are likely to miss the critical role of the ordinary, that taken for granted, in the daily functioning of our society.

The ordinary today includes one relatively new dimension that is sometimes overlooked in the analysis of disasters. Legislative actions and agency-promulgated regulations have become a sort of second-order reality that affects the lives of all of us. Some of these regulations have the effect of protecting us from dangers; many have the opposite effect, even though it is probably safe to say that none were *intended* to facilitate disaster. Let me tell you about one of a great many "ordinary situations" that prevail around the nation today. Here is a community general hospital where a spectrum of care is being provided—babies are being born, people are recovering from surgery, and so forth. Not far away is a major facility for the sick and frail elderly—nearly 500 old people, many of whom cannot move about without assistance and who require substantial care and shelter for continued survival. Between both hospitals is a railroad yard. And in this railroad yard on any given day one can often count three, four, five, six, or more tank cars filled with polyvinyl chloride (polychlorinated biphenyl—PCB). This substance is now well known to be very hazardous to the health when there is exposure to even minute amounts over a period of time. Expert opinion is also clear that exposure to large amounts (through breathing and skin contact) in a short time period could also be very hazardous to healthy adults—what about to infants, the aged, and the ill? I admit to being an interested party to this situation as director of the geriatric facility.

At the time of this writing my colleagues and I have already spent months "working through the system" to try to remove the hazard. Others, including the town itself, have also been trying to negotiate their way through layers of regulations, competing jurisdictions, and technical court rulings—as well as, it must be said, to something less than high-priority attention from decision-making officials. It is probable that some gas is leaking. The railbeds are not in good shape. Gusts of wind often blow about cement dust and whatever other contaminants might be available at the moment. Here is a situation that looks—and is—ordinary enough and that may never generate a disaster. Yet the background circumstances for a disaster exist, and nobody can really set a probability. This kind of situation with its many variants can be found in neighborhood after neighborhood, community after community throughout the nation. "Getting something done" to head off possible catastrophe or even to plan effective countermoves should a disaster develop is often frustrated by the tangled web of regulations and jurisdictions as well as by denial, indifference, and other factors already noted. Ordinary, all of it, yet potentially part of a lethal outcome.

Communication and miscommunication

No outer limit has been established for the scope of disaster that might result from failure of the warning-predicting-preventing system. Perhaps the most extensive destruction would involve the coupling of an enormously powerful threat with a tightly controlled information network. *The Day the World Ended* (Thomas & Witts, 1969)[6] is a title that scarcely exaggerates when the facts it reports are considered. The incredibly violent eruption of Mt. Pelee incinerated virtually the entire population of St. Pierre on the morning of May 8, 1902. There was no way then nor is there now to prevent the eruption. However, the fact that 30,000 men, women, and children were turned into charred corpses cannot be laid only to the natural forces involved. Vested political and economic interests convincingly denied reports that the volcano had started to erupt. Holding control of the Martinique newspaper and desiring to keep as many people on the island as possible for an upcoming election, the responsible officials deliberately lied and deceived. They even invented a nonexistent scientist to subdue any fears that might have been aroused. Instead of evacuating the island, the officials so managed the news and information network that the people of St. Pierre had no chance to escape disaster.

A more contemporary version of this type of disaster seems to be peering around the edges at us in the form of a thermonuclear accident. In the first edition of this book a reference was made to *We Almost Lost Detroit* (Fuller, 1975).[7] This was an account of an incident at the Enrico Fermi atomic reactor, located approximately 30 miles from Detroit. It was a situation in which a significant threat to thousands of lives was posed, and in which the communication process (both internally and to the public) was riddled with gaps and inaccuracies. In the past few years more incidents that threatened catastrophe have either occurred or come to the notice of investigators. Perhaps the "closest call" so far (certainly the one that has attracted most attention) was the accident at Three Mile Island. Although the details of the Three Mile Island situation had their specific and unique features, the overall pattern is essentially a repetition of what has been true of disasters and near-disasters of many types throughout this century. To concentrate on the communication dimension alone, we see at first fragmentary and conflicting reports, with the hasty assurances that all is well. Later there are multiple recriminations, passing the blame on to various persons, machines, regulations, etc. Credibility is strained, to say the least, by the mixed and defensive messages that come out of near-disasters such as the Three Mile Island incident. Each such incident (whether involving thermonuclear or other type of potential catastrophe) increases the difficulty for the public in deciding how to evaluate the whole pattern of warnings and reassurances that issue forth from what should be authoritative sources.

A recent article concerning "troubles" at the Pilgrim I nuclear reactor plant in Plymouth, Massachusetts[8] indicates increasing distrust of information provided by and about the facility. Citizens appear to be finding it difficult to acquire information they need to allay anxiety about radiation leaks that could already be having serious effect. There are charges of lies, deception, and cover-up as well as incompetence. Certain obvious violations of safety practices have been observed (e.g., conveyance of radioactive waste in a flatbed truck in the midst of afternoon city traffic), as well as official attempts to cover up such incidents. Earlier we were considering the phenomenon of people not paying enough attention to accurate warnings and predictions; the total situation also includes the deliberate failure of authorities to provide adequate warning and, at times, to deliberately mislead. A functional component of our society intended to meet one of the vital operational needs (e.g., energy supply) could also turn out to be massively involved in the *killing* component of the death system.

Technical problems can afflict the warning-predicting-preventing system in natural disaster as well. People have been lulled into believing they were not in the area threatened by storm or flood because of communication errors and ambiguities. The couple who heard reassuring news that they were not in the area endangered by flood might have been more relieved had the message not been coming through the radio of their water-filled car. Incomplete, contradictory, ambiguous, or over-

generalized communication is an invitation to misinterpretation and ineffective response. Harry B. Williams (1964) cites a classical example during a flooding of the Rio Grande. Inhabitants of a threatened town heard the following message from a sound truck: "An all-time record flood is going to inundate the city. You must evacuate immediately. (Pause) The _____ Theater is presenting two exciting features tonight. Be sure to see these pictures at the _____ Theater tonight."[9,p.91]

What then is required for effective functioning of our warning-predicting-preventing system? Accurate information is necessary, of course. But so is a communication network that is skillful and in good technical working order. Personal and social motives that might lead to evasions and distortions must be set aside. And yet, even accurate, timely, well-stated information can fail to elicit appropriate response from individuals, groups, or agencies. The sense of immunity, the misinterpretation of disaster threats as scoldings and punishments, the desire to avoid inconvenience are among the psychological factors that can interfere with utilization of information to prevent death and destruction. Furthermore, as we have seen, the resistance to taking necessary safeguards because of economic and power motives should not be underestimated.

Although this brief discussion has emphasized problems and failings, there is also basis for some optimism. Despite social and psychological obstacles, disaster-control efforts have become somewhat more successful in recent years. Warning and prediction systems have become more proficient on the technical level. Perhaps enough has already been learned about the psychology of organization, management, and communication in general that this knowledge could be applied usefully to improving both the transmittal and reception of disaster-threat information. I think it is fair to say that our society has not yet given high priority to developing disaster-prevention systems that will transcend the ordinary petty motives and practices that breed catastrophe, so our potentials in this area have not really been tested.

INTERVENTION AND "POSTVENTION"

The fate of the injured, the dying, the dead, and the survivors must now be considered. The type of disaster obviously makes a difference. In a flood, for example, there may be a large number of people suffering from exposure and injury. Finding and providing care to those in most serious condition is of high priority. After a flash flood there may be a new category of person in the community: the missing. There is a related need to rescue the missing who are still alive and to reassure their friends and family, and also a need to recover the bodies of the dead and begin the physical and social processes of consolidation after death. Furthermore, flooding is a type of disaster that can create still other hazards to survival, such as epidemic disease in a weakened population. Even though the disaster itself has ended, the stress and the potential for further death continues. By contrast, the crash of a jetliner is often an extremely lethal event that is restricted to a very limited time and place. Survivors are sought, but usually the ratio of persons killed to persons involved is much higher than in the flood, storm, or quake situation. The person who wishes to be knowledgeable or helpful on the scene of disaster would need to learn many specifics associated with the various forms in which disaster strikes. Here, however, we will concentrate on some of the more general features of intervention and "postvention."

Typical concerns after disaster strikes

How adequately society comes to the aid of disaster victims will be reflected in both the immediate and long-term outcomes. At best, we can save lives that might have been lost, and provide an afflicted community with the kind of support it needs. At worst, we increase the death toll, carve additional scars into the personalities of the survivors, and create problems that continue to plague the community decades later.

Sociologist Vanderlyn Pine (1974) has pointed out eight typical concerns that arise in the wake of disaster:

1. Those living through the disaster are cared for and given necessary medical attention.
2. Those not directly involved in the disaster or its aftermath are excluded from the general vicinity.
3. The disaster area is protected as undisturbed as possible in order to allow concerned agencies and organizations to carry out necessary investigations.
4. When there have been fatalities, it is customary to mark and record the location where the dead human remains are found, and then, these remains are removed from the scene.
5. If possible, the dead human remains are identified, and their deaths must be certified.
6. The surviving next of kin are notified of the disaster and of the death of their family member(s).
7. The final disposition of those dead as a result of the disaster is implemented.
8. The sociopsychological needs of the survivors of the disaster victims should be met effectively from the time of notification until the remains of the dead person are returned to their care.[10, p.3]

It is much easier to list these concerns than to act on them effectively in the middle of the situation. The intervention-postvention effort is likely to include both professionals and those without specialized skills. It may also include people from the immediate area and others converging from the outside. There is potential for both excellent collaboration and distressing confusion and conflict in this kind of situation. Both kinds of outcome have been observed. Local and federal agencies, for example, must be able to share responsibility and expertise. Organization and disciplined effort is valuable, but an overly formalized, inflexible, and insensitive approach to the needs of the survivors can defeat many of the good intentions. Problems have been known to develop when people who are expert in their own professions or skill areas do not realize how to put these best to the service of disaster relief.

Communication problems may continue into the intervention-postvention phase. People converging on the scene of the disaster may be speaking different technical languages and holding widely varied expectations of what should be done—and who should be in charge. The helpers may also be more or less sensitive to the needs communicated by victims and survivors. The fixed idea that one knows precisely what disaster victims need can stand in the way of discovering what they actually do need at a particular moment. Both the physical reality and the emotional climate frequently shift with the passage of time after disaster. The helper may be too busy doing and talking to *listen* carefully to the victims and survivors.

Strong feelings are likely to flourish in the aftermath of disaster. This includes a temporary "feeling of nonfeeling." Good communication is vital but also difficult to achieve in such a situation. And failures in communication in turn can result in either immediate or long-term problems. Families made homeless by flood have at times been relocated haphazardly in densely packed trailer courts instead of being helped to retain their previous community groupings. This can be both a consequence and a subsequent cause of poor communication. Survivors may then feel twice victimized—first by the disaster, then by the helpers. Psychological symptoms such as depression and phobia may then develop among the survivors to further complicate their adjustment and their ability to get back on their feet (e.g., Church, 1974).[11]

The dead and their survivors

In our society we are most familiar with the death of individuals. When a person dies after a long illness, for example, medical personnel usually are available to certify the death, inform next of kin, and prepare the body for the funeral director selected by the family. Although the death may hit family and friends with great emotional impact, it may not have been entirely unexpected; furthermore, their own lives may be moving along in reasonably stable shape.

This is not the situation when a disaster claims many lives. The deaths are unexpected; health-care personnel appear on the scene as best they can, not necessarily selected by the victims; and the survivors themselves may have experienced considerable stress and disorganization in their own lives. Even those components of the death system taken most for granted may falter under such circumstances. The location of the body itself may be in question. Problems can arise in identifying the many victims of a disaster. Imagine the feelings of those who search desperately among both the living and the dead for missing family or friends. The distress of viewing the body of a loved one after it has been carefully prepared and exhibited at a funeral home hardly suggests the reaction to human remains that have been severely disfigured in a disaster, especially when one corpse after another must be viewed in an effort to establish identity. For some people this is indeed the stuff of which nightmares are made.

Hershiser and Quarentelli[12] have shown that such problems can be held to a minimum in the wake of a flood (the Rapid City, South Dakota disaster in which 237 people died). Volunteer efforts were especially effective in the recovery of bodies and the tactful interaction with people searching for their missing friends and family. Local authorities, National Guard, and the residents themselves cooperated well. Funeral directors assisted in the identification process, agreed to provide moderately priced funerals, and worked cooperatively instead of in terms of normal business competition. These investigators, and others, have noted that survivors often express a strong need to bury the dead properly—there is a certain dignity required for the dead as well as for the dying. The research team found that *respect* for the dead was the most prominent attitude shown. The teams of helping people therefore made a serious attempt, under difficult circumstances, to treat each body in an individual and appropriate manner.

It is also impressive that community volunteers assisted in cleaning bodies and making them as presentable as possible. While in some other cultures it is standard practice for family and friends to perform this function, in America all activities involving touching and "preparing" the dead are usually delegated to specialists. Somehow, people found a way of overcoming the usual aversion toward physical contact with a corpse. Obviously, there is much to learn from observations of humane and effective as well as insensitive and confused responses of the death system. And, in the situation that has just been described, most of the participants in this effort were not permanently associated with the death system but had been recruited into it by circumstance.

MAKING SENSE OF DISASTER

Over the centuries there has been an intense interest in *explaining* why a particular disaster occurred as well as in specifying why certain people perished while others were spared. Two alternatives seem most prominent. First, we might take a simple position that has the look of objectivity. This position would restrict itself to the specific natural causes of disaster. It might also include the so-called laws of chance and probability. The "why" question should be answered by reference to whatever knowledge is available in the earth and physical sciences for certain types of disaster and in other appropriate scientific realms for other disasters. Our questions about catastrophes would be an-

swered, if at all, through detailed knowledge of how the world works.

The alternative position would utilize what is known of the physical causation and process of disasters, but would also add the human factor. Power and profit motives and individual psychological interpretations would be taken into account. Physical science might tell us *how* a slag tip grew and eventually avalanched on the village of Aberfan, South Wales, killing 28 adults and almost all of the younger generation (116 children). Psychology and other sociobehavioral sciences, however, would be more likely to reveal the *why* of it—why the slag buildup was tolerated although the danger was clear.

There is still another perspective, however. Throughout human history, three other elements seem to have been more dominant in the search for explanation.[13] First, disaster often has been associated with the mood of the universe and its governing deities. A moral or divine significance is attributed to the catastrophe. The enemy's fleet was shattered by storm—sure proof that the gods have taken our side, and confirmation of our superior virtue. Our own temple has been razed by fire or crumbled by an earthquake? This must be a message of divine discontent with the status quo in our society or with certain sinners in our midst. Disasters, then, are to be read for their true significance.

The importance of disaster interpretation often has gone well beyond response to any specific event. Both the public and personal lives of many of our predecessors were governed by elaborate precautions intended to lessen the threat of disaster, usually by placating the gods. Rituals were developed and exercised to prevent calamity, including disastrous nonhappenings such as the possible failure of the Nile to overrun its banks.

Interpretations of disaster became linked with the society's normative behaviors and attitudes. In this sense, it might be said that we have maintained a *fabric of disaster*.

An overwhelming disaster occurs only now and again. But prayers, rituals, codes of conduct, superstitions, all of these are part of the daily experience. Viewed in this manner, disaster is not an isolated rarity. It is a predictable and common phenomenon in private and institutional life because disaster is so regularly memorialized, predicted, symbolized, and warded off (as well as wished upon adversaries), even if disasters themselves do not occur every day.[13,p.69]

Second, disaster can serve as an explanation of other events. "We have not been the same since . . . ." Or "The world has not recovered since . . ." (fill in any disaster of your choice). Whether or not these explanations are historically accurate, there is a tradition of distinguishing between the way things used to be before the flood, before the fire, before the expressway went through the center of our town (an event perceived locally as disastrous).

Third, there is *power* in explanation. Individuals and society institutions with strong power motives may seek to increase their credibility by asserting that they have the definitive or inside information on disaster. The king, general, or church that can prove most persuasive with disaster explanation is in a better position to manipulate and control others. "Do as I say, or even greater disasters will befall you" may be the implicit message. Note how this ancient political device continues to find application today as, for example, among those who claim special understanding of the energy crisis and its possible disasters.

Perhaps you found the "why" question of special pertinence when you were mulling over the death-related questions of most interest to you (Chapter 7). Perhaps you wondered why some lives are snuffed out early or violently while others continue unmolested. Behind this type of question there is often a need to find—

or project—*meaning* and *intention* into the universe. Things do not just happen; they happen for a reason. To identify this need is not to reject or ridicule it. Outstanding minds continue to disagree on the possible meaningfulness of the universe and our place in it. The point here is that disaster tends to engage our search for meaning. Many of us have difficulty believing that catastrophes come by change or as the simple consequence of physical events alone. For disasters to make sense they must fit into some kind of scheme, purpose, or plan. The danger here of course is that one might arrive hastily at conclusions that serve emotional needs but circumvent reality.

A completely different orientation also has its dangers. One might close the book on the "why" question with the conclusion that there is no purpose or order. Death by disaster comes when "it" chooses, and "it" does not even choose for any reason relevant to humankind. The danger in this case is that inquiry into the specific causes of disaster is stultified, and the opportunity to warn, predict, prevent, or respond more effectively after the event is thereby relinquished. Both the placating-the-gods and the nothing-can-be-done-about-it orientations can make society more vulnerable than necessary to disaster.

SUMMARY

Disaster—life-threatening events that befall many people within a relatively short period of time—comes in many forms, all of which engage society's death system. The *warning-predicting-preventing* functions may be ineffective for a number of reasons. These include the fact that prevention of death is only one social goal among others and not necessarily the dominant goal. In our own society, for example, an increasing percentage of the population is at risk because of its preference for living in disaster-prone areas of the country. Some reasons for failure to heed disaster warnings can be found in individual orientations, such as the *sense of personal immunity*, interpretation of disaster as *punishment*, and the *unwillingness to be inconvenienced*. The culturally prevalent need to be in control of the situation, and to *deny vulnerability* is another contributing factor in disaster as well as in the individual facing terminal illness.

Analysis of many specific disasters suggests that *ordinary social attitudes and practices* often contribute to the death toll. Power and profit motives figure prominently here. Disasters can also be magnified by *failures in the communication process*, such as ambiguous or contradictory messages. The combination of *high lethal threat and a tightly controlled information network* is singled out as an especially dangerous situation.

The process of *intervention* and *postvention* after a disaster has struck is briefly examined. Attention is given to *type of disaster*, *typical concerns*, and *patterns of communication and collaboration among helpers and survivors*. The situation that arises when many die in one episode is contrasted with the more familiar situation in which a particular individual reaches the end of life.

Making sense of disaster is seen in historical perspective. Disasters have often been interpreted as signs of approval or disapproval from the gods; they have also been used to explain other events. Furthermore, there is power to be gained by winning credibility as an authority on disasters. Two orientations are contrasted: the inclination to read purpose and intention into disaster and the opposing inclination to assume that there is no pattern at all and nothing to be done in preparation or prevention.

REFERENCES

1. Harshbarger, D., & Moran, G. A selective bibliography on disaster and human ecology. *Omega*, 1974, 5, 89-95.
2. Sanderson, R. E. The role of the federal government in providing disaster assistance. In V. R. Pine (Ed.), *Responding to disaster*. Milwaukee: Bulfin, 1974.
3. Wolfenstein, M. *Disaster: a psychological essay*. New York: Arno Press, 1977.
4. Harris, J. (Ed.). The great Boston fire, 1872. *The Boston Globe*, November 12, 1972, special publication.
5. Stack, J. *The Boston Globe*, November 26, 1967, p. 1.
6. Thomas, G., & Witts, M. M. *The day the world ended*. New York: Ballantine Books, Inc., 1969.
7. Fuller, J. G. *We almost lost Detroit*. New York: Thomas Y. Crowell Co., Inc., 1975.
8. Barron, S. D. Nuclear neighborhood. *Boston*, December 1979, 123-125, 192-210.
9. Williams, H. B. Human factors in warning-and-response systems. In G. G. Grosser, H. Wechsler, & M. Greenblatt (Eds.), *The threat of impending disaster*. Cambridge, Mass.: The M. I. T. Press, 1964.
10. Pine, V. R. The social context of disaster. In V. R. Pine (Ed.), *Responding to disaster*. Milwaukee: Bulfin, 1974.
11. Church, J. S. The Buffalo Creek disaster: extent and range of emotional and/or behavioral problems. *Omega*, 1974, 5, 61-64.
12. Hershiser, M. R., & Quarentelli, E. L. The handling of the dead in a disaster. *Omega*, 1976, 7, 195-208.
13. Kastenbaum, R. Disaster, death, and human ecology. *Omega*, 1974, 5, 65-72.

CHAPTER 9

❖ INTIMATIONS OF MORTALITY
In childhood's hour

It is a long way from the violent impact of a mass disaster to a quiet garden where a fuzzy caterpillar wriggles along to the delight of a 16-month-old boy. Disaster relief teams will not converge on the scene nor will the media capture the event in words and photograph. But it is in this type of situation, and in many others that remain unknown to the adult world, that children begin their acquaintance with death.

The child notices the approach of big adult feet moving along the path. He shows an alarmed expression, according to his companion, a senior biomedical scientist who is also the boy's father. In a moment the caterpillar lies crushed. The boy bends over the remains, studying them intently. Finally, he stands up and announces in a sad and resigned voice, "No more!"

This little incident contains some of the most significant problems encountered in trying to understand the individual's lifelong relationship to death. Here are a few of the questions raised by this incident:

1. When do we form our first intimations of mortality?
2. To what extent is our understanding of death dependent on psychobiological maturation and to what extent does it depend on particular experiences that stray into our lives?
3. What is the relationship between how we think and how we feel about death?
4. How do death-related thoughts and experiences affect the individual's entire pattern of development?
5. At what point in the total life span does a person attain the final or most highly developed understanding of death?
6. How *should* parents and society in general respond to the child's death-related encounters and explorations?

Think of these questions within the context of the opening incident. The garden scene appears to have demonstrated awareness of death in a very young child. But did it really? Is it valid to conclude that such an insight could develop at so early an age, especially when the weight of opinion and evidence in developmental psychology holds that concepts of this type are not attained until many years later? The "when" question is by no means easy to answer. And yet it is not easy to put aside, either. Many of our actions and assumptions are based on what we think that other people think. If we credit the young child with either too much or too little understanding of death, we might behave inappropriately as a result.

In this incident death was brought about by an outside but human source, and the victim was a tiny subhuman creature. As the years go by this child will encounter a variety of other death-related incidents. How much of his death attitudes as an adult will depend on the number, kind, intensity, and timing of these incidents—and how much will depend on the basic processes of maturation or on the society's particular life-style? It might be argued that experiences themselves do not count for much until the child is mature enough to make use of them. But the child who witnesses the death of other children as a reality in everyday life—victims of famine, disease, and warfare in many parts of the world today—does not let these experiences pass without notice. Close attention is required to the dialectic between whatever might be universal in the development of the individual and all that is contingent on the particular circumstances in which development takes place.

Another relationship raises questions. The father reported a particular emotional orientation—sad and resigned—as well as the expression of insight. Does this mean that the first awareness of death always arouses sadness? If so, how about later encounters with death? It is tempting to suppose that there is a direct link between the thought of death and a particular emotional state, especially if we notice this tendency in ourselves and assume that everybody else must feel as we do. In this book an attempt is made to distinguish between death-related thoughts and perceptions on the one hand and the way we *feel* about death on the other. This could be an artificial distinction if carried too far. Thinking and feeling ordinarily are components of the same psychological situation to death if we suspend any assumptions about their relationship that have not been identified and analyzed.

Over the years, most textbooks on child development have said little about the possible effect of death thoughts and experiences on the total developmental pattern. The implication has been that this is not an important topic.

Let us add just a little more about the subsequent experiences of the boy in the garden. This was his favorite place for an outing with his father. After the caterpillar incident, the child seemed especially concerned about *impermanence* (not that this word was in his vocabulary). He had regularly led his father to an area of this semipublic garden in which large bright flowers flourished. Now he noticed that the largest blossom has changed. He expressed apprehension over its condition. The next day he did not approach these flowers spontaneously as he had done in the past. His father eventually led him there, however. The boy quickly took in the withered appearance of the blossom and saw petals of other blossoms on the ground. He turned and headed off in the opposite direction. On subsequent visits to the garden he made it clear that he did not want to go to that area.

This behavioral sequence suggests at least a specific and short-term effect of a death encounter. No doubt alternative explanations could be offered for the boy's behavior, and there is no way of knowing what role, if any, this episode may have played in his subsequent development. However, enough observations have been made to raise the possibility that death-related experiences and the thoughts and feelings they stimulate do not themselves pass quickly into oblivion. Early relationships with death, even ones apparently as trivial as the caterpillar and the blossom, may have significant impact on the formation of personality. At the very least, this is a possibility that we cannot afford to dismiss without careful inquiry.

Perhaps what has been reported here was the child's first encounter with death, perhaps not. It is clear that he did become mentally and emotionally involved in the episode. But how much further would his thoughts and feelings have to advance before it could be said that he has a fully mature grasp of death? Notice that we cannot say much about the relative adequacy of a child's understanding unless there is some firm criterion or endpoint for comparison. We have to know what constitutes a well-developed orientation toward death. This kind of knowledge is available for many other developmental dimensions, for example, the growth of the skeletal and nervous systems. But it is questionable that either our learned disciplines or our society in general possess a single, well-documented framework for determining what constitutes the most mature orientation toward death. Despite this limitation, it will be important to follow the continued pattern of death orientations from early childhood onward.

If you had been this boy's parent, what would have been your impulse? Would you have taken him gently but firmly by the hand and led him away from the caterpillar as soon as it had been crushed? Would you have changed the subject? Or would you have taken the occasion to deliver a minisermon on life and death? Would you have thought nothing of this incident or taken it very seriously? Would you have gone out of your way in the future to protect him from death encounters? Or would you have done just the opposite, finding or creating situations in which he would have death experiences of a type you might consider constructive? Parental decisions about how they will relate to their children on the subject of death do not always begin this early, although the opportunities to make decisions often come earlier than parents realize. Sooner or later, however, decisions are made, either consciously or by default. The study of the child's relationship with death, from the first glimmers of mortality onward, can provide useful information for all those who have children in their lives.

A CLASSICAL STUDY

We begin with one of the earliest and most influential studies. Maria Nagy[1] applied a simple but effective approach. She invited 378 children ranging in age from 3 to 10 years to express their death-related thoughts and feelings. The older boys and girls were asked to draw pictures and also to "write down everything that comes to your mind about death." Children of all ages were engaged in conversation on the subject. Nagy selected the children to be as representative as possible, coming from a variety of social and religious backgrounds with a balance between the two sexes. As she examined the children's words and pictures, Nagy came to the conclusion that a clear developmental progression had been demonstrated. Three age-related stages of death interpretation were proposed.

Stage 1

Stage 1 includes the youngest children (age 3 years) and extends through about the fifth year; in other words, it embraces the outlook of the post–toddler/preschool child. One characteristic of the child's view at this time is the notion that death is a *continuation* of life but on a reduced level. The dead are, in effect, less alive. They cannot see and hear—very well. They are not as hungry as the living. They do not do much. Being dead and being asleep are seen as similar conditions. In this respect the conception of the stage 1 child differs markedly from the adult conception that death is not the diminishment but the cessation of life.

The youngest children in this study differed from adults in another fundamental way. They thought of death as *temporary*. The dead might return, just as the sleeping might awake. It was clear that the theme of death as *departure* or *separation* was uppermost in the minds of many children. The person had gone away (e.g., to live in the cemetary) and would come back again, as people usually did after a trip.

Although stage 1 was defined essentially by the interpretation of death as partial and temporary—with strong analogies to sleep and separation—another characteristic was also noted by Nagy. The preschoolers were very *curious*. They were full of questions about the details of the funeral, the coffin, the cemetary, and so on. This questing fascination with the practical or concrete aspects of death is sometimes overlooked. Developmentalists have been quick to learn from Nagy's study that very young children do not understand death as complete and final but slow in appreciating *how active an effort* the children are making to achieve understanding. This effort perhaps is related to another aspect of Nagy's observation that has not received all the attention it deserves. Even though these very young children did not seem to understand death adequately by adult standards, what they did think about it was sufficiently powerful to arouse negative feelings. At the least, death did not seem to be much fun—lying around in a coffin all day, and all night, too. The dead might be sleeping, which is acceptable but boring, or they might be scared and lonely, away from all their friends. The combination of what the young child knows and does not know about death can arouse anxiety. "He would like to come out, but the coffin is nailed down," one 5-year-old told "Auntie Death," the name bestowed on the psychologist by her research participants. This comment suggests the fear of being buried alive that in some times and places has also been prevalent among adults.[2] It also suggests that people are being cruel to the deceased by nailing down the coffin. The possibilities for further misinterpretations and ill feelings based on this conception of death are considerable.

Stage 2

Stage 2 seems to begin around age 5 or 6 years and persist until approximately the ninth year. A major advance in the understanding of death comes about during this time. The child now recognizes that death is *final*. The older the child in this age range, the more firm the

conclusion. Nagy found another new theme emerging. Many of the children represented death as a person. We have already seen that *personification* is one of humankind's most ancient modes of expressing the relationship with death (Chapter 4). This approach seemed natural and spontaneous among the stage 2 children, although it also appeared among some of the younger and older ones as well.

One nine-year-old confided that

Death is very dangerous. You never know what minute he is going to carry you off with him. Death is invisible, something nobody has ever seen in all the world. But at night he comes to everybody and carries them off with him. Death is like a skeleton. All the parts are made of bone. But then when it begins to be light, when it's morning, there's not a trace of him. It's that dangerous, death.[1,p.11]

The personification of death as a skeleton was fairly common. As can be seen from this example, the anxiety associated with death does not necessarily diminish as the child grows older and is able to think in terms of finality. Death personifications often were fearful, representing enormous, often mysterious power.

It is interesting to notice that some children added threats or lethal wishes to their personifications. As Nagy reports, "Kill the death-man so we will not die" is a frequent comment by children. This vein of thought and feeling will be worth coming back to in a while. Also worth further attention is the fact that some children depicted death as a circus clown, supposedly the embodiment of mirth and good times. For other children, the dead are death and vice versa. Associations with angels and other spirits do not often relieve the anxiety. "The death angels are great enemies of people," declared a 7-year-old. "Death is the king of the angels. Death commands the angels. The angels work for death."

There is at least one more significant characteristic of stage 2, according to Nagy. The realization of death's finality is accompanied by the belief that this fate might still be eluded. The clever or fortunate person might not be caught by Death-man. This idea shows up also in the association of mortality with specific modes of cessation. A child might be killed crossing the street, for example. But if children are very careful in crossing the street, they will not be run over and, therefore, they will not die.

In other words, children in this age range tend to see death as an *outside* force or personified agent. "It's that dangerous, death," as one boy has already been quoted. However, the saving grace is that a particular individual does not have to die. The child does not recognize mortality as universal and personal. Stage 2, then, combines appreciation for one of death's most salient attributes—finality—with an escape hatch.

Stage 3

The level of development represented by stage 3 was found to begin around age 9 or 10 years and is assumed to continue thereafter. The child now understands death to be *personal, universal,* and *inevitable* as well as final. All that lives must die, including oneself. Discussion of death at this age shows the qualities of adult reasoning: "Death is the termination of life. Death is destiny. We finish our earthly life. Death is the end of life on earth," declared one 9-year-old boy. A 10-year-old girl adds a moral and poetic dimension: "It means the passing of the body. Death is a great squaring of accounts in our lives. It is a thing from which our bodies cannot be resurrected. It is like the withering of flowers."

This new awareness is compatible with belief in some form of afterlife, as with the 9-year-old boy who declares, "Everyone has to die once, but the soul lives on." In fact, it might be argued that the child does not really have a grasp of afterlife concepts until death itself is appreciated as final and inevitable.

HOW FAMILIAR IS THE DEATH THEME IN CHILDHOOD?

We cannot expect one study to answer all questions for us. The study itself raises some additional questions, and it is also appropriate to determine if the answers it seems to furnish hold up under further investigation. For example, this study, like any other, was conducted in a particular part of the world at a particular time. The place was Budapest, the time was the late 1940s. Would essentially the same findings be obtained with children growing up in other times and other places? Although this question cannot be answered definitively at present, several more recent studies will prove worth consulting.

In expanding our view beyond Nagy's contribution, let us begin with one of its implications that has not yet been mentioned. Apparently she did not have much trouble in persuading the children to share their death-related thoughts and feelings. The implication is that death was already a familiar theme in their lives. One might argue, however, that she forced them to think about this subject, that left to themselves they would not have done so. Whether or not these boys and girls had been thinking about death previously, the study itself indicated that they could direct themselves to this problem when it was presented to them. It would be helpful to learn if it is unusual or commonplace for children in a variety of situations to have death-related experiences and thoughts.

Our own death system betrays a strong bias on this point. It is generally assumed that young children do not think about death; furthermore, if this morbid subject does wander into their lives and minds, their attention should be distracted as soon as possible.[3,4] "They *don't!*" and "They *shouldn't!*" was the adult orientation toward childhood sexuality in the pre-Freudian era; it is still dominant on the subject of death. Our children are too pure and tender to be interested in such matters. Whether or not children *should* think about death and sex requires an assessment of personal and social values. Whether or not they *do* think about these emotion-laden subjects, however, is a question that empirical observation should be able to answer. It remains to be seen whether or not our society is ready to accept the answer.

Child's play

The play and games of children offer an excellent opportunity for observation. They provide a sampling of children being children rather than objects of inquiry bound into a research framework. Play behavior is also of particular interest because many of its forms have been in existence for centuries. A small and relatively new area of scholarship has devoted itself to comparison of child play in ancient and contemporary times. Most relevant for us of course is the death theme. It is clear that many traditional songs and games, played at various times and place throughout history, have centered around death. Other songs and games are also strongly suggestive of death.

Perhaps you already knew that the familiar ring-around-the-rosie game and song achieved popularity during the peak years of the plague in medieval Europe. "Ashes . . . ashes . . . all fall down!" The children who recited and enacted this little drama were acutely aware that people all about them were falling victim. We can imagine the security they sought by joining hands. The ritual impersonated and, in its way, *mastered* death. Psychoanalysts sometimes speak of the strategy by which we convert a passive fear into an attempt at active mastery. Quaint and innocent as the game may seem today, in its heyday ring-around-the-rosie represented both an acknowledgement of the

prevalence of uncontrolled death in the society and the impulse to confront and master at least some of the anxiety through shared activity.

The rich variety of tag-and-chase games includes some that make the death theme quite explicit.[5] Even the most see-no-death adult would have a difficult time in dismissing a game known to children as "Dead Man Arise!" This type of game has many names and local variations. In Sicily, for example, children would play "A Morsi Sanzuni."

One child lay down pretending to be dead while his companions sang a dirge, occasionally going up to the body and lifting an arm or a leg to make sure the player was dead, and nearly stifling the child with parting kisses. Suddenly he would jump up, chase his mourners, and try to mount the back of one of them. . . . In Czechoslovakia . . . the recumbent player was covered with leaves, or had her frock held over her face. The players then made a circle and counted the chimes of the clock, but each time "Death" replied "I must still sleep." This continued until the clock struck twelve when, as in some other European games, the sleeping player sprung to life, and tried to catch someone.[5,p.107]

Alongside explicit death-themed tag games can be set the basic scarey-chase motif itself. Typically, the person who is It must not see or move while the other players conceal themselves. The touch of It is scary and thrilling, powerful enough to transform the victim's position in the game even at the slightest contact. Further resemblances to death are suggested in those variations where the victim must freeze (enter suspended animation?) until rescued by one who is still free ("alive"?). There is not space to linger here in children's traditional songs and games, fascinating though they are. But the weight of observation strongly suggests that concern with death has been a common theme in children's play throughout the centuries.

Observing the personal play styles of individual children today also provides many glimpses of the death theme. Psychiatrist Gregory Rochlin[6] has shared some of his observations of young children playing on themes of death. Perhaps you have made some observations of this kind yourself. I remember a 2-year-old who enjoyed lying on his back, arms spread out in crucifixion position, eyes closed. He would ask for a "magic kiss"—at first from a parent; later a playmate or even a cat would do—and then spring up full of life. Where did this act come from? What did it mean? These questions remain unanswered. So far as anyone could tell, the whole routine was his own idea, and in a few months it had disappeared.

More open to understanding was the behavior of an 8-year-old. He was at the piano, not exactly pounding away aimlessly but not exactly playing any recognizable music either. What was he up to? "Making music for Lovey," the long-haired cat whose fatal encounter with a car or truck was still resonating within the family. The boy explained how each episode in the musical tribute recalled something about Lovey: "This is when she scratched me; this is how she used to sit in the sun." In truth, then, this was more an example of artistic memorialization—the composition of a requiem—than child's play. And yet this example (and how many others?) might have been passed off as simple childish amusement had inquiry not been made.

Other encounters with death

Information from other quarters also suggests that death themes are common in the world of childhood. A pioneering series of small interrelated studies was conducted in Great Britain just as World War II started to take shape. Sylvia Anthony[7] interviewed children, gave them little tests, and asked some of their parents to keep diaries of death-related experiences they happened to observe. Death concerns and experiences were common for both normal and emotionally disturbed children.

No support has been found for the idea that children, including the very young, are sheltered from death encounters. There is in fact some further support for the proposition that children actively seek at least certain kinds of death-related expression.[8] Consideration of the basic structure of the child's world—right here and now—reveals many influential inputs. Television is a major example. How long can a child sit in front of the glowing tube without witnessing death or death talk in some form? Cartoon characters flirt with annihilation, often returning to life after being crushed, burned, devoured, dropped off a cliff, drowned, turned inside out, and so on. On the "grown-up" programs there may be a freshly slain corpse every 5 minutes or so. News reports on television and radio present very curious direct and indirect death messages. The child hears, for example, that "200 were killed by the earthquake" in some part of the world he or she has not known about before. Two hundred *what*, 200 *who* were killed? The child learns that death of people, at least people far away, is something that happens mostly in numbers. (In a war report, it may be 200 "terrorists" who were "exterminated"—an interesting problem for a young mind to put together with its general effort to make sense of life and death and what it means to be a person.) Before the child can make a firm start at sorting out this kind of information, the announcer has moved on, with no change of intonation, to a completely unrelated item.

Taking in what the media have to present, then, poses the child with a continuing task. How does the child make sense of the information and the accompanying feeling-tone when adults speak of death? Is a person supposed to be as blank and controlled as the announcer? Is the child supposed to turn off thoughts and feelings about death and move on to something completely different, just as the scene of a fiery plane crash or a bleeding accident victim gives way to an interview with a local politician? The media certainly do not shelter either child or adult from certain types of death encounter. For the youngest viewers, we can speculate on how these messages come across and what efforts they make to catch on to the expected attitudes.

But the child's experience with death is not limited to media. Even though we live in a society where there is less visible encounter with dying and the dead than in most societies, there are many ways in which personally impactful deaths can enter a child's world. The father of a school friend dies. The family down the block had somebody killed in Viet Nam, and you feel funny when they speak about him, or you see his picture. Mother goes away to attend the funeral of a relative. Or perhaps death edges even closer into the family constellation. Death within the family, including the possible death of the child, is not so rare an occurrence as many of us would like to believe.

It is difficult to defend the proposition that children are unacquainted with death. More tenable is the proposition that often we are not sufficiently acquainted with our children's thoughts and experiences.

INTERPLAY BETWEEN DEVELOPMENTAL AND SOCIAL FORCES IN THE CHILD'S UNDERSTANDING OF DEATH
More evidence for the developmental view

The observations we have already considered indicate that death is a relatively familiar theme in childhood and also that older and younger children have rather different ideas on the subject. Several other studies support the general conclusion that what children think about death is closely related to their level of development.

Jean Piaget,[9] Heinz Werner,[10] and a number of other important contributors to the study of human development have insisted on the difference between chronological age and level of maturation. Although there is in general a relationship between age and level of development, the two are far from identical. Gerald Koocher[11] respected this difference in his study of 75 children of average mental ability who ranged in age from 6 to 15 years. All the children were tested to determine their general level of cognitive functioning, using a set of tasks devised by Piaget and his followers. This procedure enabled Koocher to divide the children into three categories that were based on the type of thought processes they had demonstrated rather than their chronological age. These categories, starting from the lowest developmental level, are known as the *preoperational*, the *concrete-operational*, and the *formal-operational*. As might have been expected, there were more younger children at the lowest developmental level, more older children at the higher levels. But it turned out that some of the youngest children showed a fairly advanced level of thinking while some of the older children were functioning at less mature levels. This means that we would be mistaken to relate a child's conceptions of death to calendar age alone. Generalizations about how a child of such and such an age thinks about death would be imprecise because of differences among children in their progress toward adult modes of thought, even if all children were of normal intelligence.

In the Koocher study, the children's thoughts about death were more closely related to their developmental levels, as established by mental performance tasks, than to their chronological age. Children at the higher developmental levels were more realistic and objective in their answers to a set of death-related questions. A preoperational child would explain "what makes things die," for example, with an answer such as, "By eating a dirty bug." A formal-operational child would speak instead of "physical deterioration." The nature of the children's understanding of death seemed fairly consistent with their overall way of understanding the world.

The groundbreaking Nagy study is both confirmed and modified by Koocher's more recent investigation. Yes, there is a developmental progression in thoughts of death, but we can be more accurate by relating this progression to direct measures of cognitive maturation rather than to chronological age. There is also something to learn from two "nonfindings" by Koocher. Taking a close look at his data, Koocher noticed that only 5% of the children discussed the possible effect of their own death on other people. Why would children fail to appreciate what their deaths might mean to others? This apparently illustrates the general developmental principle, advocated by Piaget and others, that one must pass through an egocentric mode of organizing the world before one reaches a more mature outlook. Most children cannot yet see death from the self and other perspectives. This limitation is useful to keep in mind when we interact with children on the subject of death. The other "nonfinding" is perhaps even more striking because it involves the complete absence of one type of response found fairly often by Nagy: "Not a single child in the present study gave a personification-type response, when asked what would happen at the time of death."[11,p.374] The possible meaning of this difference in results will be taken up in a moment.

Several other studies have also supported the general proposition that thoughts of death progress in accordance with developmental principles.[12-14] Additionally, each of these studies has something more to offer for our consideration. Perry Childers and Mary Wimmer[12] studied 75 children ranging in age from 4 to 10 years. They distinguished in their questions and data analysis between two aspects of

death awareness: universality and irrevocability. The idea that all living things die became increasingly clear to the children with advancing age (although, as we have seen, age is an imperfect approximation of developmental level). By age 10 years, 90% of the children recognized death's universality,[12] which is rather close support for Nagy's results. However, children at all ages seemed to have more trouble grasping the idea of death as final and irrevocable. Individual differences among the children were more common on this point, and even by age 10 years more than a third of the children either denied that death was final or could not make up their minds. These findings should caution us against taking too simple an approach to the concept of death itself; we can find either rather quick and steady growth or a longer and harder pathway to understanding, depending on the particular facet of death we have in focus.

It has been known for some time that the younger the child, the more likely he or she is to attribute life to forms that seem to move on their own, such as clouds and streams. There has been a tradition of controversy on the precise nature and meaning of animism in children,[16,17] but it is evident that ideas of what is living and what is dead must be interrelated. Margot Tallmer and her colleagues[13] found that clear distinctions between animate and inanimate forms seem to come before the child's ability to express adequate conceptions of death. This suggests that the distinction between animate and inanimate is more basic and perhaps helps prepare the way for understanding death.

The relationship between ideas of life and death was examined systematically, although with a small number of children, by Gwen Safier.[14] Interviewing 30 boys who ranged in age from 4 to 10 years, she found a three-stage developmental progression.

The youngest children seemed to interpret

both life and death in terms of a constant *flux*. "Something goes, then it stops, then it goes on again. There is an absence of the idea of absolutes."[14,p.285] At this stage of thought, death, as well as life, comes and goes.

Next, there is an intermediate stage in which the dominant idea is of the *outside agent*. As Safier puts it, "Something makes it go, something makes it stop."[14,p.286] The boys tended to see both life and death as something that is given and taken away, implying the existence of an external force. They also showed an interest in scientific explanation and expressed more curiosity about both life and death.

The highest level embodied the principle of the *internal agent*. "Something goes by itself, something stops by itself."[14,p.285] This was the view of children developmentally advanced enough to manipulate ideas with some skill. They were beginning, at about age 10 years, to establish a mental framework in which a variety of thoughts and impressions could be integrated, including thoughts of life and death.

Safier's study indicates a close relationship between thoughts of life and death at each of the three levels. It therefore tends to support some of the basic developmental principles of Piaget as well as the most general findings of Nagy. Death thoughts do not grow up all by themselves; they are part of a sort of community of thoughts, all influenced by each other and by the individual's overall level of maturation.

A recent study by Kane[15] adds further support to the general proposition that the child's understanding of death is closely linked with the general level of maturity. The participants in her experiment, ranging in age from 3 to 12 years, progressed in their death conceptualizations in a manner roughly parallel to Piaget's stages of preoperational, concrete-operational and formal-operational. This study helps to forge a link between studies of death cognitions in children and one of the major theoretical approaches to thought development in general, the Piagetian model. It also suggests that adult ideas of death may be achieved a little earlier than previous research had indicated. The 8-year-olds in Kane's study expressed death concepts that previous generations of researchers (and, possibly, Piaget himself) would have thought unlikely to be developed until the verge of adolescence. It is interesting that actual known experience with death seemed to be associated with a more "advanced" (or adult-like) understanding for the younger children in her sample (age 6 and younger), but not for the older children. While it is probably too soon to come to any conclusions about these findings, the inquiry into possible relationships between death-related experiences and maturity of death concepts is a welcome addition to the research spectrum and deserves additional attention.

Appreciation of developmental progress in the interpretation of death does not require us to neglect the influence of sociocultural forces. Several of the researchers whose work has been described here, for example, observed that the children seemed to be much affected by what they had been seeing on television. There is the strong impression that children growing up in recent years have a wider exposure to death in its various forms through the media, especially television, than in earlier decades of this century. The boys in Safier's study seemed to be more reality oriented in their death interpretations than children of the same age who had been studied in the past. Safier comments:

One must remember that Piaget worked with Swiss children in the late 1920s, and Nagy worked with Hungarian children in the 1940s. As a differentiator between those times and now, one must look to television, which most children watch for various lengths of time today. They have more accidental and violent deaths within their field of vision than any previous generation: for example, in Westerns, in mystery stories, in cartoons, etc. The greater awareness of death (in this decade with its threat of atomic annihilation) may have brought about an earlier sophistication in this area for some of the children. Many references to television were made by the boys in [the highest developmental group].[14,p.293]

Safier's frame of reference for these observations is perhaps too limited. Children in other times and places have been much more directly involved in premature or violent deaths than our own television-viewing youngsters; for example, those growing up during the plague years of the Middle Ages. Furthermore, it is difficult to pinpoint the effect of television. Many other changes have been wrought on our society over the past several decades besides the introduction of television. And the nature both of television and of our social climate has shifted over time. Writing in 1964, for example, Safier reflected an acute concern with nuclear catastrophe. This threat remains but now faces competition from other sources, such as violent street crime and consciousness raising in the media about the prevention, diagnosis, and treatment of serious diseases.

Nevertheless, it is evident that television is one of the current sources of influence in the child's discovery and exploration of death. Tallmer and colleagues[13] had reason to believe that the effects of television may vary from child to child, depending on the child's socioeconomic echelon. Studying 199 children ranging in age from 3 to 9 years, this research team examined possible differences related to socioeconomic status (SES). Half the children in this study attended urban ghetto schools, the other half were clearly in the middle-class category. Comparing children of the same age but of different SES, it was found that the urban slum dwellers were more aware of the concept of death. The data did not directly indicate why there should be such a difference, but the investigators speculate that the lower-class chil-

dren are "exposed to more real violence, an exposure which would be reflected in their fantasies about death." They argued that

because they may be in more actual danger than middle class children, they may devote more of their intelligence to useful learning than middle class youth. The effect of TV may be different for those who can relate to it on a daily, realistic basis, rather than as a pure fantasy. . . . Perhaps because their concepts are more realistic, the findings of greater evidences of feelings might have been anticipated. An example of a lower SES child's response: "A man is burying somebody. That is his job. He feels sad because the person he's burying was his friend." Additionally, lower class children show a significant increase of feelings with age while middle class children do not. The lower class children's fantasy content indicates that they are attempting to deal in a realistic, sensible manner with their environment.[13,pp.18-19]

Actually, the observations made in recent studies suggest that many children are showing a practical, matter-of-fact approach to the interpretation of death. None of the studies conducted in the United States in recent years (e.g., Kane, 1979[15]) reports the strong personification tendency that Nagy found among children in Budapest three decades ago. Is this because of the difference in time, place, or what? Whatever the reasons might be, they probably are to be found in the sociocultural arena rather than in traditional developmental phenomena studied in isolation. Koocher,[11] who noted a straight-on, detail-oriented approach in the midwestern children he studied, suggests that this represents an alternative strategy to mastering concern over death. The children attempt to gain some sense of control through matter-of-fact knowledge, as distinguished from indulgence in the supernatural or fantastic. This suggestion is at the least consistent with our society's emphasis on science, technology, and control. There is the implication that children can emphasize either magical, fantastic or realistic, objectivistic interpretations of death, depending on the surroundings in which they develop.

It remains for further research to clarify the relationship between developmental principles and sociocultural influences in the formation of a child's orientation toward death. Many developmental psychologists today are well aware of the importance of ecological considerations in general and are attempting to study development within its socioenvironmental context. Firm conclusions seem to be beyond our grasp at present, but it is clear enough that attention must be given to the full complexities of individual maturation within a particular environment if we are to understand how orientations toward death develop.

SHARING THE CHILD'S DISCOVERY OF DEATH

We do not know as much about the child's discovery of death as we should. But enough has been learned, both through studies such as those reviewed here and through the experiences of teachers, clinicians, and other sensitive observers, to suggest some guidelines. First, let us return to the child's earliest glimmers of mortality and face an apparent contradiction in the basic facts.

Too young to know?

There are two sets of observations that seem to be at odds with each other. Controlled studies (Nagy, Koocher, Safier, etc.) indicate that realistic or adult-oriented death concepts are not grasped until the child has reached a relatively advanced level of thought. The 9- or 11-year-old range appears to be the most typical time for realistic death concepts to be expressed, taking chronological age as a rough index only. If anything, this is a little younger than one might expect. According to Piaget, the flexible and integrative qualities associated with adult thought usually are not established

until early adolescence. Perhaps it could be said that 10-year-olds *know* some of death's most distinctive characteristics but are still limited in the ways they can relate this knowledge to their total understanding of the world. Only when they reach the formal-operational stage will they be able to think about death, or anything else, in an abstract and systematic manner.

The material that finds its way into textbooks and research contributions in developmental psychology suggests, then, that young children can know very little about death. However, anecdotal reports and observations of children at play suggest otherwise. It looks as though a controversy might be shaping up, with anecdotal and naturalistic observations on the one side and more structured research on the other. Still other observations can be mustered in support of the case for early recognition of mortality. These are all subject to serious methodological criticism or to alternative interpretations, yet are worth mentioning.

More than half a century ago, G. Stanley Hall and Colin Scott[18] asked adults to recall their earliest experiences with death. Many remembered encounters going back to their preschool years. Evidently, these experiences had made a lasting impression because they were recalled in vivid detail.

The child's exquisite temperature sense feels a chill where it formerly felt heat. Then comes the immobility of face and body where it used to find prompt movements of response. There is no answering kiss, pat, or smile. . . . Often the half-opened eyes are noticed with age. The silence and tearfulness of friends are also impressive to the infant, who often weeps reflexly or sympathetically.[18,p.440]

Hall adds that funeral and burial scenes sometimes were the very earliest of all memories for the adults he studied. More recent studies[19] also find death experiences common when adults are asked for their earliest memories, as I have also found in some of my own research.

Adah Maurer has argued for an even earlier relationship with death. She suggests that the infant's periodic alternations between sleeping and waking states endow it with a basic appreciation of the dichotomy between being and nonbeing. Furthermore, the infant actually conducts little experiments of its own on this existential problem.

By the time he is three months old, the healthy baby is secure enough in his self feelings to be ready to experiment with these contrasting states. In the game of peek a-boo, he replays in safe circumstances the alternate terror and delight, confirming his sense of self by risking and regaining complete consciousness. A light cloth spread over his face and body will elicit an immediate and forceful reaction. Short, sharp intakes of breath, vigorous thrashing of arms and legs removes the erstwhile shroud to reveal widely staring eyes that scan the scene with frantic alertness until they lock glances with the smiling mother, whereupon he will wriggle and laugh with joy. . . . To the empathetic observer, it is obvious that he enjoyed the temporary dimming of the light, the blotting out of the reassuring face and the suggestion of a lack of air which his own efforts enabled him to restore, his aliveness additionally confirmed by the glad greeting implicit in the eye-to-eye oneness with another human.[8,p.36]

This view implies that the infant does somehow recognize the state of being alienated from sources of support, comfort, and stimulation. Furthermore, even the 3-month-old is not too young to do something about it. Peek-a-boo, originally, according to Maurer, an Old English phrase meaning, "alive or dead?", represents an attempt at active mastery of the gap between being and nonbeing. Later pleasures of infancy and childhood such as throw-away-and-recovery games are also seen as efforts to understand and master the already recognized coming and going of phenomena.

Finally, attention should be called to the great diversity of observations made on attachment and separation behaviors in animals as well as humans. Valuable summaries and interpretations can be found in John Bowlby's pair of books on this topic.[20,21] It is clear that separation from the nourishing and protecting adult, usually the mother, is a survival threat to the very young. Although there are important differences between species, mechanisms or strategies exist for maintaining the necessary contact and communication. Within this very broad context, it should not be surprising to realize that the young in our own species have some ability to sense and communicate the need for contact, comfort, and protection.

Let us come back to the controversy now and see what can be done about it within the limits of present knowledge. The structured studies have methodological advantages over random observations of behavior in the naturalistic situation, retrospective accounts by adults, and the like. But these studies, to exercise their advantages, tend to limit the scope of inquiry rather severely. They limit themselves, for example, to children old enough to put their thoughts into words or to pay attention to a stranger's questions. A thousand studies of 10-year-olds under controlled conditions will never tell us what a 2-year-old discovers on his or her own. The two types of observation, then, are best regarded as complementary if far from strictly comparable.

Notice also that different frameworks of interpretation are employed. The controlled developmental studies are often analyzed to determine how far away the child at a certain age or level is from the adult conception of death. The researcher's eye tends to be on the final destination of the child's thoughts. But the anecdotal and naturalistic approach tends to give more attention to the child's interests and efforts for their own sake. Instead of emphasizing that the preschooler still has a long way to go in grasping death, there is more appreciation for the child's curiosity and fascination with the topic. The child's knowledge of death can be faulted when adult standards are applied, but this should not obscure the stimulus that intimations of mortality has given to the child's exploration of self and the world.

Some of the differences in the interpretation of the child's acquaintance with death also hinge on the discrimination between *perceptions* and *conceptions*. Research as different as Nagy's and Hall and Scott's reveal close attention to perceptual detail in the death discoveries of young children. Very young children seem to notice death-related phenomena and to take away some vivid impressions, even if they cannot yet interpret these phenomena on a conceptual level. This is a particularly important point on the topic of *separation*. Part of the adult conception of death is the sense of loss, separation, absence. We do not have to insist that an infant understands the meaning of death in order to credit it with a direct sense of discomfort when separated from the mothering person. By the time children are old enough to talk about their thoughts and feelings, separation does emerge as a major death-related theme.[7] The infant and young child who is encountering separation, and that would be *every* infant and young child in one way or another, is thereby becoming familiar with one of mortality's most poignant stings. In a more extensive discussion elsewhere, we have related the young child's anticipations of full-fledged death concepts to the experience of time.[2] Separation and death are at the least strong analogies for each other in the young child's phenomenological world.

There is still another facet to the differences found in naturalistic observations and those found in structured developmental research. It is my impression that those who systematize human development have a strong bias toward consistency and stability. The most relevant aspect of this bias is the conspicuous attention given to such phenomena as object constancy in its various forms. Much research and theory continues to be devoted to the processes by which children come to recognize enduring, unchanging, invariant characteristics of the world. But in truth, does not the world also include much that vanishes, changes, varies? Too often the *phenomenon of flux*, to use Safier's term, is treated as though part of an immature interpretation of the world, a sort of error factor one passes through en route to recognition of what an orderly place this universe really is. This does injustice to one major aspect of reality. It also leads us to miss the point that young children must understand vanishings and inconstancies if they are also to understand stability and order. I suggest the child is actively engaged in trying to understand both being and nonbeing at the same time, and right from the beginning of the experiences with the world. This means that the adult's conception of death is prefigured in the infant's first explorations of "no more!"

At least one other key issue remains in the controversy. Strict adherence to the traditional theories of mental development would force us to rule out the possibility that a 5-year-old, let alone a 16-*month*-old, could form concepts such as of death's finality. But if we adhere just as strictly to what we sometimes see and hear from the child, then we must at times admit that a very young child has indeed recognized one of death's cardinal features. There are two lines of explanation that seem worth exploring: (1) the possibility that developmental level is even more independent of chronological age than research has already demonstrated or (2) the possibility that young children can gain sudden insight into death-related phenomena but seem to lose it later because of their lack of a stable integrative framework in which to house this thought, and perhaps because of sociocultural pressures to keep a low profile in such matters.

In short, I think we are best advised to proceed as though a child is *never* too young to experience some form of death encounter and to have thoughts and feelings engaged by it.

Teresa learns about death: a research case history

Attention has been given to children's thoughts about death and, to a lesser extent, the attitudes and behaviors of the adults around them. Let us now look at one research case history in some detail to see how a particular parent and child have shared death experiences together.*

Teresa is a seven-year-old described by her mother as a quiet girl who enjoys her own company. "She's just a very nice girl, not afraid to express any emotions at all." Teresa is especially interested in plants and how they grow, and much involved in her family as a unit.

Has death come into Teresa's life? Her mother reports that:

My mother died, her grandmother, in January of this year and . . . we all knew she was dying. I told Teresa and I told June (her sister) that she was dying. They wanted to know, "what is dying, where is she going to go, why is she going, why is she leaving me? She's my Grandma! I don't want her to die!" . . . And . . . just very curious about the whole business of the wake and the funeral and "why do we have to do this, why do we have to do that." The big thing was, "I don't want to see other people sad, because it makes me sad."

How did Teresa respond to the death when it actually came?

She comforted me. She came to me. She would cry when I cried. She would put her arms around me and she would say, "Please don't cry; everything will be all right. Grandma isn't suffering anymore. Grandma is happy now."

---

*Verbatim excerpts from transcript of an interview conducted by Deidre Rozema as part of a study under my direction.

The death was experienced as a major loss by everybody in the family. Grandma was 54 years old at the time of her death, and had been very close to the whole family although not living with them. "My mother was my best friend and she was also my children's best friend."

What did Teresa understand about Grandma's death?

She understands that she (Grandma) was put in the ground in that cold outer casket, but Teresa realizes that she is not there. She's in spirit, beside her, watching her and loving her always. And Teresa sees a bird—my mother was a bird freak—and she said, "I wonder if Grandma can see that bird?" You know, she's very much into, very aware that Grandma is around her, spiritually, not physically.

What did Teresa not understand about this death?

She still doesn't understand . . . why. You know, why take her from us now, she wasn't old, you know, she was a young woman. Why was she so sick, you know, What did she do? Did she do something bad?

Does Teresa have any death concerns or fears?

I think she'd be very much afraid of losing me at this point because since my mother has died she's becoming extremely touchy with me; she gets a little bit upset when I leave to go out, you know. "Please come back soon!" You know, I think she relates it to losing me, to maybe her fears of losing her own mother.

How have you answered her questions about death?

Well, as far as the religious, we don't get into it at my house, you know. I don't want to get into hell and heaven and that, because I don't want them to get hung up on it. . . . I really don't think we even discussed it, you know, before it actually hit us; we never really discussed it with the children. . . .

Has it been difficult to discuss death with Teresa?

Not with Teresa, not at all. With June, yes, but not with Teresa.

How do you feel in general about your understanding about what Teresa thinks about death?

I think she's got her head pretty well together. She's really probably done better than I have. If I can elaborate a little . . . at one point . . . two or three months after my mother died, I was sitting by myself, having my crying jag and getting it all out, and Teresa got up out of bed. You know, I was sitting in the dark. I just knew it was coming. I had put them to bed. So she got up, and she came beside me and she said, "Mama, I know why you're crying." And I said, "Why, Teresa?" And she said, "Because you miss your mother." And I said, "You're right." And Teresa said, "But you always have to remember, how good she was to us, remember she used to take us uptown and buy us ice cream and she used to sing us songs and remember when she bought me this bracelet."

And within a matter of, say, three minutes, I felt so relieved, like, you know, tons had been lifted off me; from this seven-year-old child, you know, really laying it on me and tell me, come on, you know, you got to go on living. . . . And the oldest one (June) will not discuss it at all. You know, it's too bad.

Do you have any questions of your own—about what to do with a child in things related to death?

I don't know. There are things I don't know, and so I wouldn't know how to explain it to them. I don't know how to make it easier for them. . . . This is a society where everybody dies—why do we grieve then? Why is there a wake, why is there a funeral? These are things I don't understand so I'm sure they don't understand, you know, why the pain?

Before she died, I was totally agnostic. Now I just hope—that she is happy and contented and having a good time because she deserved it because she was sick for quite a while. You know, this is what I hope. I really don't have any positive feelings and vibra-

tions. . . . Everybody told me, "Oh, you'll feel her spirit, you'll feel her close to you," and I haven't gotten this, I just feel relieved that she's not suffering and I just hope that she's up there having a hell of a time, I really do!

Should parents and children discuss death together: what do you think?

It's very important, so very important. I can remember my own first experience with death and how frightened I was of it. I think it's something that should be talked about in a family and . . . I'm having a hard time expressing myself, but I really think that when people die, that we love, we shouldn't have to grieve . . . why do they put us through the wakes, the funerals? This is what we saw when we were children; we saw grieving over death—we grieve over death—and my children will grieve over death.

What is the worst thing a parent could say or do with a child in a death situation?

I would hate to stifle emotions. I would hate to say, "Stop all that crying!" Or, the other thing is, "He's gone away for a vacation. He's left us, but he'll come back." That's a bunch of lies and children see through these things.

What is the best thing a parent could say or do with a child in a death situation?

Let the children see what goes on. Let them be totally involved with the family, to be able to express with the family their own emotions and to be totally included in what goes on instead of shifted off to a friend's house.

How curious about death were you when you were Teresa's age?

I wasn't at all . . . until I was about 10 years old. . . . I lost my cat and I remember, I cried all day upstairs in my room because I thought: this is death. I'm going to lose my mother. And I cried and cried and I was so scared and I had nightmares.

How was death handled in your home when you were growing up?

It wasn't. I said to my mother once, "I'm so afraid that you're going to die." And she just said, "I'm not going to die." . . . And she died [these words spoken very softly and sadly].

Was that the way she should have handled it, or what do you think she should have done instead?

I think that if she could have drawn more out of me and really given me time that I needed, and maybe have said—well, I don't know what you can say to a child to make it any easier when there is a threat, a scare of losing a parent, but just to be able to sit down and discuss it. . . .

What are your thoughts and feelings about death now?

Since my first death was my mother, I think it was very hard because she was my mother. . . . I just accept the fact that she is dead and I will no longer see her, but I just hang on to the thought that she's not suffering and that she knew she was dying even though nobody told her and . . . . She said more with her eyes, more than anything else in the world. I feel very . . . . I feel peace within myself.

Did she tell you her thoughts or feelings at all?

No, she was aphasic . . . and paralyzed. She couldn't talk. The only thing she could do was move one arm and one hand and the night before she died, we went in there and they took her out of the special care unit and just took off the respirator and let her die and she just kept pointing up to heaven. She knew she was dying and then she just . . . made us feel at ease. Because I was glad she knew, and she knew that I knew so we wouldn't have to play the game: "Okay, Ma, we'll get you out of here in a couple of weeks." We just didn't have to play that game. It was a kind of peace, you know, that we share.

Is there anything you would like to add?

I think we should teach children about death in schools. I don't mean we shouldn't teach them at home, but in school, too. Let people know what often happens in grief, so they won't be so surprised. . . . Should start early because it's like sex education, you know, you almost don't talk about it until it happens, until there is a problem.

Some reflections and questions

Each person—child or adult—has a distinctive relationship with death based on the individuality we develop and the unique situations in which we participate. Teresa's relationship to death is not identical with that of other seven-year-olds. Somehow we need to take into account both the individuality of the particular child and the more general characteristics of people who are at a given point in their developmental careers. Here are a few reflections and questions centering around Teresa that might be helpful when our own lives intersect with those of young children and their distinctive life-death experiences.

1. Where is death as an abstraction? The death-oriented thoughts of Teresa and her mother seem dominated by a very specific pattern of events involving a person dear to both of them. It is not death in general, but the loss of Grandmother that is so much on their minds. Grandmother's death has raised or intensified thoughts and feelings about death in the more abstract sense. The burden of concern, however, is with a particular person who had long been central to their lives. This is not unusual. It is, in fact, perhaps the most typical way in which death concern surfaces in our lives—as concrete reality. Scientific and philosophical inquiries into death are valuable. We must invariably return, however, to the keenly individual and specific world in which each of us lives and in which death bears the names of real people.

2. Could we understand Teresa's orientation toward death if we focused only on Teresa? Doubtful. By enlarging our focus to include the mother-child relationship we see that experiences, attitudes, and ways of coping with death are part of the intimate flow of life between them. This does not mean, of course, that all parents and children (or even all mothers and

daughters) have the same type of interaction and mutual-influence process. But it does suggest that we recognize the limitations of even the best studies that have concentrated exclusively on the child's death perceptions and cognitions. It is useful and "legitimate" to examine the child's death thoughts separately as one part of our total approach to the subject. Eventually, however, we need to achieve a broader perspective in which the interpersonal context of death thoughts and orientations are embodied.

3. It is not by accident or whim that the research case history excerpted here is based on the mother's report. Children have fathers, too, but mothers have been more willing to discuss this subject with us. Why might that be? And what might this differential readiness to discuss the child's relationship with death tell us about the death attitudes of fathers and mothers and the role they see themselves as playing in their young child's development?

4. The interview reported here concentrated on Teresa. Some of her mother's remarks, however, indicated that speaking about death with June, the other daughter, was a different and more difficult proposition. This is not unusual. Within the same household there may be a variety of responses to death, just as there is to other situations. This is one more reason for caution in making generalizations, and one more reason for becoming well acquainted with every family configuration and every individual in the family when we really want to understand the place of death in their lives.

5. Teresa's mother is a sensitive person who favors an open communication process and who is quite capable of reflecting on her own behavior as well as her children's. This does not mean, however, that she has been able to cope with death-related problems to her own complete satisfaction. She has unresolved questions of her own in some areas (the value of funerals and the grief process in particular), and these unresolved concerns seem to create some difficulties in helping her children. Not every parent has this particular area of unresolved personal concern, but most parents we have come to know do have some areas of concern that rise up to complicate their death-related communications with their children. If we have not had or made the occasion to examine our own death thoughts and feelings carefully ahead of time, then we are more likely to run into such problems in the middle of an actual death situation.

An excerpt from another case history might be useful here. Stanley's mother has been asked what her young boy does not yet understand about death:

What the purpose of death is. Why we were put on this earth for a reason and why we're going to die. Stanley is definitely too little to understand why somebody's laying in a casket. Especially if it is somebody young. Why is that person dead? You try to explain to him that God put him on this earth but He called him back. He wanted him back. I don't think he can comprehend that at all. . . . When a little boy dies, I tell him the little boy was very sick and God wanted him back.

This mother is probably accurate in saying that Stanley does not understand the explanation given. But we cannot help but wonder what message did come across from the mother's explanation and what questions Stanley has been left to fathom for himself. "God does not want the healthy? Is it wrong to want people to live? Is God the enemy who takes my friends away? Do I have to get very sick and die in order to be loved by God?" Stanley's mother has a set of assumptions about life and death that perhaps need more sorting out and reflection on her part. She is not a person who is inclined to reflect on such matters, however, but is more comfortable in passing along a received dogma familiar to her since her own childhood. The gap between the abstraction level and tone of her explanation and the type of understanding and reassurance a boy of Stanley's age needs could present some problems. The parent who is not able to cope with a child's death-related curiosity on a simple, naturalistic level because of his or her own discomfort with the subject may be perpetuating the anxieties for still another generation.

6. Teresa's mother apparently had a warm and loving home life herself as she was growing up. And yet, the topic of death was given minimal attention, glossed over. This has made it more difficult to cope both with the death of her mother (who had promised she was not going to die) and with the feelings of her own daughters. Again, this seems to be a typical situation. Today's young mothers in general seem to be more aware of the value of discussing death with their children as part of their general preparation for life. However, most often they have not benefited from such discussions or "good examples" in their own homes while growing up. In this sense, perhaps there now exists a transitional generation of parents who are trying to relate to their children in an area that was off-limits when they themselves were young. This leads to situations in which much second-guessing of one's own response takes place ("Did I say the right thing?"), but the effort in general should make death a less divisive topic between parent and child in generations to come.

These are a few of the observations and questions that have come to mind regarding the relationship between one mother and one young daughter. You can find other implications in the excerpts given and in the experiences you encounter yourself.

A few guidelines

Although this is not a how-to book, it might be appropriate to pass along a few simple guidelines that have been found helpful in relating to children on the subject of death.

1. Be a good observer. See how the child is behaving. Listen to what he or she is really saying. Do not feel obliged to rush in with explanations, reassurances, or actions unless there is some overriding necessity to do so. You will be more helpful to the child when you are relaxed, patient, and attentive enough to develop a better idea of what questions or needs the child actually is expressing, rather than those we might assume to be there.

2. Do not wait or plan for "one big tell-all." Maintain a continuing dialogue with the children in your life as occasions present themselves. The death of pet animals, movie, newspaper, or television presentations that arouse their interest—whatever brushes with mortality the children have—can offer the opportunity for discussion. This does not mean, of course, that parents should remain forever poised to jump on a death-dialogue opportunity. But it is more natural and effective to include death as one of the many topics that adults and children can discuss together. And we are more likely to be helpful when we are not ourselves caught up in the midst of a death situation. Combine a child who has never been let in on death with an adult who is grief-stricken or uptight and we have something less than the most desirable situation possible.

3. When the situation centers around an actual death, do not expect all of the child's response to be obvious and immediate. The total realization and response is likely to unfold over a period of time and to express itself in many ways, including, for example, changes in sleeping habits, mood, relationships with other children, demands on adults, and so forth. Be patient and be available.

4. The child is truly a part of the family. Sometimes we feel the panicked impulse to remove children from the scene when death has come too close (e.g., sending them off to a relative or neighbor). Examine such impulses before acting on them. Whatever practical deci-

sions you reach, bear in mind what the children might learn from the opportunity to participate in the family's response and what lingering questions and misinterpretations might remain if they are excluded.

5. In speaking with children about death, simple and direct language is much to be preferred over fanciful, sentimental, and symbolic meanderings. Too often what we say to children turns out to be a semisermon, peppered with words and concepts that mean little to them. Try to provide them with accurate information. See if they understand what you have said (e.g., by having them explain it back to you) and if that is really what they wanted to know in the first place.

6. The child's sense of comfort will be strengthened by the very fact that you are available to talk about death with him or her. Your expression of feelings natural to the situation (worry, sorrow, perhaps even anger) are not likely to harm the child but rather to provide a basis for expressing and sorting out his or her own feelings.

We will be considering children and death in other contexts, particularly when bereavement and grief are explored more systematically (Chapters 14 and 15). In the meantime, for further discussion of relating to the child on the subject of death, you might find Earl Grollman's collection of essays useful.[22]

SUMMARY

There is reason to believe that even infants and very young children have death-related experiences that engage their thoughts and feelings. Observations of preschool children are difficult to evaluate. Nevertheless, various forms of "playing with death" have been noted. It is reasonably clear that normal children do think about death and try to test out its meanings as best they can.

Most of the structured research has excluded very young children. Nagy's pioneering research indicated that children pass through three stages of death interpretation. In the first, death is viewed as temporary and as a diminution rather than complete cessation of life. In the intermediate stage, death is recognized to be final but not necessarily universal. Children in this stage (roughly between the ages of 5 and 9 years) also tended to represent death as a person, a finding, that has *not* been replicated by other studies. In the third stage, the child sees death as universal and personal as well as final.

A number of other studies have expanded our understanding of the child's discovery of death. In general, there is support for the proposition that concepts of death develop along with the child's overall maturation, following principles already established in developmental psychology. But it was observed that sociocultural factors are also important in shaping the child's knowledge of death. The possible role of television, for example, was touched on.

It is possible to argue that children much younger than 10 years are too young to know about death. Two sets of observations are compared and contrasted. Our provisional conclusion is that children *do* set their minds to work on the problem of death very early, even if sophisticated and stable *concepts* do not arrive until years later. Several guidelines are offered for sharing the child's discovery of death.

If we should emphasize one point in this summary, it would be the *privilege* of sharing the child's discoveries. The child knows enough to take death seriously, which paradoxically includes playing and gaming with death. Appreciation of life's dangers, mysteries, and threats contribute to the sense of wonder that adults often observe in children. I personally value the opportunity to have shared with my children the mysteries of a fallen leaf or dead bird—as mysterious fundamentally to me as to them. Intimations of mortality make childhood much more vital and interesting than the fairy-tale never-neverland version that we sometimes substitute for the child's own perceptions. And perhaps there is no need to emphasize the child's need for honest and dependable contact with adults as he or she encounters death in the discovery of life.

REFERENCES

1. Nagy, M. H. The child's theories concerning death. In H. Feifel (Ed.), *The meaning of death*. New York: McGraw-Hill Book Co., 1969. (Reprinted from *Journal of Genetic Psychology*, 1948, 73, 3-27.)
2. Kastenbaum, R., & Aisenberg, R. B. *The psychology of death*. New York: Springer Publishing Co. Inc., 1972. (See especially Chapter 5.)
3. Kastenbaum, R. Childhood: the kingdom where creatures die. *Journal of Clinical Child Psychology*, 1974, 3, 11-13.
4. Feifel, H. Psychology and the death-awareness movement. *Journal of Clinical Child Psychology*, 1974, 3, 6-7.
5. Opie, I., & Opie, P. *Children's games in street and playground*. London: Oxford University Press, 1969.
6. Rochlin, G. How younger children view death and themselves. In E. A. Grollman (Ed.), *Explaining death to children*. Boston: Beacon Press, 1967, pp. 51-88.
7. Anthony, S. *The discovery of death in childhood and after*. New York: Basic Books, Inc., 1972. (Revision of *The child's discovery of death*. New York: Harcourt, Brace & World, 1940.)
8. Maurer, A. Maturation of concepts of death. *British Journal of Medicine and Psychology*, 1966, 39, 35-41.
9. Piaget, J. *The child's conception of the world*. Patterson, N.J.: Littlefield, Adams & Co., 1960.
10. Werner, H. *Comparative psychology of mental development*. New York: International Universities Press, 1957.
11. Koocher, G. Childhood, death, and cognitive development. *Developmental Psychology*, 1973, 9, 369-375.
12. Childers, P., & Wimmer, M. The concept of death in early childhood. *Child Development*, 1971, 42, 705-715.
13. Tallmer, M., Formanek, R., & Tallmer, J. Factors influencing children's concepts of death. *Journal of Clinical Child Psychology*, 1974, 3, 17-19.
14. Safier, G. A study in relationships between the life and death concepts in children. *Journal of Genetic Psychology*, 1964, 105, 283-294.
15. Kane, B. Children's concepts of death. *Journal of Genetic Psychology*, 1979, 134, 141-153.
16. Klingberg, G. The distinction between living and not living among 7–10 year-old children with some remarks concerning the so-called animism controversy. *Journal of Genetic Psychology*, 1957, 105, 227-238.
17. Huang, I. Children's conceptions of physical causality: a critical summary. *Journal of Genetic Psychology*, 1943, 63, 71-121.
18. Hall, G. S. *Senescence*. New York: D. Appleton, 1922.
19. Tobin, S. The earliest memory as data for research in aging. In D. P. Kent, R. Kastenbaum, & S. Sherwood (Eds.), *Research, planning, and action for the elderly*. New York: Behavioral Publications, Inc., 1972.
20. Bowlby, J. *Attachment*. New York: Basic Books, Inc., 1969.
21. Bowlby, J. *Separation*. New York: Basic Books, Inc. 1973.
22. Grollman, E. A. (Ed.). *Explaining death to children*. Boston: Beacon Press, 1967.

CHAPTER 10

❖ DEATH AS LIFE'S COMPANION
The adult years

We have learned that children are sensitive to death. The toddler notices wilting, separation, loss, absence. The 10-year-old tells us matter-of-factly that all living things die. From the first intimation of mortality through the more advanced thought processes of later childhood, there is an active effort to comprehend death phenomena.

It is reasonable to expect even more of adults. We presumably have the advantage not only of higher-level thought processes but also the additional years of life experience. The adult should have a firmer, more secure grasp of concepts that the child is trying hard to achieve. There should be command of "all the answers," or at least a more advanced, subtle, and philosophical level of questioning. However, the assumption that adult status necessarily guarantees a mature orientation toward death does not stand up to critical inquiry. What we might be quick to call childish in the responses of a 10-year-old can be observed of many adult minds confronted with the challenge of death.

MAN IS MORTAL: BUT WHAT DOES THAT HAVE TO DO WITH ME?

Much adult death thought is evasionary. Let us take an example that is no less "real" for having been depicted in Tolstoy's masterful short novel, *The Death of Ivan Ilych*. The same type of phenomena can be observed today, a century later.

Him, not me

The thought of the sufferings of this man he had known so intimately, first as a merry little boy, then as a schoolmate, and later as a grown-up colleague, suddenly struck Peter Ivanovich with horror . . . "Three days of frightful suffering and then death! Why, that might suddenly, at any time, happen to me," he thought, and for a moment felt terrified. But—he himself did not know how—the customary reflection at once occurred to him, that this *had* happened to Ivan Ilych and not to him, and that it should not and could not happen to him and to think that it could would be yielding to depression which he ought not to do. . . . After which reflection Peter Ivanovich felt reassured, and began to ask with interest about the details of Ivan Ilych's death, as though death were an accident natural to Ivan Ilych but certainly not to himself.[1,pp. 101-102]

As an adult, Peter Ivanovich presumably knows that death is universal, inevitable, and his fate as well as his late colleague's. Yet we catch him, with Tolstoy's help, playing a desperate evasionary game in his mind. Consider some of the possible elements in Peter Ivanovich's response:

1. He already knew of Ivan Ilych's death, otherwise he would not have been at the

widow's home, participating in an obligatory paying of respects. But it is only on viewing the corpse that the realization of death strikes him. There is obviously a difference between intellectual knowledge and emotional impact. In this instance the *visibility* of death seemed to break through his psychological barrier between acknowledgment of his friend's passing and what it betokens for him.

2. Peter Ivanovich immediately became concerned for Peter Ivanovich. His thoughts and feelings did not center either around the man who had lost his life or the woman who had lost her husband. Once his feelings had been penetrated, he found it necessary to struggle with personal anxiety.

3. Yet he could not *admit* to others that he had become frightened for himself. Why not? The implicit rules of the situation required expression of sympathy for the survivors and a show of sorrow for the deceased. One was not supposed to be so vulnerable or selfish as to turn inward. This means that other visitors might also have been as acutely afflicted as Peter Ivanovich—and as unable to share their distress with each other. There is another possible reason as well. If Peter Ivanovich heard himself admitting such fears, it might bruise his self-esteem and sense of invulnerability. He wanted to leave this house of death with an air of confidence that death had, in fact, been left behind. Admitting his uneasiness privately was bad enough; having the anxieties escape the bounds of his internal dialogue would be even worse.

4. Peter Ivanovich's basic evasionary technique in this passage is the effort to *differentiate* himself from Ivan Ilych. For an alarming moment he had experienced a sense of kinship with the deceased. A person—not so very different from himself—had died. It had taken some passage of time and the direct perception of the corpse to bring his thoughts and feelings that far. Now he had to beat a quick retreat

from this vulnerable position. Yes, people really do die; no, the kind of person that Peter Ivanovich was does not die. The proof was in the fact that he was the vertical man who could walk around, while Ivan was horizontal and immobile. We witness Peter Ivanovich stretching and torturing his thought process to arrive at an acceptable (anxiety-reducing) conclusion.

5. Once Peter Ivanovich has quelled his momentary panic, he is able to discuss Ivan Ilych's death. Even so, he is more interested in details than in feelings and meanings. He has started to rebuild the barrier between himself and death. Whatever he learns about how his friend died will serve to strengthen this barrier—all that was true of Ivan is manifestly not applicable to him.

Are these evasionary dynamics limited to characters in a nineteenth-century novel? Or do we not find them also in abundance around us today and just perhaps in our own mind as well? Let us take a few examples from the here-and-now.

It's nothing—really!

❖ Sitting in his favorite chair after dinner, the man suddenly went pale. He felt severe pain in his chest, and had to gasp for breath. His wife was by his side in a moment. "What's wrong? Oh! I'll get the doctor, the hospital . . . ." The man struggled for control and waved one hand feebly in a negative gesture. "It's nothing—really . . . . I'll just lie down till it goes away."

This scene, with its variations, has been repeated often enough to become well recognized by the health establishment. Peter Ivanovich experienced difficulty with the remainder of personal mortality that he saw on the face of his deceased friend, but he himself was in good health. Yet sometimes we manage to evade reality even when the death threat has expressed itself in our own bodies.

Again, it is useful to remind ourselves of the difference between a rational and idealized version of what should and what actually does happen. Adults not only "should" understand death at least as well as the 10-year-old but also should be alert to some of the more significant warning signs. It would be in our own enlightened self-interest to recognize potential critical symptoms and to seek prompt and expert assistance. Those who maintain that the "will to live" is the most potent of all motives have difficulty explaining situations in which mentally competent adults spurn assistance when a life threat arises. Delay in seeking diagnosis and treatment is common enough to be of concern to the medical profession.

One typical maneuver is the familiar: "If I close my eyes or don't look at it, then it really isn't there at all." Psychologists sometimes refer to this process as *perceptual defense*. Perhaps you have noticed a problem with this concept. We cannot defend ourselves against a threat until we have seen and classified it in the first place! Explanations aside, there is little doubt that sometimes we do avert our gaze when the reality is more than we can bear.

Some symptoms are subtle or ambiguous enough to escape notice. There is no point in speaking of perceptual defense every time a person misses the opportunity to recognize a possible threat to his or her life. But there is a point in looking for this defensive maneuver in the person who has not acknowledged a steady, unplanned loss of weight or a lingering, racking cough, or perhaps a series of blackouts and dizzy spells. The victim of a major heart attack (myocardial infarction) may have had one or more warning attacks that he or she managed to ignore.

This first line of defense can be overwhelmed. The pain and distress of a heart attack, for example, is nearly impossible to deny. It is at this point that a second line of defense may be used. The victim may admit to feeling pain, weakness, and fatigue. But he offers a reassuring explanation. "Just an upset stomach," he may insist, or "a little muscle spasm," or "I guess those late hours have caught up with me. Just need to lie down a while, get some rest." The defensive strategy has passed from the perceptual to the cognitive—but the individual is still holding to the position that his life is not really in jeopardy.

Curiously, exposure of the *threat* of death sometimes disturbs us more than death itself. We seem willing at times to gamble with our lives to avoid explicit recognition that a death threat does exist. And we may then pay with our lives when warning signs are ignored because the warning itself is too alarming to bear. This does not look to be rational, mature behavior, yet it can be shown by adults who are otherwise intelligent and practical beings. Whenever we observe what appears to be inappropriate and self-defeating behavior in ourselves or others the question of anxiety can be raised. Have we been so alarmed and stirred up that we address ourselves more to the reduction of the anxiety as such than to the identification and solution of the problem that has generated the alarm in the first place?

The possible link between anxiety and denial of serious illness has been studied by McCrae, Bartone, and Costa (1976) in nearly 1000 men who ranged in age from 25 to 90 years. At every age level there were some men with high, moderate, and low levels of expressed anxiety. An interesting difference showed up when highly anxious men of various ages were compared with each other on their reporting of *physical* complaints. Young and middle-aged anxious men reported *more* physical symptoms than adjusted men of the same age. But anxious *old* men reported *fewer* physical symptoms than less anxious men of the same age.[2]

Implications of this finding were elaborated by a further analysis of the available data. The investigators were able to construct a discrepancy index. This index compared the number of complaints expressed by the men and the actual findings of thorough medical examinations. The pattern of age and anxiety again showed a reversal: young and middle-aged men with high anxiety reported more illnesses than their physicians could find. But in old age, the less anxious men reported more illnesses—while, the anxious men actually *underreported* the extent of their ailments. The anxious young man was more likely, for example, to express concern about cardiovascular symptoms that the physician did not find to be life threatening. But it was the well-adjusted (not highly anxious) old man who was concerned about his health. The anxious elder underestimated the actual hazards found by the physician. It was as though the anxious old man must protect himself from recognition of an actual threat to life, while the anxious young person can afford to focus on symptoms because he does not truly think his life is in danger.

It is worth keeping in mind that the adjusted old men in this study reported many physical complaints, even more than the physicians could find. Ordinarily, this might be interpreted as neurotic behavior. The person might be said to be overly concerned with the condition of his body, exaggerating and perhaps imagining problems. Within the context of the total study, however, this does not seem to be the case. The well-adjusted old men seemed to be actively monitoring their own physical status. This is a realistic policy to follow in the advanced years of life. It is not identical with an anxious younger person's constant preoccupation with the state of his body. Does this mean that the adjusted old men had a greater fear of death than their anxious peers? We might expect men who were more anxious in general to be more anxious about death as well. Yet the better adjusted elders could face the prospect of serious illness more openly. Their concern about catastrophic illness and death

did not have to be disguised or denied. The more anxious elders had to avert their attention from their own actual health problems to keep the lid on the agitation bubbling underneath. The person who expresses direct concern about the state of his health might be behaving in his own enlightened self-interest. A high level of anxiety seems to be associated with evading actual medical problems. It would be unfair—and inaccurate—to classify the adjusted old men in this study as neurotically concerned with health or death when, in fact, the data imply that it is their relative freedom from the need to be defensive that allows them to confront their physical condition realistically.

Another interesting link with anxiety has been suggested in a recent study by Richard Schulz and David Aderman (1978).[3] They reasoned that physicians with different levels of death anxiety might somehow have differential outcomes in their work with terminally ill patients. Schulz and Aderman received surprisingly good cooperation (no turn-downs) from 24 physicians in a community hospital who completed a brief self-report death-anxiety questionnaire. Hospital records were then examined to determine for a 12-month period (1) the percentage of total patients treated who died under their care; (2) the average length of the terminal patients' final stay in the hospital; and (3) the average length of stay in the hospital of the nondying patients. The physicians were classified into high, moderate, and low death-anxiety groups on the basis of their questionnaire responses.

There were no significant differences among physicians with varying levels of anxiety with respect to the length of stay of their nondying patients, nor with respect to percentage of terminal patients treated. But "the length of final hospitalization for patients who died varied directly as a function of the physicians' death anxiety. Patients of physicians with high death anxiety were in the hospital an average of five days longer before dying than patients treated by physicians of medium and low death anxiety."[3,p.331] This study suggests, as the investigators note, that death anxiety can have behavioral effects. It is of particular interest because the anxiety was on the part of the physicians and the ultimate effects seemed to be on the patients! We cannot assume a cause-effect relationship, however, because this study was limited to a correlational analysis. Furthermore, we can only speculate on the specific ways in which the physicians' death anxiety might have been translated into behaviors that influenced the survival of the patients. It would have been more useful to know what relationship, if any, existed between the physician's death-anxiety level and the patient's anxiety and denial/acceptance orientation. This is, nevertheless, a provocative study that emphasizes the intimate relationships between how a person feels about death and what actually happens.

Emphasis in this chapter has been on the people who are in or around a death-salient situation. Are anxiety and evasion as commonplace among people who are not so caught up in the death system at the moment? In a critical review of the research literature up to 1977, Kastenbaum and Costa (1977)[4] observed that direct self-resports only rarely indicate high death concern. This might mean, of course, that just about everybody is denying death like mad. But it might mean a number of other things instead, of which the simplest would be that most people are *not* terrified of death, at least at the level of conscious self-awareness. This conclusion would be consistent with research of Herman Feifel and Allan B. Branscomb (1973), who found that several different adult populations showed little manifest death anxiety on the direct, self-report level.[5]

A recent survey by the Gallup Organization has also failed to turn up evidence of evasionary attitudes on the part of adults who are largely noninvolved in death situations. Only one death-relevant question was asked: "If you had a fatal illness would you want to be told about it, or not?" Results indicated that 90% of the national sample (1518 men and women aged 18 years and over) indicated they would want to be informed. Men, whites, and those on higher educational and occupational levels expressed somewhat more frequently the desire to be informed, but the main point was the overwhelming preference for knowledge vs ignorance on the part of the entire sample.[6] Whether or not these same people would have the same attitude if they found themselves faced with a personal death situation is a matter for speculation. It does seem wise, however, to distinguish between the way an adult looks at death when there seems to be a safe distance and what happens when the prospect or threat is of a more immediate nature. We would also want to keep in mind the difference between studies that ask only for the respondent's direct self-report and those that also attempt to assess anxiety, denial, and other feelings through other means. The Feifel-Branscomb study, for example, found evidence of death anxiety at presumably "deeper" levels within the personality of the same people who appeared without appreciable concern at the direct-report level.

YOUTH: TOO ALIVE TO DIE?

The anxiety-evasion dynamics, important as they are, do not tell the whole story. Other facets of our companionship with or alienation from death become more apparent when we continue with a life-span perspective.

Somebody else who happens to have my name may grow old some day and may even die. But that's not really *me*, is it? I am here right now, and I'm as full of life as can be. It's the only way I know to be. I have always been young, never old, always alive, never dead. Sure, I have a good imagination: but to see myself, *really* see myself as old or dead—say, that's asking too much!

This is part of the implicit credo of youth

that I have observed in our society for more than two decades. Probably it has been around much longer; perhaps it is starting to change as part of the death-awareness trend. Most of us, however, have grown up in a society that celebrates youth. The beauty, vigor, and athletic grace of the young adult are admired and rewarded. And why not? But the omissions are enormous. Little systematic preparation is provided—or even expected—to meet the challenges of later life and of death. Both aging and death appear to share a cloudy, dimly perceived existence on the far distant mental horizon. Just as it may be difficult for a middle-aged adult to realize personal mortality as an authentic fact, so the young adult may have a sense that both old age and death are conditions that do no really apply to him or her.

One of my own first studies was an attempt to learn about adolescent views of time and death. This involved 260 high-school students way back in 1959.[7] It was clear that the typical adolescent in this sample lived with an intense experience of the present and the immediate future. Everything important in life was either at hand or not very far ahead. The remote future (middle and especially old age) was seen as risky, unpleasant, devoid of positive value. Interestingly, these young men and women also did not care to think much about their past. Their typical attitude was to see themselves as having emerged from being mere children who could not control their own lives. This image of self in the past was not nearly so satisfying as their new if precarious sense of coming into their own. Overall, there was a sense of being caught up in a swoosh of rapidly passing time. There was a feeling of movement, of acceleration, that took precedence over both where they had been and where they were going in the long run.

Old age and death were viewed as very far away, not just in years but in psychological distance as well. The impression was that these adolescents did not necessarily lack the ability to think about the remote future but were making a determined effort to keep the distance between self and old age/death as great as possible. It is important to note that there were exceptions to this general rule. Some adolescents, about 15%, did seem to be taking their personal futurity into account in structuring their present lives. And we should also remember that death awareness is now more open in our society than at the time this study was conducted.

Nevertheless, there appears to be a sustaining theme in our society—shared by the individual and the culture at large—that youth is too lively and vital a time for visitations from death. At its extreme, this view holds that all that is truly exciting and worthwhile in life occurs within a few golden years of youth. Although familiar enough in our own society, it was also a strong theme with the ancient Greeks. And one of the most memorable expressions of this sentiment has been with us for over 800 years, since an Arabian mathematician and poet lamented:

> Alas, that Spring should vanish with the Rose!
> That Youth's sweet-scented Manuscript should close!
> The Nightingale that in the Branches sang,
> Ah, whence, and whither flown again, who knows!"[8]

What follows when the "sweet-scented Manuscript" does close? So long as both age and death are disvalued by a society and so long as human development is seen as essentially terminating with youth, the difference *between* old age and death may not even seem very important (until one is up close). The man or woman temporarily in possession of youth may behave much of the time as though one of the immortals. This tendency is supported by many aspects of our culture. It is also supported by our limited empathy and imagination. Many of us just find it very difficult to put ourselves in the place of either an old person or a person up against the immediate prospect of death. This is a developmental limitation more than a matter of denial or evasion as such. Very little has been done to explore the relationship between defensive maneuvers away from facing phenomena of aging and death and the empathic-imaginative abilities needed to comprehend personal aging and death in the first place. It is my impression that we are sometimes too quick to conclude that a person is "denying" death in some form or other, when it might be closer to the truth to say that this person has not been able to *encompass* death in his or her basic perspective on life.

Timely and untimely death

Both society and the individual tend to behave as though death grants special immunity to the young adult. When we hear or read of a person having suffered an "untimely" death, it usually proves to be a relatively young man or woman. I would be hard put, in fact, to recall a single instance in which this was not the case. This cultural orientation implies of course that the death of older people *is* timely and appropriate. To the extent that society disbelieves in the death of the young, then, we should not be astonished to find the same attitude in many young people themselves.

Whether untimely or not, however, death is a companion to young as well as old. Attitudes toward death can be seen in better perspective when set alongside the actual threat to life. Let us, then, briefly consider mortality statistics.

Of every 1000 15-year-olds in the United States, approximately 999 will live to celebrate their sixteenth birthday.[9] We can choose either to be comforted by these odds or to focus on the reminder that some actually die even at this favored age. The average 15-year-old can expect almost 58 more years of life. These two pieces of statistical information—mortality and average life expectancy—do appear to support the general attitude that the young are, at the

least, semi-immortal. By the same token, however, the relative infrequence of death at this age level is likely to generate more trauma when a young person does perish, because the death is so unexpected.

Let us move along one full decade. The 25-year-old still has excellent odds for continued survival. But a downward trend already can be recognized. Three 25-year-olds will have died before their twenty-sixth birthday for every two people who perished between ages 15 and 16. Furthermore, the average life expectancy has diminished by almost precisely the same amount of time that has passed in the interim. As a person enters what our society considers to be prime time, then, he already has joined a higher risk category. The future skill offers a long prospect: but it has been foreshortened by approximately one seventh of its previous length.

Another basis for comparison can be found if we compare the proportion of life already lived to the proportion of life remaining. The average 15-year-old has about one fifth of his life behind him, while the 25-year-old has moved through about one third of his expected total life span. This difference may or may not be of psychological significance from the individual's own perspective, but the statistics do represent actual weeks, months, and years of life. Although both the 15- and the 25-year-old are young, they occupy different positions of life risk and future expectancy. These differences will continue to increase substantially with each passing decade. As a rough guide, statistics usually show the mortality approximately doubling itself from one adult decade to the next.

Does our death concern or anxiety also double from decade to decade? Does our attitude toward personal mortality change in any systematic way as the odds for survival become progressively less favorable? These questions cannot be answered adequately on the basis of present knowledge. But we can at least improve our sensitivity to the relationship between life and death probabilities and the individual's personal feelings and expectations.

A person is not just a 15- or 25-year-old, of course. Many other characteristics affect both attitude and vulnerability. Consider gender, for example. Mortality rate and life expectancy are not the same for males and females. At every age level, males have greater odds against their continued survival. This differential is true at birth and remains in force into the advanced reaches of old age. The 15-year-old girl has only half the life risk of the boy who sits next to her in class. Only one female in 2000 will fail to survive between her fifteenth and sixteenth birthday as compared with one male in 1000. Additionally, the female at this age has an average life expectation of more than 61 years as compared with 54 for the male. This differential grows greater as the years go by. The 25-year-old male has twice the vulnerability that he had at age 15, while the female's probability of death has increased by less than 60%. There remains about a 7-year differential in average life expectation, still favoring females.

On the basis of mortality risk alone, then, it would be reasonable to expect some difference in death attitude between males and females. Research has not yet made it clear how gender identity contributes to death attitudes, but well-crafted multivariate studies may do so in the future. It will be important to keep in mind the changing status and meanings of gender identity in our society when the question of sex differences is eventually examined systematically.

Socioeconomic status is another important variable in our vulnerability to death. In general, lower socioeconomic status is associated with greater risk. Across a broad age spectrum, 20 to 64 years, men in the lowest of five socioeconomic categories had a mortality rate almost two times greater than men in the highest category. The difference was even greater for the younger men. The mortality ratio for men in the 20 to 24 group was nearly *four* times higher when those at the bottom of the socioeconomic ladder were compared with those at the top. This big difference became even a little bigger in the next age range studied, 25 to 34 years, and then slowly diminished through the remaining years.[10]

Just being alive means being of a particular age, functioning at a particular socioeconomic echelon, and being either female or male. Each of these characteristics, taken separately and, more fittingly, taken together, has implications for the individual's relationship to death. And there is hardly a comparison between the simple outline of vulnerability we can derive from a few selected dimensions such as these and the actual richness and complexity represented in the life of every human being. Even at the simplest level, however, we can see how inappropriate some of our culture's orientations toward death are when stacked up against the facts. The young are not supposed to think much about death, even less are they supposed to die. But a young man at the bottom of the socioeconomic hierarchy occupies quite a different position of vulnerability than a woman of the same age at the top of the hierarchy. Even within the ranks of the young, there are appreciable objective differences to be recognized as well as subjective or personal differences that elude the elegant but narrow language of statistics.

A paradox, now. It has been suggested that both the individual and society think of death among young adults as untimely. Yet there is another way of looking at the same background circumstances and coming to a different conclusion. A. E. Housman addressed these lines "To an Athlete Dying Young":

The time you won your town the race
We chaired you through the market-place;
Man and boy stood cheering by,
And home we brought you shoulder-high

To-day, the road all runners come
Shoulder-high we bring you home,
And set you at your threshold down,
Townsman of a stiller town.

Smart lad, to slip betimes away
From fields where glory does not stay
And early though the laurel grows
It withers quicker than the rose. . . .

Now you will not swell the rout
Of lads that wore their honors out,
Runners whom renown outran
And the name died before the man. . . .[11]

If we truly believe that worthwhile life terminates with youth, then it is possible to welcome a biologically premature death. This view lends itself readily to romantic embellishments. The individual attains a peak and then perishes, preferably in a burst of glory. Next to Housman's athlete dying young, we might set the soldier who lays down his life for his country or the young lovers who die in each other's arms. These are dramatic and moving situations. Yet it is possible to wonder about the relationship between death-welcoming or even death-seeking orientations in young adults and *fear of life beyond youth*.

The insights of Otto Rank, a pioneering psychoanalyst, come to mind here. He recognized that we may experience both the fear of being trapped where we are and the fear of going ahead with our lives.[12] This can be a subtle process. A person may appear to embrace death willingly. The underlying motivation, however, may be a fear of going on with the risks and challenges of life. This suggests that we might not always be wise in applauding and encouraging what appears to be a courageous relinquishment of life. The action might actually be, at least in part, a way of turning back from challenges that lie ahead if one accepted the risks and opportunities of life and development.

A few statistics have been invoked in this

section. Nevertheless, the basic question remains one for each individual to explore on a very personal basis. When a new acceptance or longing for death appears just as the first bloom of youth fades, we might wonder about a hesitancy to go on with life's new direction. Impulsive retreat from life can masquerade as death acceptance. However, a period of temporary withdrawal to gain new perspective can be beneficial. The athlete who does not die young, for example, may take time out to reevaluate the course of his or her life. Even if this reevaluation has its painful or confusing aspects, the individual may come out on the other side of the crisis as a more mature and resourceful person with a new relationship to life.

THE TRIUMPH OF TIME

Father Time leaps through the air, holding in one hand a serpent coiled into a circle, biting its own tail. The serpent is one of several symbols intended to suggest that time goes on and on in endless cycles. But what does Father Time have in his other hand? It is his own child, and he is devouring the child. Furthermore, Time's pathway is littered with the remains of human life and accomplishment. Time gives; Time takes away. Picter Brueghel's rendition of "The Triumph of Time" was not intended to set the mind at ease. It was a vivid reminder to his sixteenth-century countrymen that life is only a temporary gift to the individual, although the universe itself may continue to roll along.

I have observed adolescents responding to this fantasy painting with smiles, giggles, and the making of faces. Older adults do not seem to find as much to smile about; their thoughts and responses move inward very quickly. And no wonder. In middle and old age, time often seems to change character. Just as many of the desired things in life carry a price tag, so the adult realizes more keenly the time tag attached to all he or she values, including life itself. This new relationship to time and death has been recognized by philosophers, poets, and social scientists. Sociologist Wilbert E. Moore, for example, speaks of time as "the ultimate scarcity."[13] This is not necessarily the outlook of the young person who sees the future as the realm in which hopes and potentials can be actualized. But it does appear close to the daily experience of men and women who are pressured by time on all sides. The husband or wife may say to each other, "If only there were more hours in the day!" Meanwhile, on another psychological level, they may also be starting to feel, "If only there were more years left to life!"

Specific forms of time pressure may disturb adults who are somewhere in the not-young, not-old range. "Have I reached the peak of my career, or can I still expect to advance?" "Is it already too late to have another baby?" The individual may not yet be thinking seriously about the end of his or her life. But time limitations in certain areas of life may be rising to the surface. The race against the clock not only may become a daily contest but also shape up as a long-distance effort as well.

Time, disengagement, and death

The disengagement theory of aging has given special attention to the shifting meanings of time throughout adult life. Elaine Cumming and William Henry developed this influential, although no longer dominant, theory while analyzing life history and adjustment data for a population of normal, healthy, elderly men and women in Kansas City.[14] The theory suggests that we reach a peak of engagement with the outside world in the middle years of our lives. This is the time when there are young children to raise, careers to be established and advanced, and many social and civic responsibilities to be fulfilled. This pattern of mutual expectations can bring many rewards and satisfactions. But it also requires heavy time commitments and the ability to function in keeping with multiple schedules.

Eventually, however, the individual begins to sense that he or she does not really have all the time in the world. Life's final destination can be seen on the horizon. With this realization ripening in his or her mind, the individual begins preparation for the process of disengagement. Some activities seem less important than others, and there just is not time for everything. Perhaps certain goals and values that had been put aside in the press of daily life will not be revived and given greater priority. Why wait any longer for travel, for pursuing a long-neglected interest, for finding the time to be with one's favorite people? In short, the person must decide what is really worth attention, given the heightened awareness of time's scarcity.

Death is seen as the ultimate disengagement. But there may still be much life ahead before the final separation. During this time, the individual is likely to go through a process of altering the relationship between self and society. Less time will be spent under the control of other people's demands and expectations; more time will be retained for one's own purposes. When this disengagement process is operating smoothly, both society and the individual give each other permission to loosen their mutual ties. The functional roles this person played in society, especially in the occupational sphere, now can be taken over by younger people. Meanwhile, the aging individual has more time to devote to personal thoughts, feelings, and interests.

This way of thinking about time and death in later life also fits in well with Robert Butler's concept of the "life review,"[15] and Erik Erikson's belief that acceptance of one's unique life-career is a critical factor in accepting death as well.[16] Both interpretations of the inner dynamics of later life center around the individual's coming to terms with what he or she has experienced and become throughout the life span now that death is coming more clearly into prospect.

It would be convenient to accept disengagement theory and related concepts as though they were demonstrated facts about our changing relationship with time and death. However much sense these ideas might make, though, they have not yet been fully supported by systematic research, and there are, in fact, some observations that suggest limits to their range of applicability. Disengagement theory has lost rather than gained support over its two decades of existence, although no general psychosocial theory of aging has risen to fully take its place, and the life-review and Eriksonian concepts have served more as sensitizing guides to understanding some aspects of aging than as specific hypotheses to be critically evaluated. Nevertheless, all these approaches alert us to possible transformations in our relationships to self and society as time runs out, and suggest that the pattern we establish for ourselves in our early adult years will prove influential on our coming to terms with aging and death.

Individual differences

Some people do think about the value of time and the prospect of their own death well before the middle years of life. And some old people have never thought much about these matters and still take life on a day-to-day basis: neither reevaluation nor life review seem to be in their character. If we have the urge to establish general principles, it is frustrating to discover how many people do not seem to fit the rule. But if we are able to rejoice in the diversity of human personalities, then we can take a more relaxed and, perhaps, more practical approach.

Consider, for example, the scope of individual differences in the *realization* of personal death. Intellectually, most of us are able to understand the supposed basics of death by ado-

lescence, if not before. But some of us go on for many years without ever taking death to heart. We can be exposed to death situations and yet move through and past them without drawing substantial implications for ourselves. Ben Hecht, the author of several popular works, describes himself as a man who often was in contact with death in his days as a freewheeling newspaperman. He covered many kinds of death and also had his share of bereavement in his personal life. Nevertheless, young man Hecht "felt a childish immortality within the day he occupied."[17] The fact that he was an intelligent adult exposed repeatedly to death was not sufficient to make this reality personal to him. But eventually he did learn: "I can recall the hour in which I lost my immortality, in which I tried on my shroud for the first time and saw how it became me. . . . The knowledge of my dying came to me when my mother died." After the funeral, he felt as though he had been "to the edge of the world and looked over its last foot of territory into nothingness."[17, p. 109]

The death of a parent or of one special person often makes the difference. Simply knowing a person's age does not tell us whether he or she realizes death as an authentic personal fact. Similarly, knowing a person's age does not tell us how the future is imagined. Try for yourself the following exercise in *subjective life expectancy*.

SUBJECTIVE LIFE EXPECTANCY

1. I *expect* to live to age (*circle your answer*)

   25 30 35 40 45 50 55 60 65

   70 75 80 85 90 95 100

2. I *want* to live to age (*circle your answer*)

   25 30 35 40 45 50 55 60 65

   70 75 80 85 90 95 100

There are some people at all age levels studied who cannot bring themselves to answer either question. "I can't think about death—my death—not at all" is the frank statement we sometimes hear. Other people are afraid that if they do specify an age, then this will somehow *make* death come at that time. Still other people realize that they are not ready to answer the questions. They use these questions as an invitation or challenge to reflect more carefully on expectations that they have not yet given an airing.

Individual differences increase when we consider people who do find it possible to answer these questions (usually, more than 90% of those who are asked do respond with their subjective life expectancy). Among 20-year-olds, for example, we find some who expect to live another 60 years, or three times the length of their existence up to that point. This subjective expectation, of course, is well within statistical expectations as well. Yet other 20-year-olds expect to be dead within the next decade. They see themselves as having used up two thirds of their allotted time. Neither of these are especially extreme illustrations. And neither can be judged easily for their realism. Some respondents have predicted long lives although they are suffering what is usually considered to be a terminal illness. And some who have predicted a foreshortened life expectation have plausible reasons. One study found expectations for early and violent death to be common in a particular population of young adults.[18] These were "hard-core unemployed" men who had little opportunity for secure jobs and housing and whose life-styles did involve unusual peril. But we have also found substantial differences in subjective life expectancy within the ranks of college students as well. Whether or not the individual's expectancies are confirmed by the eventual facts, it is possible that the person who expects a long life will feel and behave differently in many situations than the age peer who believes there is not much time left.

The difference between expected and desired life span is also worth thinking about. Most people either state a preference for dying at the expected age or for living beyond that time, were it possible to do so. Yet it is not that rare for an adult in good health to state a preference for dying earlier than the expected age. Sometimes this is associated with a dread of old age. A sense of emptiness is expressed by others: "I just don't know of anything to live for after I've had some kicks and seen something of the world." And some people are unable to explain their reasons, but nevertheless feel they have been given more life than they feel like using.

The thoughts and feelings that flash through your mind in answering these subjective life-expectancy questions may be more important than the answers themselves. Perhaps you were able to catch some of your assumptions, fears, and hopes as they moved by. Would you have answered this pair of questions in the same way 5 years ago? Will you have the same thoughts and feelings about the length of your life when you are 5, 10, or 20 years older? There probably are some elements in your subjective life expectancy that other people of your age tend to share. But there may be other thoughts and feelings that are more personal, more distinctive to you. The simple fact that you have opened your mind to the projection of your future life—both what is expected and what is desired—gives you a different perspective from the person whose assumptions have never been brought to light.

As you become increasingly aware of your own thoughts about life and death, it may be that you will also become even more appreciative of the many ways in which other people orient themselves to this subject. You may be alert to the possible effect of a person's age and position in life on his view of death, but also alert to the ways in which his or her distinctive personality is coming to terms with our companion death.

"DENYING" AND "ACCEPTING" DEATH

Is this person "accepting" or "denying" death? Discussion of an individual's orientation toward death often centers around acceptance-denial dynamics, some examples of which have been given throughout this chapter. Like many other important words, however, *acceptance* and *denial* are used in a variety of ways and sometimes their meanings become so loose and blurred that they mislead more than they help. It is worthwhile to review and supplement what has already been implied about acceptance-denial dynamics in the adult's relationship to death.

Too simple a view

If we absorbed observations and opinions without reflection, it is likely we would come to the following set of assumptions:

1. People either accept or deny death.
2. Acceptance is good; denial is bad—or— denial is good; acceptance is bad.
3. Attitudes toward death are well described and understood when they have been properly classified in acceptance-denial terms.

These assumptions do not stand up well, however, when examined in the light of broad-ranging and critical observations. We will replace them with a more useful core of propositions after the following considerations.

Types and contexts of acceptance-denial

A standard dictionary of psychiatry defines *denial* as "a primitive defense, consisting of an attempt to disavow the existence of unpleasant reality." It adds that

Because denial must ignore data presenting themselves to the perceptory system and garnered by the memory apparatus, such a defense can operate only in the undeveloped, infantile psyche, or in persons whose ego is weak or disturbed (as in the psychoses), and even so, denial succeeds best against single internal perceptions of a painful nature. Denial and

negation are also used, more loosely, to refer to any form of resistance.[19, p. 199]

Resistance itself (as discussed by Freud and others with a psychoanalytical orientation) is a complex set of phenomena. An individual may "resist" at various levels of awareness, for various purposes, and in various forms. It seems to me that one of the problems in communicating clearly about a person's orientation toward death comes from an indiscriminate use of the term *denial*—implying a "primitive defense"—when the facts would better support the existence of a more subtle and functional process, some relatively sophisticated form of *resistance*. In other words, we sometimes conclude that a person is "denying" death when it is more likely that he or she is *not* functioning on a primitive defensive level, but rather is coping with a difficult situation in a relatively resourceful way. This will become clearer if we distinguish among several processes all of which can look like denial.

1. *Selective attention.* There are many things happening that are competing for the individual's attention. To focus on one or two of the dimensions or events necessarily means that other aspects of the situation will be given less attention. A person who has never been in a hospital before, for example, might find many new, interesting and challenging goings-on to notice and think about. These may, in fact, seem much more vivid and perceptually real than something as abstract as a diagnosis that will be made eventually. For the moment, other, more immediate perceptual and interpersonal phenomena call more forcefully on attention.

2. *Selective response.* In this instance, the person may have death-relevant thoughts well in mind. However, he or she judges that this is not quite the time or place to express them. "I'm not going to open up to this young doctor who looks more scared than I am;" or "There is

nothing effective I can *do* about the situation at this moment, so I will do something else (or nothing in particular) even though I know what's up." Still again: "There is something very important I must accomplish while I have the opportunity, so this must take priority over words and actions that center on my impending death."

3. *Compartmentalizing*. This process involves awareness and some response to death-salient aspects of the situation. What is missing, however, is the connection between one aspect and another, the drawing out of the full implications of what is taking place. The individual, for example, may know that he has a poor prognosis (accurate perception, nondenial). He may also be cooperating well with treatment and speak appropriately about his condition in many respects (adaptive response, nondenial). Yet the same person may be making future plans (and failing to revise other plans) just as though he were going to be around in good health for years to come. "Compartmentalizing" is a term already quite familiar in the mental health field, so we are using it here even though it does not do equal justice to all the phenomena we have in mind. What we most want to draw attention to is the type of process in which at least some aspects of dying-and-death reality are clearly acknowledged, but which at the same time stops just short enough of drawing the implications that might lead to full emotional as well as intellectual realization. It has been known to happen in academia, for example, that a student or instructor remarks, "Well, we covered death today!"—and the emphasis should really be on the "covered."[20]

4. *Deception*. People sometimes deliberately give false information to others. This takes place in dying-and-death situations as well as elsewhere. When people are telling each other lies (for whatever purpose), it makes sense to acknowledge this for what it is, and not confuse the issue by using the ambiguous term, denial.

5. *Denial* (the real thing). This is the basic defensive process at the core of the definition given earlier. The individual is not just selecting among possible perceptions and responses, limiting the logical connections between one phenomenon and the other, or engaged in conscious deception. Rather, the self appears to be totally organized against recognition of death-laden reality. Such an orientation, at the extreme, can be bizarre and may accompany a psychotic reaction. It does not have to be quite that extreme, however, and we can sometimes recognize the existence of a true denial process that weaves in and out with other, more sophisticated ways of coping.

It is important to keep in mind that each individual in a dying-death situation has some influence on and is being influenced by others. Acceptance-denial is an *interpersonal* as well as an *intrapsychic* process. Furthermore, there is both the immediate situation and the historical background to consider. Mr. A. may come from an ethnic background in which dying and death are treated in a straightforward manner (the Amish, for example). But now he might find himself in a medical establishment where death is still quite a taboo and high-anxiety topic: a potential "death accepter" trapped among the denyers. The reverse also takes place. Mr. B. may have grown up learning how to deny death—especially the deeper emotions associated with death—and is now a patient in a more "liberated" health-care establishment where staff believe that an openness and sharing of feelings is important: the "denyer" confronted with the "accepters." To understand how a particular person is coping with the acceptance-denial dynamics requires, then, some attention to the past and current interpersonal field as well as the individual's own thoughts and feelings.

Fortunately, there are now a number of sensitive observers who have recognized the complexity of acceptance-denial dynamics. Take, for example, a recent clinical study by Daniel A. Dansak and Rosemarie S. Cordes, a psychiatrist/nurse team. They point out that when terminally ill cancer patients speak little about their death fears or expectations, this silence is often construed as proving that they are *denying* (in the basic, primitive-defense sense of this term). It was found, however, that often "such patients are not truly 'denying' cancer and its consequences, but have merely decided, more or less voluntarily, to 'suppress' these thoughts as a method of coping with their illness."[21] This conclusion was reached after working closely with more than 100 cancer patients. Sometimes they found that staff made the denial interpretation when, in fact, the patient knew his or her situation very well but was cultivating whatever hope still remained and was at the same time helping to make realistic future plans with his or her family. It was common for people, in effect, to make the best of a bad situation. This pattern of adaptation seems to combine both selective attention and selective response. It is not that the person is blind to his or her situation, but it is felt that remaining time and energies can better be spent in other ways than talking about death to people in white coats with stethoscopes sticking out of their pockets.

Avery D. Weisman, one of the most gifted observers of feelings and behavior in death-salient situations, has called attention to two points that are particularly important here. Weisman notes that a person does not usually deny everything about death to everybody. More often, a careful selective process is involved. We must then go beyond the question, "Is this person denying death?" It is more useful to ask instead, "What aspects of dying or death are being shared with what other people, under what circumstances, and why?" One of the many implications of this approach is that

apparent denial on the part of the patient may derive largely from a lack of responsive people in the environment. The related point has to do with the *function* of so-called denial. "The purpose of denial," writes Weisman, "is not simply to avoid a danger, but to prevent loss of a significant relationship."[22] All of the adaptive processes we have described above might be used, then, in an effort to make The Other Person (spouse, parent, child, friend) feel comfortable enough to maintain a vitally needed relationship. It is the anxiety of The Other Person that the individual faced with death may have to struggle with just as much, if not more, than their own.

As already noted, there is research to suggest that different processes of coping with the realization of death may be at work within the same individual at the same time (e.g., Feifel & Branscomb, 1973[5]). This finding is consistent with the conclusions of a number of other observers of death dynamics. Richard G. Dumont and Dennis C. Foss, for example, conclude their survey of *The American Way of Death* (1972)[23] with the belief that society generally supports death denial on the emotional level, but supports acceptance on the intellectual level. The inevitability of death is too central a fact of life to evade, yet it is just not acceptable emotionally because it is associated with such calamities as separation from loved ones, a sense of failure, and the possibility of eternal damnation. They follow in Freud's footsteps by suggesting that

Man contains within himself a most profound contradiction. At the conscious, intellectual level he is absolutely convinced that he must die, this belief being reinforced and sustained by contacts with those around him who share it, as well as by the knowledge of the deaths of others. He can be more certain of his death than of his name. His unconscious is "immortal," however, denying the reality of his death and not allowing him to imagine himself dead. There is absolutely no way to eradicate this emotional feeling of immortality, so that the individual's emotions deny his death quite as steadfastly as his intellect affirms it.[23,pp.104-105]

It should be noted that there is a strong philosophical and speculative element in this view of acceptance-denial. I do not see that a firm data-based case has been made for the intellect-accepts, the emotions-deny interpretation, but the circumstantial case is persuasive, at least to the point that it is characteristic of humans to have both acceptance and denial dynamics going on at the same time.

Two of the simple and oppositional assumptions mentioned earlier in this section can be resolved if we are willing to deal with the more complex interplay of thoughts and feelings about death. Acceptance and denial are not necessarily either "good" or "bad" in themselves. We must examine the contexts in which these processes are used and the purposes they seem to be serving. If what we are calling denial really *is* denial, then we may be faced with a person who is making a desperate stand against catastrophe. He or she has been forced to fall back on a "primitive" defensive process that involves rejection of important aspects of reality. This person does need psychological help, and, quite possibly, help of other types as well. On the other hand, the person may not be "denying," so much as selectively perceiving, linking and responding to what is taking place. This total pattern of coping with difficult reality may have its evasionary aspects at certain times with certain people, but there is method, judgment, and purpose at work. Even flashes of "pure denial" may contribute to overall adaptation, as when challenges come too swiftly or are too overwhelming to meet in other ways. A little later, the individual may have found another and more characteristic way to deal with the same challenge, once the first impact has been partially warded off and partially absorbed.

A more realistic view

Let us now replace the simplistic assumptions about acceptance and denial with the following:

1. Most people most of the time probably have both acceptance- and denial-type dynamics in process at different personality levels, and with different degrees of dominance.

2. States of total acceptance and total denial of death do occur, but these are in fairly extreme circumstances: the individual letting go of life after achieving a sense of completion and having struggled as long as struggling seemed worthwhile, or the individual massively resisting catastrophic reality when it first bursts on him or her.

3. Much of what is loosely spoken of as "denial" can be understood more adequately in terms of adaptive processes through which the person responds selectively to different aspects of a difficult situation.

4. The individual's pattern of adaptation to death as companion should be considered within the context of acceptance and denial that characterizes the large interpersonal network around him or her.

5. "Acceptance" and "denial" can be evaluated only when we are in a position to understand what the person is trying to accomplish and what he or she is up against.

6. Important as the acceptance-denial dynamics are, our relationship to death is more complex, more nuanced than these terms suggest.

SUMMARY

Becoming an adult does not guarantee a firm appreciation of personal mortality. *Evasionary thought* is common. This includes the acceptance of the general proposition, "man is mortal," without drawing the logical personal implications. A passage from Tolstoy's *The Death of Ivan Ilych* reveals a person's desperate need to *differentiate* himself from the kind of man who dies (him, not me dynamics). We also recognize the tendency to deny a death threat even when it is one's own body that has been seized with painful and serious symptoms ("It's nothing—really!").

Our society appears to have special difficulty in believing that young people can die. The death of a young person is seen as untimely, implying that death is quite timely for older adults. Nevertheless, persons do die even in the favored years of early adulthood. In fact, we see a *steady rise in mortality* well before the person enters middle age. Sex and socioeconomic class differences are associated with different mortalities and life expectancies for people of the same age. Understanding a person's attitudes toward death requires some knowledge of the background of life risk that he or she faces at a particular point in the life span.

Paradoxically, some people regard youth as the most timely occasion for death. This apparent acceptance lends itself to romantic embellishments. However, it may conceal a hesitation to explore what life has to offer beyond youth. Dying young in a blaze of glory, in other words, may be an image based on the fear of growing up and growing old.

The individual's relationship to time and death tends to change with advancing age. Often there is an increasing sense of time pressure in daily life. Gradually there comes an awareness of time running out. *Disengagement theory* portrays the person as heavily obligated to family, occupational, and civic demands during the middle years of life and therefore much under the control of social time. But as the person grows older he or she seeks freedom from some of these responsibilities (some of which naturally fade away), and to have more of the remaining time left for personal interests. It is thought that a major reorientation in life-style comes about as the aging individual recognizes death's proximity and the need to decide what

best to do with the time that still remains. The concept of a *life-review* process suggests that the prospect of death impels the elderly person to reevaluate all that he or she has been in order to face death with integrity and equanimity. The disengagement and life-review concepts, along with Erikson's concepts of aging and death, although valuable, cannot be taken as established and comprehensive principles of the adult's orientation toward time and death. Individual differences, for example, have been relatively neglected.

We remind ourselves that people come to their very personal *realizations* of death at different points in the life span, and that there are appreciable individual differences in when, if ever, a person is ready to reevaluate the direction life is taking. Examples of individual differences at the same age level are given through an exercise in *subjective life expectancy*.

Acceptance-denial dynamics are particularly important in understanding our life-span relationship to death. These concepts are sometimes used both loosely and simplistically, however, and so we examined them more closely than is usually the case. Theoretically, death is everybody's companion throughout the entire life span. We do not all acknowledge death's absent presence in the same way, however, and there is no good substitute for trying to understand each person's orientation on an individual basis.

REFERENCES

1. Tolstoy, L. *The death of Ivan Ilych.* New York: The New American Library, Inc., 1960. (Originally published, 1886.)
2. McCrae, R. R., Bartone, P. T., & Costa, P. T. Age, personality, and self-reported health. *International Journal of Aging and Human Development*, 1976, 6, 49-58.
3. Schulz, R., & Aderman, D. Physician's death anxiety and patient outcomes. *Omega*, 1978, 9, 327-332.
4. Kastenbaum, R., & Costa, P. T., Jr. Psychological perspectives on death, *Annual Review of Psychology*, 1978, 28, 225-250.

5. Feifel, H., & Branscomb, A. Who's afraid of death? *Journal of Abnormal Psychology,* 1973, *81,* 82-88.

6. Blumenfield, M., Levy, N. B., & Kaufman, D. The wish to be informed of a fatal illness. *Omega,* 1978, *9,* 323-326.

7. Kastenbaum, R. Time and death in adolescence. In H. Feifel (Ed.), *The meaning of death.* New York: McGraw-Hill Book Co., 1959.

8. Omar Khayyam. *The Rubaiyat.* (c. 1120 A.D.). New York: Avenel Books, 1970.

9. Metropolitan Life. Expectations of life in the United States at a new high. *Statistical Bulletin,* April 1975, *56,* 5-7.

10. Metropolitan Life. Socioeconomic mortality differentials. *Statistical Bulletin,* January 1975, *56,* 2-5.

11. Housman, A. E. To an athlete dying young. In Housman, A. E. *A Shropshire lad.* New York: Avon Press, 1966, pp. 63-65. (Originally published, 1896.)

12. Rank, O. *Will therapy.* New York: Alfred A. Knopf, Inc., 1945.

13. Moore, W. E. *Man, time, and society.* New York: John Wiley & Sons, Inc., 1963.

14. Cumming, E., & Henry, W. E. *Growing old.* New York: Arno Press, 1980. (Originally published, 1961.)

15. Butler, R. N. The life review: an interpretation of reminiscence in the aged. *Psychiatry,* 1963, *119,* 721-728.

16. Erikson, E. H. *Identity and the life cycle: psychological issues.* New York: International Universities Press, 1959.

17. Hecht, B. *A child of the century.* New York: Ballantine Books, Inc., 1970.

18. Teahan, J. E., & Kastenbaum, R. Future time perspective and subjective life-expectancy in "hard-core unemployed" men. *Omega,* 1970, *1,* 189-200.

19. Hinsie, L. E., & Campbell, R. J. *Psychiatric dictionary* (4th ed.). New York: Oxford University Press, 1970.

20. Kastenbaum, R. We covered death today. *Death Education,* 1977, *1,* 85-92.

21. Dansak, D. A., & Cordes, R. S. Cancer: denial or suppression? *International Journal of Psychiatry in Medicine,* 1979, *9,* 257-262.

22. Weisman, A. D. *On dying and denying.* New York: Behavioral Publications, Inc., 1972.

23. Dumont, R. G., & Foss, D. C. *The American way of death.* Cambridge, Mass.: Schenkman Publishing Co., 1972.

CHAPTER 11

❖ DYING
Transition from life

What image comes to mind when you think of a dying person? Perhaps you find yourself thinking of a deathbed scene. The dying person is at home, in his own bed, surrounded by the people who mean the most to him. Everybody is intent on communicating love and concern. Finally, the dying person utters his last words and expires.

Perhaps instead your image is dominated by religious meanings. The dying person is attuned to the mysterious transition from the life he has known to the new form of existence he anticipates "on the other side." It is the priest or minister whose presence is most crucial. Peace with himself and with God is the most vital consideration now as life slips away.

Still again, your image may take the form of an intensive care unit in a large modern hospital. The atmosphere is stark, efficient, professionalized. No homey touches are in evidence. Several pieces of medical equipment surround the patient. You recognize the intravenous (IV) tube hung on a pole near the bed, dripping a clear fluid into a vein in the patient's arm. Perhaps you also visualize a catheter designed to carry off urine, an oxygen mask, a nasogastric tube, or a device to monitor cardiac activity and other vital signs. Hospital staff come and go with brisk purpose. The person himself? It is hard to say much about him. He seems to be a part of the medicotechnological network

rather than a human being with a distinct personality of his own.

These are among the more common images of the dying person. Each of these images has actual counterparts in real life. There *are* family deathbed scenes, significant confrontations with the meaning of life at the point of death, and all-out control of the dying person's body through elaborate use of life-support systems. But these images greatly simplify the life experiences of most people who are afflicted with a terminal illness. In earlier chapters we saw that *death* is a word with many usages and meanings. *Dying* is another term that must be approached with care. To know that a person is dying is not necessarily to know very much about what is actually taking place or what might be done to enhance the quality of his remaining life.

All three images of the dying person that have been sketched here, for example, emphasize the situation in which death is in very close prospect. There is a dramatic urgency. What will the last words be? Will he find peace and blessing before departing life? Should the life-support system be maintained or should somebody pull the plug? If these are sometimes actual situations, they are also frequently the stuff of dramatic imagination, familiar to us through presentations in books, television productions, and motion pictures. "They didn't seem to be getting it right. They weren't behaving the way they were supposed to, none of them. Then I realized—hey, this is the *real* hospital with *real* people in it. I guess I was expecting things to happen the way they do when, you know, somebody is dying on one of those TV programs." In reviewing her recent visit to a terminally ill friend, this young woman realized how much her expectations had been shaped by the conventions of the media rather than by actual personal experience. Difficult though it may be, let us try to detach ourselves from the images that have come to us from various sources and examine the dying process in a more systematic manner.

WHEN DOES DYING BEGIN?

The most secure definition of dying could be made by waiting until the death event has occurred. At that point it could be said that the deceased had moved through a process of decline that culminated in death. Another person may have seemed just as ill a few months ago, but this person recovered. Therefore we cannot be sure that an individual actually is dying until the process has concluded.

Such a cautious approach is seldom applied in practice. We do not wait until death to judge that a person is dying. This means of course that we will be in error some of the time. A "dying" person recovers; a "nondying" person meets his death. These errors are tolerated because classification of a person as "dying" has significant implications in our society. It makes a difference to most of us if we believe we are in contact with a dying person, not least of all when that dying person is ourself.

The lack of a clear definition of dying presents many difficulties. We may fail to distinguish adequately between everything that the individual does and experiences and the dying process as such. At any point in time, what is "dying behavior" and what is not? This is not an easy question to answer, and requires inti-

mate knowledge of the particular individual and situation. But if we are not even aware of the question, then we might develop an extreme and simplistic view that interferes with our capacity to help and understand. "That's just the way dying people think" can be a hasty and inaccurate response to preferences, ideas, and behaviors that have their roots in the individual's basic selfhood or in current reality factors. It can be, in other words, a way of dismissing the full and distinctive reality of the individual in favor of a stereotyped notion of the dying process. Are all the individual's thoughts, feelings, needs, and bodily states determined by or locked into that special process we call dying? Is the individual a dying person and a dying person only? These are not assumptions to be quickly snapped into place.

For reasons such as these it is useful to approach the definition of the dying process by starting where the process itself starts. But where is that?

Abstract views of the dying process

You may have heard it said that "we die from the moment we are born." This is a fairly popular bit of philosophy. It has one strong point to make. We are reminded that life is continuous and always related to death. A person does not suddenly become exposed to mortal peril; we live, and have always lived, in peril. This proposition may be particularly useful in warning us not to establish strong psychological boundaries between ourselves and those who appear to be in more immediate jeopardy. The individual who takes this view to heart will not be astonished when events remind him of personal mortality.

There are several problems with this conception, however. One of these problems is associated with the way this view is often used. Typically, this philosophy is expressed by a person who is poised for flight. He recognizes that a death situation exists and is not willing to deny it completely. Yet personal emotions run too strong, or he feels at a loss for coping with the situation. "We die from the moment we are born" recommends itself as an intellectual response that accepts the general but neutralizes the specific. It is as though the person had said instead, "There is nothing really special here. Maybe you *are* dying, but everybody is dying, and isn't it a lovely day?" An intellectual formulation that helps us to keep our poise and extricate ourselves from a demanding situation at the same time can be a valuable asset— but should not be taken on face value if we are interested in a solid understanding rather than simply an anxiety-reducing strategy.

This conception is also questionable if taken as a direct statement of fact. It is true that there is continual death among the cells that comprise our bodies all through life. The outer layer of the skin, for example, is comprised of dead cells that are replaced in turn by other dead cells. Certain forms of tissue death are programmed to occur at particular times in our psychobiological development. The loss of the umbilical cord after birth is one of the clearest examples in our species of a biological structure phasing itself out after its function has been served. The principle of programmed death as part of normal development appears to be well established in biology.[1]

Nevertheless, it is peculiar to insist that the normal turnover of cells or the atrophy of unnecessary structures comprises a process of dying for the organism as a whole. The fact that each day that is lived theoretically brings one closer to death does not establish that an actual process of decline and failure is operative. The compelling fact about the infant and child remains the surge of growth. The *person* is maturing psychologically, socially, and biologically. The overall course is one of development, the emergence and perfection of structure and function. When the balance is so heavily in favor of life and growth, there is little

credibility in maintaining that the person is really dying. If the term "dying" is used so loosely to make a quasi-philosophical point in the midst of development, then we would simply have to find a new term to represent the very different processes observed when life actually is in jeopardy.

A more challenging conception has also been with us for many years. Three centuries ago, Jeremey Taylor, chaplain to King Charles I of England, conceived of old age as "a longer sickness," a "middle state between life and death-bed." He likened aging to the faltering and collapse of a used-up timepiece in which first the ornamental and then the most vital components

become useless, and entangled like the wheels of a broken clock. *Baldness* is but a dressing to our funerals, the proper ornament of mourning, and of a person entered very far into the regions and possession of death: and we have many more of the same signification; grey hairs, rotten teeth, dim eyes, trembling joints, short breath, stiff limbs, wrinkled skin, short memory, decayed appetite.[2,pp.4-5]

Aging, then, is a form of terminal illness: it is no longer life, even if it is not yet death. Taylor notes that the loss of baby teeth at age 7 years serves as one of the "prologues to the tragedy," but it is only in advanced age that to live is also to die. Deterioration of body and mind argue that aging is dying. Furthermore, there is an acute awareness of *time:* "and while we think a thought we die; and the clock strikes, and reckons on our portion of eternity; we form our words with the breath of our nostrils, we have the less to live upon for every word we speak."[2,p.7] This is a vision in which human suffering relentlessly increases once the early prime of life is passed, although suffering is likely at any age. His mind seems to function like a motion-picture camera that can reveal how what we call "aging" is identical with what, in accelerated motion, we also call "dying."

This conception of aging as dying is thought provoking. It has more impact than the proposition that dying begins with life. Parallels can be seen between certain phenomena of aging individuals and phenomena characteristic of the dying person. And it is a mind-stretching idea to consider the possibility that aging might be slow dying, and dying, fast aging. Although there may well be a place for this conception in our overall view of death and human development, it is far from a sufficient basis for defining the dying process. There is not much point in linking dying with aging when we have yet to learn when *aging* begins! This is a question worth attention in its own right and complex enough to resist easy solution. Furthermore, the life of elderly people cannot be reduced to the dimensions of dying. The more we learn about how elderly people actually function, the more variety and vitality become apparent.[3,4] There is much more to aging than dying, even if the basic connection be granted at a general level. Pragmatically, it is also difficult to equate the two processes. A young person may die because of a specific bodily failure (e.g., an unexpected drug reaction) even though otherwise in good health and not at all resembling the aging person depicted by Taylor.

Abstract views about the dying process are helpful in shaking us out of the assumptions that accumulate when we are faced with one individual instance after another. There is a place for general and somewhat philosophical propositions. But there is also a place for an up-close view of the dying process, such as now follows.

Dying begins: pragmatic definitions

Dying usually begins as a psychosocial event. Theoretically, there may be one moment when the person is not dying and another moment in which a biological event has occurred that will lead to death. But in practice these moments, if they do occur, often pass without adequate observation. Whatever the underlying organic situation might be, it is on the level of thoughts, feelings, interpersonal communications, and actions that the onset of the dying process usually defines itself. We will consider some of the contexts in which the onset of dying is discovered or certified.

Dying begins when the facts are recognized. The physician's office is visited by people with varying amounts of concern for their health. These concerns themselves may or may not represent their actual health status. Included are the person who has been convinced for years that he is dying and the person who has just come in for a routine checkup—yet the latter individual may be the one who actually has a life-threatening illness that is about to be discovered. For this reason one might decide to mark the beginning of the dying process from the time that the biomedical situation is recognized by a person with the appropriate background to make an accurate assessment. We might want to rely, then, on the physician's judgment. The physician, in turn, is likely to place some reliance on clinical and laboratory diagnostic procedures. "This person is dying" is a conclusion the physician will not reach in advance of the facts. From this perspective, then, the dying process begins when the physician has obtained and analyzed enough critical information to make such a judgment. The physician might suspect that the patient has been on a terminal trajectory for some time before the diagnostic evaluation was established. But this had not been "official" dying; it is only now that the person will be regarded in terms of this new status.

Becoming a dying patient can be compared in this sense with other rituals of transition. An adolescent male in a tribal society might have been as strong and brave last week as he is this week. But only now has he been accepted as an adult member of the community because he has in the intervening time passed through the necessary tests and rituals. He is a man because the tribal elders take him to be a man. A person becomes a dying patient because the physician takes him to be one.

Dying begins when the facts are communicated. There is a big difference, however, between the physician's prognosis and the patient's awareness. Perhaps it makes more sense to date the onset of the dying process from the moment at which the physician informs the patient. This would mean that there are *two* beginning points of the dying process, not counting the theoretical moment when the bodily changes shifted critically to a terminal course. It may seem peculiar to think of dying in this way. But the patient and the physician clearly are different people with very different frameworks for perceiving and interpreting the terminal process. Instead of jumbling together these two different outlooks, it is useful to respect both frames of references.

There is likely to be a lag between the physician's formulation of the diagnosis and prognosis and the time this is shared with the patient. Seldom do physicians break the news at the same instant they reach their conclusion. There may be a lag of days, weeks, or even months before the physician tells the patient precisely what has been found. Furthermore, sometimes the physician never does tell the patient. The patient who wants to discover the truth about his condition may have to find out in some other way. We cannot entirely depend, then, on the physician's communication as the definitive starting point of the dying process from the patient's standpoint. Why a physician might choose to communicate almost immediately or to delay the communication indefinitely is a question that all of us have the right to be curious about. But even when the physician does share the findings with the patient, can this be taken unequivocally as the onset of the dying process?

Dying begins when the patient realizes or accepts the facts. More than one nurse has returned from the bedside of a patient almost bursting with anger at the physician. "Why hasn't he leveled with this patient? This man is dying, and nobody has told him what's going on!" At times, this concern is well justified. The physician has not provided the terminally ill patient with a clear statement of his condition, whether it be the doctor's own failure of nerve in disclosing such information or some other reason that stands up better to scrutiny. But at other times, the patient's apparent lack of knowledge cannot be laid at the physician's doorstep. The patient was told, but he "didn't stay told." Somehow the patient was able to "forget" or misinterpret the central facts. He was not psychologically ready to accept the news.

We sometimes have difficulty in accepting news that changes our view of ourselves or the world, quite apart from tidings of terminal illness. It may take us a while to get our minds and feelings around a challenging new fact. This phenomenon sometimes occurs during the course of a terminal illness and should not really surprise us. Notice also that the physician's communication can be subtle or direct, couched in clear language or technical jargon, thorough or sketchy. Often we do not know precisely what the physician has told the patient, and, just as importantly, *how* he or she has told the patient. Was the patient given time to let the message sink in or did the physician turn and rush away? Did the physician say one thing with words and something else with facial expression and tone of voice?

The physician's ability to communicate can make a big difference in how quickly, accurately, and fully the message comes across. Howard G. Hogshead has compiled a succinct set of guidelines from his own experiences as well as those of other physicians. He recommends the following approach to physicians who are sensitive to this problem:

1. *Keep it simple.* Perhaps as a result of apprehension or uneasiness, there is a tendency to go into too many details and technicalities.
2. Ask yourself, *"What does this diagnosis mean to this patient?"* Many patients are simply unable to comprehend the nature of the diagnosis, in which case methods must be found to gradually educate them.
3. *Meet on "cool ground" first.* It is very unpleasant to walk in to meet people whom you have never met before, knowing you have to give them a piece of really bad news. It is always easier to handle if you have some earlier relationship to the patient or his family, and have some notion of their background and possible reaction to the news.
4. *Don't deliver all the news at once.* . . . People have a marvelous way of letting you know how much they are able to handle. . . . This may mean that the full disclosure has to be spread out over two or three sessions.
5. *Wait for questions.* A long pause will allow the question that tells you where to go next.
6. *Do not argue with denial.* . . . This usually leads to loss of rapport. . . . In general, the patient will "hear" the message when he is ready to accept it.
7. *Ask questions yourself.* Ask the patient to tell you what you have told him or ask him what it means. Oftentimes, you will be surprised at the answer. Or, ask the patients what the doctors at such-and-such a hospital have told him.
8. *Do not destroy all hope.* There are a hundred ways of handling this, and it requires real tact and experience to acquire the necessary skill.
9. *Do not say anything that is not true.* This would be the most cruel blow of all.[5,p.129]

There can be another time lag, then, between communication and realization of terminal illness, dependent on many factors including the physician's communication skills. A person is not dying *to himself* until he clearly realizes his situation. In this sense, the dying process cannot be dated from the medical prognosis or the act of communication, if there is one. We must be aware of the individual's thoughts and feelings. This often leads to disagreement as to whether or not a person knows. Disagreements can arise because some of us are better observers than others. Furthermore, some of us are looking for clues to support a particular opinion. Human behavior is complex enough to provide support for opposite opinions here as in other areas. A terminally ill person may talk about a relatively minor although distressing symptom. This leads me to assume that the patient is not aware of the more critical situation that threatens life. But *you* may notice instead that he slips into the past tense when talking about family and occupational life, suggesting that he does not project himself far into the future. We come to different conclusions, based on relevant but inadequate observation.

Disagreements may also arise because the terminally ill person, like most other people, behaves somewhat differently depending on the situation. The person may express a different attitude toward his or her illness when with a member of the immediate family than when with a physician, a colleague, or a stranger. Most of the health-care staff may be under the impression that the patient does not know, but one nurse may realize that he is keenly aware of the situation because he has selected her as the person with whom to share his most personal thoughts and feelings.

Additionally, the person's own estimation of his or her condition may shift from time to time. Avery D. Weisman, an outstanding clinical researcher in this area, speaks of "middle knowledge."[6] It is not necessarily a question of knowing or not knowing. The individual probably knows, suspects, or senses what is taking place in his body. But this awareness is not always on the same level of consciousness, nor does his overall interpretation of his condition remain constant. Depending on our relationship with the person and his total life situation at a particular time, we might come away either with or without the impression that he sees himself as dying.

Dying begins when nothing more can be done to preserve life. This is a pragmatic definition with important consequences for the care of very ill people. The physician may have known for weeks, months, or even years that this person was suffering from a condition that was likely to prove fatal but might have had good reason not to classify the person as dying. Despite the fact that a life-threatening process was at work, the person might have been functioning well and still have the prospect of going on for some time before experiencing incapacitating effects of illness. The physician might have been distinguishing between a dying and a doomed person. The healthy prisoner awaiting capital punishment would be another example of a doomed person, as would the occupants of a jetliner that is about to crash into the side of a mountain.

But more importantly, the physician may not have classified the person as dying despite the diagnostic signs because avenues of treatment remained open. The person was not doomed for certain. The physician would know that individuals with this particular condition have a certain probability of death within a particular range of time (e.g., 6 months, 5 years). Perhaps this patient would be one of the survivors. Furthermore, the probabilities themselves might shift as a new treatment mode is introduced or an existing mode is refined and improved. The physician can take into account the seriousness of a patient's condition through his or her knowledge of probable outcomes without necessarily having to classify the person as dying, at least not until all treatment possibilities have been exhausted.

Even with this pragmatic approach, however, there is room for diagreement. The internist or family physician may have a different orientation from the doctor who specializes in the particular condition that afflicts the patient. The specialist in chemotherapy and the surgeon may have different orientations toward treatment and prognosis, one of them being less ready in a particular circumstance to classify the person as dying. So long as there is one more procedure that might be carried out to halt or reverse the pathological process, some member of the medical team may decline to think of the patient as terminally ill.

On the current scene, much attention has been given to what appears to be the unnecessary or unwise prolongation of life when recovery seems to be out of the question. Vital functions such as circulation and respiration may be kept going through mechanical devices. Some people who see or hear about this kind of situation conclude either that the person is dying or that for all intents and purposes is already dead. The medical establishment is then criticized for overreaching its appropriate powers and functions. This can be seen as a situation in which at least some of the medical people still hesitate to classify the person as dying. The patient is seen as having a very high probability of death, but there is reluctance to conclude that the process cannot be halted or reversed.

As you can see, the definition of dying and its onset may be closely related to the definition of life. It may be linked more specifically to the definition of life as a human being, which implies more than physiological functioning. Medical personnel may disagree among themselves, just as we might, as to whether a person is dying who has passed a certain point of responsiveness or experiencing. Perhaps he or she should be considered dying when phenomenological life starts to fade and dead when phenomenological life appears to be extinguished. But perhaps the patient is neither dead nor dying, because the mechanical life-support system has stabilized his condi-

WHAT ARE YOU READY TO HEAR?
A thought exercise

Guidelines have been offered for the physician who wants to communicate sensitively and effectively when there is "bad news" to convey. But what about the recipient, the listener?

Suppose that you have a medical problem and have undergone a series of physical examinations and laboratory tests. You will be seeing your physician soon. Right now you do not know the nature of your ailment, its severity, likely outcome, or recommended method of treatment. But you will be seeing your physician soon, and he or she may have this information available.

The "news" might be good. But it might also be the case that you are afflicted with a life-threatening condition. This condition itself could range from one with a high probability of lethal outcome, to one that, although posing a definite life threat, might respond well to treatment.

Develop guidelines for your own interaction and communication with the physician! Think carefully about what you might say and do that would (1) help the physician to be most effective in communicating whatever information is available to be shared and also (2) accord with your own personality, values, and mood. Formulate at least five guiding principles for yourself and indicate briefly why you have established these.

Guideline: _____

_____

Basis: _____

_____

Guideline: _____

_____

Basis: _____

_____

Guideline: _____

_____

Basis: _____

_____

Guideline: _____

_____

Basis: _____

_____

Guideline: _____

_____

Basis: _____

_____

tion, even though at a very low, vegetative level.

The other extreme has been relatively neglected in the past few years because of the attention given to the dubious prolongation of vegetative existence. Yet over the centuries there has been more concern about the hasty judgment that a person was on a terminal course that could not be modified. The physician, or somebody else on the scene in an influential position, might prematurely conclude that the person was dying and that nothing could be done to alter the outcome. About a century ago, for example, there was public alarm in both Europe and the United States that people actually were being pronounced dead and subsequently buried while life still lingered within them.[7,pp.132ff] Even short of this extreme, the health-care establishment has been second-guessed on occasion because of an apparent willingness to give up life-fostering efforts too soon. An ambulance driver with limited training and supervision, for example, may judge that there is nothing to be done for the accident victim or comatose person he is bringing to the emergency room. This decision is likely to be made even more quickly if the victim has alcohol on his breath, appears disheveled and poorly groomed, is of advanced age, or belongs to an ethnic or racial group toward which attitudes of discrimination exist. By words and actions, the ambulance worker may indicate that this individual does not require high-priority attention from the busy emergency-room staff and thus deprive the person of his last chance for survival.

The onset of dying can be interpreted as starting either too soon or too late, in terms of the practical consequences that flow from this judgment. The judgment is made too soon, for example, if it results in a failure to take action that might lead to recovery. As late as the eighteenth century in a city as sophisticated as London, special efforts had to be made to persuade

the establishment that victims of drowning could be restored to life and health by prompt emergency treatment.[8] Today it is perhaps even more difficult to determine, with certainty, when it is too soon to suspend active treatment in certain disorders. By contrast, we might consider that the classification of a person as dying is made too late if painful or isolating treatments are continued beyond realistic hope of success while preventing the person from living his final days as he might have chosen if the terminal prognosis was clearly accepted.

Fears and misperceptions

Differences among perceptions of the dying process can be extreme. Consider a few examples: (1) a child believes that his mother will die soon because she donated blood to the Red Cross; (2) a woman has discovered a lump on her breast and is seized with the panicked conviction that she is dying; (3) a man goes through a GI series (a diagnostic procedure) and decides that he must be dying, because he knows somebody who went through these procedures and did die; (4) as a woman is prepared for surgery, she becomes pale and withdrawn, feeling that she will start to die as soon as the anesthesia takes effect; (5) a man has been in the hospital longer than he expected; as a priest enters the room, he suddenly thinks with alarm that his days are numbered.

In all of these instances, it may be only the particular individual mentioned who believes that the dying process is at work. The health personnel know differently. The difference may reflect level of medical education and access to the facts. Poor communication and unexamined personal fears may also contribute to the misinterpretations. Adults might not think of the possibility that some routine procedure could be seen in a more menacing aspect by a child, and the child may keep his anxieties to himself unless a supportive adult notices his distress. It is easy for many of us to assume that hypodermic needles, medications, x-ray examinations, and other familiar procedures are understood and accepted by everybody. But there is the occasional person, not only the child, who misinterprets such procedures and suffers in consequence.

Adults whose knowledge of their bodies is undependable may be overtaken by anxiety when something goes wrong. The principle that a little knowledge is a dangerous thing can apply, as in the premature self-diagnosis that a lump in the breast means cancer, and that cancer means dying and death. Fortunately, many health personnel recognize how concerned a person is likely to be when discovering a possible sign of cancer and will take care to explain and reduce inappropriate alarm. But it may be less evident to everybody that the person who is being prepared for a fairly routine surgical procedure is picturing himself at death's door. The death fear of a woman about to undergo a cholecystectomy may be as intense and disorganizing as that experienced by a person who does in fact face a high-risk procedure.

Some people have limited awareness of a life-threatening disease that actually exists, while others perceive themselves as dying when the situation is not that critical. The wise physician and nurse make an effort to learn what the patient himself believes his condition to be. The family that encourages open communication on all important topics will also reduce the likelihood that one of its members would persist in a serious misinterpretation of his health status.

A few reflections

We have seen that there is no simple, infallible answer to the question, "When does dying begin?" Seldom is there a clear, well-established moment when everybody in the situation, including of course the patient, knows for certain that the condition has become terminal, irreversible. Most often, classification of a person as dying is a psychosocial process. It reflects the background, information, needs, and motives of the person who is making the classification, as well as the objective facts themselves. Because each person has his own framework, it is not surprising that the onset of the dying process often registers at a different point in time in the minds of the various people involved. The patient for example may begin dying to himself when he loses a certain function, for example, the ability to move around on his own or to control bladder and bowel. This self-definition may or may not be shared by others. If it is out of phase with medical judgment, this could lead to behavior that is mutually puzzling. Why did this cooperative and resilient patient suddenly withdraw and turn aside from treatment? Sometimes it is because he has privately redefined himself as a dying person. The physician may initiate a shift in the situation by coming to an implicit conclusion and not sharing it directly with the patient. The patient may then feel frightened and abandoned. He learns that his condition is terminal or hopeless by indirect but convincing observations, the subtle shifts in what is and what is not being done for him, and how frequently the physician shows up or looks him in the eyes.

To say that we should try to understand each person's point of view is not to say that we must refrain from criticism or attempts to change the situation. Rather, our attempts to improve the care of a seriously ill person are likely to be more successful if we can see the situation from several standpoints in addition to our own. We might, for example, recognize the appreciable differences that exist even within the medical profession. Much of the commentary and research in this area has addressed itself to the doctor in general. There have been numerous critiques of the physician's lack of skill, sensitivity, or personal strength in relating to the dying person.[9-11] These critiques deserve to be taken seriously by the medical profession.

However, a careful look at the specific role and problems faced by physicians in a variety of specialty areas brings out differences in the definition of the dying process and in doctor-patient interaction. Rea, Greenspoon, and Spilka[12] studied the attitudes and practices of 151 physicians who represented a broad spectrum of specialty areas. They found that physicians who encounter many terminally ill people in their practice were the ones most likely to inform their patients fully, regardless of what the family desires. They were also most likely to spend extra time with dying patients. The researchers had the impression that the physicians with experience in working with terminally ill people were more open and compassionate than physicians in general.

Pediatricians and cardiologists were less likely than some of the other physicians to share a terminal diagnosis directly with their patients. They relied more on family members to communicate on this subject. But Rea and colleagues point out that

the authoritative role of parents in all matters relating to children might explain the presence of pediatrics here. Cardiologists repeatedly stated that they could not be as sure of a terminal diagnosis as their fellows in other specialties, and this perception may lead to the feeling that the family should be the prime decision making group.[12,p.299]

In other words, even when a physician does not personally and fully provide the terminal diagnosis to the patient, there may be other factors that should be taken into consideration besides the possibility of insensitivity.

This research group, like others before them, did find considerable resistance on the part of the physicians to dealing with death-related questions. They noted that "many if not most of the physicians were deeply troubled by

the topic." Yet there was also the impression that most of the physicians studied were sensitive and compassionate: "the humanity of these physicians cannot be questioned." Physician as well as patient, then, have subjective involvement in the dying process. By recognizing both the objective and the subjective side of each person's view of the dying process we are more apt to develop a constructive perspective rather than one that seeks out villains or scapegoats.

Health-care provider and patient may also be influenced by ideas and anxieties that are current on the larger social scene. Susan Sontag,[12a] for example, points out that not many years ago the diagnosis of tuberculosis was often received as though both a death sentence and a scandal. The physician had to take into account that it was not just a matter of communicating a medical diagnosis with (at the time) serious and perhaps lethal implications. He or she was also confronting the patient with something bordering on sinfulness or criminality: it was "wrong" to have this mysterious ailment. When such an idea prevailed throughout society, it added greatly to the distress of the person who had a form of disgrace to experience as well as the possibility of dying. Tuberculosis no longer is associated with the myths and metaphors described by Sontag, but cancer has taken on a similar, although not identical, role. She compares cancer with another major life-threatening illness today:

Someone who has had a coronary is at least as likely to die of another one within a few years as someone with cancer is likely to die soon from cancer. But no one thinks of concealing the truth from a cardiac patient: there is nothing shameful about a heart attack. Cancer patients are lied to, not just because the disease is (or is thought to be) a death sentence, but because it is felt to be obscene—in the original meaning of that word: ill-omened, abominable, repugnant to the senses. Cardiac disease implies a weakness, trouble, failure that is mechanical; there is no disgrace, nothing of the taboo that once surrounded people afflicted with TB and still surrounds those who have cancer. The metaphors attached to TB and to cancer imply living processes of a particularly resonant and horrid kind.[12a,p.8-9]

It should be made clear that Sontag is not declaring that either tuberculosis or cancer is necessarily horrid or fatal, not is she unaware of continued shifts in our attitudes, especially toward cancer. The main point is that society tends to attach differential images and feelings to various types of life-threatening disorder, and these should also be taken into account in understanding what the individual is likely to experience on learning that he or she is suffering from a particular disease process.

DYING TRAJECTORIES: FROM BEGINNING TO END

We have been exploring the *onset* of the dying process as interpreted by the various people involved. The *end* of the dying process usually takes place in a hospital or nursing home. This was not always the case. It was easier to think of birth and death as natural events that belonged primarily to the family in years gone by. Now it is more typical to think of birth and death as events not only shared with but presided over by experts. Something has been gained and something has been lost in this shift.

Recently there have been indications of a movement to restore a more personal and humane quality to both birth and death. Ideally, this would retain many of the positive achievements developed by health establishment but place them in the service of human values. Dr. Frederic Le Boyer's approach to welcoming an infant across the threshold into the postnatal world is a good example of providing a favorable entry scene.[13] The hospice movement (Chapter 13) is a good example of the effort to create a more favorable exit scene. Those who are concerned only with birth or only with death may not be aware that this warming current is making itself felt in *both* areas.

But the reality for many people today is that the later phases of the dying process will occur in a traditional hospital setting. This suggests that attention be given to the course of dying as it is interpreted by hospital personnel. Barney Glaser, Anselm Strauss, and their collaborators have carried out what may be called a classic study in this area. They observed dying as a social phenomenon in six medical facilities in the San Francisco area. Most of their conclusions are reported in a pair of books, *Awareness of Dying*[14] and *Time for Dying*.[15] The latter book is of particular relevance here, although both are highly recommended.

It is important to understand the perspective and methodology of these researchers. Their field research approach gave Glaser and Strauss the opportunity to move rather freely through the hospital environment. They watched doctors and nurses at work and also in their more informal moments. They sat in on staff meetings. They asked a few questions here and there and conducted more lengthy and formal interviews. They absorbed what was happening in the hospital both day and night. Theirs was, in other words, a flexible, semistructured approach that placed a premium on the investigator's observational skills and ability to become intimately involved in the environment without making his or her presence too disruptive. This field-research approach offers the opportunity to acquire a wide range of information and impressions and obtain a general feel for what is taking place. It also offers the opportunity to organize these impressions into a more objective perspective than the people in the environment themselves are likely to possess. Each physician, nurse, and patient is involved in his or her own functioning; the field researcher can put the entire pattern together, if they are skillful enough.

We should also keep in mind that the field

researcher does not have the responsibility for patient care that occupies so much of the energies of the hospital staff. Furthermore, the researcher is not the huband, wife, or child of a dying patient nor himself terminally ill. This emotional distance gives the field researcher a unique role. The findings may strike us as too scientific or cold and aloof. This does not necessarily mean that the research lacks human compassion any more than the physicians and nurses do but simply that he is taking advantage of his distinctive viewpoint to see things the way that others with their more involved needs and function cannot. This note on methodology is intended as a reminder that observations and interpretations of the dying process should always be considered in terms of their origins, angles of vision, and limitations.

Glaser and Strauss organize many of their observations around the concept of *dying trajectories*. All dying processes take time; furthermore, all have a certain shape through time. The combination of duration and shape can be seen, and even graphed, as a trajectory. The dying trajectory for one person might best be represented as a straight downhill line; for somebody else, the trajectory might be represented instead as slowly vacillating (getting better, getting worse) over a long period of time, and so on. The Glaser and Strauss approach to understanding dying trajectories is consistent with what has already been presented in this chapter:

Neither duration nor shape is a purely objective physiological property. They are both perceived properties; their dimensions depend on when the perceiver initially *defines* someone as dying and on his *expectations* of how that dying will proceed. Dying trajectories themselves, then, are perceived courses of dying rather than the actual courses. This distinction is readily evident in the type of trajectory that involves a short reprieve from death. This reprieve represents an unexpected deferment of death. On the other hand, in a lingering death by-

standers may expect a faster death than actually occurs.[15,p.6]

Certainty and time

According to Glaser and Strauss, the staff must answer two questions for itself about every patient whose life is in jeopardy: Will he die? If so, when? These are the questions of certainty and time. The questions are important because the staff tends to take its treatment and attitudinal clues from the answers that are developed. In general, it is easier for the staff to organize itself around the patient when the answers are clear. A hospital relies much on standard operating procedures. It is uncomfortable and disrupting when a patient's condition does not lend itself to straightforward expectations such as "This man will recover" or "This woman will die eventually, but not for some time."

We are reminded by Glaser and Strauss that the time framework can vary a great deal depending on circumstances. In the emergency room the staff's uncertainty about a patient's recovery or death can change to certainty in just a few minutes. The fate of a premature baby may be determined in a few hours or a few days. But the outlook for a cancer patient may remain indeterminate for months.

Taken together, certainty and time yield four types of death expectations from the staff's viewpoint (which is not to say that all staff members necessarily hold the same expectations): "(1) certain death at a known time, (2) certain death at an unknown time, (3) uncertain death but a known time when certainty will be established, and (4) uncertain death and an unknown time when the question will be resolved." The detailed observations by the Glaser-Strauss team suggest the staff interaction with patients is closely related to the particular expectations they have formed about time and certainty of death. Whether or not the staff happens to be correct in its expectations, the kinds of experiences it provides for the patient are influenced by its expectations. Especially important are situations in which staff expectations change. One of the examples given is that of a physician's decision to stop further blood transfusions. This is a clue to others that implies there is no hope for recovery. Yet the nurses may decline to take this hint and continue instead to do everything within their power to give the patient still another chance.

This is a useful example of how subtle the expectation and communication process can be. As Glaser and Strauss put it:

Since the doctor has said nothing official, even nurses who believe the patient is dying can still give him an outside chance and stand ready to save him. They remain constantly alert to counterclues. "Everybody is simply waiting," said one nurse. If the doctor had indicated that the patient would die within the day, nurses would have ceased their constant watch for counterclues and reduced their efforts to save him, concentrating instead on giving comfort to the last, with no undue prolonging of life.[15,p.11]

It is possible, then, for one member of the treatment team to come to a conclusion but still leave room for others to follow an alternative course. In some situations this disparity might interfere with systematic care. But in other situations it might offer that extra opportunity for favorable outcome that would have been denied by a more insistent and authoritarian decision. The example given here shows the death system in action. The physician has decided that the *prevention* function of the death system cannot be achieved, but the nurses manages to continue with the *caring-comforting* function while still maintaining the possibility of a reprieve.

In classical socioanthropological language, Glaser and Strauss see the same situation as an example of "status passage." Society, in this case the health personnel on the scene, must decide whether or not this person should be redefined. Once he was a person. Later he became a patient. Is he now to be redefined as a *dying* patient? Dying and death are distinctive, yet the sociologists have a point when they make comparisons with other processes in which the individual's status alters in the eyes of society. It is not within the scope of this book to pursue the parallels, but it is possible our understanding of the dying process would be improved by a careful comparison of dying trajectories with other status-change phenomena (e.g., from youth to adult, from worker to retiree).

We will now consider three dying trajectories observed by Glaser and Strauss: "lingering," "the expected quick trajectory," and "the unexpected quick trajectory."

Lingering

When life is fading slowly and gradually toward death, there is a characteristic tempo and emphasis on the part of the care givers. Custodial services may be more prominent than in vigorous and aggressive treatment. Many physicians and some nurses do not seem to find the care of the chronic patient very challenging or rewarding. Ambitious young professionals may spend some time working with patients who are on a lingering trajectory, but most of the care is provided by lower echelon, and usually rather low-paid, staff.

There is seldom a dramatic rescue scene. The staff tries to keep the patient comfortable and viable on a day-to-day basis. But when he is clearly failing, the staff is inclined to believe that is has already done what should have been done and that the patient has earned his death after a long downhill process. In the geriatric ward, for example, the apparition of specialists pouring in from all over the hospital and a battery of heroic measures being placed in position is quite uncommon. A quiet fading out seems to be expected and accepted by the staff as fit conclusion to the lingering trajectory. Perhaps the death that terminates a lingering trajectory is more acceptable because the person has been considered socially dead for some time. Even within the institution itself, some patients may be considered more alive than others. Glaser and Strauss observed, as a number of other researchers have also noted, that staff become attached to some patients very closely as they interact with them through the months. Yet, although the staff is likely to feel sad about the patients' passing, this reaction is held in check by the belief that their lives no longer had much value to either themselves or society. In one way or another, death is seen as an appropriate event when it happens to a person who has been on the lingering trajectory. For every patient who has somehow attracted the special attention and sympathy of staff members, however, there are other who have remained until the day of their death impersonal beings without distinct identities and characteristics.

According to Glaser and Strauss, the patient on a lingering trajectory seldom has much control over the management of his condition. Family members also seem to leave it all to the staff, especially as time goes on. In fact, the frequency and duration of visits from family members characteristically falls of when the lingering nature of the patient's trajectory has become established. Other patients usually do not show much response when a death occurs; often it was questionable whether or not they were even aware of the death. Furthermore, the slowly dying person usually does not speak of final things to family and friends. Glaser and Strauss pass along these last two observations with the clear awareness that what they have seen might not be all that transpires. We will report other observations on the response of terminally ill patients to their own condition and the reactions of other patients later in this chapter.

In overview, the lingering trajectory most often does not produce obvious disruptions in the environment. Staff tend to assume that the patient himself also moves rather gently toward death. "These patients drift out of the world," say Glaser and Strauss, "sometimes almost like imperceptibly melting snowflakes. The organization of work emphasizes comfort care and custodial routine, and is complemented by a sentimental order emphasizing patience and inevitability."[15,p.64]

But the picture is not always so tranquil and orderly. Occasionally there is a patient, family member, or even a doctor or nurse who does not accept the impending death. Glaser and Strauss also noticed incidents in which a person would upset and confuse the staff by showing too much emotion or making a commotion after a patient had died. Perhaps strong reactions to a patient's death challenged the staff's customary assumption that the social loss of a lingerer did not amount to much.

More could be said about the lingering trajector, from both the work of Glaser and Strauss and the work of others. We could notice the difference, for example, between the person who is gradually failing over a long period of time *in an expected way* and the person who is taking *too* long to die. The patience of family and staff may be strained when a patient neither makes a recovery nor dies more or less on schedule. And we could notice how a lingering trajectory gives both the patient and his family *time*, time to grow accustomed to the idea of dying, time to make plans, time to work through old conflicts and misunderstanding, time to review the kind of life he has lived, and so on.

The process of dying, if we could ever agree on a reasonable definition, seems to take more time for more people today than in past years. We are more likely to avoid or recover from acute diseases but, then, more likely to develop chronic conditions that directly and indirectly lead us toward death. The lingering trajectory is not the image of dying that usually seizes the imagination of the media. However, it is the reality of dying for many of us and therefore well worth our attention.

The expected quick trajectory

Glaser and Strauss maintain that the American hospital system is best prepared to cope with emergency situations. Human and technological resources are mustered most splendidly when there is an acute life-death crisis. The emergency room, the intensive care unit (ICU), and the perpetual readiness of specialists to rush to the scene are life-saving resources we have become accustomed to expect from the modern medical facility.

Time truly is of the essence when a patient is defined as being on an expected quick trajectory. The staff organizes itself with precision to make the most effective use of the time remaining on the side of life. This is in marked contrast to the more leisurely, drifting pattern that surrounds the patient on a lingering trajectory. As the staff devotes itself to the patient there may be a series of redefinitions in their minds; for example, "He is out of immediate danger but probably will not survive for an extended period of time" changing to "I think he is on the road to complete recovery."

Several types of quick trajectories were observed. Each involved a different pattern of interaction with the staff. In a *pointed trajectory*, the patient is exposed to a very risky procedure, one that might either save his life or itself result in death. In this situation the staff often has enough advance time to organize itself properly. The patient may have the opportunity to exercise some control and options (share some precious minutes with a loved one, make some decisions or requests, etc.). The *danger-period trajectory* is one that involves more watching and waiting. The question is whether or not the person will be able to survive a stressful experience such as high-risk surgery or a major heart attack. The patient

may be unconscious or only partially aware of his surroundings as compared with the alert state that one might possess in the pointed trajectory. The danger period may vary between a few hours to a few days. This is the type of situation in which the family may remain at bedside or in the corridor, with doctors and nurses maintaining close vigilance all the while.

The *crisis trajectory* imposes still another condition on both the patient and those concerned for him. The patient is not in acute danger at the moment. Perhaps he will not be in acute danger at all, but his life might suddenly be threatened in an hour, tomorrow, or at almost any time. This is an especially tense situation. It will persist until the patient's condition improves enough to place him out of danger or until the crisis actually arrives and rescue efforts are made.

Different from all of these is the *will-probably-die* type of *trajectory*. The staff believes that nothing effective can be done. Essentially the aim is to keep the patient as comfortable as possible and wait for the end to come, usually within a few hours or days. As examples of this type of trajectory, Glaser and Strauss note the person returning from unsuccessful surgery, the accident victim who is beyond saving, and the individual whose suicide attempt failed to end life immediately but did place him on a terminal course.

These are not the only types of expected quick trajectories observed by Glaser and Strauss, but they serve to illustrate the range of experiences and situations that exist even within the special group of people who face death in near prospect. There are also some common problems that arise in connection with the expected quick trajectory. The family, for example, is likely to be close by the patient. This confronts the staff with more implicit demand for interaction and communication. What should those people in the waiting room be told? Who should tell them? Is this the time to prepare them for the bad news, or can it be postponed a little longer? Should all the family be told at once, or is there one person in particular who should be relied on to grasp the situation first? The staff must somehow come to terms with the needs of the family while still carrying out its treatment activities. Obviously, this is a situation to challenge the staff's judgment and interpersonal skills.

Hospital policy can lighten the responsibility of the individual staff member. He or she may be relieved to invoke rules and regulations instead of making a personal decision. However, restrictive regulations can make it difficult for the staff to accede to the family's wishes. Some families need a sense of close physical involvement with the dying person, for example, which may complicate the staff's pattern of management. A relative might even topple over life-supporting equipment or faint and need medical attention himself, as Glaser and Strauss observed.

What are the salient features of the expected quick trajectory situation? We see the urgency of time, the intense organization of treatment efforts, the rapidly shifting expectations, and the volatile, sensitive staff-family interface. In the midst of this pressure errors can be made. This can include, as Glaser and Strauss note, attempts to save a patient from a disease he does not have. A person may arrive at the hospital in critical condition but with no readily available medical history to guide the staff. The pressure of time may then force medical personnel to proceed on the basis of an educated guess rather than secure knowledge. This contrasts with the lingering trajectory, which provides the staff with abundant time and opportunity to comprehend the patient's condition and anticipate possible crises.

There is another observation about the expected quick trajectory that is especially important. The physical condition of the patient proved to be only one of the factors that determined the nature of the trajectory. In some instances, whether or not there was a fighting chance to save the patient's life depended on the available resources in the particular hospital or even the particular ward. The lack of an oxygen tank on the ward or of a kidney machine in the hospital would make the difference between the will-probably-die type of trajectory and one with more hope. Even more significant, perhaps, was the observation that the *perceived social value* of the endangered person could spell the difference between an all-out rescue attempt and a do-nothing orientation. This is expecially apt to happen when the medical team has pressing decisions to make about who will receive emergency treatment first or be given the benefit of life-support apparatus that is in short supply. "When a patient is not 'worth' having a chance," say Glaser and Strauss, "he may in effect be given none." By contrast, when a prominent person enters the hospital on a quick trajectory, or suddenly "turns bad" in the hospital, the implicit definition that he is dying may be set aside in favor of an intensive campaign of heroic precedures. The person is considered too important to die. Glaser and Strauss believe that at least in some instances, the difference in social value the staff attributes to a quick trajectory patient is literally the difference between life and death. The psychosocial definition of dying is no less critical at the end of the process than it is at the onset. This also reminds us again that social quirks that consider one "type" of person more "important" than another (whether on basis of age, sex, race, economic status or whatever) can play a direct role in the death system, as when quick decisions must be made about priority and extent of life-sustaining effort.

The unexpected quick trajectory

The significance of the interpersonal setting in which dying takes place is emphasized again by the unexpected quick trajectory. Personnel in the emergency room, for example, expect to be called on for immediate life-or-death measures. The experienced ER team adjusts quickly to situations that would immobilize most other people. But in other areas of the same hospital the staff has a pattern of functioning and a belief system that is less attuned to a sudden turn of events. "The appearance of the unexpected quick trajectory consitutes crisis. On these wards there is no general preparation for quick dying trajectories—at least of certain kinds—and the work and sentimental orders of the ward 'blow up' when they occur."[15,p.121]

What Glaser and Strauss are talking about here may still appear peculiar or mysterious to those who assume that hospitals function strictly according to rational and utilitarian principles. The field researchers are taking into account that hospital personnel, like the rest of us, need to maintain a frame of reference that can get them through the challenges of their work. Over the years, both the hospital and its individual personnel develop a relatively comfortable and reassuring framework for interpreting and anticipating experience. I have often come across the attitude, for example, that "there are sick people here . . . but nobody is going to die . . . on my ward . . . at least, not today."

Perhaps the concept of "middle knowledge"[16] should be applied to personnel as well as to terminally ill patients. The staff in non-emergency areas *know* but do not *believe* that a life-or-death situation might arise at any moment. It would be too stressful for them to function every day with that expectation in mind, an expectation that is also at variance with the kind of care they are called upon to deliver on a more routine basis. In this sense, something does "blow up" when a patient unexpectedly enters a crisis phase on the "wrong" ward—it is the staff's security-giving myth of an orderly and manageable universe that is at least temporarily punctured.

Some unexpected deaths prove more disturbing than others to the staff. The medically interesting case is one of the most frequent examples. The staff is more likely to be taken aback and to regret the death of a patient who presented unusual features to them. Personnel also tend to be affected more by the death of a patient whose life they had tried especially hard to save. They see their unusual investment in time and energy fading away. This is not the same as mourning the loss of a patient as a person. Instead it is the loss of the staff's effort that is felt as a blow. Glaser and Strauss report that it is the "poor physician who tried so hard" that receives the sympathy of other staff members rather than the patient himself. The patient may never have come across to the staff as an individual human being during the course of the intensive life-saving efforts. The patient who dies for the wrong reasons also dismays and alarms the staff. Treatment may have been focused on one critical aspect of the patient's condition, but death may have come through a different route.

A major theme running through observations of the unexpected quick trajectory is the staff's need to shield itself against surprise, to maintain as far as possible an orientation that everything is under control or as expected. This is worth a moment's reflection. How much of the emotional energy of medical personnel is diverted to this purpose? Does the need to maintain such a powerful self-protecting orientation deprive the staff of the energy and flexibility they might otherwise bring to the treatment process? It cannot be easy to respond fully to the demands of the dying situation, or even to perceive the situation clearly, when one's own security is under attack. Also, professionally trained people who have reason to expect crisis situations do not necessarily cope with the terminally ill person more successfully than the lay person. The entrenched, well-practiced, institutionally supported defenses of the physician or nurse may give way, or be dangerously exaggerated, when reality overwhelms the sense of control.[17] Perhaps this makes it even more understandable that the turn for the worse in a patient's condition might immobilize or disorganize a spouse, parent, child, or close friend. Not only is his relationship to the threatened person much more intense and intimate, but the lay person may lack the professional's expertise in concealing vulnerability.

Unfortunately, the hospital itself at times precipitates an unexpected quick trajectory. Glaser and Strauss give such examples as confusion in the mobilization of treatment resources, the turning of attention away from some patients in order to concentrate on one urgent case, accidents attributable to carelessness or poor safety practices in the institution, and a variety of specific problems that can arise when a hospital is seriously understaffed.

The combination of time pressure and the surprise factor can lead to what Glaser and Strauss term "institutional evasions." Essentially, there is not the time and opportunity to make the moves that are officially required in the situation, and the available staff must improvise a response or use an alternative approach that could expose them to reprimand or even to legal action. There may not be time to bring a qualified physician to the scene, for example. Yet nurses on the ward may have the experience and skill to engage in life-saving procedures. If they proceed to do things that officially require a physician's personal direction, then they have exposed themselves to serious criticism, but if they do not use their skills promptly, the patient may die before the physician has time to arrive and size up the situation. There are many variations of this situation. The departures or evasions of institutional rules may be minor or substantial. The institution itself may choose to notice or ignore the infractions. One extra source of tension with the unexpected quick trajectory, then, is the conflict between doing what seems to be best

for the patient immediately and abiding strictly by all hospital regulations.

LEARNING FROM THE PSYCHOLOGICAL AUTOPSY

In the preceding section we explored some dimensions of the dying process as seen through the eyes of a sociologically oriented field-research team. Many of their observations have also been made by clinicians and other investigators, but Glaser and Strauss were in an unusually good position to see the whole institutional system at work. Now we will explore, more briefly, some aspects of the dying process as seen from a different methodological approach, the *psychological autopsy*. There are many similar findings, but we will concentrate on some phenomena that show up more clearly with the psychological autopsy technique.

The psychological autopsy as a method

Psychologists Edwin Shneidman and Norman Farberow[18] introduced the psychological autopsy (PA) as a method of establishing the *intentionality* of people who died under ambiguous circumstances. Was this a suicide? An accident? The result of an unexpected complication of an illness? A homicide? Families and acquaintances of the deceased were interviewed, and efforts were made by a multidisciplinary team to reconstruct the victim's lifestyle and determine to what extent, if any, the individual participated in bringing about his own death.

The method later was modified by Weisman and Kastenbaum to study a broader spectrum of people who died in the hospital situation.[19,20] It is now used for clinical and teaching as well as research purposes in a number of settings throughout the world.[16] The first systematic use of the modified procedure was in a hospital for the aged where a larger study of dying and death was already in progress. In common with the somatic autopsy or postmortem, the PA at-

---

OUTLINE OF PSYCHOLOGICAL AUTOPSY TOPICS*

1. *Final illness*
   a. What was the patient's terminal illness?
   b. Did this illness differ substantially from the admission diagnoses?
   c. Was the death expected or unexpected at this time?
   d. Was death sudden or gradual?
   e. Was autopsy permission granted?

2. *Preterminal period*
   a. What was the patient's mental status and level of consciousness prior to the terminal illness?
   b. What happened that drew attention to mental, physical, or social changes?
   c. Did the patient ever refer openly to death and dying or give other indications of going downhill?
   d. Other that direct declarations about death, were there unusual utterances or behavior that may have served as premonitions?
   e. What was the extent and nature of his relationship with other people during the preterminal period?

3. *Hospital course*
   a. What was the extent and nature of the patient's relationship with people (other patients, staff, relatives, vistors, etc.) during his overall hospital course?
   b. How was the patient regarded by those who were in contact with him?
   c. What personal problems or crises developed, and how were they met?

4. *Prehospital situation*
   a. What was the patient's medical condition and mental status at the time of admission?
   b. What were the medical, social, and personal circumstances that led to hospitalization?
   c. What was the patient's attitude toward his admission?

*From Weisman, A. D., & Kastenbaum, R. *The psychological autopsy: a study of the terminal phase of life.* Community Mental Health Journal Monograph. New York: Behavioral Publications, Inc., 1968.

tempts to reconstruct and coordinate all relevant information, contribute insights that will improve care of the living, and advance basic research and understanding. Special attention is given to distinguishing between what staff and family assume or hope and the actual events and experiences that comprise the terminal phase of life. The investigators here are concerned not only with the deceased patient's intentionality, but with the entire sociomedical context of death, including the quality of the life that preceded the death.

The research team develops background information about the deceased and then conducts an intensive case conference in which there is participation from as many people who worked with the patient as possible: nurses, social workers, chaplains, occupational therapists, physicians, volunteers, and so on. The proceedings are tape-recorded and analyzed. In reconstructing the patient's life and death, the PA moves backward from the moment of cessation to the course of the individual's career before entering the hospital. A very general outline of the topics explored is given in the boxed material. In practice, many more specific inquires are generated from the discussion.

Although the PA was developed primarily as a method for generating new knowledge about dying and death, it also provides an opportunity for staff to express their feelings and exchange perspectives. People who might never have shared their reactions to a particular death have the opportunity to open up and to learn from each other. At times the PA serves a therapeutic function for the staff, although there are also occasions when it uncovers disturbing phenomena that leave the participants with newly perceived problems to solve.

Many of the PA participants have played key roles in the care of the deceased person, while others are limited to a research and evaluation function. This interplay is one of the factors that gives the PA a distinctive perspective on the dying process. The fact that it is not conducted until after the death but makes use of all available information previously obtained also gives the PA a distinctive orientation. We would expect, and we do find, some types of information and insights turning up that are less visible with other methods.

Is death noticed?

As mentioned earlier, Glaser and Strauss found that patients usually did not show much response to the death of one of their peers and that the dying person himself usually did not discuss this topic with the staff. The PA method places a different perspective on these observations. Attention will be limited here to PA research conducted in the geriatric hospital situation.

A general pattern was discovered in which staff turned off attempts by patients to discuss impending death. It was not surprising that verbal communication on this subject was limited; the aged men and women quickly learned that comments of this type were unwelcome. Staff tended to reassure patients that they were not going to die, rapidly changed the subject, or even flatly contradicted the patient: "You don't mean that." Not all staff members followed this pattern, but it was more common than not for patient's tentative explorations of death-related topics to be rebuffed or set aside.

However, the retrospective integration of information accomplished by the PA often indicated that the patients persisted in finding some way to express their awareness of impending death. Participants in the PA eventually learned to read clues that previously escaped their attention. One clue, for example, was the decision of some patients to give away prized possessions. A patient considered to be in no immediate danger of death would visit a friend in the hospital and give him a radio or television set, or perhaps his favorite pair of slippers. The staff had noticed this action, but it did not register as a possible leave-taking behavior until it was later connected with the fact the patient died just a day or two later.

Some patients spoke openly or symbolically about death even though ignored by staff. This was the case with a 75-year-old former stonemason. He had gradually lost some of the vigor he had shown earlier in his hospital stay, but otherwise appeared to be in reasonable condition. One morning he asked for directions to a cemetery near his former home. Although he made the direct statement that he was expecting the undertaker, this was not taken up by the staff as a clue to impending death or even as a topic worth exploring. It was just a statement that didn't make much sense. On another occasion he told several people that his boss (going back many years, in reality) had called for him; he was supposed to help dig graves for eight people. This time the delusion persisted. He stayed around the ward so he could be found when the people came to take him to the cemetery. Two days before he died, the patient had several teeth extracted. He then told staff that it was time to call his sisters, about whom he had never spoken previously. His death came as a surprise to the staff although, apparently, not to himself. Cause of death was determined to be cerebral thrombosis. Despite all the clues this man had given, no notice had been taken. His "crazy talk" seemed even less crazy when, during the PA, it was learned that he had outlived seven siblings—his reference to digging a grave for eight people no longer seemed so arbitrary.

It was learned not only that many patients did communicate about their death concerns but that it was fairly common for people to anticipate their demise before the staff had any reason to do so. This could have been one of the reasons for the patient-staff communication problems. The patient may have sensed himself to be starting on a relatively quick trajectory, while the staff considered him to be on a lingering, almost stable, trajectory. In retrospect, many staff members were amazed to discover how many clues of patient awareness or concern about death had passed them by.

The implicit staff attitude that death communications were not welcome also played a role in the response of other patients to a death. This was reinforced by unofficial hospital practices that tended to cover up death. Patients often were placed in the position of having to guess what happened to the person who used to sleep in the bed on the other side of the room; the hospital wasn't offering any information. The PA team came across many examples of response to another patient's death, usually of an indirect nature. When a patient had died on the "wrong" ward, for example, neither patient nor staff were likely to initiate discussion of the event. But during the next several nights there would be an increase in insomnia and mid-night confusional states. Patients found various reasons for having to be up and about, preferably with a light on and some human companionship nearby.

Thoughts and feelings before death

At the time the PA method was first applied to this area, it had been generally assumed that terminally ill people, especially the aged and dying, most often lapsed into a nonresponsive state as death drew close. This was thought to include not simply a last few minutes or hours of comatose functioning but the preceding days and weeks as well. By contrast, it was learned that most of the terminally ill aged maintained some appreciable degree of mental alertness close to, if not right up to, the end of life. Mental status ranged from clear and consistent alertness to an oscillation between foggy and clear periods. The hospital's conservative use of mind-affecting drugs may have contributed to the maintenance of mental status in some patients who elsewhere might have been subjected to massive chemical control. It was not difficult to detect limitations and problems in mental functioning in many of the terminally ill patients, yet close attention usually revealed that the person *did* remain in contact with at least the most significant aspects of his situation. We learned how often it would have been a mistake to treat the patient as though phenomenologically dead, incapable of understanding or caring about what was left to his life. This is another example of a research finding that had some immediate impact upon clinical practice.

Another rather popular assumption at the time was that terminally ill people have a more or less standard way of orienting themselves toward their death. This view was held by some of the hospital and the PA staff, as well as by outsiders to the dying process who imagined how the final scenes should be played. After 120 PAs, as well as related studies and clinical experiences, this assumption was set aside for lack of support. Case after case indicated that people died in a number of different ways. Rigorous analysis and evaluation of the available information also forced us to conclude on some occasions that nobody really knew enough about what had happened to make any definitive statement.

Having failed to prove that all people, or even all aged people, die in approximately the same manner, we described some of the most frequently seen patterns. Many of the preterminal orientations could be classified as either *acceptance, apathy, apprehension,* or *anticipation.*

Acceptance refers to patients who spoke about death in a dispassionate and realistic way; apathy describes patients who seemed indifferent to almost any event, including death; apprehension refers to patients who openly voiced fear and alarm about death; and anticipation applies to patients who showed acceptance plus an explicit wish for death.[19,p.22]

In a later analysis, attention was limited to the patients whose life and death had been best documented.[20] Acceptance again emerged as one of the basic orientations, in fact marginally the most common orientation observed. The next most common orientation, however, seemed best described as those who were *interrupted* by death. People in *both* groups recognized the prospect of imminent death. They differed, however, in their response to this realization. A very independent-minded 90-year-old woman, for example, systematically prepared herself for the end. She decreased her range of interactions and activities, initiated arrangements for her own funeral, and told the staff precisely what she did and did not want to have done for her during the terminal process. As death came very near, she refused medication and insisted that any attempt to prolong her life would be a crime. She was ready for death. (The staff did, in fact, respect the wishes of this woman they had long admired.)

An 82-year-old former schoolteacher typified the other most frequently observed orientation. She was depressed, resigned, and ready for death when she entered the geriatric hospital. This transitional event signaled the onset of the dying process to her. But after a few weeks she discovered that life went on rather actively for some of the patients. There were, indeed, some very sick people in the hospital,

but also many other who were not quite so bad off. She regained her spirits and became an active, popular member of the institutional community. Three years later, she faced death as though it were a regrettable interruption of a still cherishable life. This sentiment was reciprocated by patients and staff who felt that her impending death would take away one of the most enjoyable and valued people on the scene.

These two very different life-styles in the face of death raise questions for those who would insist on a standard attitude or management technique. Which of these women had a better or more authentic orientation toward death? One altered her behavior, but in keeping with her own principles, as death approached, accepting the inevitable. The other seemed just as much aware of her fate but demanded that death catch her on the run; she would do all she could as long as she could. Those of us who knew such people could not answer this question. We found ourselves simply respecting individual differences in death as well as in life.

SUMMARY

Many of us have been influenced by melodramatic presentations that portray dying as a scene played out just before the final curtain falls. There is usually much more to dying, however, than a few hours or days that abide by some conventional story line. Pathways from life to death are complex and varied. Often both the terminally ill person and those close to him or her live with the prospect of death over a more extended period of time. If we wish to understand the situation of the dying person we cannot afford the simplification of focusing on the last moment to the exclusion of all that has gone on before.

It is illuminating to start with the question: *When does dying begin?* In one sense, this question does not even become relevant until death has occurred, because not all people succumb to a life-threatening condition. Although logic might be on the side of suspending the classification of "dying" until the death event, we seldom wait this long. Much feeling, thought, and behavior are organized around the judgment that a person either is or is not "dying." This judgment is not so easy to make as it might appear. Every person in the situation may have a different conception of what "dying" *is*, and also a different perspective for observing and interpreting the facts.

In this chapter we first considered some abstract views of the dying process. The popular phrase, "We die from the moment we are born," reminds us that life is continuous and always related to death. On analysis, however, this view reveals both logical deficiencies and a tendency to play into psychological defenses that subtly deny death at the same time they seem to be acknowledging its reality. While it may deserve a place in our general orientation toward death, the living-is-dying conception is a questionable foundation for intensive understanding of the dying process. Aging as "slow dying" is a more provocative concept. There are some parallels between certain phenomena of aging and dying. The parallels are imperfect, however, and "aging" itself is better considered a process in need of explanation rather than as an explanation for anything else. Additionally, the lives of elderly people cannot be reduced to the dimensions of dying without senseless distortion.

The position taken here is that *dying usually begins as a psychosocial event*. Four common pragmatic modes of defining the onset of dying are explored:

1. Dying begins when the facts are recognized.
2. Dying begins when the facts are communicated.
3. Dying begins when the patient realizes or accepts the facts.

4. Dying begins when nothing more can be done to preserve life.

Because judgments about dying are made within psychosocial contexts, often there are lags, miscommunications, and disagreements. A person may be considered terminally ill by some people and not by others. This is not an idle fact. Differences in treatment are often related to classification of the person as dying or not dying, as are differences in how the afflicted person feels about himself. Many fears and misperceptions go unrecognized, for example, a child's dread of a routine medical procedure on the belief that it might kill him, or an adult's hasty assumption that a self-discovered symptom means certain death. Research indicates that there are appreciable differences within the medical profession itself in the approach taken to patients with life-threatening illness. Improved communication at all levels—within the family, within the health-care professions, and between patient, family, and health professionals—can alleviate some of the unnecessary suffering sometimes associated with the dying process. Some guidelines are offered for improving physician-patient communication.

Whatever the circumstances in which "dying" is thought to begin, there is a high probability that the final course will be run in a medical facility of some type. This makes it important to learn about the dying process as it takes place in our hospitals and nursing homes. Particular attention is given to the systematic field research of Glaser and Strauss in a variety of medical settings. Many of their observations are organized around the concept of *dying trajectories*, essentially, the duration and "shape" of the individual's passage from life to death. Glaser and Strauss emphasize the human or subjective side of the trajectories. It is how everybody *expects* a particular individual's situation to develop that is really important.

Certainty and *time* are the two basic dimensions in question: Will this person die, and if so, when? The hospital staff has a keen interest in developing expectations about certainty and time for each patient because this makes it possible to organize both the work that must be done and the staff's own feelings. There is a characteristic tempo and emphasis on the part of the caregivers for every trajectory. In the *lingering trajectory,* custodial services are the most prominent. Dramatic rescue scenes are rare. A quiet fading out is usually expected and accepted by the staff. Often the person thought to be on a lingering trajectory is seen as having used up most of whatever social value he or she originally possessed. The patient on a lingering trajectory seldom has much control over the management of his condition, and family involvement also tends to be limited. This trajectory typically does not produce disruptions in the institutional environment. It is seen as the inevitable and natural end to a life that cannot and need not be much prolonged.

The *expected quick trajectory* often is seen in the emergency room and the intensive care unit. The American medical system is at its best in coping with this kind of emergency situation, according to Glaser and Strauss. Time is much more important here than in the lingering trajectory. The staff's decisions and activities must race against a rapidly failing condition. Several types of expected quick trajectory are identified, each with its own implications for the activities and feelings to the staff. One of the most anxiety-arousing aspects of this trajectory is the likelihood for expectations to change radically and swiftly; another is the sensitive and emotion-laden relationship with any family and friends who may be on the scene. There is the danger of making serious errors under time and emotion pressure, but also the danger of delaying definitive action too long. From a psychological standpoint, one of the most significant aspects of this trajectory is the influence of the patient's *perceived social value.* This may determine whether or not an all-out rescue effort is made.

The *unexpected quick trajectory* often brings about a crisis atmosphere. It is not just that a life-or-death situation has emerged, but that it has taken place without being clearly anticipated by the staff. A patient receiving relatively routine care suddenly takes a serious turn for the worse—and thereby upsets the staff's personal and social defenses against being taken by surprise. At times the caregivers may be caught in a bind between obeying all the official rules and procedures and doing what might save the person's life. This can lead to "institutional evasions" that open the staff to potential criticism if they concentrate on the stricken patient and set a few rules aside.

Another view of the dying process is obtained through the clinical research procedure known as the *psychological autopsy.* The method is described, and illustrative results given, from a study of aged men and women in an all-geriatric hospital. It was found, for example, that staff tended to turn off attempts by patients to discuss their impending death. Nevertheless, many old people found subtle ways of expressing their knowledge of death; often they seemed to know that they were dying before the underlying medical changes could be detected by staff. Surviving patients were "protected" from knowledge of death by the hospital's "silent treatment." Yet the behavior of patients after one of their wardmates had died often made it clear that they had noticed and were affected by this event.

Most of the terminally ill aged studied by this method maintained some degree of mental alertness until the very end of their lives. As this fact became known, staff became more careful and sensitive in their relationships with patients they previously assumed were out of contact.

There was no support for the proposition that everybody (or even all aged people) dies in the same way. Many individual differences were noted. The two most common orientations were quite different from each other. Some people *accepted* their approaching demise and systematically withdrew from previous activities and relationships. But others acknowledged the approach of death without shifting their daily routines. For these people, death came as an *interruption* in a life they pursued as long as they could. The investigators learned to respect such individual differences in the face of death and would not conclude that people either do die or should die in any one "standardized" way.

REFERENCES

1. Saunders, J. W., & Fallon, J. F. Cell death in morphogensis. In *Major problems in developmental biology.* New York: Academic Press, Inc., 1967.
2. Taylor, J. *Holy dying.* London, 1651. (Reprinted by Arno Press, New York, 1977.)
3. Hendricks, J., & Hendricks, C. *Aging in mass society.* Cambridge, Mass.: Winthrop Press, 1979.
4. Kastenbaum, R. *Growing old.* London & New York: Harper & Row, Publishers, 1979.
5. Hogshead, H. P. The art of delivering bad news. In C. Garfield (Ed.), *Psychosocial care of the dying patient.* New York: McGraw-Hill Book Co., 1978, pp. 128-132.
6. Weisman, A. D. *On death and denying.* New York: Behavioral Publications, Inc., 1972.
7. Kastenbaum, R., & Aisenberg, R. B. *The psychology of death.* New York: Springer Publishing Co., Inc., 1972.
8. Royal Humane Society for the Recovery of Persons Apparently Drowned or Dead. *Annual report.* London: John Nichols & Son, 1820.
9. Aronson, G. J. Treatment of the dying person. In H. Feifel (Ed.), *The meaning of death.* New York: McGraw-Hill Book Co., 1959.
10. Feifel, H. The function of attitudes toward death. In *Death and dying: attitudes of patient and doctor.* (Vol. 5, Symposium No. 11). New York: Group for the Advancement of Psychiatry, 1965.
11. Cassell, E. J. Treating the dying: the doctor vs. the man within the doctor. In C. Garfield (Ed.), *Psychosocial care of the dying patient.* New York: McGraw-Hill Book Co., 1978, pp. 93-99.
12. Rea, M. P., Greenspoon, S., & Spilka, B. Physicians and the terminally ill patient: some selected attitudes and behavior. *Omega,* 1975, 7, 291-302.
12a. Sontag, S. *Illness as Metaphor.* New York: Farrar, Straus & Giroux, Inc., 1978.
13. Le Boyer, F. *Pour une naissance sans violence.* Paris: Editions du Seuil, 1974.
14. Glaser, B. G., & Strauss, A. *Awareness of dying.* Chicago: Aldine Publishing Co., 1966.
15. Glaser, B. G., & Strauss, A. *Time for dying.* Chicago: Aldine Publishing Co., 1968.
16. Weisman, A. D. *The realization of death.* New York: Jason Aronson, Inc., 1974.
17. Kastenbaum, R. In control. In C. Garfield (Ed.), *Psychosocial care of the dying patient.* New York: McGraw-Hill Book Co., 1978, pp. 227-244.
18. Shneidman, E. S., & Farberow, N. (Eds.), *The cry for help.* New York: McGraw-Hill Book Co., 1961.
19. Weisman, A. D., & Kastenbaum, R. *The psychological autopsy: a study of the terminal phase of life.* Community Mental Health Journal Monograph. New York: Behavioral Publications, Inc., 1968.
20. Kastenbaum, R., & Weisman, A. D. The psychological autopsy as a research procedure in gerontology. In D. P. Kent, R. Kastenbaum, & S. Sherwood (Eds.), *Research, planning, and action for the elderly.* New York: Behavioral Publications, Inc., 1972, 210-217.

CHAPTER 12

❖ DYING
Reflection on life

How do people die? How *should* people die? These questions sometimes are jumbled together. It is difficult to keep our hopes and fears out of the picture long enough to determine the basic facts of the situation. And yet hopes and fears are themselves part of the human reality. An entirely objective view of the dying process may be an unattainable goal. The scientist and the clinician have their feelings and biases, as do the family, the caregivers, and the dying person himself. Furthermore, a relentlessly impersonal analysis of the terminal phase of life might introduce its own kind of distortion. We have already commented on the tendency of many individuals to master death concern by adopting a think-but-do-not-feel orientation.

It is possible, however, to respect both the hard facts and the feelings involved in the dying situation and attempt to integrate them into a reasonable perspective. Let us first take a few examples in which facts and feelings have not been adequately distinguished.

Greg, as we will call him, was a college student who lived for more than 2 years with the knowledge that he would probably die within the near future. He suffered from a form of leukemia that posed an unusual puzzle to his physicians. Greg acknowledged the disease itself as a central problem. But often he was more concerned about the ways in which other people related to him. "I have had to develop almost a whole new set of friends," he said. "My good old buddies just felt awfully uncomfortable around me. They couldn't be themselves anymore. I realized they'd be relieved if I would just sort of drift away from them."

What seemed to disturb Greg's friends most was a discrepancy and ambiguity. Greg still looked like the kind of person who might be described as a strapping fellow. He was powerfully built and had a history of health and vigor. This appearance made it difficult to accept the premise that he was in the grip of a life-threatening disorder. None of the "good old buddies" could relate to *both* facts: that Greg looked healthy enough and functioned well enough and that he also might be considered terminally ill. Most of his friends and family chose to relate to Healthy Greg. "I guess it was my own fault. If I wanted to make things easier for everybody, I could have just shut up about my condition. But I didn't think I had to. I mean, you talk about important things with your best friends, don't you? I didn't go on and on about it. When something new happened, or I started feeling shaky about it, I would say something. Oh, man—they just couldn't handle it!"

This type of situation had come to our attention before. In the circle of friends and relations there usually were some people who could handle terminal illness if it followed a pattern that made sense to them. Two patterns were the easiest to comprehend: (1) the sick person's health obviously was failing; deterioration was visible and extreme; (2) the sick person cooled it, that is, kept his thoughts and feelings to himself so others would not be disturbed. In the first instance, the individual could be treated in a special way as befitted his condition. The evident illness made this person different. People around him could therefore be supportive and sympathetic. In the second instance the tacit agreement not to discuss dying and death allowed relationships to continue in at least superficially good order.

Greg, however, posed a problem for his friends as well as his physicians. He touched on his illness often enough to make it hard for them to ignore but often he looked well enough. When he did have an acute episode he would be in the hospital. Afterward he would keep it to himself for a while. "I didn't like to show my face around when I felt rotten." This pattern crossed up his friend's expectations. Everybody knew that a dying person looks different, so Greg *should* have looked different. Similarly, it was assumed that dying was the last thing a dying person would want to talk about. A young man would be especially keen to preserve his macho image by concealing if not subduing any signs of pain, weakness, or fear. Greg was a deviant, then, in behaving as a dying young man should not.

Perhaps it would have been easier for Greg had his friends not made these assumptions about the "facts" of dying. But again, perhaps it was their concern both for him and for their own feelings that led to these assumptions in the first place.

Another type of situation sometimes develops when a sick and debilitated old person is admitted to a hospital.

An old woman is admitted to a hospital. Her family anticipate her death. Arrangements are made to set things in order. This may include putting a pet dog or cat "to sleep" and breaking up the apartment or house in which the woman had been living. The logic is that this sick old woman will not return home again, certainly will not be able to care for a pet or maintain a household. Furthermore, she should not be burdened with these responsibilities and loose ends. These actions on the part of the family sometimes pivot around a misreading of the actual situation. Yes, grandmother (or mother) is old and very sick. But she might survive longer than anticipated with good care and her own recuperative powers. It can be a crushing, demoralizing blow to learn that very personal links to life have been sundered. That hard-to-define attitude known as *will to live* may dissolve when the patient realizes her cherished little world is no longer waiting for her. Even if she does not survive longer than expected, the last days may be blighted by a sense of abandonment and betrayal.

Why has this happened? Often the family's distress in experiencing the old person's decline seems to precipitate questionable actions. The lingering trajectory means lingering pain for the family. Life cannot go on as before. Normal family plans and activities are clouded over by this depressing and unsettled situation. It is in this context that we may hear somebody say, "It would be a kindness if she could go quickly." This sentiment can be read in two directions: foreshortening the dying person's suffering, and relieving the family's anxious tension. Instead of just waiting for the inevitable, then, the family may try to set its own house in order by dismantling what remains of the dying person's life outside the hospital. In short, the need to reduce one's own distress leads to certain assumptions about the patient's condition. It is easier to dispose of the cat, for example, if one can believe that a terminally ill person would not really care, and it is easier to make financial and housing decisions for her if one believes that such practical affairs also are beyond her interest or competence.

Another facet of the family's difficulty in relating to an old person on the decline has come to my attention more recently. The "adult child" (a peculiar but apt term) may be forced to contend with two realities at the same time. Here is Mother or Father, apparently much altered by advanced age and illness. Physical death may be in near prospect, but even while still alive, the parent does not seem to be the same person. The "real" parent may be represented by an image in the adult child's mind. It is a strong image because it formed many years ago and has had a core function in the adult child's own life. How can the individual cope simultaneously with these two realities— the image of the healthy, intact parent who has meant so much for so many years, and the severely impaired person who retains the parent's name but no longer looks or behaves like Mother or Father? It is not easy to do emotional justice to both realities at the same time. Finding a way of relating to the impaired/dying parent might be difficult enough; the same would be true of mourning the deceased parent. But—doing both at the same time? My colleagues and I are now studying this difficulty both in terms of the adult child's own thoughts and feelings, and what type of interactions continue to occur between the adult child and the impaired/dying parent. It is already clear that one pattern of coping involves a turning away from the still-living parent to protect one's memory of that parent, which is still very important to the adult child's own identity. At times this leads to misperceptions of the parent's actual physical, mental, and emotional situation.

Consider one more example in which questions of fact and value or need become jumbled. This case study is drawn from a master's thesis in nursing science by Beatrice Schaberg, who did a series of interviews with women dying of breast cancer.[1]

Mrs. B was a 47-year-old married black Prot-

estant woman, a college graduate and mathematics teacher in an elementary school. She had three children ranging in age from 10 to 17 years. Her husband worked for a large Detroit-based company. Mrs. B herself discovered the lump on her breast and feared the worst. Neither surgical removal of the affected area (mastectomy) nor chemotherapy could bring under control the malignant growth that had been found. She was now in the hospital, well aware of the seriousness of her condition. Mr. B visited daily and was "my mainstay." The family was managing in her absence, and friends had been helpful.

As hope for recovery or prolonged survival ebbed, Mrs. B often thought about her children:

All of a sudden I wanted them to hurry up and grow up. I want to know their careers before I pass away, that kind of cheats them out of childhood. I wouldn't ordinarily have done that. I don't want to push but right now I want them to choose things I think are worthy—because of me. I think time is running out.[1,p.23]

She seemed to accept her coming death: "There is nothing you can do about it, so you might as well resign yourself." Yet she retained attachment to life and specifically hoped that she would be able to go home when the radiation therapy treatments were finished. To be at home with her family once more, even if not for long, was perhaps the one hope she permitted herself.

It was at the conclusion of the planned course of radiation therapy that a key incident occurred. Mrs. B asked the physician if she would be allowed to go home now. The answer was, "No, we would like to give you a round of chemotherapy first. But before we can do that we have to wait for your platelet count to come up." She asked how long that would take. "We don't know. It is 50,000 now and has to go to 100,000 before we can do the therapy."

According to Schaberg, "Mrs. B's face fell. She said no more to the doctors. During the interview that followed this she acted differently. She seemed very tired and slow moving. . . . She admitted reluctantly that she was disappointed. Her affect was flat. She avoided direct eye contact."

Mrs. B lived another three weeks, but did not again mention going home. "The last time I saw her she seemed to recognize me, she smiled, and then her eyes lost the look of recognition. She died the following day."

What happened here? The physician had replaced Mrs. B's values with his own. Furthermore, he had disguised his values in professional-scientific terminology. Both Mrs. B and her physician knew that she had only a short time to live. The physician preferred to interpret the situation in terms of platelet count. It was the impression of Schaberg and myself that this was the physician's way of sweeping aside personal feelings and values that could not be discussed as easily as platelet counts. Mrs. B's desire to be home with her family again—and the family's need to have her back for a final leave-taking—were not given a hearing. The patient was told she could not go home as though this were a straightforward medical decision. In actuality, it was the physician's personal judgment about where a person *should* die. The medical staff in general, according to Schaberg, seemed to have no realization that Mrs. B had been doing so much emotional work about life and death, and what significance she attached to the hope of going home again.

In these three examples we have seen how friends, family, and physician can respond to a dying person in ways that increase distress and demoralize the spirit. Greg was, in part, a victim of the attitude that a person should not be afraid of death and, even if he is, should never admit it. This reaction confronted him although his expressions of concern were moderate and

realistic. The sick old woman was treated to some extent as one who is socially dead. This was based both on misconceptions of her actual condition and needs and on the family's discomfort with a lingering trajectory. Mrs. B was denied the opportunity to choose the way in which she would prefer to live out her last days because staff substituted their values for hers and presented them in the guise of indisputable facts. These are but a few of the situations in which anxiety generates confusion between fact and value, and then affects people's lives in times of great vulnerability.

INDIVIDUALITY AND UNIVERSALITY IN THE EXPERIENCE OF DYING

Consider three possibilities: (1) people die essentially in the same way, and there is not much that can be done about it; (2) people die essentially in the same way, but it is possible for the experience to be influenced appreciably for the better or worse; (3) each person dies in his or her own way, therefore it is not appropriate to put forth general propositions about an ideal *modus terminalus*.

Although seldom expressed quite this directly, all three views have their advocates. We see people withdrawing from a dying person on the assumption that there is nothing really to be done in the presence of the inevitable. Or, in a more constructive vein, we see people advocating a particular course of action intended to improve the situation of the dying person in general. Emphasis on the individuality of a particular dying person is encountered most frequently when the experience has become a memorable one for the survivors or care givers. It is not a dominant theme in the more systematic writings and studies.

The possibility that individual differences might be more important than universal characteristics is often felt as a threat to the establishment of a secure body of knowledge. This is true in many fields, not just in the area of dying and death. Traditionally, scientists hope to emerge with powerful laws or principles. At the least, they want to specify relationships that can be observed and predicted over and over again and generalized from one situation to another. Dependable generalizations yield a kind of *control*. We feel more powerful when we know what to expect, and sometimes this knowledge actually permits us to manipulate the situation, to change the course of events. Those of us who are not scientists may also value knowledge for the sake of power and control. Are you a hospital administrator? If so, you would feel more in control of the situation if you knew for a fact who would die when. Are you a person encountering your first experience with a friend or relative who appears to be terminally ill? You would probably feel more secure if you knew what was going to happen next. This might help you master some of your own feelings of uncertainty and distress and enable you to relate more positively to the dying person.

In other words, it would be at least a little easier for most of us—scientists, caregivers, or people living among other people—if valid generalizations could be made about the dying person. The generalizations of fact might then be supplemented by generalizations of value or preference. Universality has its lures. I suggest that we do not succumb too quickly to the temptation of imagining a typical dying person. This can lead to premature closure of efforts to gain thorough knowledge of dying as a human experience. It can also lead us to relate more to the image of a dying person than to the unique individuals whose lives are endangered.

This discussion has not been intended to deny the possibility that significant commonalities might exist in the experiences and needs of people who are dying; it has been more in the nature of a caution that we refrain from seizing upon an assumption just because it promises to ease our own feelings a bit. I would not feel obliged to observe, analyze, and compare if I could convince myself that there are no useful generalizations to be made about the dying process. More importantly, I would perhaps feel less responsibility for thinking through the implications of "good" or "bad" dying if general standards were out of the question. The need for achieving an appropriate *balance* between appreciation of what is distinctive in the terminal-phase experiences of a particular individual and what might be important to all or most terminally ill people is of practical as well as theoretical significance. It is, for example, one of the major considerations for those involved in developing hospice systems (Chapter 13).

We turn now to some of the factors that influence the nature and experience of dying. The present state of knowledge limits the conclusions that can be drawn. However, it is possible to guide our personal thoughts and observations by taking into account the following selected factors. You will recognize as we go along that each of these factors or areas of concern has relevance to *any* person who is on a dying trajectory but that the particular relevance and significance varies from individual to individual. We can begin, then, with respect for both universal and individual dimensions of dying.

Age

Everybody, whether healthy or dying, has an age. Chronological age is the simplest although not necessarily the most accurate index of the individual's position in the total life span. Among the dying there are infants, young children, older children, adolescents, and young, middle-aged, old, and very old adults. The characteristics that distinguish, say, a young child from a middle-aged adult do not dissolve because both are dying. Age tends to be associated with extent and type of life experience, strength, coping ability, attitudes, and mental functioning. All these factors have a bearing on the individual's orientation toward dying and death. It is not necessary to maintain that age "causes" a certain style of coping or a particular constellation of attitudes and cognitions. Such a contention would in fact be inconsistent with findings obtained by sociobehavioral gerontologists.[2] Chronological age can be regarded instead as a general index and starting point for exploring what the individual brings with him to the dying situation.

We have already seen that there are age differences in the individual's interpretation of death (Chapters 9 and 10). The very young child, for example, may not grasp the finality of death, while most adults should comprehend it. Given such an important difference in what the individual understands about death, we might look for differences in the person's adaptation to the total situation. Recognition of differences in the interpretation of death and therefore in adaptation to terminal illness might in turn suggest somewhat different approaches to care and emotional support. A study conducted at the City of Hope Medical Center in Duarte, California, indicates that important differences may exist among children of varying ages as well as between children and adults. Natterson and Knudson[3] studied children ranging in age from less than 1 year to almost 13. All were suffering from cancer-related conditions with poor prognoses. The youngest children appeared to be most alarmed about the separation from their parents. These were the preschool boys and girls who would have been at home with their mothers had not severe illness struck. Children in the 5 to 10 years of age range appeared to be most upset by the nature of the diagnostic and treatment procedures. Natterson and Knudson make it clear that this fear and distress had strong roots in reality. Procedures such as bone-marrow aspiration and venipuncture involve physical invasion of the integrity of the body. Pain and

mutilation, even in the service of medical treatment, could hardly fail to be threatening. Anxiety about dying and death as such was found mostly with the oldest children. This is consistent with the studies of death cognitions in healthy children; the 11- or 12-year-old usually grasps both the finality and the universality of death.

If we were in a position to comfort a child who is living in the midst of such pain and distress, we might then improve our sensitivity by responding to the concerns that are most dominant at his particular age level. Almost all the children seemed frightened and depressed by the imposed separation from home and parents. Any way that could be devised to alleviate some of the separation-linked anxiety probably would be of significant comfort to the child, regardless of age. But we would proceed in the knowledge that separation was an especially harrowing problem for the youngest children. Similarly, we would have to address ourselves to the alleviation of the fear of mutilation if we intended to comfort the slightly older child. A more direct appreciation and sharing of fears related to dying and death would be necessary if we wished to meet the concerns of the oldest children head on. Recognition of the child's most urgent concerns does not in itself guarantee that we will be effective in reducing apprehension and suffering, but it does at least give appropriate direction to our efforts. Research findings can help to guide these efforts. It has been found, for example, that 11- and 12-year-olds with higher self-esteem tend to have less death anxiety.[4] This suggests that whatever might be done in general to strengthen a child's good feelings about himself as a person might prove to be valuable in meeting specific losses and stresses associated with life-threatening disease.

Whatever we understand about the resources, vulnerabilities, and needs of people at a particular age level can be helpful in relating to the terminally ill person. This is one of the reasons it does not necessarily require a death expert to help meet the dying person's needs. Often what is needed is a person sensitive to what a child is likely to think, the hopes and vulnerabilities of an adolescent, or what an aged person holds precious. It is not a generalized person who is facing death. Instead, it is a young man who had been expecting a long life ahead, or an old woman who has outlived most of the people who mattered to her—always a *particular* person who is at a particular station in life.

Attention to age as a factor in the dying process can introduce its own problems, however, if one is held captive by stereotyped attitudes. Some adults, for example, persist in regarding childhood as a prolonged visit to make-believe land. The concerns of a young boy or girl are treated as childish fears almost by definition. We have seen, though, that even very young children are sensitive to separation and abandonment, and that death-related perceptions find their way into the lives of many youngsters who are in good health. The child who is exposed not only to his own illness but to other very sick children in the hospital has to contend with experiences that are all too real. The adult may be tempted to deny that the child could possibly understand what is happening. Adult fantasies and needs, then, threaten to interfere with vital communication and support. Whether or not the child in fact grasps the central facts, he is probably trying hard to make sense of the situation and master his anxiety.

Surprisingly, perhaps, mistaken assumptions about the nature of children sometimes can be found even among professional health-care givers:

It is quite remarkable that for a long time it was believed by the medical profession that infants did not experience pain to the same extent as adults, and even in my lifetime I remember operations, such as the removal of tonsils and circumcision,

being done on children without the use of anesthetic. From the results of a study I did in the last year on the treatment of leukaemic children in hospital, it was obvious that this mistaken idea was still with us. Changing of dressing, taking of bone marrow samples and the insertion of needles into the spine are procedures which often cause a great deal of pain to children and yet they are still done without adequate analgesia. In a modern hospital there is no excuse for any child to suffer pain from such diagnostic or therapeutic measures.[5,p.56]

To understand the relationship of age to the situation of the dying person, we must therefore examine our habitual assumptions about what an individual of a certain age is like. Take a pair of examples from the other side of the age spectrum, as reported by the medical director of a nursing home.[6] A 92-year-old woman returned to the nursing home after her second bout of surgery for a broken hip. Although the operation was successful, she developed an infection that led to shock and coma. While in the comatose state she also was afflicted by aspiration pneumonia. Until this illness the woman had been in good spirits. Family members had been affectionate, attentive, and patient with her.

With the onset of the comatose state, however, the physician withdrew all drugs, stopped all feeding processes, and advised the nursing staff to "do nothing." He further stated, "This patient is better off dead than alive. Let her alone." The nursing staff, however, had become devoted to this patient during her long stay in the institution and voiced dissent with being committed to a "do-nothing" program and having been designated, without consultation, as the agent of the death process.[6,p.161]

The director of the nursing staff managed to persuade the physician to permit a treatment program that would give the old woman at least a chance for survival. With restorative nursing she did in fact recover and at the most recent report was engaged in a rehabilitative nursing program.

The family of a confused and pain-ridden 86-year-old woman changed its attitude toward her when she stopped eating, slumping down whether placed in a chair or on her feet, and became incontinent. She admitted, after much questioning, that she was both afraid of death and wished to die. The family now asked over and again for the staff to let the old woman die. "Why not let her go, isn't she vegetating?" The attending physician did nothing to institute a treatment regime that might restore her health and spirits. But again the nursing director helped to turn the situation about, calling on the institution's medical policy committee to take action. Permission was finally granted for restorative nursing. Furthermore, social workers discovered the patient's own self-destructive tendencies and their probable causes. The old woman was reassured that she was alive and was going to be helped to stay alive. The family was also assured by the social workers that

the patient had a right to live and that she was entitled to all the services and skills at the command of the rehabilitation team. In addition, the family was informed forthrightly that the institution and its staff members had a clear commitment to maintain life and had no obligation to be the agents of death for the patient, family or physician.[6,pp.161-162]

The patient did recover, becoming ambulatory again and having control over her body functions.

As the author of these case histories, Michael B. Miller, observes, it is easy to assume that old people are ready to die, especially those who are showing obvious symptoms or who express self-destructive tendencies. Systematic research has indicated that dying and senility are conditions that are often treated as though equivalent even by health professionals who should know better.[7] In our cultural death system it is the old person who is seen as ripe for the grim reaper. This encourages family and care givers to withhold treatment that might both extend life and improve its quality. Fortunately this general tendency can be successfully combatted, as these examples indicate.

Stereotyped ideas about old people contribute to a pattern of discrimination throughout our society.[8] These stereotypes can be life-threatening when "sick" or "depressed" quickly becomes translated into "dying" and "hopeless" in the minds of those whom the old person relies on for care. Understanding the old person's adaptation to the dying process begins with a resolve to determine the facts for ourselves rather than relying on commonplace assumptions.

Sex

Our personal identity throughout our lives includes our gender and sex-related roles. This does not mean of course that either all men or all women are alike. But it would be naive to neglect the many ways in which our sex roles influence our experiences and actions. The dying person remains either a male or a female. This means, for example, that a man with cancer of the prostate may be concerned with the threat of becoming impotent as well as with the risk of his life (although in practice, timely diagnosis and treatment sharply reduces both risks). Cervical cancer may disturb a young woman not only because of the life risk but also because one of the treatment possibilities, hysterectomy, would rule out any subsequent pregnancies. Both the man and the woman described may be troubled about the future of their initimate relationships even if the threat to their lives is lifted. Some people interpret physical trauma affecting their sexual organs as punishment for real or fantasied transgressions. Others become preoccupied with the physical condition in a way that interferes with affectional and sexual relationships. "I'm no good anymore" may be a self-tormenting thought for either the man or the woman, each experiencing this in his or her own way. Even if the treatment is completely successful, there will have been a period of time during which concern about death was intensified by doubts as to the individual's intactness as a sexual being. These are not the only types of reaction people have to cancer of the reproductive system but simply illustrate some of the interactions between sex role and disease.

Serious illness of any type may pose different threats to men and women. This is most easily seen in families that operate within the traditional sex-role patterns of our society: the husband goes off to work, the wife stays home and looks after children and house.

When the woman is faced with a life-threatening illness, she is likely to have concerns about the integrity and well-being of the family. Will the children eat well? Can her husband manage the essential household tasks? In general, will they be able to manage without her? Her concern may extend to some special hopes and plans for the family that are jeopardized by the illness. At any particular moment, what most troubles the woman-wife-mother may be the fate of her family more than her own.

The man-husband-father in this traditionally oriented family is likely to have distinctive concerns of his own. Has the illness destroyed his career prospects? Will he lose his job or his chance for advancement even if he makes a good recovery? Has he provided well enough for his family in case he doesn't pull through? Is he, in effect, a "good man" if he cannot work and bring in the money? There may be a crisis in self-esteem if he finds himself confined to hospital or home for a protracted time, away from the work-oriented situations that support his sense of identity as a valuable person.

Research in progress by myself and my colleagues suggests that men and women in our society may have different hierarchies of concern about death while they are in good health

and examining their expectations in the abstract. This should be clearly distinguished from studies involving people who are in the midst of a life-threatening illness. Some data are being obtained through a slightly revised form of a procedure introduced by James Diggory and Doreen Rothman.[9] Respondents are asked to indicate the relative amount of concern they feel about a set of possible consequences associated with their own death.

Our first respondents were 427 undergraduates (240 female, 187 male) on three urban university campuses during the early 1970s. College men and women differed most in their rankings of two pairs of possible consequences. The men were most concerned that "The process of dying might be painful" and that "All my plans and projects would come to an end." Notice that both these consequences focus on the situation of the dying person himself. The women expressed relatively more concern that "My death would cause grief to my relatives and friends" and that "I could no longer care for my dependents" (in the case of many undergraduate women this meant projecting themselves into their future roles as mothers). Both of these consequences focus on the situation of the people who survive the dying person herself. These sex differences in death concern should not be overinterpreted. They represent group trends only, although clear enough so far as such trends go. Furthermore, there were points of close agreement between respondents of both sexes.

A second series of studies was conducted with new samples of young adults, both high-school and college students (314 women, 218 men). Before a few of the more relevant findings are cited here, you might find it interesting to think about how you would answer one of the questions added for the second study. In the study itself the respondents were presented with the opportunity to rate each of the alternatives separately on a four-point agree/

INTEREST IN CONTINUANCE OF SELF

Which of these ways seem most preferable or appropriate to you? Indicate your first choice by writing the number "1" in front of it. Indicate your second choice with "2," and so on, until you have arranged the alternatives in a rank order that represents your thoughts and feelings about this question at the present time.

_____ A. I would like to have some achievements or accomplishments that live on after my death.

_____ B. I would like to bring children into this world, in part for the purpose of keeping something of me alive.

_____ C. I would like to have people remember me after my death.

_____ D. I would like to have my thoughts and personality placed on a computer program and made available to succeeding generations.

_____ E. I would like to live forever if I could.

_____ F. I would like to have some form of life after death in which my mind and personality continue.

_____ G. I want an impressive funeral and a beautiful and well-marked resting place as a reminder of my existence on earth.

---

disagree type scale as well as in the combined form given here.

Listed here are some of the ways in which people have expressed an interest in the continuance of their selves beyond death. People differ in their preferences.

Both young men and women in our sample most frequently selected the "live forever" option.[10] Continuance by procreation was the second most frequent choice for both sexes. Major points of difference between the sexes included the young women's greater interest in life after death and living on in the memories of others, as compared with the young men's higher priority for achievements and accomplishments. Computerized immortality and an impressive funeral and resting place were low priorities for both men and women. The larger study also found that many young men and women felt that having children would represent a form of self-continuation and might make them feel less anxious about death—yet consciously rejected the idea of bringing children into the world for this reason. This was associated with a disinclination to name children after themselves or others in their families. The general impression was that many of the respondents did not want to burden possible children-to-be with their own ego needs, but rather to let them be free to become themselves. This seemed to be in contrast with a perhaps more traditional orientation in which the child links one generation to the next as a sort of "name-soul." The overall pattern of findings in this study suggests that life and death orientations characteristic of each sex are in the process of change and that we should be alert to possible sex differences without jumping to fixed and premature conclusions.

Sex differences in the dying situation may be important from the standpoint of professional caregivers as well as that of the patient. Direct care to the dying person is usually provided by women, often registered nurses, licensed practical nurses, or aides. Responsibility for the total care plan, however, is often in the hands of a male physician. The physician may be more plan and achievement oriented, a characteristic that favors survival of the rigors of medical training. He may therefore be more persistent in cure-oriented treatments but also quicker to withdraw when failure looms on the horizon. The nurse may be more sensitive to the patient's relationship with significant people in his life and less apt to regard impending death as a failure.

Changing patterns of sex roles in our society might show up in adaptation to terminal illness as well as in other situations. When one marital partner is disabled, the other may have more experience in the ailing one's sphere of responsibility and be better able to maintain the integrity of the family. It is more likely now than in past years, for example, that the wife is a current or potential wage earner and that she is familiar with financial management. Similarly, the husband of today may have had more time with the children and more responsibility for running the household than in the past. This pattern is becoming more common as young couples share and exchange responsibilities with less concern for man's work and woman's work than had become traditional. Furthermore, the healthy one may be more attuned to the needs and concerns of the sick partner because there has been more commonality in their experiences.

Ethnic background

Staff in one of the nation's most prestigious hospitals had difficulty in maintaining poise when a particular little old man was admitted in critical condition. It was not so much the patient himself, but rather the fact that a veritable tribe accompanied him and seemed determined to stay on the scene. One nurse did recognize that this was "just standard operating procedure for the gypsies—but it sure raised hell with *our* SOP!" The fact that hospitals in our society are not arranged to accommodate families and swarming relatives is of interest.

Hospitals, by their physical structure and established practices, bespeak a focus on the professional care of the patient. There is literally no place for the community to maintain its relationship to the patient or participate in the care process. This sets up a situation of mutual culture shock when a close, possessive group of people insist on keeping the ailing member in their midst while at the same time seeking high-quality medical attention. The point here is not that hospitals should be expected to adapt themselves to every possible variation in ethnic background, but that there *are* built-in expectations and constraints, many of which have the effect of distancing the terminally ill patient from those who would be close to him.

The incident mentioned here is but one of many that illustrate the possibility of conflict and miscommunication when the ethnic background of the dying patient differs from that of those in a position to provide care or make significant decisions. I have seen a woman in terror not because she was facing the prospect of death but because hospital routine had destroyed her personal security pattern that was supported by behaviors and rituals that our society would consider superstitious. Medicine could not save her, and folk-magic defenses were neither understood nor respected.

The miscommunication does not have to be dramatic to influence the patient's experiences. Health personnel with an Anglo-Saxon stiff-upper-lip philosophy may disapprove of the moans, groans, and complaints of a patient whose own heritage condones and expects forthright signs of distress. The pinching shoe is sometimes found on the other foot: a physician of Latin-Mediterranean background underestimated the suffering of her predominately WASP-Yankee patients until she learned how hard they were working at keeping their pain to themselves. Studies of the pain experience[11,12] make it clear that there are appreciable individual differences that, in turn, often are related to ethnic background.

Think for a moment of your own ethnic heritage. Do you belong to a tradition in which, for example, faith in afterlife is one of the sustaining features? Is death itself acknowledged as a central fact of life? Are funerals major occasions or formalities to be moved through as quickly as possible? Is it customary for the family to expect its members to have their needs met out there in society, or is there a determination that all of "our people" stick closely together, especially on crucial and intimate matters? These are a few of the ethnically related considerations that have a bearing on the individual's relationship to dying and death. The more we know about the traditions that speak through the individual, the better position we will be in to understand what he might be experiencing as death moves into prospect. Studies focusing on ethnic attitudes toward dying and death within the general U.S. population are just starting to appear,[13] although there are many anthropological reports that demonstrate distinctive orientations in various parts of the world. The concept of ethnicity itself must be examined carefully, including the interaction between background heritage and the current scene, especially when the current scene is a health-care facility.[14]

Sometimes the awareness of impending death alters the individual's relationship to his ethnic heritage. The person who has come to think of himself as a 100% homogenized American, for example, may feel drawn back to a heritage that had not seemed relevant for many years. This can take the form of renewed religious interest or a longing to see the old country or to be in contact with others who represent a continuing tradition. It is premature, in terms of research findings, to conclude that people with a deep sense of ethnic belongingness die "better," but integration into a tradition does constitute one potentially helpful set of supports for a person who might otherwise feel alone and abandoned in the face of death.

Interpersonal relationships

Ethnic background, although important, is not the only type of relationship that binds one person to another. The extent and quality of the dying person's links to other people is one of the most critical factors to be considered. A recent study—one of the best yet available from the research craftsmanship standpoint—makes this point very clear.

Avery D. Weisman and J. William Worden performed a psychosocial analysis of cancer deaths,[15] using a controlled case-study approach evolved from the psychological autopsy method.[16,17] They studied 46 cancer patients, of whom 35 died during the course of the investigation. Weisman and Worden purposely sought out patients who were likely to die within a short period of time (as it turned out, the deaths occurred in a range between 4 weeks and 1 year from point of entry into the study). The patients were receiving comprehensive medical and nursing care in a major urban hospital. There were 18 men and 17 women among those who died. All but four of the patients were 40 years old or older; the largest concentration was in the age 60 to 69 years range. The typical patient was white, Catholic, and married, although other race, religious, and marital status conditions were also represented.

From their previous experience, the investigators theorized that interpersonal relationships are so significant that they might markedly affect the patient's length of survival. This view was consistent with observations made by a number of others who have worked with dying people and their families, but it had not previously been tested through systematic research. To investigate this possibility, Weisman and Worden devised a *Survival Quotient* (SQ):

$$SQ = \frac{\text{Observed survival} - \text{Expected survival}}{\text{Standard error of estimated survival}}$$

This quotient was based on information collected on a large number of cancer patients throughout the Commonwealth of Massachusetts by a tumor registry service. How long a particular person survived could be related to the average length of survival not for cancer in general but for the particular form of the illness, as well as the patient's age and sex, type of treatments received, and so on. The standard error component of the SQ utilizes a statistical technique to create a z, or standard score, that makes it possible to compare individuals suffering with a variety of different cancers. In this study the types of cancer were distinguished according to their primary site: breast, cervix, colon, lung, lymphoma, and stomach. Information about each person was developed using an elaborated form of the psychological autopsy technique described in Chapter 11. An SQ score was computed, and all the data examined through the use of statistical procedures known as factor analysis and multiple regression analysis. For those unfamiliar with these procedures, it can be said that they are techniques for sorting out complex information and then determining which components or items are the best predictors of specified outcomes. In this case, of course, the most important outcome was length of survival, as indexed by the SQ.

One of the key findings was that patients who maintained active and mutually responsive relationships survived longer than those who brought poor social relationships with them into the terminal stage of life. Early separation from one or both parents during the patient's childhood and adolescence was associated with a shorter period of survival. The patients who died rapidly also tended to have "few friends, distant relationships with families, or a series of hostile but dependent associations with others." Weisman and Worden offer a composite picture both of those who survived longer than expected and those who died sooner than expected on the basis of the available background data for their specific conditions. The quality of interpersonal relationships is one of the major differences between these two groups:

Longer survivals are associated with patients who have good relationships with others, and manage to preserve a reasonable degree of intimacy with family and friends until the very last. They ask for and receive much medical and emotional support. As a rule, they accept the reality of serious illness, but still do not believe that death is inevitable. Hence, at times they may deny the gravity of illness or seem to repudiate the fact of becoming more feeble. They are seldom deeply depressed but may voice resentment about various aspects of their treatment and illness. Whatever anger is displayed, it should be noted, does not alienate others but commands their attention. They may be afraid of dying alone and untended, so they refuse to let others pull away without taking care of their needs.

Shorter survivals occur in patients who report poor social relationships, starting with early separations from their family of origin, and continuing throughout life. Sometimes they have had diagnosed psychiatric disorders, but almost as often talk about repeated mutually destructive relationships with people through the years. At times, they have considered suicide. Now, when treatment fails, depression deepens, and they become highly pessimistic about their progress. They want to die—a finding that often reflects more conflict than acceptance.[15,p.71]

In a subsequent report the same investigators observed that interpersonal difficulties associated with widowhood, a troubled marriage, or membership in a "multiproblem" family were more common among those cancer patients who were highly distressed during the early months of their illness.[18] The nature and extent of the individual's ongoing interpersonal problems proved to be a useful predictor of response to cancer and treatment in the months ahead.

There is no reason to believe that the quality of interpersonal relationships is important only in terminal illness related to cancer. The person who has become alienated from others would seem to be at greater risk from virtually any life-threatening illness. The *links* between interpersonal relationship and survival still have to be carefully researched, as do a variety of conditions other than cancer. Did some of the people in the Weisman-Worden study, for example, die prematurely because they felt they had nothing to live for? If so, how could this psychological attitude have become translated into the physical events that foreshorten life?

Take a less mysterious example. Each winter there is an upsurge in the sudden deaths of men with known cardiovascular ailments. They are stricken, literally, with snow shovel in hand. In some instances the man may have exposed himself to a fatal heart attack because of his desire to continue in his role as a strong, competent male. This pathway to death, then, may be associated more closely with sex-role identity than with interpersonal relationships, although the two are mutually influential. But in other instances, there may have been no one on the scene to caution the man, to persuade him not to take this risk and offer an alternative solution to the snow-disposal problem. With poor interpersonal relations, the victim may have been entirely on his own—or have contributed *subintentionally* (Chapter 15) to his death by taking this invitation to self-destruction. You can probably think of many other examples in which the availability of people who really care about an individual can make a life-or-death difference in practical ways, even apart from the more difficult to establish links between attitude and longevity.

The quality as well as the duration of life is influenced by the pattern of interpersonal relationships. Elisabeth Kubler-Ross[19] and others have written compellingly about the loneliness and isolation of many terminally ill people. Most often, attention is given to the ways in which family and staff may turn from the patient because he is dying. The dying person is an aversive stimulus in our society; we are un-

comfortable in his presence.[20] We prefer to maintain a large social distance between ourselves and the dying person.[21] Those who venture to bring up the topic of dying and death themselves are likely to find the communication rejected, distorted, or turned aside.[22]

But emotional abandonment by family and staff does not account for all the interpersonal problems that may be encountered by the dying person. As indicated by the Weisman-Worden study, some people have a lifelong pattern of alienating others. They tend to approach the terminal phase of life as loners. Their isolation is not occasioned but only emphasized by the new situation. Aged people and some others may have outlived or moved out of contact with the friends and relatives who have most mattered in their lives. The dying person may have had a warm and sociable life-style, but for various reasons few if any of his intimates may be on the scene.

To understand the experiences of the dying person, then, we must appreciate both the type of interpersonal relationships he has developed through the years and the pattern of relationships that demonstrates itself in the immediate situation. A person who is secure in his social worth and acceptability on the basis of lifelong experience, for example, may be better able to bear the peculiarities of existence in a hospital milieu. Similarly, the person who has had previous experience with institutional life may find that there are fewer adjustments to make when his world has again come down to the confines of an institution. Well acquainted with environments that run by the book and with clear chains of command, such a person may become the kind of patient who is readily accepted by the staff.

The pattern of interpersonal relationships an individual brings with him can be quite distinctive. Similarly, he may strike quite a distinctive response from the new people (physicians, nurses). In this sense, each person has at least the possibility of moving through a different set of significant experiences in the terminal phases of life.

Personality/life-style

We have touched on four major influences: age, sex, ethnic background, and interpersonal relationships. These are all a part of the person who is facing death (which, in the broadest sense, is the least exclusive category on earth). Yet the person is not simply an accumulation of factors and influences. Each individual is an unique personality. This is more than a general, philosophical proposition. It also means, for example, that if we group together several people of the same age and treat them in the same way we are probably behaving inappropriately. Whether the individual is 10 years old or 110, the characteristics of individual personality shine through and deserve appreciation in their own right. Statistical predictions based on age alone or on sex, ethnic background, or interpersonal relationships, usually fall short of the mark. Similarity of background factors does not guarantee identical personality. Two 50-year-old women of Old Yankee background and similar family configurations, for example, may be as different as night and day in their personalities and life-styles, although sharing some beliefs and habits.

It is important to appreciate the background and interpersonal network of a terminally ill person. But *who* this person really is must be regarded as a question to be posed in its own right.

Sensitivity to the individual personality of the dying patient has been expressed by a number of people who have accepted clinical responsibilities for the seriously ill. "We all try hard to be ourselves," notes Loma Feigenberg, a Swedish cancer specialist who developed a second career as a psychiatrist to meet the emotional needs of his patients.[23] He sees the acceptance of the patient's individuality as one of the major requirements of anyone who

would be therapeutic. This is one of the reasons why he does not approach a new relationship with a terminally ill person with a particular formula in mind; the needs, motives, and resources of each patient are to be explored and respected.[24] It is not assumed that any two people will bring quite the same constellation of needs and resources to the terminal situation.

A study in Great Britain indicated that several characteristics of personality or life-style may be particularly important in the individual's adaptation to terminal illness. John Hinton explored the relationship between preillness personality and the state of mind during the the period of final illness.[25] The patients were 22 men and 38 women, all suffering from some form of cancer in an advanced stage. There were some limitations of the study, imposed by the conditions in which it was carried out, and these are acknowledged by Hinton.

People who faced problems throughout their lives seemed more able to adapt to terminal illness. They were more likely to indicate that they knew their condition was probably fatal and more likely to approve of the care they were receiving in the hospital. But "people who had not coped so well in the past made it apparent to the nurses that they were troubled and unhappy in their last illness."[25,p.98] People who were decisive, not the same characteristic as problem-facing, also seemed more aware of the nature of their prognoses and more accepting of the situation. Based on nursing reports, indecisive people were more likely to appear depressed and withdrawn.

One of the advantages of controlled research is the opportunity to subject common assumptions to critical scrutiny. In this study one frequently held assumption about personality and adaptation to terminal illness failed to be supported. People with neurotic life-styles did *not* show more depression or anxiety during their final illness than did other people. Nervous people did seem more troubled over the prospect of dying, but their daily mood and behavior was not much different from people with more stable or adjusted life-styles.

But differences were found with respect to another important personality characteristic. Those who viewed their entire lives as satisfying or fulfilling maintained a more positive mood during the final illness. They expressed less distress both about the process of dying and about the probable outcome. Patients with a good marital relationship also showed a more positive mood and less distress about dying, reinforcing points already made regarding interpersonal relationships. The association between personality characteristics and maintenance of interpersonal relationships during this period of stress is commented on by Hinton in his summary of the findings:

The capacity of facing or not facing problems in the past affected the mood during the terminal illness. Those . . . less able to cope were observed to be more resentful and isolated. It was the most important factor amongst those studied here in determining whether a person would maintain social relationships or withdraw in the ward situation. Past difficulties in coping also increased the likelihood of current depression and anxiety. In this way it differed to some extent from the element of decisiveness or its opposite. Although the latter had an influence on the mood of the dying, its effect was demonstrated more in that the decisive people were apt to show greater recognition that they might be dying. They also gave more praise for their care.[25,p.109]

The possible relationship between personality and coronary heart disease has been discussed and studied for years. The greatest impact has been made by the research and writing of cardiologists Meyer Friedman and Ray R. Rosenman.[26] Their major study included more than 3000 men who were studied for almost 5 years. The men who proved most vulnerable to coronary heart disease tended to show one type of personality configuration, while those who were least vulnerable showed a distinctly different type of personality. These have become known simply as type A and type B behavior patterns.

What is the type A pattern? Friedman and Rosenman found 13 characteristics of this pattern when it appears in its fully developed form. The type A person:

1. Speaks in a hurried and explosive style, betraying "excess aggression or hostility."

2. Moves, walks, and eats rapidly all the time.

3. Shows impatience with the tempo of people and events around him. Things are not moving fast enough or getting done quickly enough to suit him.

4. Often tries to think or do several things at the same time (to save time). This characteristic is called *polyphasic* thought or performance.

5. Always attempts to bring conversations around to topics that interest him, only pretending to listen to what others have to say when they discuss their own interests.

6. Almost always feels guilty when he relaxes or does nothing for a few days or even just a few hours.

7. Fails to observe interesting and attractive features of the environment (probably because too intent on his own plans and schedules).

8. Does not have time to spare for enjoyment because he is preoccupied with the getting of things.

9. Operates with a "chronic sense of time urgency." He tries to do more and more in less and less time, thereby setting himself up for crises when the tight, pressured schedule goes awry.

10. Behaves aggressively and competitively toward other type A people. "This is a telltale trait," say Friedman and Rosenman, "because no one arouses the aggressive and/or hostile feelings of one

type A subject more quickly than another type A subject."

11. Uses characteristic gestures or nervous tics that suggest he is in the midst of a continual struggle (e.g., pounding one fist into the palm of the other hand, clenching the jaw).

12. Believes that his success has been based on an ability to do things faster than others can or will, and feels he must continue to do everything as fast as he can.

13. Prefers to evaluate his own activities and those of other people in terms of numbers—how much accomplished in what period of time.

This is the full-blown type A pattern. Many people have type A characteristics that have not reached the proportions just outlined. In fact, Friedman and Rosenman report that type A behaviors are very common in our society.

What is type B life-style? It is perhaps most easily defined as the *absence* of the characteristics noted for type A. The type B person can relax without guilt, is not haunted by a sense of chronic time urgency or the need to challenge every possible competitor. He does not carry about an excess load of aggression or hostility. He has the time and inclination to enjoy life and appreciate what is beautiful and interesting in the world around him. The type B person is also thought to have a clearer sense of his own resources and limitations. He is less likely to overreach himself in an effort to prove his worth, more willing to trust his own judgment of his value as a person.

The type A pattern is thought both to increase an individual's likelihood of developing coronary heart disease (CHD)* in the first place and to magnify the risk to life once this disorder has appeared. Personality or life-style,

---

*CHD is defined as coronary artery disease that has become severe enough to produce symptoms or actual injury to cardiac muscle.

then, bears on the "choice" of terminal illness. Furthermore, because the illness is in some way engendered by life-style, it is not only the nature of the condition but the timing of death that is influenced. The Friedman-Rosenman research suggests that many people have perished with severe CHD who might otherwise be alive and healthy today. This is certainly an example of taking personality or life-style very seriously as a factor in terminal illness.

There is an important question of sequence here. Does a particular life-style *lead* to a particular life-threatening illness? Or is it more accurate to conclude that certain personality characteristics develop *in reaction* to the disease? This question could not be answered if we met a person for the first time when he was already far advanced on a terminal trajectory. We could not then determine with any confidence whether his personality style at this point had preceded or followed the onset of severe illness. However, because Friedman and Rosenman did follow the same men over a period of years, they were in a position to observe that well-established type A behavior often preceded CHD.

When Friedman and Rosenman decided to share their basic findings with the general public they also made an effort to provide helpful advice and suggestions. It was clear to them that it is already too late for some people to prevent the development of coronary symptoms, but they felt that modifications in life-style could still make an important difference. They offer a set of drills to guide people with type A behavior patterns to a less stressful life-style. Essentially, these guides would increase the individual's sensitivities to the needs of other people, reduce the sense of overwhelming time pressure, and bring him into a more serene relationship with the world. A type A person who could modify his approach to life in the ways suggested by Friedman and Rosenman would probably become more relaxed and comfortable. This new orientation might then extend his life, and at the same time bring a quality to his experience that had been missing for many years. They emphasize that a modification of personality or behavior patterns is the most important "treatment" a person can pursue for himself: "If you can't succeed in altering your behavior pattern, you aren't being protected against heart disease, no matter how little cholesterol you now eat, how little cigarette smoke you inhale, or how many miles you run each day."[26,p.240]

A person with CHD may not be dying in the sense that this term most often is applied. However, the more severe the symptoms, the greater is the probability of death within the relatively near future. The findings and suggestions of Friedman and Rosenman can be appreciated as quite relevant to the situation of the person whose death may be in close prospect.

There is another facet of the CHD-personality relationship that should be made explicit. The discovery of an apparent relationship between type A behavior and premature illness and death has led quickly to advocacy for preventing or changing this pattern. This advocacy seems plausible enough. Shouldn't people be spared the suffering of CHD and the foreshortening of their lives? And isn't the type A pattern a distressful one for both the individual himself and those around him? I am tempted to answer both questions affirmatively. But I hesitate a moment. Advocacy for changing type A behavior is not simply a public health or medical issue. It is an issue of values and priorities as well. In the service of preventative medicine or of mental health we might inadvertently find ourselves campaigning against a certain life-style. Is this what we *want* to do? And is such a campaign, in fact, consistent with our cultural values that emphasize many of the traits embodied in type A behavior? The value question has been raised: What is your answer?

In point of fact, it is very difficult for many people to change their life-style even when there is reason to believe that certain changes might appreciably reduce the likelihood of premature death. A national Multiple Risk Factor Intervention Trial has been in progress in the United States for the past few years, encouraged in part by findings such as those of Friedman and Rosenman. There have been favorable results for some of the volunteer participants (people at higher than normal risk for life-threatening illness), but also many examples of people who seem unable or unwilling to alter their behavior to save their lives. As the authors of a recent literature review on this topic indicate, many of us routinely engage in self-destructive behaviors whose outcomes are death by illness.[27] It cannot be assumed that we will change our smoking, drinking, eating, or physical activity habits just to stay alive. Another way of saying this, perhaps, is that longevity is not necessarily our primary and dominating motive, no matter what some people have been saying about the "drive to survive" for many centuries.

Environment

Individual differences among terminally ill people sometimes appear to be obscured by environmental constraints. A ward comprised entirely of withdrawn, unresponsive patients might lead the observer to conclude that this is the natural or universal reaction to impending death. There is an alternative possibility, however. Lack of stimulation and a general ward milieu in which individuality is discouraged can be the primary factor responsible for the apparent homogeneity.

There is widespread appreciation among social scientists and others for the impact of the environment on the individual. This can be seen in large-scale efforts such as conservation of natural and historical resources throughout the nation. It can also be seen in the burgeoning literature on creating a liveable environment for the city dweller, the factory worker, the office clerk, and so on. The reader who is not already acquainted with important developments in our knowledge of enviromental impact has many sources to consult (e.g., Proshansky et al., 1970[28]; Odum, 1971[29]).

Environmental factors can be of particularly great significance for the dying person. The weakness and immobility that often accompany the later phases of the dying process increasingly limit the individual's environmental options. He cannot be in the place that might bring most comfort, perhaps, because of nursing and medical needs that seem to require hospitalization. There is progressively less control over the environment. This includes both physical and social components. The dying person may not be able to choose who will be in his vicinity. It may be a person he has never seen before, also on a terminal trajectory. He has little control over the routines of the day. Most of the sights, smells, and sounds belong to the place rather than to the individual. The old woman in a nursing home or hospital, for example, is not sniffing the familiar aromas of her German or Spanish kitchen; the furniture lacks the textures and contours of the chairs, tables, and beds she has known for years; and so on.

The typical dying person tends to be increasingly alienated from the familiar circumstances of his life and increasingly powerless in controlling or influencing the environment.

This means that anxiety, withdrawal, anger, confusion, and a variety of other states observed in the terminally ill can be interpreted as understandable responses to a threatening or inadequate environment. Many of us would also feel anxious, withdrawn, angry, or confused if constrained indefinitely within a closed-system environment that bears little relationship to the kind of person we are and the kind of lives we have led. The sensory and social deprivation of some dying places seems to encourage a loosening of the ties to consensual

reality. The mind is left to its own resources, fears, and preoccupations. A combination of psychosocially depleted environment, illness, and medication can easily develop into a picture of confusion or despair. "That is what dying is all about!" one person might say. "No, that is what we impose on people *because* they are dying!" is an appropriate rejoinder.

Consider a few of the psychosocial dimensions of the dying person's environment. Is this individual the *only* person dying here? If so, then it is more likely that special treatment patterns will be applied, special in either a positive or negative sense. But if this is a situation where *everybody* is dying a quite different pattern might evolve. Is this an environment in which dying and death can be openly discussed? Or do family or staff operate under the assumption that denial and evasion are the best policies? Imagine yourself facing death in both of these situations. Although you are the same person, the nature of your experiences is likely to be quite different. In one situation you would find people ready to recognize and discuss your questions and needs with the clear understanding that death is in prospect. In the other situation you would find yourself under strong, if only implied, pressure to keep your unspeakable death to yourself. An observer's impression of the dying process in general or of you in particular might vary considerably depending on the environment in which he encountered you.

We do not know how much of the dying person's experiences depend on specific characteristics of the environment. In one sense, this is a research problem. We might envision a major study to examine the detailed relationships between terminally ill people and various aspects of their environments. But there is no need to wait for such a study to use our own eyes, minds, and hearts. Improved care of the dying person means, to some extent, an improved set of environments in which to live and to die.

Disease and treatment

A person does not just die. He dies of "something"—or of many things. Discussion of the dying person sometimes ignores the specific medical problems that so keenly affect his welfare. Similarly, the nature of the treatment being carried out, and how the patient responds to the treatment, also deserve consideration. We are spinning off observations and ideas in the abstract unless we continually bear in mind the symptoms and treatment patterns for specific life-threatening illnesses.

Think, for example, of the difference between a person whose likely cause of death will be kidney failure and its complications and a person suffering severe inroads into his respiratory functioning. There is no intention here of claiming that there is a single pattern with any one disease entity—this would run counter to the multifaceted approach we have been trying to convey. Nevertheless, there are some features more often observed in one form of advanced illness than in another.

The person with kidney failure may fade away as waste products accumulate in the body. Over a period of time, he may become more lethargic, less alert, less able to sustain attention and intention. There may, however, be intermittent periods of better functioning when the person seems more like his old self. The very final hours or days may be spent in a comatose condition.

A degenerative respiratory condition is apt to produce more alarming symptoms and experiences. Perhaps you have seen a person with advanced emphysema struggle for breath. An episode of acute respiratory failure is frightening to the individual himself and likely to arouse the anxiety of those around him. Once a person has experienced this kind of distress it is difficult to avoid apprehension about future episodes.

Some conditions are accompanied by persistent pain and discomfort. Other conditions can reach peaks of agony that test the limits of the individual and the state of medical comfort giving. Nausea, weakness, and a more generalized sense of ill-being may be more dominant than pain for some terminally ill people. It is difficult to appear serene and philosophical when one is wracked by vomiting or diarrhea. All the possible symptoms of all the possible pathways of terminal decline need not be catalogued here. But the friend, relative, caregiver, and researcher would do well to appreciate that the particular person is not dying in an abstract sense; there are specific impairments and symptoms that directly affect thinking and mood.

Different types of treatment may be carried out for the same condition, depending on characteristics of the patient and the hospital. Just knowing the nature of the illness, then, does not tell us everything about what the person has been experiencing. Some of the more advanced forms of treatment today for life-threatening illness require isolation. The patient is placed in an environment especially designed for its freedom from possible contamination—biologically, a nonliving environment. This is done, for example, when the patient has lost his immunity defenses and could not ward off even minor infections. Isolation as part of treatment is still isolation. At a time when the individual may be much in need psychologically of support, interaction, and familiar faces, every effort is made to keep him in a sterile situation. Whether or not the person survives this treatment physically, the experience itself introduces appreciable stress. In medical settings where the more advanced procedures are not available, the patient with the same condition may experience life rather differently.

It makes a difference whether a person is suffering from a condition for which a standard regime has been well established or for which experimental treatments dominate. The fact that a treatment is experimental often means that the patient's life is controlled down to the smallest detail in order to permit careful evaluation of the results. Sociologist Renee C. Fox has published these instructions for patients on a metabolic endocrine research ward:

> Patient can eat only what is given on his tray. Absolutely nothing else. He must eat every crumb of food on his diet, every grain of measured salt, if any, every bit of butter, sugar, bread, etc.
>
> Patient is to drink only the distilled water which is given him in his carafe. He is not to drink water from the faucet or fountain.
>
> Repeat. Repeat. Repeat. Patient may have no candy, cake, fruit, soda or chewing gum which visitors might bring in. Only foods on the diet may be eaten.
>
> Patients may not use regular toothpaste because it contains calcium.
>
> Each patient has his own urinal and bedpan in the utility room marked with his name. . . . Remind patients to empty bladder when voiding. Urinal should be left on shelf in utility room with tag noting patient's name and time of voiding.
>
> Special time for Voiding
> a. Between 6–7 AM to complete 24-hour collection.
> b. Between 9:30–10:30 (before going to bed).
> c. Before defecating.
> d. Before going to bath.
> e. Before going off the ward for any reason.
> Procedure for Defecating:
> a. Ambulatory patients void, then place a white enamel stool inside the commode. Can and lid are left on shelf in utility room and tagged with patient's name and time of defecation.
> b. Bed patients void in urinal, then defecate in separate bedpan which has been lined with 2 layers of wax paper.[30, pp. 122-123]

We have reprinted this entire list to convey the extraordinary degree of control that may be exerted over a person's life for purposes of treatment and research. The individual himself would hardly dream up this kind of regime if he were resolved to live out the final days in a manner consistent with previous personality and values. The example given here is fairly extreme but not altogether uncommon. It points

to a frequent trade-off: the person with a life-threatening illness surrenders options and controls over much of his existence in an effort either to receive the direct benefits of medical advances or to contribute to the eventual development of successful treatments.

The nature of the disease and its treatment has been barely touched on here. The same may be said for the previous topics covered. But perhaps enough has been conveyed to revise the lingering image of dying as a rather abstract process or a dramatic moment.

Stages of adaptation

We have examined a variety of influences on the experiences and behaviors of a person whose death is in close prospect. At least one important set of phenomena remains to be considered: adaptive strategies, reactions, or stages that become evident during the dying process. The focus now is on what the individual does in response to his situation of jeopardy.

The basic idea that a dying person might develop a strategy for adapting to her perils and limitations was unfamiliar to most people until recent years. People who did not have responsibilities that brought them into intimate contact with the terminally ill seldom thought systematically about this subject. The learned disciplines were the most part silent. There was no developmental psychology of dying, for example, no well-formulated psychiatric or psychobiological expectations. Before taking up the question of specific adaptational strategies, then, we might acknowledge that this is a relatively new approach, although there are some historical forerunners.

The writings and lectures of Elisabeth Kubler-Ross have drawn widespread attention to the psychological world of the dying person, most notably her book *On Death and Dying*.[19] Her basic points are so well known by now that only a brief summary is required. The following conceptualization was based on her interviews with approximately 200 patients in a Chicago-area hospital. Subsequently she has interviewed several hundred other patients throughout the country. Kubler-Ross believes that the dying person passes through five stages. These begin when the individual becomes aware of the poor prognosis. The stages are normal, or nonpathological, ways of responding to the prospect of death and the miseries of dying. The individual begins with a stage known as *denial*, and moves through the remaining stages of *anger, bargaining, depression,* and *acceptance.* Some people do not make it all the way through to acceptance. A person may become arrested at any of the stages along the way. Further, there can be some slipping back and forth between stages, and each individual has his own tempo of movement through the stages.

Denial is the first response to the bad news. "No, not me, it cannot be true!" is the typical statement or feeling that is communicated. The denial stage can be expressed in many ways. Kubler-Ross cites, for example, a woman who insisted that her x-ray films had been mixed up with some other patient's and who subsequently shopped around for other doctors, hoping to find a more optimistic prognosis. Denial is fueled by anxiety and usually is a temporary defense. It could also be described as "a state of shock from which he recuperates gradually."[19,p.37]

Anger wells up and boils over after the initial shock and denial response has passed. "Why *me?*" is the characteristic feeling at this time. The patient's rage and resentment can be expressed in many directions. A pious person might even vent anger at God. It is as though somebody must be blamed for his overwhelming disaster. The patient is likely to become more difficult to relate to at this time because of his struggle with frustration and fury.

Bargaining is the middle stage. The dying person attempts to make some kind of deal with fate. He may ask for an extension of life, just long enough, say, to see a child graduate from high school or get married. The bargaining process may go on between the patient and his caregivers, friends, or family or in an internal dialogue with God. Kubler-Ross compares the shift from anger to bargaining with the child whose request for an overnight visit with a friend has been rejected. The child stamps his foot and shouts defiantly, "No!" Then, a little later, he comes around to ask, "If I am very good all week and wash the dishes every evening, then will you let me go?"[19,p.72]

Depression eventually follows as the person experiences increasing weakness, discomfort, and physical deterioration. He can see that he is not getting better. The symptoms are too obvious to ignore. The stress and strain have taken too much out of him. The psychological picture of depression may include feelings of guilt and unworthiness. There may also be explicit fear of dying at this stage and a loosening of relationships with other people. The person is withdrawing, becoming less responsive. A sense of great loss dominates his thoughts and feelings.

Acceptance, the final stage, represents the end of the struggle. The patient is letting go. This shows up in a lifting or amelioration of the depression. However, acceptance is not necessarily a happy or blissful state. "It is almost void of feelings. It is as if the pain had gone, the struggle is over, and there comes a time for 'the final rest before the long journey' as one patient phrased it."[19,p.100]

Interwoven through all five stages there is the strand of *hope.* The unexpected shift from realistic acknowledgement of impending death to hope of miraculous recovery is seen often enough that it is hardly unexpected any more. Subtle though its expression may be, the maintenance of hope occurs throughout the whole sequence.

In addition to describing these stages, Kubler-Ross indicates some of the typical problems that arise at each point and suggests ways of approaching them. She emphasizes, for example, the need to understand and tolerate the patient's anger during the second stage rather than to retaliate and punish him for it.

Evaluating the stage theory

The stage theory of dying requires careful evaluation. It was accepted quickly by some people as though a definitive and comprehensive account. Soon after the first Kubler-Ross book was published and its message repeated in hundreds of lectures, there was a social phenomenon worthy of analysis in its own right. Many readers and listeners behaved as though memorizing the five stages is equivalent to knowing what the dying process was all about and, therefore, what should and should not be done. This conceptualization exerted so much appeal that attempts at objective evaluation were decidedly unwelcome. Even subsequent efforts by Kubler-Ross to discourage rigid adherence to stage theory could not catch up to this phenomenon. Like any other attempt to understand human experience, the stage theory of dying must be examined with all the thoroughness and sensitivity that can be brought to the enterprise. The fact that it is concerned with life-and-death matters cannot be taken as a reason for lowering standards of evidence; if anything, this intensifies our obligation to evaluate the theory with great care. We can make only a beginning here. The first set of points presented here concentrate on the negative side; this is followed by another set of observations that concentrate more on the positive or supportive side.

1. *The existence of the stages as such has not been demonstrated.* Dying people sometimes use denial, become angry, try to bargain with fate, lapse into depression, or into a depleted, beyond-the-struggle way of being. These phenomena themselves have been clearly described by Kubler-Ross and others. However, her conceptualization aspires to be more than a catalogue of moods or orientations shown by dying people. No evidence is presented that any of these phenomena comprise what scientists ordinarily would understand as a "stage" (see, for example, definitions and discussions of stages in developmental biology or in Piaget's work on cognitive maturation). A person may bargain, for example, and yet have many other thoughts, feelings, and maneuvers in operation at about the same time. What is the basis for specifying this as a bargaining stage? Furthermore, because of the lack of clear definitions and criteria for stages per se in this theory, it is possible that other responses to the dying situation might qualify as well as those presently included. Some people, for example, seem very concerned with *controlling* what happens to them. Others are especially interested in assuring a kind of *continuity* between themselves and those who will survive them. These are just two of the other dynamics that can be observed among dying people. Which dynamics are powerful and universal enough to be fixed as stages? What criteria and evidence should be used? At present there is no clear evidence for the establishment of *five* basic orientations among dying people, as distinguished from any smaller or larger number, and no evidence that any of the terms employed by Kubler-Ross meet criteria appropriate for a stage.

2. *No evidence is presented that people do move from stage 1 through stage 5.* Examples of behavior said to comprise stages are given in the form of brief clinical descriptions involving various patients. But evidence that the *same* person goes through all the stages is not offered. There are a number of ways in which clinical observations such as those made by Kubler-Ross could be presented and analyzed to test the possibility of sequential modes of functioning. This was not done either in the origi-

nal book nor in subsequent presentations. For the better part of a decade, then, the basic stage conceptualization has been taken on faith.

3. *Limits of the method have not been recognized.* The conclusions come from observations made—and then interpretered—by one person. The method is the psychiatric interview, more specifically, it is the psychiatric interview as conducted by an individual with a particular personal and professional background. This is a natural and sensible approach for exploring a problem area, making observations, acquiring insights. The conclusions drawn, however, do not acknowledge the special conditions and limitations within which the observations should be viewed. Other psychiatrists or clinicians have made other observations and interpretations of the dying person's situation. This is not surprising, for the interview method relies heavily on the particular experience, personality, and purpose of the interviewer and the type of relationship formed with the interviewee. The step from observation to interpretation is a significant one, but neither the basic observation nor the process of interpretation has been checked against the judgment of other qualified people. Furthermore, what the dying person says and does in the presence of a psychiatrist is not identical with his entire mode of functioning. The nurse who cares regularly for the patient's physical needs may see important aspects of the total functioning that do not show up in an interview, and the same may be said of the physician in charge and family members and friends. Behavioral studies might reveal a different perspective, as might a diary kept by the patient himself. In other words, one valuable source of information about the experiences and needs of the dying patient has taken the place of extensive, multilevel, cross-validated approaches. This is *not* a criticism either of the clinical method or of Kubler-Ross's skill in its use; it is simply an acknowledgement that a set of con-

clusions have been widely accepted without concern for the specific limitations of the data-gathering method used.

4. *There is insufficient distinction between description and prescription.* Stage theories in general often fail to take a clear position on the distinction between what happens and what *should* happen. Once a stage framework has been established it is typical for people to attach positive values to rapid movement from one stage to the next. Protests from Jean Piaget have not prevented some educators and developmentalists from devising programs to speed up the child's maturation. Kubler-Ross similarly has cautioned against trying to rush a patient through the stages. But the impulse often can be observed among caregivers or family who are acquainted with the basic idea of the stages. People draw the implication that the patient should be heading from denial right through to acceptance. This generates pressure that may or may not be desirable from other standpoints. And it establishes the image of acceptance as the universally desired outcome of the dying person's ordeal.

We may place subtle but compelling demands on the individual to meet our expectations, without having clear in our minds the distinction between modal and desirable patterns of adapting to the prospect of death. The dangers here are intensified by the fact that most deaths occur in institutional settings. The concept of universal stages thus lends itself to misuse by those who would find their tasks simplified and anxieties reduced through a standardized approach to the dying person.

5. *There is a questionable balance between emphasis on response to the dying situation and the totality of the individual's life.* The stage theory has tended to make the dying person seem very special. This has its positive aspects. Yet it engenders an attitude of hedging our relationships with the dying person around with rules and expectations presumably specific

to his situation. The supposed universality of the stages has already led to the dying person being treated by some people as a kind of specimen moving along predetermined paths rather than as a complete human being with a distinctive identity. But we have already reminded ourselves that the dying person is male or female, of one ethnic background or another, and at a particular point in his or her life cycle. We have seen that the nature of the disease, its symptoms, and its treatment can have a profound effect on what the dying person experiences. Perhaps most important of all, *who the person is* deserves prime consideration in the dying situation as in any other. Even if the stage theory were clarified and proven, it is unlikely that it would account for nearly as much of the dying person's experiences as has been widely assumed. The person takes the entire course of his life with him into the final months and weeks. Emphasis on the still hypothetical stages of reaction to terminal illness tends to drain away individuality, or at least our perception of individuality.

6. *The resources, pressures, and characteristics of the immediate environment can also make a tremendous difference.* There are still medical environments, for example, in which almost everybody "denies" core aspects of terminality almost all of the time. This obviously has an influence over the individual patient who supposedly begins with a denial reaction. Note that the same terminally ill person might respond quite differently if located in a death-denying as compared with an Amish environment or, again, in a hospice-oriented environment. Too much has been learned about environmental dynamics for us to treat these in a simple or neglectful manner when considering the experiences of the terminally ill person.[31]

7. *The available evidence, although not definitive, fails to provide support for a stage theory of dying.* Studies have not generally confirmed the five-stage model.[e.g.,32,33] It remains surprising that no truly systematic, well-

controlled investigation seems to have been carried out on an appropriate scale to properly evaluate the stage model. Available research and much of the clinical experience that has accumulated over the past decade, however, suggest that much caution be used in applying the model to the experiences and behavior of terminally ill people in general.

Against these selected criticisms should be set considerations such as the following:

1. The value of Kubler-Ross's work in improving sensitivity to the needs of the dying person has not been called into question. The criticisms have been limited to the stage theory and some of its implications. The stage theory is not essential for appreciation of many of her useful observations and insights.

2. It is not necessary that the stage theory be accepted or rejected in all its particulars. From my own experience, for example, it appears that some form of denial very frequently occurs soon after the person is confronted with the prospect of dying and death. Specific phenomena described by Kubler-Ross could be examined in more detail and placed into perspective without having to accept the total theory as it now stands.

3. Some of the practical problems that have arisen in the wake of Kubler-Ross's presentations can be attributed to hasty and uncritical application rather than to her observations and ideas as such. With more death education courses now available and, we hope, a growth of experience and sophistication in general, her work may receive more appropriate application.

4. The idea that there might be adaptive stages in the terminal process is worth attention. This first theory needs better documentation and perhaps extensive revision as well. But it has pointed the way to one of the possible approaches for conceptualizing the dying person's active participation in life's final scenes.

In sum, the need for a guide to understanding the plight of the dying person—and to keep our own anxieties under control—has led to a premature acceptance of the Kubler-Ross conceptualization. It has also led to simplistic and overly rigid use of her observations. These range from the dismissal of a patient's legitimate complaints about poor treatment as "just what you would expect in stage 2" to the assumption that further research is not really important because the stages tell us all. Evaluation of her specific contributions may take many years. It is already clear, however, that she has done much to heighten awareness of the dying person and his needs, making it possible, at least, for many people to begin the dialogue.

SUMMARY

The dying process reflects much of what has given a particular life its distinctive character. The conditions of life are so complex and multileveled that it is possible to arrive at rather different interpretations of the dying person's experiences depending on our own selective attention. This is illustrated here by examining several biographical factors that each person brings to the last scenes: *age, sex, ethnic background, interpersonal relationships,* and *personality* or *life-style*. Each individual is at a particular age or place in his total life span when death becomes a near prospect. The fact that one person is, for example, in early childhood and another in late middle age has important bearing on his ways of coming to terms with dying and death. Examples of sex-role and ethnic differences were also cited. Additionally, each person has become part of an interpersonal network comprising friends, relations, perhaps colleagues. There is evidence that the nature of this interpersonal network influences the dying person's experiences and may even affect the duration of life. Individual personality or life-style can influence the "choice" of final illness and also the quality of experience during this time.

Yet there is much more to understand about the dying person's situation. What about the disease or life-threatening condition itself? The *specific disease and treatment* must be taken into account. When we ignore the symptoms and trajectory of the particular life-threatening illness, we are apt to develop an unrealistically abstract view of the dying process. Similarities and differences in the dying experience are not to be found entirely on the basis of age or personality, for example, but also on the basis of the types of pain, discomfort, or disfiguration associated with a particular illness and its treatment.

Furthermore, a person does not die in a generalized or abstract place. He lives in an *environment* whose resources and constraints are likely to exert much influence over his experience. Two people with the same life-threatening illness may have vastly different experiences. One might, for example, be treated entirely as a patient within a totally medical situation; the other might be in a more homelike situation in which his distinctive life-style can continue to express itself and be appreciated.

Let us return now to the question whether people die primarily in a universal manner or in distinctive, individual ways. A narrow answer to this question might focus on any one of the factors noted: for example, a person dies the death of his disease or of his people. In other words, there are important similarities in the way that certain groups of people meet death. Yet a person has many characteristics and cannot be considered exclusively a third-generation Japanese-American, for example, or exclusively a victim of coronary heart disease.

We might ask, then, what is the likelihood of any two people having precisely the same pattern of age, sex, ethnic background, interpersonal relationships, and personality—and then developing the same life-threatening illness and ending up in the same environment? The closer we look at these variables, the more the probabilities shrink. The same environment, for example, may not really be the same for both people, especially if separated by a period of time.

The individual's total life pattern is likely to be so distinctive that his way of meeting death will also be distinctive. It should be quickly added that individuality can be deprived of expression by factors such as a limited or oppressive environment. If we come on a number of people who seem alike in their withdrawn and unresponsive or agitated and anxious orientations, it is not necessarily the case that this is the way people die. Instead, it may be that we have entered an environment in which sensory deprivation, emotional isolation, and over-dependence on pharmaceutical means of control are salient, or an environment in which the staff's own insecurity around death has exercised a contagious influence on the patients.

There is still another consideration: the individual's way of adapting himself to the specific stress and challenges of the dying process. This was represented in our discussion by Kubler-Ross's *stage theory of dying*. The emphasis here is almost exclusively on what might be termed the adaptive strategies of the dying person. These are conceptualized in terms of stages. There is a strong implication of universality: all dying people move through these stages (although with some variations in rate of movement and how far they proceed). This theory has been accepted rather hastily and uncritically, resulting in some unfortunate misapplications. However, it is valuable not only for the specific observations and insights made along the way but also because it raises the possibility that there might be some basic, universal modes of adaptation to terminal illness.

On balance, the possibility of characteristic stages of dying is best seen within a larger framework. Even if a person does experience and express some feelings in common with any other dying person, he does so within the unique pattern of a life that no other person

has lived, and within a particular environment while suffering from a particular disease syndrome. What is *distinctive* about this person's life may be more significant at a particular moment than the universal situation he has in common with many others.

It is hoped that, as care giving and research improve, it will become possible to do more justice both to the individual and to the universal. We will be more prepared to understand predicaments relatively specific to an adolescent or an aged person who is facing death, for example, but also to understand this *specific* young or old person.

REFERENCES

1. Schaberg, B. Emotional development in patients dying of breast cancer. Masters thesis, Wayne State University School of Nursing, 1970.
2. Eisdorfer, C., & Lawton, M. P. (Eds.), *The psychology of adult development and aging.* Washington, D.C.: American Psychological Association, 1973.
3. Natterson, J. M., & Knudson, A. G. Observations concerning fear of death in fatally ill children and their mothers. *Psychosomatic Medicine,* 1960, *22,* 456-466.
4. Wass, H., & Scott, M. Middle school students' death concepts and concerns. *Middle School Journal,* 1978, *9,* 10-12.
5. Mennie, A. B. The child in pain. In L. Burton (Ed.), *Care of the child facing death.* London: Routledge & Kegan Paul, 1974.
6. Miller, M. B. *The interdisciplinary role of the nursing home medical director.* Wakesfield, Mass.: Contemporary Publishing, Inc., 1976.
7. Markson, E. The geriatric house of death. *International Journal of Aging and Human Development,* 1970, *1,* 37-50.
8. Butler, R. N. *Why survive?* New York: Harper & Row, Publishers, 1975.
9. Diggory, J., & Rothman, D. Z. Values destroyed by death. *Journal of Abnormal Psychology,* 1961, *63,* 205-210.
10. Kastenbaum, R. Fertility and the fear of death. *Journal of Social Issues,* 1974, *30,* 63-78.
11. Crowley, D. M. *Pain and its alleviation.* Los Angeles: University of California at Los Angeles, School of Nursing, 1962.
12. Zborowski, M. Cultural components in responses to pain. In D. Apple (Ed.), *Sociological studies of health and sickness.* New York: McGraw-Hill Book Co., 1960.

13. Kalish, R. A., & Reynolds, D. *Death and ethnicity: a psychocultural study*. Los Angeles: University of Southern California Press, 1976.

14. Kastenbaum, R. Reflections on old age, ethnicity, and death. In D. E. Gelfand, & A. J. Kutzik (Eds.), *Ethnicity and aging*. New York: Springer Publishing Co., Inc., 1979, pp. 81-95.

15. Weisman, A. D., & Worden, J. W. Psychosocial analysis of cancer deaths. *Omega*, 1975, *6*, 61-65.

16. Weisman, A. D., & Kastenbaum, R. *The psychological autopsy: a study of the terminal phase of life*. New York: Behavioral Publications, Inc., 1968.

17. Weisman, A. D. *The realization of death*. New York: Jason Aronson, Inc., 1974.

18. Weisman, A. D., & Worden, J. W. The existential plight in cancer: significance of the first 100 days. *International Journal of Psychiatry in Medicine*, 1976, *7*, 1-16.

19. Kubler-Ross, E. *On death and dying*. New York: Macmillan, Inc., 1969.

20. Kastenbaum, R., & Aisenberg, R. B. *The psychology of death*. New York: Springer Publishing Co., Inc., 1972/1976 (concise edition).

21. Kalish, R. A. Social distance and the dying. *Community Mental Health Journal*, 1966, *2*, 152-155.

22. Kastenbaum, R. Multiple perspectives on a geriatric "death valley." *Community Mental Health Journal*, 1967, *3*, 21-29

23. Feigenberg, L. Care and understanding of the dying: a patient-centered approach. *Omega*, 1975, *6*, 81-94.

24. Feigenberg, L. *Terminalvard*. Lund: Liber Laromedel, 1977.

25. Hinton, J. The influence of previous personality on reactions to having terminal cancer. *Omega*, 1975, *6*, 95-112.

26. Friedman, M., & Rosenman, R. R. *Type A behavior and your heart*. New York: Alfred A. Knopf, Inc., 1974.

27. Henderson, J. B., Hall, S. M., & Lipton, H. L. Changing self-destructive behaviors. In G. C. Stone, F. Cohen, & N. E. Adler (Eds.), *Health psychology*. San Francisco: Jossey-Bass, 1979, pp. 141-160.

28. Proshansky, M. H., Ittelson, W. H., & Rivlin, L. G. (Eds.). *Environmental psychology*. New York: Holt, Rinehart & Winston, 1970.

29. Odum, H. T. *Environment, power, and society*. New York: Wiley-Interscience, 1971.

30. Fox, R. C. *Experiment perilous*. Glencoe, Ill.: The Free Press, 1959.

31. Schulz, R., & Aderman, D. Clinical research and the stages of dying. *Omega*, 1974, *5*, 137-144.

32. Metzger, A. M. A Q-methodological study of the Kubler-Ross stage theory. *Omega*, 1979, *10*, 291-302.

33. Shneidman, E. S. *Voices of death*. New York: Harper & Row, Publishers, 1980.

CHAPTER 13

❖ DYING
The hospice and other innovations in care

A few years ago, *hospice* was a term known to only a few people, and only a few actual examples were to be found. Today, citizen groups in many communities throughout the nation are involved in detailed planning if not the direct operation of a caring and support system based on hospice principles. It is clear that significant changes are taking place right now. It is also clear that many of the changes are for the better, motivated by humane impulses. The hospice movement, however, is not an isolated phenomenon, nor is it free of pressure, conflict, and critical decision points. Some attention to the larger "death-awareness movement" would be valuable in helping us to develop a perspective for understanding the hospice and other innovations in terminal care.

THE DEATH-AWARENESS MOVEMENT: A BRIEF PORTRAIT

Those of us who are not professional historians tend to measure human events by the dimensions of our own lives. Most relevantly, our sense of the death-awareness movement will depend much on "when we came in." The point of entry for the largest number of people may have been only about a decade ago when the writings and lectures of Kubler-Ross[1] brought the predicament of the dying person to general attention. Others may have been around and paying attention a decade earlier when Feifel[2] discovered that *The Meaning of Death* in our society was largely shrouded behind a "taboo" orientation. One might, in fact, make a strong case that the death-awareness movement in the United States started soon after the end of World War II and has, essentially, moved from taboo to hospice during that time. Even a brief and selected portrait of the death-awareness movement, however, should offer both more breadth and more detail.

Before the "discovery" of death

There is no harm in starting with a simple view, one that is reasonably accurate within its limits. If we were to revisit the 1950s, we would be likely to make observations of the following kind:

1. Nobody was dying or had died. People might "pass on," "expire," or "go to their Great Reward," but direct, explicit death words were seldom used. This was generally true in both medical and lay realms.

2. Institutionalized denial could be found almost everywhere. By "institutionalized denial," we mean that this was so much a characteristic of society in general, that it hardly made sense to speak of particular individuals as denying dying and death. Evelyn Waugh's fictional account of morticians arranging philo-

sophical smiles on the faces of their clients[3] was not far off the mark of actual verbal and non-verbal behavior in real life.

3. Not only were "death-education" courses virtually unheard of, but few courses of any type considered the topics of dying, death, and bereavement. One could become "an educated person" with any number of advanced courses in psychology and related fields without being called on to deal with these topics.

4. Very little clinical and research literature was available on these topics for those who might have been inclined to seek knowledge. Scattered articles and books would appear from time to time, but generally disappear into a cloud of indifference regardless of their merits.

5. Both dying and death were moving out of the province of the family and into medical and funeral "establishments" organized along increasingly technical, impersonal, and bureaucratic lines. The dying and the dead—and their families—were more frequently being "processed." This phenomenon was part of a more general tendency in American society (increasing "massness" and specialization) and, perhaps for this reason, not fully recognized at the time as presenting new problems for the personal identity and well-being of those engulfed by death situations.

6. Most critically, there was little appreciation for the terminally ill person as an individual, as a total person. During these "silent years," it was as though most people had signed a secret contract to pretend that dying and death did not exist. Any actions that acknowledge the reality of death would threaten this tacit arrangement.

One of the most important aspects of this overall pattern was that it all seemed so proper. It was not just that people happened to employ euphemisms instead of direct language, or that nobody seemed to be researching, teaching, developing improved methods of care and the like. Rather, there was an underlying assumption that this was the way things were supposed to be. It was odd if not outrageous, perhaps even obscene[4] to acknowledge dying, death, and bereavement as significant human events that deserved serious attention.

Recognizing the taboo

Currents of change began to swirl in the late 1950s and early 1960s. The general scene did not change much, but individuals and small groups here and there made sharp observations of the prevailing situation and had their own encounters with the "establishment." Herman Feifel, whose name has already been mentioned in this regard, exemplifies this period of "stirring around." A psychologist with good credentials in clinical research, Feifel also was conversant with existential philosophy and sensitive to changes in the attitudes of society since the experiences of Word War II. He tried to pursue exploratory studies with people who were directly facing problems associated with aging or dying. Feifel immediately found himself facing problems—not so much from the individuals at risk, but from an establishment that actively and fiercely resisted attention to this sealed-off domain. It was Feifel who first clearly described the taboolike characteristics of our society at that time around the subject of death.[5] He persisted in his work, despite rebuffs and ridicule, and did much to prepare the way for subsequent efforts. Other people in a variety of disciplines—nursing, psychiatry, social work, sociology, and so on—were starting to make their own independent forays into taboo territory, and often had to face similar antagonism. The dying person was being so well "protected" against human contact that an individual who expressed any inclination to be with the terminally ill was likely to be treated as a crazed invader. It may be difficult for some people to believe that this attitude was well entrenched just a few years ago, but these were the early experiences of many people who became the founders of today's death-awareness movement.

This was a period of time in which the occasional and exceptional person would respond to human needs by offering psychotherapy to the terminally ill,[6] beginning to chart the full range of psychosocial concerns that accompany life-threatening illness,[7] or otherwise taking an active role. Most of these people worked without social and scientific support systems for their own efforts and had to develop their own knowledge and techniques as they went along. This was also a period of time in which the psychological meanings of suicide and systematic efforts to prevent suicide began to take shape (e.g., Farberow and Shneidman[8]). We will not be following this component of the death-awareness movement in detail here. Important as it is in its own right, the suicide-prevention effort has continued to develop largely as a separate component in our culture's death system. This itself is a curious situation because there are in fact many significant interrelationships between dying/death/bereavement and suicide dynamics. Some of these have been recognized by various writers, but the death-awareness movement and suicide prevention as such have tended to go somewhat independent ways.

"Death talk," concern, and criticism

The situation had changed again by the time we turned the corner from the late 1960s into the early 1970s. Most of the "negatives" so commonplace in the 1950s could still be observed throughout the United States. There was now a counterforce to be reckoned with, however. Enough public attention had been engaged that one could actually speak of a true "death-awareness movement." At this time, the reasonably attentive observer might have noticed developments such as:

1. The exceptional popularity of a book that focused on the experiences of the dying person,[1] along with great public interest in lectures and workshops featuring author-psychiatrist Elisabeth Kubler-Ross.

2. A general increase in the number of publications on this topic, many of these embodying data, insights, and concepts that continue to provide a useful core to what has become a recognized domain of research and professional activity (even if it does not quite have a recognized and accepted name; *thanatology* probably comes as close as any, although not everybody likes this term). Illustrative of this development was the transition of a mimeographed death newsletter into *Omega*, an international journal concerned with death and dying that has now been officially alive since 1970.

3. The introduction of "death-education" courses in many forms and at many levels and contexts of instruction. Some of these courses failed, but many survived and on occasion were the most "exciting" or popular courses on a particular campus. Death-relevant material was also turning up now with some frequency in a variety of other courses (e.g., human development) and on the programs of many professional and scientific societies.

4. "Death talk" as a new theme in the media. There was a rather sudden shift from "taboo" to "curiosity" and then to (or over) the brink of "fad." We had rapidly transformed ourselves from a society in which the subject was improper and tacitly forbidden into one in which many people felt that "death talk" was almost obligatory.

5. Much of the "death talk" in the media and in professional and educational circles as well was of a critical nature. The needs of the terminally ill person and his or her family were often presented in vivid and compelling terms, while the health-care establishment was portrayed as insensitive and overbearing, if not downright arrogant and cruel. The most typical image, then, was of the suffering of the dying person and the aloof, technologically oriented

behavior of the health-care establishment, with the family to be counted as another victim of the process.

During this major phase in the death-awareness movement there was more talk than action. The talk had its effect: once the taboo had been removed, it was not likely that dying and death would go "back into the closet." Furthermore, the discussion helped many people to express feelings and experiences that had been weighing on them for years, while some people became activists and are now among the helpers and the teachers. By the early 1970s one could find an appreciable number of individuals and groups who felt ready, or almost ready, to do something useful in this area and were starting to explore the practical problems involved. *Hospice* was a beaconlike concept for those mostly concerned with improving the care of the terminally ill. In general, however, this was a brief era important chiefly for heightened awareness of dying and death and the beginning of a solid core of knowledge.

Practical action

Some people continue to "discover" death and have local taboos to break through. There are hospitals, schools, neighborhoods, and families in which the topic remains as threatening and "improper" as it was years ago. However, the growing edge of the death-awareness movement—and a rapidly growing edge it is—has now moved resolutely into practical activity. This momentum is obvious even in the short period between publication of the first edition of this book and the second edition you are now reading. The hospice concept required introductory exposition then, and one pointed naturally to the achievements of St. Christopher's Hospice in London and to the in-progress work in New Haven for major examples. Hospice organizations now exist in many forms and many levels of development throughout the United States, with the numbers increasing

so rapidly that a figure cited at the time of this writing (even if a dependable figure could be obtained) might well be dated by the time the book was published.

The nature of the discussion has changed as well. Much more attention is given to practical matters: coordination of services with other caregivers, selection and training of volunteers, financing, and so forth. There seems to be less need for people to convince each other about the need for improved care to the terminally ill person and his or her family. Large organizations and small, spontaneously formed community groups are working at the important details required for establishing and operating a hospice.

• • •

We will pick up now on the hospice movement in particular. Attention will be given both to the aims and methods of hospice care and to the social context in which these have been developing.

STANDARDS OF CARE FOR THE TERMINALLY ILL PERSON

By the early 1970s criticism of the care received by terminally ill people and their families had become fairly widespread. But precisely what was to be done? The hospice model already existed, most notably in the form of St. Christopher's Hospice (London). Was this to be the preferred approach to improved care? Some people closely associated with the death-awareness movement decided to work together as an international task force and took as one of their first challenges the establishment of standards of care. The participants represented many of the disciplines concerned with providing direct care or pursuing research and evaluation problems.

It was quickly agreed that there were no explicit standards of care in most places where people passed their last months, weeks, and hours. Practical action could be pursued more effectively if there were some standards or at least guidelines. The task force then decided to cast the unwritten, unofficial assumptions and practices that governed the care of the terminally ill person into the form of explicit standards. As you read this list, bear in mind that these were *not* the standards that the task force intended to recommend—rather, it was their way of setting out on the table the "hidden standards" that seemed to be implied by the way that many terminally people actually were treated.

Hidden or implicit standards of care

1. The successful death is quiet and uneventful. The death slips by with as little notice as possible; nobody is disturbed.
2. Few people are on the scene. There is, in effect, no scene. Staff is not required to adjust to the presence of family and other visitors who might have their own needs that upset the well-routined equilibrium.
3. Leave-taking behavior is at a minimum.
4. The physician does not have to involve him- or herself intimately in terminal care, especially as the end approaches.
5. The staff makes few technical errors throughout the terminal care process and few mistakes in medical etiquette.
6. Strong emphasis is given to the body during the caregiving process. Little effort is wasted on the personality of the terminally ill individual.
7. The person dies at the right time, that is, after the full range of medical interventions has been tried but before the onset of an interminable period of lingering on.
8. The patient expresses gratitude for the excellent care received.
9. After the patient's death, the family expresses gratitude for the excellent care received.
10. The staff is able to conclude that "we did everything we could for this patient."

11. Physical remains of the patient are made available to the hospital for clinical, research, or administrative purposes (via autopsy permission or organ gifts).
12. A memorial (financial) gift is made to the hospital in the name of the deceased.
13. The total cost of the terminal care process is determined to have been low or moderate: money was not wasted on a person whose life was beyond saving.[9]

This was seen as the typical pattern of a "good" or "successful" death from the perspective of the facility in which a terminally ill person spent his or her final days of life. The task force proposed a rather different set of standards. The particular wording given in the proposed standards to follow should be taken only as suggestive rather than fixed or definitive. Many hospice groups and others concerned with improved terminal care have since developed their own guidelines that represent variations or elaborations of the standards as presented here. This is quite in keeping with the task force's hope that standards of care will be carefully considered and discussed by all people responsible in some way for terminal care.

Some proposed standards

Patients, family, and staff all have legitimate needs and interests.

The terminally ill person's own preferences and life-style must be taken into account in all decision making.

These were perhaps the two most general and basic guidelines, from which the others follow. The first proposition should help to promote honest interactions and reduce unnecessary conflicts and extremism of any type. In some settings the family has been essentially left out in the cold while staff has tried to manage its own needs and anxieties (privately), while at the same time attempting to meet those of the patient. In other settings, there has been more of a staff-family network in operation, motivated to some extent by what these people need for their own emotional protection and less by the thoughts and feelings of the patient. In recent years there has been an apparent increase in patient-family as a team coming into a conflict with staff. Recognition that everybody in the situation is human and has legitimate needs and interests would seem to be a valid and important starting point for appropriate care.

The proposition about the terminally ill person's own preferences and life-style suggests that treatment should not be overly standardized. The common practice should be to recognize individuality. This means that strictly uniform, rigid rules of care cannot be laid down in all particulars and applied unvaryingly to the individual. Stated more positively, *particular criteria for care should emerge from consideration of each terminally ill individual's own personality.* Implementation of this general standard or guideline requires some "going against the grain" of usual professional and administrative practice (especially the latter), which often is inclined to favor the routinized, standardized, and essentially "automatic-ized."

Many of the following suggested guidelines emerge directly from the two general points just made.

PATIENT-ORIENTED STANDARDS

1. *Remission of symptoms is a treatment goal.* Terminal status, in other words, cannot be taken as a reason for neglect of medical or nursing efforts to reduce distressful symptoms. Even if it is expected that the person will die within hours or days, efforts should be continued to maintain functional capacity and relieve distress. A dying person should not be made to endure unnecessary thirst, for example, or gasp for breath when a change of position might afford relief.

2. *Pain control is a treatment goal.* Although pain control is part of the larger task of symptom alleviation, it is specific and important enough to be counted as a standard in its own right. Uncontrolled pain not only intensifies the anguish of dying very directly but also disturbs interpersonal relationships and demoralizes. The patient's ability to maintain psychological equilibrium is severely tested by pain.

3. *The "living will"* (see boxed material) *or similar document representing the patient's intentions will be respected as one of the determinants of the total pattern of care.* This does not mean that every expressed wish of the patient would automatically be granted. The rights and responsibilities of family, staff, and society as represented, for example, by the legal system must also be taken into account. But such a document will be considered appropriate and salient information clearly expressing the patient's preferences and intentions. (The "living will" itself is not a legally binding instrument. Some states have now passed and others are considering specific legislative acts that bear on the rights of the terminally ill person. The legal credentials of each such legislative action are themselves subject to challenge in the courts. As far as standards of care are concerned, the main point is the willingness of family and health-care providers to take seriously any document that expresses the patient's own wishes, whatever their legal status, as such, might be.)

4. *The patient should have a sense of basic security and protection in his or her environment.* This standard is met when the dying person feels he can depend on the caregivers to perform their functions and maintain appropriate communications. The patient should feel safe. He should be able to count on the people around him instead of living in apprehension of surprise tests, brusque treatment, or failure of

THE LIVING WILL

To my family, my physician, my lawyer, my clergyman
To any medical facility in whose care I happen to be
To any individual who may become responsible for my health, welfare, or affairs

Death is as much a reality as birth, growth, maturity and old age—it is the one certainty of life. If the time comes when I, _____, can no longer take part in decisions for my own future, let this statement stand as an expression of my wishes while I am still of sound mind.

If the situation should arise in which there is no reasonable expectation of my recovery from physical or mental disability, I request that I be allowed to die and not be kept alive by artificial means or "heroic measures." I do not fear death itself as much as the indignities of deterioration, dependence, and hopeless pain. I therefore ask that medication be mercifully administered to me to alleviate suffering even though this may hasten the moment of death.

This request is made after careful consideration. I hope you who care for me will feel morally bound to follow its mandate. I recognize that this appears to place a heavy responsibility on you, but it is with the intention of relieving you of such responsibility and of placing it on myself in accordance with my strong convictions that this statement is made.

Signed _____

Date _____

Witness _____   Witness _____

Copies of this request have been given to _____

_____

medication and meal routines. More critically, perhaps, the patient should feel safe emotionally—as though among people who truly care for him.

5. *Opportunities should be provided for leave-takings with the people most important to the patient.* This is likely to require flexible visiting hours and a more relaxed policy for admitting people often discriminated against by "the rules" (e.g., children or grandchildren). This standard also assumes that the environment is reasonably adaptable to simple but important needs of people who are seeing each other for perhaps the last time: a good place to sit, privacy when desired, freedom from interruption, and the like. The patient should also have the opportunity to take leave of other patients and staff if desired.

6. *Opportunities should be provided for experiencing the final moments in a way that is meaningful to the patient.* For example, the patient should be afforded the opportunity to listen to music or poetry of his choice. Physical contact should be made possible if desired, unless there is some overwhelming counterindication (e.g., a highly contagious disease). This includes the possibility of a dying man or woman being held in the arms of a spouse or other survivor if this is what they both want.

FAMILY-ORIENTED STANDARDS

1. *Family should have the opportunity to discuss dying, death, and related emotional needs with the staff.* It will not be appropriate for the staff to disregard requests for informa-

tion or expressions of the need to share feelings. While this increases the tasks of and time demands on staff, it helps the family maintain its own integration, and to be of comfort to the patient.

2. *Family should have the opportunity for privacy with the dying person both while living and while newly dead.* This might include, in some family constellations, participation of close kin and friends in dressing the corpse and accompanying it to the funeral home. Or it might include simply being alone with the dead spouse, sibling, or parent for an hour or so without interruption by staff. Any automatic preparation and routing of the deceased for purposes of hospital convenience should give way to providing the family an opportunity to express their feelings in their own style and begin the difficult process of grief and recuperation.

STAFF-ORIENTED STANDARDS

1. *Caregivers should have adequate time to form and maintain personal relationships with the patient.* This is not a priority now in most medical facilities. Implementation of this standard would require a revised attitude toward the role and scheduling of personnel. More attention might be given to the primary nursing system in which a particular staff member takes basic responsibility for a particular patient.[10] Better patient-staff relationships are desirable not only in themselves but also as a resource in treatment.

2. *A mutual support network should exist among the staff, encompassing both the technical and the socioemotional dimensions of working with the terminally ill.* Care for the terminally ill can become a draining, depleting experience, especially in a situation where there are frequent deaths. It is important that fellow workers be sensitive to each other's needs and limits and offer constructive suggestions and emotional support. The most humane and effective caregiver can lose perspective at

a particular moment. The most buoyant spirit can require comfort and support from others. A medical facility in which there is little discussion of staff responses to care of the terminally ill and no place for the individual physician or nurse to turn with his or her own feelings would not be seen as functioning acceptably, despite whatever modern resources and skills the facility might offer.

THE HOSPICE APPROACH

One practical aim of people concerned with improving care of the dying person is the modification of existing hospitals and health-care systems to meet standards of care such as those just given. This is a very difficult task in most traditional hospital settings and would seem to require a long-term effort. Furthermore, should not the same general principles of care extend to the terminally ill person, his family, and caregivers no matter where they are? An alternative is to create a different kind of system right from the beginning. Such systems of care—developed explicitly for care of individuals with limited life expectancy—have become known most widely as *hospices*. These have the advantage of beginning with a fairly clear set of priorities and a minimum of inertia and resistance to work against. There are also "in-between" solutions, such as the palliative-care unit, that might be established within an existing and more or less traditional medical setting but which itself is dedicated to the hospice philosophy and approach.

St. Christopher's: a model hospice

The hospice approach perhaps can best be exemplified by St. Christopher's, a facility that has been serving London since 1968. It quickly became an international mecca for those who would draw inspiration and insights for improved patterns of care. As a core part of her definition of St. Christopher's, Dr. Cicely Saunders, founder and director, states that "It is a Medical Foundation, aiming to offer the best professional standards of care to patients with chronic or terminal pain, both in its wards and in their own homes, especially, though not exclusively, to those with advanced malignant disease." But this is not all. It is also "a community of people gathered together to welcome and help the family during such illness and after the patient's death and to involve them as part of the caring team."[11,p.6]

Clearly, the hospice is not a "house of death" where people are shut away to die. The best available professional care is made available to all the clients; in fact, St. Christopher's has become notable for its contributions to the alleviation of pain and other types of distress. One of the most important points about a hospice is that the person continues to receive careful and appropriate medical-nursing care throughout the most advanced stages of illness. The caregivers do not turn away and say in effect, "there is nothing more we can do for you" when it becomes improbable that cure or remission can be achieved. Furthermore, the hospice is not just a place. Guiding principles for good care are followed in the patient's home or wherever he or she may be at a particular time. This means that some of the most important achievements of a hospice may not require a "place" as such—and therefore that helping organizations who lack appropriate inpatient services can nevertheless pursue hospice goals out in the community. Whether in or out of a hospice building, the concept of "community" and "caring team" is emphasized. Professionals neither abandon the terminally ill nor rush in to take over functions that are best served by family and friends.

The preceding statements have tried to overcome some of the more common misconceptions of what a hospice is by emphasizing what it is not. Put in more positive terms, a hospice is a system of care in which the active efforts of family, friends, and professional caregivers are integrated in the service of quality-of-life goals. For some individuals this involves one or more periods of residence within a hospice facility as such. Not every person who is terminally ill requires placement within a hospice facility, nor is everybody who resides in a hospice at a particular time necessarily destined to die there. Some people at St. Christopher's do enjoy periods of remission ("Although many are so frail that it is indeed the end of the journey just under 30% of those who live through their first week here will be discharged home much improved. Maximum independence in their own place of choice of suitability is the aim of hospice care.")[11,p.11]

Perhaps something of the character of St. Christopher's can be illustrated by an incident I happened to witness in the first few minutes of a visit there.

❖ Word has received that a person was arriving for admission. A station wagon had pulled up to an entrance facing the hospice's attractive garden plaza. The patient-to-be was a frail, emaciated woman who looked to be in her 60s. She was accompanied by a younger man. Dr. Saunders and the woman greeted each other as sunlight propitiously broke through the cloudy London skies. The woman smiled and said, "Well, I finally made it!" On her face there was the mark of physical ordeal but no indication of anxiety, anger, depression, or confusion. The patient was immediately introduced to the nurse who would be responsible for much of her care and then assisted to what would be her own bed (which had been transported by elevator to the ground-floor entrance). Just a few minutes later while touring the hospice we came on this woman again. She was already settled into her own place, sipping tea with the man who had driven her to the hospice. As it turned out, he was her husband. The woman was appreciably younger than her physical appearance had indicated because of the debilitating effects of advanced cancer.

This simple incident tells much about the aims and techniques of the hospice. The patient and her family had already been well acquainted with the hospice before time of admission. Consequently, there was a sense of having made the next logical stop on her journey through life rather than a jarring transition from home to an impersonal institution. Much of St. Christopher's effort is devoted to a home-care program. This has become true of many other hospices as well, and some hospice organizations consist only of the home-care component. With the guidance of hospice personnel, some families are able to provide high-quality care to their terminally ill members throughout the entire course of the illness. Patient and family know that the hospice is there when and if they need it. *Hospice* can perhaps be thought of more aptly as a process and a spirit of mutual concern rather than a place.

The sociophysical environment of the hospice facility, when one does in fact exist, is designed for life as well as death. In the little incident that has been described, for example, staff recognized the importance of the first few minutes of the admission process. There was a certain kind of efficiency made possible by current technology (e.g., having the patient's own bed ready to meet her). Many other up-to-date techniques are used throughout St. Christopher's when these are seen as beneficial to patient care. But there was also the affirmation of human contact by both the medical director and the nurse. The prompt welcoming of the husband through the tea service further signaled the hospice's interest in encouraging the maintenance of interpersonal relationships and comforting habits. These are small details. But Saunders and her staff value the significance of

details such as these as well as the more obviously important aspects of patient care.

The family of the terminally ill person is not merely tolerated at a hospice such as St. Christopher's. Instead, the family is both a provider and a recipient of care. The philosophy of care encompasses the entire family unit. Many family members not only visit with their own kin but also befriend other patients. This permeability of the hospice much reduces the likelihood of social isolation for the patient and the sense of helplessness for the family. It does raise the possibility, however, that the family might spend so much time and effort at the hospice that they do not look after their other needs adequately. To place a limit on family involvement, St. Christopher's has established a weekly "family's day off." This allows the family a useful "vacation" without any sense of guilt attached.

The philosophy of care also encompasses the staff. Saunders notes, for example, that

The fact that we have a playroom for the children of the staff has played an enormous part in maintaining a continuity of staffing. This enables a married person, trained or untrained, who has a desire to come back to nursing or care for people, to return to a field of nursing where she has a tremendous amount to give and also finds satisfaction.[12,p.519]

In many ways St. Christopher's Hospice represents an attempt to embody the emerging standards of care for the dying person. One might also say that the standards are a way of articulating some of the major goals that St. Christopher has been pursuing since its inception.

A person who has been with seriously and terminally ill patients in other environments is likely to observe a different attitude among most patients at St. Christopher's. There appears to be less anxiety and suffering, more serenity, and a stronger sense of security. One also gets the impression that it is neither the general atmosphere nor the specific treatment procedures that produce the favorable effects. Rather it seems to be the *integration* of the humane impulse and the clinical expertise. The hospice staff has made itself particularly expert in the management of chronic pain. Relief from seemingly endless and meaningless suffering makes it possible for many terminally ill people to call on their own personal resources to adapt to their situation and be more responsive to others. When the high priority given to pain management is successful, it makes a dramatic difference in the patient's sense of well-being and, obviously, a difference to the family and staff as well.

It is important to realize that many patients make their pain worse by anticipating it. Consequently *we* should do the anticipating . . . we use our drugs to prevent the pain from ever happening rather than trying to get on top of it once it has occurred. This means a careful analysis of the total situation—the other symptoms, attention to details, a lot of careful nursing, and just listening so that we know what their sensation is like, and so that they know we are interested. I had a patient say to me, "And then I came here and *you listened*. The pain seemed to go by just talking." She was not trying to be polite; her perception of pain had really been influenced by our attention and time.[12,p.64]

Is the hospice approach proving successful?

The impressions of staff and visitors at St. Christopher's suggest that the hospice approach is achieving its aims. This conclusion remains tentative, however, until we have an adequate base of systematic research not only at St. Christopher's but concerning other hospice organizations as well. This requires us to face another set of reality factors: (1) High-quality research is invariably very difficult to carry out in complex "real-life" settings, especially when the well-being and sensitivities of so many people must be taken into consideration. (2) Techniques for effective and relevant research into

care of the terminally ill person are presently at an early stage of development. (3) Research and evaluation priorities generally come well down the list—the primary goal of the hospice, of course, is improved care. Energies and funding for evaluation take a secondary place even for those caregivers who recognize the importance of continuous and thorough examination of the caring process and its outcome. The smaller hospice endeavors and those at an early point in their development seldom have energy and funding to spare in evaluation efforts. Furthermore, compassion and commitment to hospice objectives on the part of organizers and staff members does not guarantee research expertise. Hospice development at the moment seems to be running well ahead of the research and evaluation components that will be necessary at some point to see if the new approach is really making an appreciable difference. It is more than a matter of just finding out if the hospice approach "works." We also want to know what it is about the total hospice approach that is most useful, what problems should be identified and dealth with more adequately, how staff and volunteers can best be selected, trained, and helped to weather the stresses associated with their work, and so on.

Useful clinical studies are just starting to appear. C. Murray Parkes, for example, reports that only 8% of those who died at St. Christopher's suffered unrelieved pain, as compared with 20% who died in hospitals and 28% of those who died at home.[13] This study had several methodological limitations that were difficult to avoid under the circumstances, and so it is premature to come to firm conclusions. Nevertheless, here is at least an indication that there can be substantial benefits for individuals receiving hospice care. At the same time, the fact that pain control seems to be managed better at St. Christopher's Hospice than in tradicial hospitals or in the home setting suggests that applying hospice-learned expertise to these other settings could reduce the differential in the future.

In another recent study John Hinton[14] compared the attitudes of terminally ill patients at a hospice, a "foundation home" (a British near-equivalent to a nursing home), and acute hospital radiotherapy wards. Most aspects of care were rated equally in all three settings, but the hospice patients appeared least depressed and anxious—and preferred the more open, straightforward type of communication climate available to them there. The first research reports emerging from Hospice, Inc. of New Haven, Connecticut (generally considered the pioneering hospice venture in the United States) also suggest some quality-of-life differentials. Sylvia Lack and Robert Buckingham[15] report less anxiety, depression, and hostility among terminally ill patients receiving hospice-associated home care as compared with others who resided outside their cachement area and were without such services. Family members also seemed to benefit in terms of their overall social adjustment and ability to express their thoughts and feelings with less distress. These studies also have flaws and limitations that were difficult to avoid under the circumstances. The results, as far as they go, are encouraging to hospice advocates, but do not constitute a firm basis for drawing conclusions about the extent and nature of possible advantages associated with the hospice approach.

It is not surprising that many of the reports and evaluations that are emerging from the first wave of evaluation emphasize the relative cost of hospice care as compared with traditional hospitalization. Many people today are keenly aware of the enormous cost of hospitalization in general and are seeking ways to bring this under control. The cost factor is certainly important, but we remain concerned here more single-mindedly on the quality of life for terminally ill patient, family, and staff. Because

availability and sources of funding for hospices, as well as the expenses involved, continue to be in flux, the interested reader will need to keep up with current and local as well as national developments in this area. Useful background reading for perspective on the practical development and management of hospices—including ways in which hospice endeavors can fall apart—is provided by Paul M. DuBois in his recent book, *The Hospice Way of Death*.[16] A special issue of the journal *Death Education* is also devoted to the hospice movement and includes useful description of cost and other practical considerations involved in a variety of hospice-type approaches to terminal care in the United States and Canada.[17] What I wish to emphasize here is the hope that the question of cost does not gain undue prominence. Most of the people who have brought the hospice movement as far as it has come presently seem to have been motivated largely by the desire to improve care for the terminally ill person and the family. On the present scene, however (and, certainly, *behind* the scenes), financial concerns appear to be rapidly taking precedence. Some people appear ready to support an alternative care system such as the hospice if it promises to save money—whether or not this also results in actual improvement of care. Others seem to be playing into this bias by putting forth the hospice alternative as a kind of bargain (subsidized to some extent by significant free labor supplied by volunteers). I will not try to conceal my concern that financial issues may warp our expectations and affect our ability to concentrate on the caring process itself and its adequate evaluation. It will not be easy to place a price tag on quality of life for the terminally ill person (at least, I *hope* it will not be easy!). Without underestimating the importance of the financial aspects, it is still human lives we are concerned with here, and how well the hospice approach addresses itself to core human concerns when death is in prospect should remain our top priority. End of (please excuse me) sermon!

An experience with hospice home care

While systematic research and evaluation of hospice programs is still in its early stages, more and more people are directly experiencing the hospice approach. In the United States this is often limited to the home-care component, as only Hospice, Inc. (New Haven) has reached the point of constructing its own free-standing physical facility designed especially for that purpose. Let us take just one example of the context of death for a family that has participated in a home-care hospice program. Favoring detail over scope, we focus on the deathbed scene itself as recalled—vividly—by one family member, the young adult daughter of a woman who had been terminally ill for several months after a lifetime of good health.

❖ The next day I woke up and went in to see my mother. I noticed the difference immediately. She had this rattle in her throat. She kept trying to talk, but all her words were garbled by the mucus in her throat. . . . And I called the doctor, and he gave me a good idea of what was happening. It was very hard for me to believe that she was so close (*"to death" were the words implied but not spoken by the daughter*). She looked so calm and so serene. In her room and among all her things. She looked really OK. She didn't look like she was in distress. She looked like she was just *glowing*.

And my sister came over. She brought over a tape made by a priest on death and dying. We put it on and we let my mother listen to it; isn't that awful? And it was talking about acceptance of death and it seemed to be quite appropriate at the time. And then my sister went to the movies and I stayed around with Emma (*a housekeeper with some experience in caring for invalids,*

employed by the family to help out at this time). And my sister had left a picture of her little boy so my mother could see him. And it was just as if everything was in preparation.

I got out her makeup and lotion and started to make her up. Put lotion all over her skin. (*Did she know what you were doing?*) She did, because she held out her arm like this, and moved a little here and there to make it easier to make her up. But I was afraid in touching her body—she was so *frail*, I was afraid her skin might break if I touched her too hard or hugged her. Before this time she hadn't wanted to be touched, because it hurt. But now it didn't seem to hurt her at all; her pain had all diminished. I put blush on her face . . . and lipstick on . . . and I brushed her hair.

And then I explained to her that I was going out for a cup of tea, because Emma said, "Why don't you go out—you deserve a break, just take a small break. It's good for you to go out." OK. After I finished making her up, I told her I was going to go out for a cup of tea and I would be *right back*.

As I bent down to hug her, she—her body—I don't know how to describe it: she opened her mouth as I was holding her, and blood came out. And I thought at first, "What's wrong, what happened?" And Emma said, "It's OK. It's nothing. She's fine. She'll be OK. You go and get your tea." But it was hard for me to let go of her. A part of me felt like "that was *it*," but, oh, no, it couldn't have happened. When I looked at her again, she looked—beautiful.

She was glowing. She looked so smooth. She was just—beautiful. It was the only time I saw her look so beautiful during her whole illness. . . .

And when I came back the hearse was in front of our house. And I said, "Oh, no! You're not going to take my mother away!"

And my father was there, and all these people were already there. The people he had listed in his preparation. The people who were supposed to be there; the things that were supposed to happen. . . . I resented it all. "They're not going to go into the room. I'm going into the room first!" I wanted to touch her. I wanted to be alone with her. I went in and closed the door. And I touched her all over, and took her all in. And then I realized. I realized . . . she had gone without a struggle. It was really right, it was all right, you know? She looked very good. *She looked as if it was right*. It wasn't painful. It was the right time, and she was ready to go.

This is part of just one person's experience with death. If it were to be enlarged on further, we would see that the other family members were able to respond in their own distinctive ways to the situation. The father, for example, did much planning and managing, his way of coping with the impending loss. The other daughters had their own ways of relating to their mother and her illness. The daughter who has shared her own experience with us had a very close relationship with her mother and, as we have seen, was able to continue this relationship on an intimate basis not only up to but through the moment of death itself. Does an "appropriate death" perhaps mean an ending that allows loved ones to respond freely in their own distinctive ways, as well as an ending that appears appropriate to the dying person herself? If so, then this might well have been an "appropriate death."[18] It might have been much more difficult for the family members as well as the terminally ill woman to have felt and acted like the distinctive people they were if restricted by a hospital and medically managed situation.

Other positive features are also obvious. The woman apparently died free of pain and suffer-

ing. The final impression that *"it was right"* could well be a valuable core around which the daughter integrates her mother's death into her own ongoing life. The daughter also took full advantage of the opportunity to relate intimately with her dying mother. She will not have to live with regret, self-recriminations, or anger about her own actions. Would she have felt comfortable in lotioning and making up her mother if the scene were in a hospital? Would this even have been permitted? Would she have been allowed to stay to the very end, or shooed away by hospital staff? Would she have been allowed to return for a few minutes of privacy with her mother after death?

The hospice (in this instance, Hospice of Miami) was one source of support for this family. It may have made the difference, but the strength obviously was in the family itself, the feelings that members of an intact and affectionate family had for each other. Perhaps the hospice offered just enough to help the family be itself through the entire period of crisis. This does not mean, however, that the relationship between hospice and family was smooth at all times. The family at first had some resistance to the approach made by the hospice because it confronted them with the realization that their mother actually was terminally ill. Even now, the daughter quoted above wonders what the *expectancy effect* might have been on the mother and the entire family. How was the mother's length of survival as well as her quality of life influenced by the hospice influence? This is a relevant question, but it also can be asked when terminal care is mediated through traditional medical and hospital systems. The likelihood that a different set of expectancies is involved, or that the expectancies are communicated differently when a hospice approach is involved, deserves careful consideration and is among the many questions awaiting research. It should also be recognized that "Emma" was not a person carefully selected and trained by the hospice organization itself. How she behaved during the terminal crisis situation differs in some respects from the way that most hospices would prefer their volunteers, staff, or other affilitates to conduct themselves.

The experience reported here was not "successful," if the aim of terminal care is to keep everybody's feelings under control and maneuver the death event through with minimal impact. The daughter's life had changed at the moment she first learned of her mother's terminal illness some months before. The circumstances of her dying and death have influenced her much, and she is now pursuing a career that involves providing care and comfort to others. It is not "life as usual" for this woman; she regards both the basic fact of her mother's death and the particular circumstances under which it occurred as strong motivation for her own continued growth as a person. And it is very clear that she would not want to have been deprived of the opportunity to be with her mother to the end and in the freedom and familiarity of their own house.

SOME QUESTIONS ABOUT HOSPICES AND OTHER INNOVATIONS IN TERMINAL CARE

The hospice as such is perhaps the most evident practical outcome of the death-awareness movement at this time (alongside the marked increase in death-education courses at many academic levels and in many forms). The *palliative-care unit* is a significant variation, involving a small, specialized service that applies hospice principles within a larger, more traditional medical setting (e.g., Wilson et al., 1978[19]). A variety of helping groups have come into existence within recent years, which also pursue humanistic aims for the terminally ill and their families. One can learn much from the example of the SHANTI Project in the San Francisco Bay area of California, founded by psychologist Charles A. Garfield and his colleagues.[20] In this project, as well as in many other efforts around the nation, the role of the volunteer is a critical one. This leads to one set of questions: Are there enough suitable volunteers available for hospice and related projects to succeed? Will people volunteer over prolonged periods of time when the "financial pinch" is leading so many men and women today to seek additional sources of income and, thus, reducing time and energy for voluntarism? Will volunteers be used appropriately, as they seem to be in places such as St. Christopher's and SHANTI, or will they be exploited and overextended as a way of cutting expenses? Should the latter situation develop, then the hospice movement might become severely distorted. Those components of the "establishment" that are relatively insensitive to human suffering could serve up what seems—but only seems—to be a hospice approach when in fact what they are doing is to cut terminal care adrift from the mainstream of quality care.

This leads us to a second set of questions. Is it desirable to develop an elaborate alternative or set of alternatives to traditional medical care? Or would it perhaps be a sounder policy to go right after the health-care establishment as it presently stands and try to introduce hospice-type reforms through and through? The standards of care for terminally ill people are not really that different from the various "patient's bills of rights" that have come to the fore in recent years. And, for that matter, the patient's bill of rights is largely a restatement of those basic principles embodied in the Constitution for all citizens regardless of their health status. It is conceivable that a hospice movement successful on its own terms could actually intensify the split between "humanists" and "technicians" in the health-care field. Those who prefer to work with new and fancy equipment and practice aggressive health care at the growing edge of "state-of-the-art" knowledge could continue to do so. They would be less encumbered by the growing demands and recriminations associated with humanistic protest. Let the terminally ill (i.e., "failed") patient go someplace else and be under the care of soft-hearted health professionals (or volunteers)! The situation could deteriorate even further: the technically competent, the really first-rate physicians and nurses might stay in one realm, and the less competent practitioners drift into hospice care. This perhaps is putting the matter harshly, but it is one of the possible outcomes unless steps are taken to strengthen expression of the humane impulse in the traditional medical setting and to maintain the highest standards in hospice-type alternatives.

Many other questions must also be addressed. Just a few of these will be touched on here.

1. Can the hospice approach succeed for indivduals who do not have the support of an intact family to call on? Many hospices favor or require the existence of an intact family before entering the picture themselves.

2. How successful can the hospice approach be in settings where the religious or spiritual element is not manifest as obviously as it is in the mecca, St. Christopher's? Although difficult to define objectively, it certainly looks as though a sense of shared faith (not identical with membership in any particular religious group) plays a role in some of the most effective hospice settings.

3. How successful can the hospice approach be when people suffering from a variety of life-threatening conditions other than cancer can included? The hospice movement has been closely linked with care of people afflicted with advanced, nonresponsive stages of cancer. This is changing somewhat, but what has been learned and accomplished so far has been largely with cancer patients, and this is but one of many conditions that can contribute to death.

4. What is the relationship between the hospice movement as now conceived and practiced and the still-increasing trend for people to die in old age and in some type of institution? Is or should a nursing home be a hospice? Not much thought or action has yet been given to the hospice spirit in general and the fact that old men and women often end their lives in deplorable situations. It is true that some elderly people have become hospice clients, but in general there has been little relationship established between hospice care and geriatrics.

These are but a few of the questions that should be examined further, but which would take us beyond the scope of this book. For a readable general history and current description of the hospice movement, fortunately there is Sandol Stoddard's recent book[21] to consult. This helpful introductory book, along with a few more pragmatic approaches (e.g., DuBois[16] and Kastenbaum[22]), will serve as useful guides, but none of us can afford either to leap onto or off of the "hospice bandwagon" without exercising our own powers of observation and judgment. The hospice movement, after all, is emerging from the same society whose death system is notable for its complexity, contradictions, peculiarities, and, often enough, penchant for self-defeat. It is fair to say that we are at a point in the current death-awareness movement when it is time to act as well as to talk—but this does not mean it is time to stop thinking!

BEING WITH A DYING PERSON

Set aside for a moment all that is happening elsewhere to improve the situation of the dying person. Focus on a simple, personal situation: being with a dying man, woman, or child. Intelligent and resourceful people sometimes avoid this situation at any cost. "I should see him, but I just can't bring myself to do it." Some people who do overcome their own resistances also express anxiety. "I feel so helpless just standing there," is the way it is sometimes said, "I don't know what to do, what to *say*." Perhaps you have not been in such a situation. And perhaps you would not experience these difficulties if such a situation did arise. But enough of us do have problems in being with a dying person to warrant some suggestions.

And underline *suggestions*. I find it repugnant as well as unnecessary to prepare a "how-to" book for relating to the dying person. We are defeated before we begin with that kind of approach. It assumes that a dying person is a special case or exotic specimen that we must handle with a ritual of approved sayings and techniques. The most fundamental suggestion is simply to relate to a dying person with the best qualities we are able to bring to *any* relationship. The particular person you are and the particular person he is—these form the most secure basis for a relationship.

It follows that there is no one proven way to be with a dying person. Your good relationship with a dying person may be quite different from another good relationship that somebody else has with the same person. There is no evidence that a fixed, stereotyped kind of relationship, no matter how humanistically conceived, is an advantage to the dying person. Rather, we are probably bringing more to the situation when we come with our own natural personality. This means, for example, that it may even be more helpful to say something stupid that is in character instead of uttering a carefully rehearsed "sensitive" phrase. When you are yourself with the dying person you are keeping him or her in contact with at least one authentic point of interpersonal support.

Listening is an active process. When you are really listening to what a person has to say you are not doing nothing. Hearing what the dying person is trying to communicate requires a knack of tuning out some of our own expectations and concerns. If I think he is or should be concerned about some particular problem,

I may not take in the fact that he has something very different on his mind. I may also conclude that *he* is depressed today when it is my own feelings that are drooping. The fact that you are taking the time and effort to listen carefully will come across.

This does not mean, by the way, that you must be silent or very quiet. It is possible to listen during animated discussion. You can bring energy and a broad range of news, gossip, remembrances, and ideas into the discussion. But if you listen well you will catch yourself before a fresh flow of ideas turns into a babble that has some as yet unrecognized purpose. The person who talks too fast and too loud has found a way to limit what the other person can say and to cover up his own inner doubts with verbal smokescreens. Confident that you are tuned in to the dying person's communications, however, you will feel free in keeping up as active a part in conversation as seems appropriate and natural.

Is this a moment when your friend needs your companionship to air his thoughts about the future or concerns about important uncompleted business from the past? A moment when the prospect of death will be discussed with depth and candor? Or does he need something else of you right now? Perhaps this is a time when he would like to relate to you as though he were not dying. You are not obliged to discuss, let alone bring up the subject of death on every possible occasion. A person who knows well what lies ahead may have other interests on his mind, too. Preferring to talk about something else is not necessarily an act of denial, let alone of pathological denial. It is adaptive to take a vacation from dying, even if it is but an occasional vacation of the mind. You can relate to many of the experiences and interests you have in common on those occasions. It may take you by surprise if he speaks one day of plans and expectations that go far into the future. It was just a few days ago that he was asking you to look after a few things for him after he has died. But in all probability he is not being absurd or losing his mind. Instead he is affording both of you some momentary relief from a reality that neither of you has forgotten.

There may well be other moments when death is in the center of his consciousness. He will find a way of letting you know, with or without words. What will you do then? You will let him know that you are *with* him. He will see that your relationship is strong enough to contain these ideas and feelings. He will not be expecting you to cure him, nor will he demand the impossible in any other way. There may be some specific feelings or incidents to work through in your relationship—patching over an old argument, saying things to each other that good friends may just take for granted but which need expression at certain times.

Many a person has approached a dying friend with trepidation, expecting a scene or a demand that he could not possibly cope with. And the same person has come away with the realization that "he just wanted me to think well of him after he's gone," or "he had the feeling that I was the person who could hear him out without passing judgment or changing the subject, just listening and accepting."

You will feel comfortable enough with your friend that you will not start glancing furtively at your watch the moment you arrive at his bedside. You will maintain normal eye contact. If touching comes naturally in your relationship or seems to be appropriate at some moment now, you will not hesitate to affirm your relationship with physical contact. You will acknowledge obvious aspects of his condition rather than indulge in elaborate rituals to pretend that you haven't noticed weakness, fatigue, or discomfort. The more you can accept of the realities of his condition, the easier it will be for him to do so as well, or, perhaps more significantly, the more choice he will

have of the ways in which he would prefer to regard his situation. You will sense that it is not very helpful to exclaim, "Say, you're really looking . . . um . . . great today," when the opposite is what meets the eye. In general, you will not lead off with many evaluative-type statements. You will give him leads that he can take in whatever direction he prefers at the moment.

But what if seeing your friend ravaged and weak is too much for you? What if the awareness of his impending death suddenly breaks through in a way you cannot control? This might have been one of your secret fears. Yet if such a moment does arise, you should realize now that tears can also be a gift of friendship. You have shown your abiding concern by being with your friend through the vicissitudes of the illness, the hopes and the disappointments, the remissions and the relapses. You have spoken and you have listened when there were words to say. And if there is now a moment for tears and silence together, well, what of it?

In short, you will find you and your dying friend keeping much of yourselves and your relationship intact. But separately and together, you will also be undergoing some deepenings and transformations. Some of these will be painful, but less so because shared. You will not have expected yourself to become a Dr. Miracle or your friend to win the Heroic Death of the Year award. And, as the years go by, you will value ever more the hours you spent together.

SUMMARY

What can be done to improve the situation of the terminally ill person and his or her family? The *hospice* approach has emerged as the leading alternative to the established pattern of care that has been the target of much criticism over the past few years.

Perspective on the hospice approach is offered through a brief examination of the *death-*

awareness movement. This movement is traced through several phases. A period that might be described as "conspiracy of silence" was followed by exposure and attack on this "taboo" against dealing openly with death. Breakthrough of the taboo was first expressed mostly by an enormous increase in "death talk" and by sharp and bitter criticism of then-current modes of care. At the same time, research, clinical, and educational contributions of some stature were starting to provide an underpinning of knowledge for the new movement. The growing edge of the field has now moved ahead into a more action-oriented phase in which the actual development and operation of hospice-type services is featured.

Attention has been given to the formulation of *standards of care* for the dying person, the family, and for the caregivers as well. *St. Christopher's Hospice* (England) has become the model and mecca for hospice development around the world. St. Christopher's offers a full range of services for terminally ill people and their families—including residence in a facility designed especially for this purpose, when the need arises. The hospice is not primarily a place, however. It can be better regarded as a caring system or network that attempts to support a high quality of life in its clients wherever they might be. Family members and volunteers usually have very important functions to serve in hospice efforts.

Impressionistic information and the few research reports available so far suggest that the hospice approach does represent a clear improvement in the caring process for terminally ill people and their families. Much more research and evaluation are required, however, and a number of difficult questions must be faced before the contribution of the hospice movement can be properly assessed. Some possible dangers and distortions associated with the growth of the hospice movement are noted (e.g., an exaggeration of the present split be-tween those who prefer to provide aggressive, but narrow and emotionally aloof health services, and "soft-hearted" humanists). The extent to which the hospice philosophy should be cultivated as a separate wing of the health-care establishment as compared to its diffusion through the entire establishment should be a matter of careful consideration in the years directly ahead of us.

Being with a dying person is a situation not limited to professional care givers. Many of us have already had this experience; none of us are exempt in the future. A few suggestions are made in response to the fears and insecurities that we sometimes bring with us to the bedside of a terminally ill person, even if that person is somebody we have known well for years. The process of dying and the prospect of death, formidable as they are, do not necessarily shatter human relationships. (This comes through clearly in a vignette drawn from one individual's recent experience with the death of her mother.) What has been good and strong in our relationships with other people can continue and deepen through the phase of living known as dying.

REFERENCES

1. Kubler-Ross, E. *On death and dying.* New York: Macmillan, Inc. 1969.
2. Feifel, H. (Ed.). *The meaning of death.* New York: McGraw-Hill Book Co., 1959.
3. Waugh, E. *The loved one.* Boston: Little, Brown & Co., 1948.
4. Gorer, G. The pornography of death. In W. Phillips & P. Rahv (Eds.), *Modern writing.* New York: McGraw-Hill Book Co., 1959, pp. 157-188. (Reprinted in Gorer: *Death, grief, and mourning.* New York: Arno Press, 1977.)
5. Feifel, H. The taboo on death. *American Behavioral Scientist,* 1963, *6*, 66-67.
6. LeShan, L. Psychotherapy and the patient with a limited lifespan. *Psychiatry,* 1961, *24*, 318-323.
7. Abrams, R. D. The patient with cancer—his changing pattern of communication. *New England Journal of Medicine,* 1966, *274*, 317-322.
8. Farberow, N. L., & Shneidman, E. S. *The cry for help.* New York: McGraw-Hill Book Co., 1965.

9. Kastenbaum, R. Toward standards of care for the terminally ill. Part II: What standards exist today? *Omega*, 1975, *6*, 289-290.

10. Marram, G. D., Shlegel, M. W., & Bevis, E. *Primary nursing: a model for individualized care.* St. Louis: The C. V. Mosby Co., 1974.

11. Saunders, C. *St. Christopher's Hospice, Annual Report, 1978-1979.* London: St. Christopher's Hospice.

12. Saunders, C. St. Christopher's Hospice. In E. S. Shneidman (Ed.), *Death: current perspectives.* Palo Alto, Calif.: Mayfield Publishing Co., 1976.

13. Parkes, C. M. Home or hospital? Terminal care as seen by surviving spouses. *Journal of the Royal College of General Practice*, 1978, *28*, 19-30.

14. Hinton, J. Comparison of places and policies for terminal care. *Lancet*, 1979, 29-32.

15. Lack, S. A., & Buckingham, R. *First American hospice: three years of care.* New Haven: Hospice, Inc.

16. DuBois, P. M. *The hospice way of death.* New York: Human Sciences Press, 1980.

17. *Death Education*, 1978, *2* (Nos. 1, 2). Special issue on the hospice. Washington, D. C.: Hemisphere Publishing Corporation.

18. Weisman, A. D. *On dying and denying.* New York: Behavioral Publications, Inc., 1972.

19. Wilson, D. C., Ajemian, I., & Mount, B. M. Montreal—The Royal Victoria Hospital care service. *Death Education*, 1978, *1-2*, 3-20.

20. Garfield, C. A., & Clark, R. O. A community model of psychosocial support for patients and families facing life-threatening illness: the SHANTI Project. In C. A. Garfield (Ed.), *Psychosocial care of the dying patient.* New York: McGraw-Hill Book Co., 1978, pp. 355-364.

21. Stoddard, S. *The hospice movement.* New York: Stein & Day, 1978.

22. Kastenbaum, B. K. *The nurse and the hospice.* St. Louis: Benchmark Press (in press).

CHAPTER 14

❖ BEREAVEMENT, GRIEF, MOURNING

❖ She has been standing there for several minutes, the telephone receiver still in her hand. Now she examines the telephone in a dreamlike manner, as though seeing it for the first time. Everything is in slow motion. Time just sits in the room as if it had no place to go.

Her face twists into a sudden grimace. She tightens her grip on the telephone, squeezing and shaking it as though it might be made to take back what it has said.

Later (minutes, hours, days?) she sits alone in the dark room. The fingers of her right hand ceaselessly rub back and forth across the gold band on the third finger of her left hand. From the next room the sound of a clock beats upon her. It has never sounded so loud before—or so bizarre and menacing. Somehow it happened. Between one tick and the next. A wife then. A widow now. How could this be true? Unbelievable, ridiculous! Yet her life was now at a stop, while the clock continued heedlessly to mark a time that had no relationship to her. Why did the clock bother? Why didn't it end this mocking torment that life was supposed to go on?

Bereavement. Grief. Mourning. The words are not adequate to convey what transformation a death can bring on the survivors. But let us at least begin with these words and see how they can best be understood.

INNER AND OUTER EXPRESSIONS OF LOSS

Bereavement is an objective fact. We are bereaved when a person close to us dies. It is also a change in status. The child may have become an orphan, the spouse a widow or widower. Bereavement is a recognized social fact, then, as well as an objective fact.

Bereavement status often shows up directly or indirectly in statistical portraits of our population. The more elderly people there are in a particular city, for example, the greater the number of widows and widowers (especially the former). Does this mean more loneliness? More living in the past? More tendency toward suicide or other forms of premature death? Perhaps. But bereavement status itself can only suggest what survivors might be experiencing and how they have adapted to the loss. It is a clue to possible psychological distress, then, as well as an objective and social fact.

When we shift from the individual to a death-system perspective, bereavement can also be seen as an outcome of large-scale social phenomena. Widowhood and orphanhood are major consequences of war. The effects of war are to be gauged not only in territories seized or relinquished but also in the short- and long-range effects of breavement. British, French, and German observers who lament that the cream of their youth was destroyed in World War I, for example, cannot be accused of exaggeration. The social consequences from the deaths of young men by the tens of thousands defy calculation. Each nation not only was deprived of the talents and energies of these men but left with a population of survivors who could not be expected to pick up their lives as usual when the war ended. How much of human history since World War I has been affected by the slaughter and bereavement of that one major conflict alone? And what has been the effect of other wars before and after? There is no way of answering these questions satisfactorily—but the consequences of individual bereavements massing together within the same society at the same time must surely exert strong influences on the quality of life for many years thereafter.

War is just one of the more obvious large-scale events that influence who is bereaved when. Bereavement points to many other social phenomena as well. The number of widows in our society, for example, has been increasing in recent decades. Furthermore, the proportion of widows to widowers has also been increasing.[1]

These are facts about bereavement. Precisely what these bare facts indicate about our changing pattern of life in the United States is still under investigation, but it is likely that cultural attitudes toward remarriage for men and women as well as differential life stress for both sexes play a part.

Grief is a response to bereavement. It is how the survivor feels. It is also how the survivor thinks, eats, sleeps, and makes it through the day. The term itself does not explain anything. Rather, when we say that a person is grief-stricken, we are only directing attention to the way in which his or her total way of being has been affected by the loss. Grief requires understanding: it is not a word that can be taken as a simple and automatic explanation of what is being experienced and why.

Furthermore, grief is not the only possible response to bereavement. There may be anger or indifference, for example. Some individuals show what psychiatrists term a "dissociative flight" from the impact of death, a pattern of denial that can become so extreme as to form the core of a psychotic reaction. Some people clearly recognize their loss but appear unable or unwilling to grieve. We cannot assume, then, that a bereaved person is experiencing grief at a particular point in time. Nevertheless, the grief response is so frequent and so painful that it is of primary importance for those who wish to understand and comfort the bereaved.

What, then, is grief? From his pioneering clinical study, Erich Lindemann declared that:

> The picture shown by people in acute grief is remarkably uniform. Common to all is the following syndrome: sensations of somatic distress occurring in waves lasting from 20 minutes to an hour at a time, a feeling of tightness in the throat, choking with shortness of breath, need for sighing, an empty feeling in the abdomen, lack of muscular power, and an intensive subjective distress described as tension or pain.[2]

Other symptoms also were commonly seen: insomnia, absentmindedness, problems in concentrating, failures of memory, and the tendency to do the same things over and over again.

This classic description by Lindemann should be seen within its context. He was working with people who had been stunned by the sudden death of loved ones in the Coconut Grove (Boston, 1942) fire in which 400 people perished within less than 15 minutes and others died later because of severe burns and smoke inhalation. Subsequent experience indicates that the total symptom picture seen by Lindemann may not be expressed by every person who has an acute grief reaction, but his description still conveys a vivid sense of what it is like to be overwhelmed by grief.[3]

It is evident that grief can affect all spheres of life. The grieving person's body doesn't work very well. Some clinicians and researchers believe that the physical side of grief is so severe that it can properly be considered a disease process. George Engel[4] suggested that an intensive or sustained grief reaction can precipitate serious illness, even death, in bereaved individuals who have underlying physical problems. The biochemical and physiological concomitants of grief place additional strain on the weak links in the bereaved person's physical systems, with the particular type of somatic reaction that develops depending on the particular weak link or defect that preexisted in the bereaved. Jerome K. Frederick[5] has proposed a specific pathway by which the grief reaction might trigger serious physical disorder. He cites a variety of studies indicating that the incidence of infections and neoplastic (cancer) conditions increases in the weeks and months directly following a major bereavement. (Additional studies of this type have been reported since Frederick's analysis, and these tend to confirm and extend a connection between bereavement and increased vulnerability to illness.) It is not vulnerability to illness, but also the mortality rate that increases for bereaved people and remains at a higher than average level for at least several years.[e.g., 6]

After examining both his own work and that of other investigators, Frederick has proposed that the loss experience sets the following sequence of events into motion:

1. The pituitary releases more adrenocorticotropic hormone as part of the body's reaction to stress.
2. This leads to stimulation of the adrenal cortex, which then either activates or releases corticosteroids.
3. The corticosteroids act to depress the body's immune mechanism.
4. If this response pattern continues (as it might with continuing psychological stress), the high activity of corticosteroids suppresses more and more of the immune responses that protect our bodies both from infection and the development of neoplastic disorders.
5. Disease processes themselves (infectious or neoplastic) become evident, generate new stress, and threaten the bereaved individual's own life.

It should be noted that this is not the only possible pathway through which an interpersonal event (death of a loved one) might lead to jeopardized health in the survivor, nor has Frederick's theory been conclusively proven. However, it is clear by now that survivors are themselves at increased physical risk, that grief can be regarded at least partially as a generalized stress reaction that has potential for major physical change even though it seems to begin on a psychological level. The telephone call, knock on the door, or "look in the doctor's eyes" convey meanings, and somehow these meanings are rapidly converted into a pattern of biochemical and physical as well as phenomenological events.

Physical aspects of distress can be intensified by what the person does or fails to do in response to the loss. Going without proper nutrition and rest and general neglect of self-care form one characteristic pattern that sometimes accompanies the grief syndrome described by Lindemann and others. Both behavioral and physiological responses to the stress of loss, then, can place the bereaved person at heightened risk.

The mind of the grieving person may not work very well either. In addition to the concentration and memory problems already mentioned, the grieving individual may not take things in as readily as usual. This increases the person's risk to others as well as himself—as an inattentive driver, for example, or as a parent who fails to notice household hazards or a worker who becomes careless on the job.

It is the emotional side of grief that besets the survivor with the greatest distress, however. The person may be tossed between opposite extremes of reaction:

When I got home from the morgue, I was just out for the rest of the day. I just couldn't help myself. I thought I would have a nervous breakdown, and my heart was going so fast. The man at the morgue said, "Well, if you don't stop crying, you're going to have a nervous breakdown." But all I could do was cry. That's all I could do. And I told him, "If I don't cry, God, my heart will burst." I had to cry, because he wasn't going to be back no more.[3,p.47]

This woman had just found herself transformed from wife to widow. She first experienced shock, could not feel or think at all. And then she could not stop herself from feeling and crying. Her alarm built up further as she feared for her self-control and sanity. It is not uncommon for people in acute grief to feel that they are "going crazy," that they will keep "getting worse and worse and then just fall all apart." This is one reason why people who have previously experienced grief experiences in their own lives and since found their way back can be very helpful to those who are in the midst of such experiences.

Distress does not end with the first wave of shock and grief. After the realization that a loved one is dead, there often is the later realization that life is supposed to go on. Depending on the individual and the situation that exists at the time of the death, there are likely to be further waves of confusion, anxiety, rage, and other painful inner stages. The sense of numbness can also return, sometimes to linger as though it would never go away.

The grieving person suffers. We should make no mistake about that.

Mourning refers to the culturally patterned expressions of the bereaved person's thoughts and feelings. Geoffrey Gorer[7] observed striking changes in mourning behavior within the same culture within his own lifetime. When his father died in 1915, aboard the Lusitania, victim of a torpedo, his mother became "a tragic, almost a frightening figure in the full panoply of widow's weeds and unrelieved black, a crepe veil shrouding her . . . so that she was visibly withdrawn from the world." But within a few months the death toll from World War I had become visibly represented throughout all of England: "Widows in mourning became increasingly frequent in the streets, so that Mother no longer stood out in the crowd." Eventually, signs of mourning were modified, reduced. Too many people were being touched too closely by death. The functioning of society as a whole would have been impaired had every bereaved person pursued every step of the traditional mourning ritual, which included a long period of withdrawal from everyday life. The previous tradition of mourning maintained its place so long as death was occasional; a new pattern had to be developed when death was rampant in everybody's neighborhood almost all the time—a recollection of other times in human history when death and therefore bereavement were occurring on a mass scale.

There are times when the bereavement and grief of individuals finds clear expression even in a heterogeneous society such as ours. The gold star in the window of many a home in the United States during World War II indicated that a very particular life had been lost. But that death represented part of a national, shared cause. Each gold star mother had her special bereavement, but collectively they signified a loss felt by the entire nation. Where, one might ask, are the "gold star mothers" for Americans who died in Viet Nam? Acknowledgment, sympathy, and support for families who experienced grief related to Vietnamese casualties has been much less in evidence than in most previous military engagements. By the time American armed forces had withdrawn from Viet Nam, the war had lost much of whatever it may have once possessed of being a national, shared cause. Social support for individual grief, then, can either be heightened or diminished by the general spirit of the times, even though the context of death (e.g., battle-field casualty) may be the same.

In our society and most others there are also occasions when the death of a prominent and respected person is expressed through forms of general mourning. The flag stands at half-mast. The train bearing the coffin rumbles slowly across the nation, observed by silent crowds. The city swarms with people as the old leader who for so long has been a part of the national identity (Churchill, de Gaulle, Franco . . .) is given his historic funeral.

Mourning is on a smaller and more personal scale for most of us in private life. Still, the ways in which we express the recognition of death reflect the attitudes and customs of society. A nation as heterogeneous as our own offers many patterns of mourning: compare those of Americans who are of Chinese, Italian, or Central European-Jewish heritage, for example. Furthermore, most traditions of mourning are in constant change, some more rapidly than others. There are reasons to be concerned about the expression of mourning in our society today and in the support that is available for the bereaved in general. This problem will be examined later in this chapter. The point here is that we do have some expectations that the bereaved person will experience grief and that the grieving person will mourn.

These expectations are often confirmed. However, any and all of these expectations may be confounded in a particular instance. Here is a person who experiences no grief. Neverthe-less he or she engages in the culturally pat-terned expressions of mourning—perhaps out of courtesy for others who are grieving or out of fear of being thought insensitive. And here is another bereaved person who grieves deeply but does not mourn—perhaps because he or she has become alienated from subcultural pat-terns in general and feels it inappropriate to conform now, or because the patterns require a network of others who share the same ap-

proach to mourning and who are not available. The fact that the bereavement-grief-mourning sequence is subject to such variation suggests that the specific sense of each of these terms be kept well in mind.

There is some evidence[8-10] that the core ex-perience of grief is much the same throughout the world. Expressions of mourning, however, may be specific to a particular culture. It is possible, then, for people in one culture to conclude that people elsewhere do not feel deeply when they are bereaved when the fact is that the others simply *express* their grief dif-ferently. The notion that life is cheap in the Orient, for example, has been fostered by in-sensitivity to the individual's response to death stemming from misinterpretations of culturally expressed modes of mourning. While our diffi-culties in comprehending what another person is experiencing when bereaved are often com-pounded by cultural differences, there is lack of understanding within our own culture about what the bereaved person goes through.

We turn now to one of the best studies on the survivor's reaction to death of a spouse; then we will move on to consider bereavement in other contexts.

WHEN A HUSBAND OR WIFE DIES

The Harvard Bereavement Study concen-trated on the experiences of relatively young men and women who lost a spouse by death. This is only one type of bereavement, but the limited focus makes it possible to obtain in-depth knowledge. The material presented here (unless otherwise identified) is drawn from *The First Year of Bereavement*,[3] an excellent book-length report by Ira Glick, Robert Weiss, and C. Murray Parkes.

Purpose, method, and scope

As the title indicates, this study was in-tended to improve our knowledge of what hap-pens in the life of a bereaved person soon after the death. Emphasis was on both sociological and the psychological sides of bereavement. Sociological questions included the effect of bereavement on the survivor's place in society and the ways in which social processes influence adjustment. Psychological questions included the patterns of individual adjustment to loss, the inner experiences of the bereaved, and the "normal" trajectory and limits of grief. The researchers were careful not to assume that there is one fixed, "normal" way of responding to marital bereavement but did want to establish whatever might be the most usual or expected pattern. There was also keen interest in learning what helps or interferes with recovery from the stress of bereavement. They asked, for example: "Are there early symptoms of difficulty that might alert observers to the likelihood that a particular individual may in part or in whole fail to recover?"

The participants were 49 widows and 19 widowers, none of whom were over 45 years old. They were contacted by project staff while they were still newly bereaved. Those willing to participate were given a series of informal, open-ended interviews that were tape-recorded and transcribed. The ethnic, racial, and religious composition of the widows and widowers in this study reflected that of the Boston area in general. This means more Irish-Catholic widows (31%) than might have been found in some other metropolitan areas. Newly bereaved black women were somewhat more willing to participate in this study than their white counterparts. Men and women whose spouse had died of cancer seemed especially willing to participate.

The immediate impact of bereavement

The response to bereavement is best considered separately for men and women, although there are some important similarities.

Most of the widows had known for some time that their husbands were seriously ill. But approximately one in five experienced a completely unexpected bereavement (by accident or sudden heart attack, for example). Another one in five knew that their husbands were not in good health but did not think their lives were in immediate danger.

Did these varied expectations make any difference when bereavement actually occurred? Yes, but in a slightly complicated way. Most women who had been expecting their husband's death felt that they had been grieving *before* the event actually came to pass. This is a phenomenon that Lindemann called "anticipatory grief" and that has been discussed increasingly over the past few years. Often a woman expressed relief that her husband's long period of suffering had terminated. However, the "anticipatory grief" did not eliminate the impact of the actual death; the wife felt pained and desolate when the end did come. Those who found themselves suddenly transformed into widows did tend to suffer more intensively, however, feeling overwhelmed, anguished, as though there were no limits to the catastrophe that had befallen them. The newly and suddenly bereaved woman might feel so numb that she feared she would never again move, act, or think—or she might cry as though she would never be able to stop. Both states might alternate in the same person soon after she had learned the news. While these reactions were not limited to the women who experienced sudden bereavement, usually they were more intense under these circumstances. An independent study by Justine Ball[11] has since come up with findings consistent with the Harvard study: grief reactions are common among all newly bereaved women, but those for whom the death has come with little or no warning tend to have the most severe reactions. However, neither study supports the idea that one can somehow "pay" the emotional price of loss in advance—anticipation may help keep the response within certain bounds, but the husband's death still has a strong impact when it comes.

Some of the wives had been told explicitly that their husbands were dying. However, few used this information as the basis for making plans for life as a widow:

Most widows, although they consciously believed that it would be good for them to have plans, could not bring themselves to make them. They may have feared that planning would somehow hasten the spouse's death or indicate that they wanted it; or they may have been unable to deal with the pain they felt when they considered their own impending widowhood. Or they may simply have been unaccustomed, after years of marriage, to planning for themselves.[3,p.32]

The husband who became a widower usually responded to the impact of the death very much as the widows did. The men differed, however, in how they interpreted their feelings and related the death to their entire life patterns. While the women often emphasized a sense of *abandonment,* the men reported feeling a sort of *dismemberment.* The women would speak of being left alone, deprived of a comforting and protecting person. The men were more likely to feel "like both my arms were being cut off." The authors suggest that these different emphases are related to what marriage had meant for widow and widower. Marriage had sustained the man's capacity to work, while for the woman it had provided a sphere of interpersonal engagement. This meant that the newly widowed woman could more readily find some expression of her interpersonal needs by going to work, while the man was more likely to become disorganized in his existing work patterns.

Emotional and physical reactions soon after bereavement

Bewilderment and despair often continued beyond the first impact of loss. There were still periods of weeping, although widowers were more apt than widows to feel choked up, rather than to express themselves through tears. Many physical symptoms appeared and sometimes lingered for weeks or months. Aches and pains, poor appetite, loss of stamina, headaches, dizziness, and menstrual irregularities were reported by many. Sleep disturbances were especially common and distressful. A widow would go to bed hoping to forget her cares for a while and to wake up the next morning with more energy and a brighter outlook. Often, however, she would wake up instead in the middle of the night and remain tormented by grief and the reality of her partner's absence. Instead of offering temporary relief from sorrow, the night often held anxieties of its own. Some women tried to knock themselves out by working hard and staying up late. Others turned to sleeping medications. The dread and emptiness of facing the night alone was relieved for some of the bereaved by having close friends or relatives who could listen to them and keep them company until sleep finally took over.

Most of the widows tried hard to maintain emotional control. This was a difficult effort. Often the newly bereaved woman would long for somebody else to take over and organize life for her. While some widows did express this need directly, most attempted to resist it. The typical widow doubted her ability to meet the challenges, but still assumed a stance of responsibility and competence. Each woman had to find her own balance between the desire to receive help and the fear of becoming dependent on others. Most women avoided a state of general collapse during the first few weeks after bereavement. However, some had increasing difficulty later. "The failure to begin to reorganize satisfactorily may not display itself until several weeks or months have passed."[3,p.67]

The widowers were more likely than the widows to be uncomfortable with direct emotional expressions of their distress. The typical widower attempted to maintain control over his feelings because he considered it unmanly, a weakness, to let go. The men also tended to emphasize realism more prominently. Such statements as "It's not fair!" were seldom made by men, although fairly often by women. The men seemed to require more rational justification for their reactions to bereavement. Although less troubled by anger than the women, the widowers did have difficulty with guilt. They were more likely to blame themselves for what they did or did not do in relation to their wives' deaths: "I wasn't sensitive enough to her," "I should have made things easier." When a wife died during childbirth, the widower sometimes felt guilt related to having been responsible for the pregnancy. The widower's guilt reaction, however, tended to subside fairly soon, although the need for rational control over all responses to the death persisted.

Leave-taking ceremonies

The realities of daily life continue during the process of grief and recuperation. One of the major demands of the period soon after bereavement is the necessity to bid farewell to the lost spouse through some type of funeral process. The leave-taking ceremonies went well for most of the bereaved in the present study. They often found it helpful to hear from others that they had done their part to ensure a proper farewell. This bolstered their sense of confidence in managing difficult affairs despite their shock and suffering. The widows were usually seen as the central and responsible individuals, even though they were provided with significant assistance. The widow was seen by all as the final authority on what should be done, regardless of different wishes that, for example, the husband's family might have. In this way, the widow was beginning to gain public acceptance as the new head of the family, a transition not usually involved when the bereaved person was the husband.

The frequently heard criticisms of funerals and funeral directors were *not* in evidence in this study. "These ceremonies were of great emotional importance for all respondents; there was nothing of empty ritual in widows' participation."[3,p.102] The widows often felt that in arranging the ceremonies they were able to continue the expression of their love, devotion, and attachment. "And those widows who felt their marriages had been only too deficient in these respects saw in the ceremonies of leave-taking a last chance to repair the lack."[3,p.102]

The funeral directors usually were seen as supportive rather than as obtrusive businesspeople. Nevertheless, there were painful moments despite all the support available. Some widows suddenly felt the full pangs of their late husband's death at a particular point during the funerary process, such as the last viewing of the body. The funeral, in this sense, emphasized the reality of the death, cutting through the haze of unreality in which many of the newly bereaved functioned despite their outward control and competence. The complete realization of the death, however, did not seem to dawn on the bereaved at any one moment in time, although some of the moments were critical steps toward this realization.

The role of the clergy in the leave-taking ceremonies was not as prominent as might have been expected, at least from the widows' perspective. Most widows seemed to be operating on very limited emotional energy. They neither sought out nor took in what the clergy might have had to say. Understandably, the widows tended to be absorbed in their own feelings. Many of the widows were religious, however, and seemed to find some comfort in clergymen's repetitions of traditional beliefs about the continuation of soul or spirit after death.

The leave-taking ceremonies did not seem to be quite as important to most of the widowers in this study. They gave less attention to the details and did not express as much gratitude toward the funeral directors. They were also more likely to feel that the cost of the funeral was too high. The emotional significance of the funeral itself may have been relatively less important for the men because they were primarily concerned with how they would manage in the months to come. The funeral and all that it involved was something that they had to "get through," rather than the milestone it represented for many widows. These differences of emphasis should not obscure the fact that the leave-taking ceremonies were important to all the bereaved, whether men or women.

Grief and recovery

And *after* the funeral? This study found what many have already observed in their own lives: community, colleagues, neighbors, relatives—all are inclined to turn back quickly to their ordinary concerns. This has the effect of a turning away from the bereaved person. For a short period of time there was concentrated attention on the needs of the bereaved person. But the deceased spouse remained dead, and the bereaved person's emotional and pragmatic problems continued day after day. The long months after the funeral often seemed to be the most difficult ones for both widow and widower.

The widows. The widows were left with the realization that they had to reorganize their lives, but now they lacked the clustering of help that had been available to them in the first days after bereavement. Most did not show much mourning behavior during this period, but continued to sorrow and grieve almost constantly. Typically, they would withdraw somewhat from ordinary social life to signify their mourning status, but seldom did anything conspicuous to emphasize it. From this study it was not possible to determine how aware others were of the anguish that continued within the widows. For their part, the widows seemed to feel that they should not burden others with their sorrow. Here was another situation, then, in which the widows had to balance two impul-

ses: to express their feelings outwardly and to avoid the impression of asking for sympathy. They felt that a "decent" amount of time had to pass before they could reenter ordinary life, and yet did not feel comfortable with a full-blown expression of mourning such as has been customary in some societies.

We will return to the widows' rather quick departure from the role of the mourner. This could be one important part of the puzzle of grief and mourning in our society at the present time.

Some features of the internal process remained intense even though the outward and formal signs of expression quickly diminished. Many widows engaged in *obsessional review.* Events surrounding the husband's death were relived over and over. The women often realized that this process was taking up much of their time and energy. They wanted to turn off the obsessional review but often could not. The review seemed to perform a vital function for them. As Glick and his colleagues suggest, it may have helped the widow to integrate the realities of her loss into her ongoing life. Mulling over the death, then, may not have been a useless exercise, but part of the recuperation process. This interpretation has similarities to Freud's analysis of "grief work."[12] Freud believed that the bereaved person must slowly and systematically detach his or her intense feelings from everything that linked him or her with the deceased. This takes time and repeated effort. Although the concepts of obsessional review and of grief work are not the same, both suggest that we might be more tolerant of the time required for a bereaved person to recuperate.

The obsessional reviews often were concerned with what *might* have happened instead of what actually did happen. How could the accident have been avoided? How might it all have turned out differently? In this way, the reviews provided an outlet for temporary escape through fantasy but came back with renewed realization that there was—in reality—no way to undo the past.

Additionally, the widows frequently searched for meaning through these reviews. *Why* had their husband been taken away? This was more of a philosophical than a pragmatic quest. It was not the name of the disease or the technical reason for the accident that primarily concerned the widow at this time. Rather, it was the need to make sense of the death. If "Why me?" is the question some people ask when they learn of their own terminal illness, "Why *him*?" seems to be the survivor's parallel question. It is also, as we have seen, one of the questions that a society's death system attempts to answer in general. It does not appear that our society at present offers much support to the individual who is trying to fathom either the "Why me?" or the "Why him?" question nor, for that matter, the more abstract, "Why death—and why life?"

The passage of time, and with it the psychosocial processes that occur with time, often relieved these questions of some of their original intensity. The question of meaning may linger indefinitely, however. There did not seem to be any indication in this study that persuasive answers were found by the bereaved, at least within the time period encompassed.

Throughout the course of grief and recovery, most widows paid close attention to their own reactions. Although they could not overcome sorrow or put their lives back together simply by monitoring their feelings, this was a way of checking to see if they were making progress. About 2 months after the death, for example, many women judged that they were coming back from the earlier shock and turmoil. This sense of revitalization helped to reassure them as they continued to struggle with both the emotional and pragmatic consequences of bereavement.

Frequently the widows were immersed in memories of their husbands. These were usually comforting thoughts. While it remained painful to review the events leading up to the death, memories of the husband himself and of shared experiences generally were positive. This was especially true in the early weeks and months. A tendency to *idealize* the lost spouse was observed here, as it has been in many other studies. The deceased husband was the best man who ever lived, a wonderful husband, a marvelous father, he had no faults whatsoever. Later, a more balanced view usually emerged. The widow would still think about him frequently and positively, but now some of his quirks and imperfections gained recognition as well.

Surges of anger—sometimes very intense—occasionally broke in between the early tendency to idealize and the later, more balanced view. The widow might find herself suddenly angry at the husband, for example, for leaving her with the children to raise by herself. Some women then became even more upset when they caught themselves with harsh feelings toward the dead spouse and reacted with guilt or confusion. In general, however, these invasions of negative feelings into the idealized memories seemed to be part of the long-run process of developing a realistic attitude that the widow could live with over the years.

Often the widow's feelings about her husband went beyond vivid memories. She might have a strong sense that he was still there, still with her. This impression would make itself felt soon after the death or a few weeks later. Once the widow developed the experience of her husband's presence, it was likely to remain with her, off and on, for a long time. This sense of remaining in the presence of a significant person who has died has been reported by many other clinicians and researchers as well. The present study adds the finding that the sense of presence was especially persistent for women whose bereavement came without advance notice. The sudden loss of a spouse, allowing no opportunity for emotional preparation, seemed to lead to more extensive haunting experiences. For most of the widows it was comforting to feel that the husband was still there somehow. But even when the sense of his presence had all the vividness of an hallucination, the widow knew the difference. She knew that her husband was really dead, even though her sense of his presence was also real in its own way. It was neither unusual nor crazy for a widow to have this sense of presence.

Throughout the first year of the widow's bereavement there was a gradual movement away from absorption in the loss and toward reconstruction of her life. This was not a smooth process by any means. By the end of a year, though, most of the widows had found more energy to channel into the obligations and opportunities of daily life. They might still experience episodes of anguish sometimes known only to themselves (e.g., when a situation reminded them poignantly of what they had lost). There was seldom a decisive severing of thoughts and feelings about the past. Instead, the widow continued to feel a sense of attachment to her deceased spouse, but had called back enough emotional energies to cope more adequately with the current life situation.

Widows with children in the house usually recognized their responsibilities clearly and felt that the need to provide parental care helped to keep from becoming lost in their own grief. They attempted to help the children feel that the world was still a good place, that life could and would go on. Often there was a new resolve to be a good mother. These efforts were complicated by conflicting needs and values: to be straightforward and realistic with the children, yet to shelter and protect them, keep their spirits up. The conflict would become acute in some situations, such as trying to tell the children what had happened to their father, and why. The "Why?" question again!

Often unable to answer the question themselves—or to keep from asking it—the widow was in a difficult position in trying to provide answers to her children. The fact that the children were at various ages and levels of cognitive development also complicated the communication process.

The widowers. The widowers in this study seemed to accept the reality of the death more rapidly and completely. Although the newly bereaved man was almost as likely to feel the presence of his wife soon after the bereavement, as time went by this phenomenon became much less common than it was for the widows. The man's need for control and realism expressed itself also in the tendency to cut off obsessional review after just a few weeks. The widower did not seem as tolerant of his impulse to dwell on the past; he pushed himself right back to the immediate realities although, like the widow, he too felt a desire to replay the circumstances of the death.

What has often been noticed about the attitudes of men in our society showed up in the aftermath of bereavement as well. The widowers were not only control and reality oriented but also less likely to speak openly about their feelings. They did not usually seek out the opportunity to share either the events themselves or their personal reactions, although most men would response to direct questions by the interviewers. Despite this more limited reaching out to others, the widowers did receive assistance from friends and kin. The sex-role differences came out here as well. Instead of trying to help the widower with his sorrow or anxiety, the people who rallied around him emphasized practical deeds that would help him to manage the house and the children. In short, society responded to the widower by trying to replace some of the support he had been receiving all along from his wife. Women most often were the providers of this kind of assistance.

Widowers expressed more independence,

more sense of confidence in recovering from the loss by themselves, although they often did make use of the practical assistance offered to them. And when widows and widowers were compared at the same points in their bereavement, it usually *seemed* that the men were making a more rapid adjustment. However, the researchers had reason to doubt that the widowers were actually recovering more rapidly. It was true that they did return more quickly to their previous roles and functions. They were also even less likely than the widows to go through a period of conspicuous mourning. The typical widower gave no outward sign of his grief.

Yet a close look at the quality of the widower's personal life, including the occupational sphere, indicated a decrease in energy, competence, and satisfaction. This was especially true when comparisons were made with non-bereaved men. The researchers were led to make a strong distinction between emotional and social recovery. The widower usually made a more rapid *social* recovery that the widow, but the evidence suggests that *emotional* recovery was slower for the men. The widower usually started to date again earlier than the widow, and the same was true of eventual remarriage. But this did not mean that he had worked through either his attachment to his former wife or the feelings stirred up since her death. The widower who had not sought out female companionship a year after his wife's death was much more likely than the widow to feel lonely and depressed.

Types of recovery from the impact of marital bereavement

There were other differences in the type of recovery made, apart from the sex differences already described. It has already been seen that the death of a spouse made a strong impact whether or not the survivor had any reason to believe it was an imminent possibility. How-

ever, the absence of an opportunity to prepare oneself emotionally for marital bereavement had a major effect on the intensity and duration of the trauma. In his independent analysis of data from this study, C. M. Parkes[13] found that lack of preparation for the loss, especially in cases of death through accident or coronary thrombosis, was associated with poor recovery.

What was meant by "poor outcome"? After slightly more than a year had passed, the spouse who had experienced sudden, unexpected bereavement was more socially withdrawn than the person who had had the opportunity for advanced knowledge. He or she remained more preoccupied with details of the death, had more difficulties in accepting the reality of the loss, and, in general, was experiencing more disorganization in daily life. Such a person was likely to be anxious and have a pessimistic future outlook. Virtually every index of adjustment showed that lack of preparation for marital bereavement was related to poor outcome.

From findings such as these it is obvious that much attention should be given to the situation of a man or woman who suffers sudden marital bereavement. The effects of bereavement per se are intensified by the shock of the unexpected. Furthermore, we cannot rely on the passage of time by itself to facilitate good recuperation from the trauma. To acknowledge this problem is not to be fatalistic. Instead, we are thus in a better position to try to understand and help the person whose life is wrenched apart by sudden death of a spouse. A recent study by Raymond G. Carey,[14] for example, provided further evidence that men and women whose spouses died with little or no advance warning had more difficulty in adjusting not only at the moment but also over the next year. This study added the finding, however, that follow-up visits by clergy and physicians were decidedly helpful to the survivors. Respondents in the Carey study further indicated that the help of neighbors had been very welcome in the early days after bereavement and would have continued to be welcome (the neighbors in this case, as in other studies, mostly withdrew from the scene after a short period of expressed concern).

Parkes also found that the response to early bereavement provides useful clues as to how the individual will respond as the months go by. Those who were most disturbed a few weeks after the death usually were the ones who continued to be disturbed a year or so later. The person who had strong feelings that the death was unreal and who tried to behave as though the spouse were still alive also was likely to have more difficulty than others over an extended period of time.

The death of a spouse from cancer often was associated with more rapid and less distress-ridden recovery on the part of the survivor. This may be, as Parkes notes, because cancer is a condition that provides time for both the terminally ill individual and the family to adjust to the prospect of death over a period of time. (It should be understood that we are speaking here only of those people whose cancer proved fatal; it is erroneous to equate "cancer" in general with "terminal illness.")

The quality of the marital relationship had some bearing on the course of the grief and recovery process. When the partners had very mixed feelings toward each other, the experiences associated with bereavement often were more disturbing. Similarly, it was harder for the survivor to adjust if the relationship had been based on a clinging dependency. If soon after bereavement the surviving spouse felt cast adrift, empty, and helpless because the mate was no longer around to make life run properly, then difficulties in adjustment were likely to be more prolonged.

Some clinical experience is necessary to make an informed judgment about the survivor's probable response to bereavement.

Yearning for the lost spouse is a feeling that many bereaved people experience, for example, but the intensity of this feeling and its place in the individual's overall reaction to the death differs from person to person. Research findings therefore must be used with caution but can be helpful in sensitizing us to both what the bereaved person is experiencing and how vulnerable he or she may be to continuing emotional problems after the first impact was subsided.

When bereavement has been not only sudden but also under especially traumatic circumstances, there is increased likelihood that the grief and recovery process will be further complicated. Consider suicide, for example. Many negative attitudes toward suicide exist in our culture (Chapter 15). The survivor may be left with more sense of guilt or shame, anger, or self-doubting than in other forms of death—and be forced to continue to function in a society that shares these attitudes toward the victim of suicide. One potential danger in this situation is that the survivor may also be drawn into suicidal thinking.

I'm going into the same thing now as Phil—I don't want to be with people, I'm lonely. Phil hated to be alone—I want to be alone, but—I want to live alone, and when I say that I mean I think about when he used to live alone and stuff. And the reason he killed himself is that he didn't want to go back living alone, he said he couldn't do it. And that scares me. [15,p.146]

After Suicide, [15] a book devoted largely to the self-reports of women widowed by suicide, is a useful source for those who want to heighten their awareness of the bereavement experiences that occur in this kind of situation. Both a sense of identification with the deceased husband and a longing for reunion are feelings that widows sometimes experience whatever the modality of death, but when it happens to be suicide, then this may beckon as at least a temporary or occasional "way out." Understanding and social support can be particularly important at this time to help the survivor overcome intermittent inclinations toward self-destructive actions.

Whatever the particular circumstances of the death, however, the grief process can be so disabling that the person is essentially out of commission for an extended period of time. Suicidal attempts and severe depressive reactions requiring psychiatric treatment are among the risks. There is a need to distinguish between "normal" bereavement—enough of an ordeal itself—and responses that are exceptionally intense, debilitating, or prolonged. Most of the bereaved men and women in the Harvard study made their way through their distress without reaching extremes of despair or self-destructiveness. But there are others whose vulnerability increased so much that the concept of grief as disease (Engel, Frederick) appeared applicable. Parkes[16] elaborates on this concept from a more socially oriented perspective:

Illnesses are characterized by the discomfort and the disturbance of function that they produce. Grief may not produce physical pain but it is very unpleasant and it usually disturbs function. Thus a newly-bereaved person is often treated by society in much the same way as a sick person. Employers expect him to miss work, he stays at home, and relatives visit and talk in hushed tones. . . . On the whole, grief resembles a physical injury more closely than any other type of illness. The loss may be spoken of as a "blow." As in the case of a physical injury the "wound" gradually heals; at least, it usually does. But occasionally complications set in, healing is delayed, or a further injury reopens a healing wound. In such cases abnormal forms arise, which may even be complicated by the onset of other types of illness. Sometimes . . . the outcome may be fatal.

In many respects, then, grief can be regarded as an illness. But it can also bring strength. Just as broken bones may end up stronger than unbroken bones, so the experience of grieving can strengthen and bring maturity to those who have previously been protected from misfortune. The pain of grief is just as much a part of life as the joy of love; it is, perhaps, the price we pay for love, the cost of commitment. To ignore this fact, or to pretend that it is not so, is to put on emotional blinkers which leave us unprepared for the losses that will inevitably occur in our own lives and unprepared to help others to cope with the losses in theirs. [16,pp.5-6]

BEREAVEMENT IN CHILDREN

Marital bereavement has been taken as one significant example of the response to grief in adult life, and it is only one example, of course. What happens when death takes somebody who is important to a child?

A death in the family can draw attention and energy away from the needs of the children. When one parent dies, for example, the surviving parent's grief can interfere with the ability to care for the emotional or even the physical needs of the children. While some newly bereaved women try to make their relationships with the children a core around which their lives can be steadied and reorganized, it is often difficult for lone parents to manage both their own sorrow and the needs of the young.

Sometimes it is a sibling who dies. In this situation the parents may be so involved in the plight of the dying child that other children are neglected. This means that the child is apt to face two sources of stress. He may be deprived of some of the normal support expected from the parents because of their own involvement in the bereavement. He may not be as well protected from accidents, for example, or given sufficient access to a loving, receptive parent. Furthermore, the child has his own bereavement response to suffer through. He may feel isolated in his own distress if the adults in the situation fail to appreciate his level of understanding or to read his bereavement response accurately. The sensitive adult will take into account both the child's developmental level and the role that the deceased person had played in his life. What did this child understand about separation and death? Was he in a transitional period of thinking in which the difference between permanent and temporary loss by death was still elusive? Or had he recently discovered for himself that death is final and universal? The developmental considerations already explored (Chapter 9) again become relevant. The specific meaning of the loss must also be understood. Was the deceased person an older sibling that the child had been looking up to? Was it a younger sibling whom the child had resented as a competitor for parental attention? Was it perhaps a grandparent who seemed to have more time for the child than any other adult did?

Furthermore, the quality of the child's personal and family situation before the bereavement deserves consideration. Had this been a tightly knit family and a child with a strong sense of love and security? Was it a broken or bent family characterized by anxiety and insecurity? These are among the questions that are worth examining in every individual situation. The impact of bereavement will depend to some extent on the child's developmental level, the specific loss that has been experienced, and the previous pattern of family security and affection.

The bereaved child may express distress in ways that do not seem closely associated with the loss. Serious problems in school may crop up for the first time. He may turn on playmates with sudden anger. Fear of the dark or of being alone may reappear. There are many ways in which the child's life pattern can show the effect of bereavement without an obvious show of sorrow. In fact, when the surviving parent has made it clear that the children are expected to be "brave," and when the parent keeps his or her own tears away from them, they may find it difficult to express their feelings openly.

Studies of bereaved children have found some types of response that might often be overlooked. Erna Furman and her colleagues,[17] for example, have observed that young children tend to express their memories of the lost person through specific activities that were associated with them. An adult can preserve a valued relationship by replaying memories in private or sharing with others. But a 2-year-old is more likely to express his longing and sadness over his father's death through actions.

For weeks he spent much of his time repeating the daily play activities that had constituted the essence of his relationship with his father. He also insisted, over and over, on taking the walks he had taken with his father, stopping at the stores where his father had shopped and recalling specific items.[17,p.55]

The toddler's need added to the mother's emotional pain, but she recognized that it was the best way he had to adjust to the loss.

The memory of children is more likely to be focused around a relatively few strong images, while the bereaved spouse has many recollections stretching over the years. The young child carries much of the remembrance of the lost parent in the form of highly cathected (emotionally invested) scenes and activities. Years after the death the child may suddenly be overwhelmed with sadness when he encounters a situation that touches off a now precious memory.

Furman and her colleagues were surprised to learn how long bereaved children were capable of experiencing and bearing up under their emotional suffering. The mental image of the lost parent remained with them. This is important to keep in mind. Adults sometimes make it easier on themselves by assuming that a child forgets easily, forgets even a significant death. The child may contribute to this assumption by his own apparent lack of grief and mourning by adult standards. He goes back to watching television, a behavior that suggests to the adult that he probably doesn't understand what has happened. This assumption is contradicted by most clinicians and researchers who have observed childhood bereavement in detail. Although "some children could bear an astonishing amount of pain alone . . . most needed a loved person who could either share their grief or empathize with them and support their tolerance and expression of affect."[17,p.57] The silent sadness of the bereaved child can be painful for the adult to share. But how are we to support and comfort unless we can accept the reality of the child's suffering?

It can be even more difficult to accept the child's response when it includes anger at the deceased. The surviving parent may be horrified to hear criticisms of the deceased parent coming from the children. This may happen precisely at the time that the widowed spouse is at the peak of idealizing the lost husband or wife. And yet such expressions may be a necessary part of the child's adaptation to the loss. They do not mean that the child does not love and miss the lost parent—quite the opposite. One of the reasons some adults find it very painful to accept the child's expression of mixed feelings toward the deceased is that these feelings are within them as well. Whoever helps a bereaved spouse express grief openly and begin the long process of recovery is also helping the children by returning the strength and sensitivity of their remaining parent.

The effects of childhood bereavement are not limited to childhood. Loss of a significant person in childhood can have an important effect on subsequent development. Major physical and mental illness occurs more often in the adult lives of those who were bereaved as children. Robert Bendiksen and Robert Fulton[18] have not only confirmed previous findings on the adverse long-term effects of childhood bereavement, they have contributed additional information as well. These researchers followed up on the life experiences of 256 men and women who had participated in a study more than 30 years before. Children whose parents had divorced while they were young showed many of the problems usually characteristic of those bereaved in childhood. Both groups had experienced more difficulties than those who grew up in intact homes. In some ways the children of divorced parents seemed to have had a worse time. They were described by Bendiksen and Fulton as "double victims." In addition to the loss of normal family interactions and support, they were exposed to issues of guilt and blame and to a separation and desertion that lacked the conclusive end and explanation of death.

This study reminds us that bereavement is not the only form of significant loss and not in every instance the most devastating. Nevertheless, evidence continues to accumulate that the child who suffers loss by death of one or more parents is likely to be more vulnerable to emotional and physical problems throughout all of adult life than the child who does not.

Many clinicians have observed that the effect of bereavement sometimes shows up most strikingly at a particular point in adult life that harks back to the time of the bereavement itself. The little girl whose mother dies may become depressed, suicidal, and desperate when she has reached the point of becoming the mother of a little girl herself.[19] Josephine Hilgard and her colleagues studied such "anniversary reactions" in adults who had suffered either paternal or sibling bereavement when young.[20,21] Enough examples of this phenomenon were discovered to merit continued alertness to the long-delayed as well as the quickly seen effects of bereavement.

One of the examples concerned a distinguished lawyer. When "Mathew" was 12 years old his brother died suddenly and unexpectedly of encephalitis. The older brother had been a brilliant student who conformed to adult expectations and wishes, while Mathew had barely passed his classes and showed a belligerent attitude. The mother of these boys placed great emphasis on education. With the older son no longer on the scene, she took special interest in Mathew. Psychological testing revealed that he was much brighter than people had been assuming. He went on to an outstanding career that was still on its way up until he poisoned himself on the day after *his* boy, Mathew, Jr., celebrated his twelfth birthday. Later it was learned that the suicide victim had told people he felt guilty because his success came only as a result of his brother's death. Had his brother lived, then he, Mathew, would have turned out as a failure, perhaps a criminal. Instead he became a criminal lawyer, a career choice that might easily be interpreted as a defense against his own early antisocial tendencies.[21]

This example has been passed along here to illustrate some of the remote yet powerful ways in which the response to childhood bereavement can operate in later life. It is not meant to prove that all children who undergo a significant bereavement will on that account face severe distress later. Such outcomes, however, do alert us to the complex ways in which bereavement experiences interweave with the child's total developmental pattern. The whole story is not told in the first few weeks or months after bereavement.

A story with a very different outcome might be useful for contrast. Charles Darwin retained all his life the memory of his mother's black velvet gown, the deathbed and worktable, but hardly anything of her appearance and his conversations with her. His memory of the death of his mother, occurring when he was 8 years old, was vivid but fragmentary—being sent for, going into her room, being greeted by father, crying afterward. Yet Darwin had much more detailed recollections of the funeral of a

soldier that he attended a few weeks later. Ralph Colp, Jr., one of many who have examined the role of developmental influences on Darwin's personality and career,[22] was struck by the apparent repression of many of his memories of his mother and her death, while details of the soldier's death remained fresh in his mind. Colp finds that death-related themes were closely interwoven with Darwin's work throughout his life. Even Darwin's dreams and his notes in the margins of books have been analyzed as part of the psychological detective work. One of the major themes disclosed was a "keen instinct against death." Colp and others believe there is a connection between Darwin's ardent advocacy of life and his fascination with the generation of new life forms (evolution). Darwin's own observations confronted him with a challenge both on the personal and the scientific level. His growing perception that there might be a process of "natural selection" in which entire species became extinguished—a form of mass slaughter—resonated with the feelings he still carried from the time of his mother's death (and other early-life bereavements). Around the middle of his life he expressed fear of sudden death and treated his theory itself as a potential survivor. Darwin had more bereavements to suffer through in his adult life, notably the death of his much-loved daughter, Annie.

Above all, Darwin's personal experiences with death and his scientific perspective on the destruction of entire species contributed to an ardent love of life. Not able to believe in any doctrine of survival of death, Darwin had to bear with his own "intolerable vision of slow and cold death—death irrevocably, and finally, ascendant over all life."[22,p.200] Yet he also had the example of his father to inspire him. The elder Darwin had lived to age 83 with a lively mind right up to the end; vivid memories of a father admirable throughout a long life seemed to help sustain him during the course of a life's work that was so freighted with death-related experiences and observations.

Near the end of his life Darwin felt too ill to pursue major research, but returned to the first creatures that interested him as a young boy: worms! As a child he enjoyed fishing and had mixed feelings about sacrificing worms to do so. As an elderly man, Darwin did little studies on the feeding of worms. In Colp's words, "Thus, the old man, who as a boy had killed worms, now, 'night after night,' observed how he would soon be eaten by worms."[22,p.200] This line of thinking was not as unrelievedly "morbid" as it might sound. It was, after all, a continuation of Darwin's incessant fascination with life and death. Scientist Darwin respected worms as coinhabitants of planet earth who, in fact, have a key role in maintaining the living ecology by literally passing the earth through themselves. That he, too, Charles Darwin, would become part of the worm and part of the earth again, was not a cliché or a horror story, but an acceptable part of the natural functioning of the world.

Ten thousand examples would provide ten thousand different stories of the direct and indirect ways in which childhood bereavement influences the entire life course. One person cannot shake off unresolved feelings of guilt on the death of a sibling during childhood and commits suicide (thereby passing a tremendous burden on to his surviving son), while another young boy goes on to make scientific contributions of the first magnitude based in part on feelings engendered by loss of his mother in childhood. The impact of childhood bereavement should not be interpreted in a simplistic manner, but neither should it be neglected for both its short- and long-range influence on the developing individual.

BEREAVEMENT IN LATER LIFE

Much less is known about bereavement, grief, and mourning in later life. This gap in knowledge is probably best attributed to still-prevailing stereotypes about elderly men and women. Along with the generally low priorities that have been given both to care and research with the elderly until recent years, there are a number of attitudes and assumptions about dying and death that have inhibited interest in the topic. These include the assumption that elderly people have "lived their lives" and the attitude that they should be ready to embrace their own deaths with philosophical equanimity and a sense of grateful release. Attitudes of this type sometimes tell us more about the people who hold them than those toward whom they are directed!

Nevertheless, there are some foundations available for approaching the study of bereavement in later life. It has been suggested that elderly men and women are more likely to develop a condition that might be called *bereavement overload*.[23] The long-lived person is more apt to have survived many people to whom he or she was deeply attached. Furthermore, there are personally significant losses other than death that can lead to grief responses. Loss of physical abilities, of employment, of social respect, of familiar environments—all of these life changes can trigger responses similar to what occurs when an interpersonal relationship is terminated by death. Elderly people tend to accumulate such losses, one on top of the other.

It is possible that many of the dysphoric and unadaptive behavior patterns sometimes associated with "old age" have much more to do with bereavement overload than with biological changes intrinsic to old age as such.

What changes would we expect in a person (of any age) who has been forced to contend with too many losses in too short a period of time? He might attempt to reconstitute his personal world by replacing the losses. This process often requires a great deal of time even under the best of circumstances. And if there were *no* appropriate replacements available (as in the death of a life-long friend), then his response would have to take another form. One might lose himself in work or other engrossing activities, at least until the burden has lightened. But this alternative often is closed to the elderly. What now? The person may simply take these emotional blows 'on the chin.' I am referring here to the process of developing bodily symptoms when grief cannot be handled adequately by the psychological structure. The person becomes increasingly preoccupied with bodily functions, often is in a state of discomfort, seldom has free energy to invest in new activities or relationships. Furthermore, the experience of multiple losses may lead to a sense of extreme caution. "I had better not care about anybody or anything else. Sooner or later I will lose these people and things as well. And I just cannot bear to lose and mourn again."23,pp.48-49

The whole constellation of "old behaviors," then, could develop from multiple, unbearable bereavement. Suicidal attempts, both direct and indirect, might well be generated from such a psychological state. The individual may give up when stricken by a relatively minor ailment and allow his condition to worsen, or reduce his activities so drastically that both body and mind are in poor tone to respond to any kind of stress. Such considerations suggest that bereavement in old age is a condition deserving careful and systematic attention.

Recent studies have begun to document what previously had been clinically based impressions. James K. Lynch[24] cites many of these studies as well as his own work in suggesting that illness and mortality rates increase for elderly as well as younger bereaved adults. *Loneliness* is identified as possibly the most critical problem for the bereaved adult. Many elderly people experience loneliness from a variety of circumstances (e.g., less opportunity to stay in contact with people important to them because of financial or transportation factors). Additional bereavements in old age can intensify the existing sense of loneliness and contribute further to the exacerbation of many physical problems. Yet we should not jump to

conclusions. As Lynch and other careful researchers point out, the particular methods used in a study have much bearing on the results. We still do not have a clear picture of the relationship between bereavement and health status in old age because the number of methodologically sound investigations remains limited. It would be useful to know, for example, if the apparent rise in physical symptoms 6 months after bereavement in one sample of elderly people represents a general tendency— the widowed individual seeming to adjust well at first, but then "coming apart" a few months later.[25]

HOW WELL DOES OUR SOCIETY SUPPORT THE BEREAVED PERSON?

One test of how well a culture's death system is functioning can be made by examining the support it provides for the bereaved. There are some signs that our society at present does not pass the test.

Some observations have already been made about the reduction in conspicuous signs of mourning. The men in the Harvard Bereavement Study, for example, did little to show the world that they were suffering the impact of a spouse's death. This seems to be in keeping with a mass, efficiency-oriented society. Mourning gets in the way. It may not seem to serve any real purpose. Pressures have been increasing against the expression of loss in almost any form. There are still places in the United States where people will stop what they are doing when a funeral procession goes by. Pedestrians stand in respectful silence and motorists wait patiently, whether or not they know the identity of the deceased. But the funeral procession is a target of efficiency practitioners in many metropolitan areas. Abolition or restriction of this practice has been urged because it slows traffic and may be conducive to accidents. Similarly, there are pressures against the use of land for cemeteries. In some parts of the nation it is now almost impossible to open new cemeteries, and existing cemeteries have been criticized as wasteful and out of joint with the times.

The cultural pattern dominant today seems indifferent or antagonistic to reminders of death. At least one of the new planned cities that has attracted much attention for its innovations has excluded funeral directors, burial grounds, and any visible evidence that its residents might possibly be numbered among the mortals. Each of the specific actions that has been taken to reduce the prominence of mourning or evidence of the dead can be defended in one way or another. What we are concerned with here is the overall pattern and its implications for the bereaved, although the reader might also be curious about the motivations for disenfranchisement of the dead.

Our society seems to have taken a direction that informs the bereaved person that his loss is not a matter of profound general concern. Memorialization of the dead and support for the bereaved has fallen relatively low on the priorities of our death system. People still gather around for the funeral and for a short period of related ritual and visiting. After that, however, the bereaved often is on his own. How long do colleagues sympathize with somebody who has suffered a significant loss? How long are relatives and neighbors prepared to be sensitive and supportive? We have noticed an increasing impatience with the grief of the bereaved. He is supposed to shape up after a short while and let everybody else get on with their own lives. Within this cultural context, it is not surprising to come across a dissertation featuring "a prescribed degriefing intervention method (DIM)" that requires but a single treatment session.[26] Quicker is cheaper; quicker is better, more "cost effective." Are we really prepared to line up for "degriefing" when overcome by profound sensations of sorrow and loss?

Perhaps our *impatience* with grief is one of the reasons why so much attention is given to the question of how long grief is "supposed" to endure. It is one of the questions most frequently raised by the public, as well as bruited about by professionals. At times it appears that society feels that no grief should be felt or expressed after the funeral. It is hard not to think in this context about the type A personality (Chapter 13). The sense of chronic time urgency that characterizes some individuals also seems to characterize much of our society in general. We are reluctant to pause for death. Thinking about the dead is a "waste of time."

From the scientific standpoint, the case for a clear-cut distinction between "normal" (just enough) and "pathological" (too much) grief is not nearly so firm as one might at first imagine. Extremes of physical and psychosocial distress after bereavement can usually be identified clearly, but there remains a range of individual differences that is too often obscured by generalizations. One of the most useful attempts to examine this question freshly is provided in recent and continuing work by Catherine M. Sanders.[e.g.,27,28] She notes:

a tendency to think in such terms as "good grief," "bad grief," "pathological grief," even "sick grief." The use of these expressions suggests that bereavement itself is a malady, a psychological impairment, or weakness as it were, from which the bereaved person must be extricated or cured. And the sooner the better. This stereotypic notion of the way people experiencing grief should behave places unrealistic limitations on the need to cope in their own characteristic ways. This notion also presupposes, quite erroneously, that all persons possess equal quantities of those elements which go into individual personalities—elements such as ego strength, optimism, frustration tolerance, and emotionality.[28,p.183]

Sanders' research involved interviews with men and women who had lost a spouse, parent, or child within the prior 3 months. The MMPI was used to help classify respondents in terms of their general coping styles, and a Grief Experience Inventory to assess specific feelings and behaviors since bereavement. The participants were seen again between 18 months and 24 months after bereavement. She found four distinct types of bereavement patterns: (1) a disturbed group; (2) a depressed, high-grief group; (3) a denial group; and (4) a normal, grief-controlled group. The latter group, it should be emphasized, was not made up of emotionally cold or bland people—they had strong feelings of loss and sorrow, but were able both to express the feelings and move ahead with their lives. Each of these groups showed a relationship between general style of coping with life problems and the way in which they tried to cope with bereavement in particular. Furthermore, each group showed a characteristic pattern of response to grief over time. Some people, for example, showed a general pattern of trying to maintain a "stiff upper lip," covering up any signs of weakness, shortcomings, or distress (based on MMPI scores). Those who used these denial-type coping strategies were of particular interest because of the assumption that people will break down if they fail to talk about their grief or "ventilate" their emotions. This danger did not seem to materialize. Most of the "stiff-upper-lippers" had their grief responses under reasonable control both at the time of initial contact and 2 years later. The "normals" showed reductions in level of grief intensity over the 2-year period, while most of the "disturbed" people remained almost as anxious as they had been soon after bereavement. The "depressed" participants were also still experiencing symptoms usually associated with acute grief after 2 years had passed, but were making some progress. Many of these people were beset by continued or new forms of stress that made it particularly difficult for them to work through the grief experience itself.

Another provocative finding by Sanders was that the type of person seemed to be more important than the type of bereavement. How the individual coped with stress in his or her life in general proved to be more closely related to bereavement outcome 24 months later than did the specific nature of the bereavement (child, parent, or spouse).

In general, this study indicates that it can be quite misleading to set a "time limit" for grief and expect all people to be at a certain level of recovery at a particular point. Individual lifestyles must be respected and taken carefully into account. This has implications not only for the distinction between so-called normal and pathological grief but also for our general interventions and expectations. Not everybody, for example, seems to have a powerful need to "open up" and discharge feelings generated by bereavement, even though the need is strong for many people. It might, then, be as inappropriate to try to force certain people to open up and express their grief directly as it is to demand that other people keep their feelings under tight control. While continued research will refine our understanding in this area, it remains for each of us to be sensitive to the unique personalities of the particular bereaved people we encounter rather than to apply a rigid formula-type approach. It also remains for subsequent research and clinical experience to develop a fully adequate concept of grief-as-disease that does not involve the overextended stereotypes mentioned by Sanders, yet takes into account the physical and psychosocial parallels with disease that have been described by Frederick, Parkes, and others.

The prevailing social climate seems to favor the *denying*-type response more than the *expressive* one. The widower is reducing his colleague's anxieties when he goes right back to work and gives no indication that he expects special concern. "I am OK," he is saying in effect, "I am not mourning." The widow releases others from the more obvious forms of obligation by refraining from displays of mourning. "She's a strong woman," her friends say with admiration. The bereaved person among us tends to be more socially acceptable if signs of mourning are set aside. But the absence of mourning behaviors too easily gives the illusion that the person is "over" the grief reaction. This may be one of the reasons why some bereaved people have fears of "going crazy." All of the anxiety and confusion, all the depths of feeling, seem to be on the inside. The rest of the world continues to move along in its usual way. With little social recognition or tolerance for grieving, the individual can be made to feel as though his response were abnormal or pathological.

My impression is that the term "abnormal" could be applied more appropriately to our society's withdrawal of support from the bereaved. Within some religious and ethnic groups there does remain a sense of closeness, of reconfirming our bonds with each other. This may even include a "legitimized" relationship with the dead. The survivors may have prayers to say, offerings to make, vigils to keep. Within such a context there is time and opportunity for personal grief to find expression in a socially approved form. The newly dead can be maintained as an important person during a critical period of psychological adjustment to the loss. The bereaved need not pretend that the funeral marks the end to his relationship with the parent, spouse, sibling, child, or friend. It is possible to have thoughts and feelings about the deceased, even to sense the presence vividly, without violating social norms. In this sense, societies that have functioned with less technological sophistication than our own often have embodied more insights into the psychological needs of the bereaved. As a society we may be uncomfortable with the seeming irrationality or inefficiency of grief. If so, this says rather more about our dominant values than about the realities of core human experience. We agree fully with Parkes:

The pain of grief is just as much a part of life as the joy of love; it is, perhaps, the price we pay for love, the cost of commitment. To ignore this fact, or to pretend that it is not so, is to put on emotional blinkers which leave us unprepared for the losses that will inevitably occur in our own lives and unprepared to help others to cope with the losses in theirs.[16,pp.5-6]

SUMMARY

As one life ends in death, a new phase begins in the life of the survivors. *Bereavement* is a term that signifies the state of loss: somebody important to this person has died. The impact of bereavement often leads to *grief*, a state of shock, sorrow, and anxiety. The grieving person experiences both physical and emotional distress. All spheres of functioning are likely to be affected. It is not only an emotionally painful condition, but one that increases vulnerability to all of life's hazards, including physical illness. *Mourning* refers to the socially patterned expression of the bereaved person's sorrow. Cultures differ in the specific signs of mourning, but it is almost universal for the bereaved to engage in some type of public behavior that acknowledges the reaction to death. Usually it is expected that a bereaved person grieves and that this condition is expressed outwardly through signals of mourning. But this is not always the case. The bereaved person may not grieve; the grieving person may shun the signs of mourning; the outward show of mourning may be exercised by somebody who does not really feel the pangs of grief.

The effects of *marital bereavement* are examined in detail as one example of grief and mourning in adult life. Most of the data are drawn from the Harvard Bereavement Study, whose participants were relatively young men and women. Bereavement made a powerful impact on almost all of these people. Those who had had the opportunity to prepare themselves emotionally for the loss of their mate usually were better able to put their lives back together during the ensuing months, but "anticipatory grief" did not prevent the anguishing impact of the loss itself when it did occur. Widows and widowers had many similarities in their grief experiences, but there were also noteworthy differences. The funeral and the leave-taking process in general seemed to be a more profound experience for the widow. She was also more likely to express her sorrow to others, engage in obsessional reviewing of the death, search for its meaning, and weep. The widower was more likely to keep his feelings to himself and reject any personal tendencies that seemed "unrealistic." The widower tended to make a more rapid *social* recovery, but a slower *emotional* recovery than the widow. Neither the widow nor the widower typically expressed grief through conspicuous signs of mourning. Both attempted to remain in control of their lives, although the widow in particular felt she had to resist the impulse to ask others to take over for her. Idealized memories of the deceased spouse often were created soon after the bereavement, gradually giving way to more balanced mental portraits. It was common to have a sense that the dead husband or wife was still present. While this sometimes took vivid, almost hallucinatory form, it did *not* mean that the individual was going crazy. Survivors sometimes did fear that they were headed for a nervous breakdown because grief was so severe and apparently without limits. Nevertheless, most of the bereaved persons moved toward a reconstruction of their lives as time went on. Those who had a particularly difficult time within the first few weeks after bereavement often had more difficulty over the long run as well.

Bereavement in childhood exposes the individual to both short- and long-term vulnerabilities. The bereaved child is subject to stress from two sources: the interruption of the normal care and interaction patterns necessary for security and growth and his own emotional response to the loss. The child's developmental level, the significance of the particular death, and the previous family climate are among the important factors to consider in trying to understand and help the bereaved child. When

such help is not forthcoming, the child may encounter serious problems later in life that are related to unresolved feelings about the bereavement. *Bereavement in later life* has been a relatively neglected topic. There is reason to believe, however, that multiple losses (of physical function, familiar environment, occupational or other roles, etc., as well as the death of significant people) often create a condition of *bereavement overload*. This burden-beyond-bearing may have much to do with the development of the entire configuration of dysphoria and dysfunctioning that is sometimes taken to be an inevitable aspect of aging as such. New studies are emphasizing the contribution of grief and feelings of loneliness to problems associated with growing old in our society and may therefore also contribute to more sensitive care and understanding.

It was suggested that *our society fails to support the bereaved person*, especially during the extended period of transition after the funeral. Emphasis on efficiency and rationality, and a growing tendency to disenfranchise the dead, exerts pressure on the bereaved to return to social functioning without "wasting time," and to keep their fears and sorrows to themselves. Recent studies indicate that important individual differences exist in response to bereavement, and that expecting everybody to be on the same "recovery timetable" or to use the same coping techniques would be unrealistic.

It is highly doubtful that our culture can eradicate or foreshorten the basic human response to grief. It can only isolate the bereaved and add to the suffering by insisting on "business as usual" soon after a loved one has died.

REFERENCES

1. Lopata, H. Z. *Women as widows: support systems.* New York: Elsevier North Holland, Inc., 1979.
2. Lindemann, E. The symptomatology and management of acute grief. *American Journal of Psychiatry,* 1944, *101,* 141-148.
3. Glick, I. O., Weiss, R. S., & Parkes, C. M. *The first*

year of bereavement. New York: Wiley-Interscience, 1974.

4. Engel, G. L. A unified concept of health and disease. In D. Ingle (Ed.), *Life and disease.* New York: Basic Books, Inc., 1963.

5. Frederick, J. F. Grief as a disease process. *Omega,* 1976, *7,* 297-306.

6. Rees, W. D., & Lutkins, S. G. The mortality of bereavement. *British Medical Journal,* 1967, *4,* 13-16.

7. Gorer, G. D. *Grief and mourning.* New York: Doubleday & Co., Inc., 1965. (Reprinted by Arno Press, New York, 1977.)

8. Clayton, P., Desmarais, L., & Winokur, G. A study of normal bereavement. *American Journal of Psychiatry,* 1968, *125,* 168-178.

9. Yamamoto, J., Ohonogi, K., Iwasaki, T., & Yoshimura, S. Mourning in Japan. *American Journal of Psychiatry,* 1969, *126,* 74-82.

10. Hobson, C. J. Widows of Blakton. *New Society,* September 14, 1964.

11. Ball, J. F. Widow's grief: the impact of age and mode of death. *Omega,* 1976, *7,* 307-333.

12. Freud, S. Mourning and melancholia (1919). In *Collected papers* (Vol. 4). New York: Basic Books, Inc., 1959.

13. Parkes, C. M. Determinants of outcome following bereavement. *Omega,* 1975, *6,* 303-324.

14. Carey, R. G. Weathering widowhood: problems and adjustment of the widowed during the first year. *Omega,* 1979, *10,* 163-174.

15. Wallace, S. E. *After suicide.* New York: Wiley-Interscience, 1973.

16. Parkes, C. M. *Bereavement.* New York: International Universities Press, 1972.

17. Furman, E. F. *A child's parent dies.* New Haven, Conn.: Yale University Press, 1974.

18. Bendiksen, R., & Fulton, R. Death and the child: an anterospective test of the childhood bereavement and later behavior disorder hypothesis. *Omega,* 1975, *6,* 45-60.

19. Moriarty, D. M. (Ed.). *The loss of loved ones.* Springfield, Ill.: Charles C Thomas, 1967.

20. Hilgard, J. R., & Newman, M. F. Anniversaries in mental illness. *Psychiatry,* 1959, *22,* 133-128.

21. Hilgard, J. R. Depressive and psychotic states as anniversaries to sibling death in childhood. *International Psychiatry Clinics,* 1969, *6,* 197-211.

22. Colp, R., Jr. The evolution of Charles Darwin's thoughts about death. *Journal of Thanatology,* 1975, *3,* 191-206.

23. Kastenbaum, R. Death and bereavement in later life. In A. H. Kutscher (Ed.), *Death and bereavement.* Springfield, Ill.: Charles C Thomas, 1969.

24. Lynch, J. K. *The broken heart: the medical consequences of loneliness.* New York: Basic Books, Inc., 1977.

25. Gerber, I., Rusalem, R., Hannon, N., Battini, D., & Arkin, A. Anticipatory grief and aged widows and widowers. *Journal of Gerontology,* 1975, *30,* 225-229.

26. DiMeo, V. V. Mourning and melancholia: a prescribed degriefing intervention method (DIM) for the reduction of depression and/or belated grief. Unpublished doctoral dissertation, Washington, D.C. United States International University, 1978.

27. Sanders, C. M. Typologies and symptoms of adult bereavement. Unpublished doctoral dissertation, University of South Florida, 1977.

28. Sanders, C. M. The use of the MMPI in assessing bereavement outcome. In C. S. Newmark (Ed.), *MMPI: Current clinical and research trends.* New York: Praeger Publishers, 1979.

CHAPTER 15

❖ SUICIDE

The victim of suicide—literally, self-murder—is neither more nor less dead than the person who perishes after a long, debilitating illness. Yet suicide has a special set of meanings for most of us. And not just for us. Cultures much different from our own have also distinguished suicide from other modes of death. The suicide victim has been denied burial in sacred ground because his action was sinful. His hands have been severed and his body interred at a crossroads so that he will be less likely to rise and find his way back to avenge himself on his enemies. But he has also been honored and idealized as a hero.[1] Whatever the particular views held by a culture at a particular time, suicide has usually commanded special attention.

Suicide remains a matter of special concern here and now. The bare fact that more than 25,000 Americans are certified as official victims of suicide each year only begins to tell the story. Experts insist that the true incidence of suicide is appreciably higher but is obscured by the process of reporting and classification. Furthermore, many deaths by accident, illness, or even by homicide seem to have strong self-destructive components. The impact of suicide spreads well beyond the death of the individual. The survivors are likely to experience both short-term and long-term bereavement responses that bear the marks of this traumatizing action. The apparent increase in the incidence of suicide among certain groups within our general population is still another reason for concern. The fact that many people are troubled enough to consider or attempt suicide merits attention, whether or not a completed suicide eventually results. The prevalence of suicidal intent tells us something about the quality of life in our culture that no thoughtful social observer can afford to ignore.

For all its importance, however, the statistical prevalence of suicide is not our core concern here. Instead, we begin by asking: What does suicide *mean*? Self-murder is after all an intentioned act. When there is reasonable doubt that the deceased intended his own death, it is usually not classified as suicide. What, then, does the suicidal person intend to express or accomplish through this extreme act? What does the suicidal action mean to the rest of us, both as a total society and as individuals? Cultural as well as individual meanings will be explored, even though the complexities involved defy simple conclusions.

Focusing on the meaning of suicide will prove useful on the practical level, too. Is suicide to be prevented? Tolerated? Encouraged? It is doubtful that we can convey a clear message to the potential victim of suicide if our own assumptions, values, and meanings are murky or self-contradictory.

SOME CULTURAL MEANINGS OF SUICIDE

Cultural and individual meanings of suicide can be separated only for purposes of analysis or emphasis. In practice, cultural meanings are expressed by individuals. The meanings discussed in this section, however, owe much to cultural traditions even if it is always the individual who either attempts or refrains from suicide.

Suicide is sinful

One of our strongest cultural traditions regards suicide as sinful. This position has been held for centuries by defenders of the Judeo-Christian faiths. Despite areas of disagreement, Catholics, Protestants, and Jews generally have been taught that suicide is morally wrong. Condemnation of suicide, accompanied by sanctions against the act, has perhaps been most emphasized by the Catholic Church, whose position was made firm as long ago as the fourth century.

But why? What about suicide is so appalling that it must be condemned and discouraged by all the authority that an organized religion can command? St. Augustine helped to establish the Catholic position by crystallizing two fundamental objections to suicide. One of these objections depends on articles of faith that are not shared by all followers of the Judeo-Christian tradition, namely, that suicide precludes the opportunity to repent of other sins. However, the other objection appears equally relevant to every person whose religion encompasses the Ten Commandments. The Sixth Commandment declares, "Thou shalt not kill." Suicide is not exempt from this commandment, in St. Augustine's judgment.[2]

Yet this influential interpretation did not express all that was implied by the moral condemnation of suicide. In the thirteenth century, St. Thomas Aquinas reaffirmed Augustine's conclusion but made another objection more explicit. He argued that God and only God has the power to grant life and death.[3] The sinfulness of suicide, then, is not based exclusively on the specific nature of the act. Rather, suicide is sinful because it represents a revolt against the ordained order of the universe. The self-murderer is engaging in a sin of pride, of self-assertion in a realm that is meant to be ruled by deity.

This point has been made by many others over the years. It was forcefully advocated by a man whose ideas of human nature and society exerted great influence over the founding fathers of the United States. John Locke refused to include self-destruction as one of the inherent liberties. "Every one . . . is bound to preserve himself, and not to quit his station wilfully." A person who abandons his station thereby transgresses the law of nature.

The offender declares himself to live by another rule than that of reason and common equity, which is that measure God has set to the actions of men for their mutual security, and so he becomes dangerous to mankind; the tie which is to secure them from injury and violence being slighted and broken by him, which being a trespass against the whole species. And the peace and safety provided for by the law of Nature.[4,p.26]

As the handiwork of God, we are possessions that are not at liberty to dispose of themselves.

This fierce moral condemnation of suicide allows few if any exceptions. Great suffering does not entitle a person to suspend the "law of Nature" and take life into his own hands. As part of his quest to understand the meaning of pain and suffering, David Bakan,[5] a contemporary psychologist, has analyzed The Book of Job. He emphasizes again the willful and therefore sinful character of suicide in the major religious tradition of the Western world:

The Judeo-Christian tradition has for centuries properly recognized the pride and sin associated with suicide. To "long for death" and to act on this longing, is to arrogate to one's own will what has been imposed on everyone for the "original sin" of being born; and it is not proper to pre-empt the role of the executioner.[5,p.127]

Bakan believes there is an intimate relationship between self-injury and *sacrifice*. Both are audacious acts in which the human trespasses into the domain of God. But a "pure" sacrifice—one that is demanded by God and complied with in the proper spirit—is free of sin. Bakan cites the death of Christ as the supreme example of sacrifice, an event taken as a cornerstone by Christianity.

Reflect a moment on suicide as sinful. Notice that this interpretation of suicide need not be identified with the individual's personal motivation. The individual may kill himself for a number of different reasons. The desire to be willful, rebellious, or prideful in the face of God may be far from his mind. But the suicidal action nevertheless will be *interpreted* as sinful by those who accept that religious dogma that has been sketched here. For an imperfect analogy, we might think of the motorist who drives through a red light. This act could be interpreted as disregard or defiance for law and order even if this was not the motorist's intention. This is one of the reasons that clergy reiterate the moral sanctions against suicide. The potential self-murderer should be advised how serious an act he is contemplating.

Individuals who accept the cultural tradition that views suicide as sinful might therefore be expected to have one more line of defense than others who are tempted to do away with themselves. There is, in a sense, more to lose by suicide. The survivors seem to have more to lose as well. Suicide of a family member could bring a strong sense of shame as well as the feelings of loss and grief that accompany bereavement from death produced by other causes. Suicide, in other words, can be a moral stigma not only for the individual but for those who become contaminated with it by association.

The moral stigma associated with suicide generates self-protective dynamics. We do not want it known that a person close to us died as a sinner. "One must not underestimate the taboo nature of the suicidal label." cautions Theodore J. Curphey, the Los Angeles County coroner who helped to develop interdisciplinary approaches to understanding and preventing suicide.[6,p.76] He is but one of many officials who have been pressured by family members to certify some other cause of death to avoid the stigma of suicide. Curphey and other suicidologists believe that actual incidence is considerably underreported in areas of the nation and the world where a strong moral sanction against suicide prevails. This practice does not always require outright falsification. Definitions of suicide vary somewhat from one cultural context to another, and deaths in which there is any ambiguity of cause can be classified at the discretion of local authorities.[7]

Condemnation of suicide as a violation of the Sixth Commandment, however, is difficult to square with the tradition of warfare and violent death that has been not only condoned but at times actively pursued by those who see themselves as defenders of the faith. Religious wars and the persecution of heretics have repeatedly violated the edict, "Thou shall not kill." As Jacques Choron observes, "during the Middle Ages, mass suicide was frequent among persecuted sects of Christian heretics and non-Christian minorities. . . . The category of non-Christians included Moslems and Jews, who refused to be converted to Christianity and preferred to commit suicide."[8,pp.25-26] Violation of the Sixth Commandment therefore led directly to suicide. The persecuted victim might be regarded as a sinner for committing suicide, but the persecutors, acting in the name of their religion, would not be sinners if they either threatened the dissidents to the point of suicide or killed them outright. The idea that "God is on our side" in terrorism and warfare persists today. It is hard to reconcile the ease with which religious justification has been found for bloodshed on a large scale with the insistence that an individual's personal violation of the Sixth Commandment—with himself as victim—must be interpreted as sinful.

This paradox suggests that there is more to

the moral condemnation of suicide than what has been made explicit up to this point. Can it be that our religious heritage is at least half in love with death, as some have suggested? The image of the crucifixion, so powerful in our tradition, is a sacrifice of suffering unto death with strong suicidal connotations. Some of the early Christian thinkers, in fact, regarded the death as suicide,[9] as did such deeply reflecting Christians of later times as John Donne.[10] Choron[8] suggests that suicide through martyrdom became all too tempting to those who tried to follow along Christ's pathway. It was glorious to die as a martyr. The Church found it advisable to protect some true believers from themselves, to reduce the attractiveness of death now that immortality had been proclaimed, and to discourage widespread emulation of the early martyrs. Admiration of martyrdom has persisted, however, and so has the moral condemnation of suicide. (But it should be kept in mind that martyrdom is not identical with suicide in general: it is a self-chosen death that occurs in a particular way, in service of a particular cause or idea, and requires the "cooperation" of others.) As both Alvarez[9] and Choron remind us, the Old and New Testaments do not directly prohibit suicide nor do they even seem to find this action particularly remarkable. This tends to support the idea that condemnation of suicide as a sin might function as an attempted safeguard against the allure of self-sacrifice in the Christian tradition.

Suicide is criminal

Is suicide a sin or a *crime?* This distinction has not always been considered important. If society—as well as the physical universe—is a manifestation of God's will, then self-destruction might be seen as an act of rebellion against both social institutions and divine authority. The intertwining of church and state made it easy to regard suicide as both criminal and sinful. Recall that even Locke, with his radical ideas of equality and liberty, spoke of the per-

son who would lift his hand against himself as an "offender," one who is "dangerous to mankind" and commits "a trespass against the whole species." Certainly the sinful and the criminal interpretations of suicide have something in common. Both regard self-destruction as a willful violation of the basic ties that relate the individual to the universe.

Over the years, however, the civil and divine realms of authority have become more independent of each other. This has also led to a more independent status for the view that suicide is a crime, and not necessarily a sin. Suicide-as-crime has been an influential tradition up to the present day, although it has always been accompanied by dissident voices. As Edwin Shneidman notes, the word *suicide* itself seems first to have come into use around the middle of the seventeenth century.[11] The earliest citation given by *The Oxford English Dictionary* attributes the following statement to Walter Charleton in 1651: "To vindicate ones self from . . . inevitable Calamity, by Sui-cide is not . . . a Crime."[11]

The question whether or not suicide should be considered a crime in any or all circumstances has been with us as long as the term itself. Theologian Paul-Louis Landsberg argues that

It is purely and simply impersonalist to try to decide such an intimately personal question as to whether or not I have the right to kill myself, by reference to society. Suppose I die a little sooner or a little later, what has that to do with a society to which, in any case, I belong for so short a space? . . . The weakness of the social argument can be seen . . . clearly in [Immanuel] Kant. According to Kant, the man who feels tempted to commit suicide should consider whether the principle on which his decision is based could become a principle of general legislation. But man knows very well that he is faced every time with a particular situation, and that he is, as a person, unique.[12,p.84]

He rejects the idea that a person has no right to commit suicide because this represents abandonment of important duty to either society in general or one's own family in particular. Few of us occupy positions of great social responsibility, Landsberg notes, and some families are "shattered or detestable." The notion that one simply must stay alive as a matter of social duty "reeks of complacency." For Landsberg, "death is above all so much a personal and individual thing that the problems it creates transcend the social life of this planet . . . the question is really far too personal to be decided by such [social duty] arguments."

The distinction between crime and sin has not been an empty one, even where church and state have been closely related. Although philosophically the two interpretations might have a common source, when suicide is considered criminal as well as sinful it is more apt to be punished by human authority. If it were a sin and only a sin, then perhaps answering to God would be quite a sufficient consequence. As a crime, however, suicide has occasionally brought severe punishment on top of the moral condemnation. This has included torture, defamation, and impoverishment. Surviving family members have sometimes been punished as well by having their possessions confiscated by the state.

The interpretation of suicide as crime is waning. Shneidman reports that only nine states continue to list suicide as a crime of any sort, and even in these domains the emphasis is on prevention rather than punishment. Police and community were startled when a person picked up after a suicide attempt was charged with a criminal offense in Prince George County, Maryland, just a few days before this paragraph was written. The intention was to protect the individual from his own self-destructive tendencies for a short period of time and find help for him. A judge quickly overturned the public prosecutor's effort to make the attempter stand trial as a criminal. Criminal laws either have been erased from the books or are not vigor-ously enforced.[11] There are at least 18 states, however, in which a person who aids or encourages somebody else to commit suicide may be charged with a felony. Criminal penalties for those who attempt suicide as well as the unenforceable penalties for those who complete suicide have been abolished throughout England and do not seem to be gaining favor any place. Another indication of attitude change can be seen in life insurance policies. It was once common for insurance companies to treat suicide as though it were a special kind of crime—one intended to defraud the underwriters. It is now possible to have death benefits associated with suicide, although with certain limitations and restrictions built into the contract.

Decriminalization of suicide is based in part on the unworkability of most laws that have been enacted, but also on the realization that such penalties have not served as effective deterrents. It may also be in keeping with a social climate in which the meanings of life and death are being reevaluated in general (e.g., the euthanasia controversies). Law enforcement agencies have now become effective front-line resources for suicide prevention in some communities, being liberated now from the legal responsibility of having to look on the attempter as a criminal.

Suicide is weakness or madness

When a person commits suicide it means that he has cracked. There is some flaw or limitation or deviation within him. This attitude toward self-destruction on the part of a culture should be distinguished from the individual's own attitude. It is not that a person tells himself, "I am out of my mind—therefore, I will take my life." Rather, it is society that sometimes declares, "A person who kills himself must be out of his mind."

The fact is that some people who commit suicide can be classified as psychotic or severely disturbed, but some cannot. David Lester[13] found general agreement among the available studies of mental disorder and suicide to the effect that individuals with diagnosed psychiatric conditions tended to have a higher suicide rate than the population at large. People diagnosed as "depressive psychotics" tend to have the highest rates of completed suicides. (Difficult as it is to be certain about the dependability of completed suicide statistics, it is even more difficult to compare groups of people on suicide *attempts, threats,* or *preoccupations* because of various problems associated with the reporting of same.) Studies since the Lester review have not materially changed this picture. If we are concerned with the probability of suicide in very large populations, then mental and emotional disorder is a relevant variable to consider: it will help us a little to identify people at risk and to make some predictions. However, psychiatric disorder is far from satisfactory as explanation or predictor of suicide. Even when a psychopathological state is present, this in itself does not explain, let alone motivate, the action. Many people go through disturbed periods without attempting suicide. And it is only through a gross distortion of the actual circumstances that one could claim *all* suicides are enacted in a spell of madness. It would be tempting to believe that a person "has to be crazy to commit suicide," but this is a far from adequate explanation.

What about the related explanation that suicide is the outcome of *"weakness"*? This view seems to have intensified as a result of the "survival of the fittest" doctrine that has now been with us for more than a century.[14] During this time many special-interest groups have interpreted Charles Darwin's theory of evolution in terms of their own values and only secondarily on the scientific evidence as such. Those who favor a rough-and-tumble, highly competitive struggle for power have tried to rationalize these tactics by analogy with the so-called

survival-of-the-fittest principle. This approach is meant to justify the raw pursuit and exploitation of power. Those who fall by the wayside? Well, they just didn't have "it." Seen in these terms, suicide is simply one of the ways in which a relatively weak member of society loses out in the junglelike struggle. It is a cultural meaning of suicide, then, in which prevention or compassion for the victim would be seen as regressive. Suicide is one of nature's ways to preserve the species by weeding out the less fit. (This interpretation is not necessarily one that would have been endorsed by Darwin himself, who had little control over how society chose to use or abuse his ideas.)

This position is not taken quite so openly today as in the heyday of rugged individualism and naive social applications of evolutionary theory. Nevertheless, one can still see it in operation. It is perhaps even easier to discern these dynamics if we broaden our scope to include self-destructive behaviors other than direct suicide. Sales representatives and executives who are "down on their luck" or under extreme pressure at work sometimes turn to drink. It may appear to colleagues that the increasing use of alcohol has become detrimental both to the individual's work performance and health and adjustment in general. The troubled person may eventually show up as a suicide statistic or as one who died in an automobile "accident" under circumstances suggestive of suicidal intent.[15] Whether or not premature death terminates the downhill spiral, many other socially and personally destructive consequences may follow abuse of alcohol. Often there is no serious effort at intervention by those who observe the process. Their colleague has proved to be a weakling in the competitive business jungle—tough, but that's life, isn't it?

"If you can't stand the heat, get out of the kitchen!" was one of the types of comment heard after a spectacular suicide in New York City not long ago. A man at the top, a ranking executive of a major international corporation, leaped to his death from offices high above Manhattan. Media coverage emphasized the length of time that his fallen body tied up traffic and other circumstantial aspects of the death. Little attention was given then or later to his state of mind, the meaning of his suicide, or the impact on survivors. Other executives around the nation commented off the record that some people just can't take the gaff. There was a note of pride in such comments: "I am strong enough to cope with adversity, that other fellow wasn't."

Both the weakness and the madness interpretations of suicide seem to have filled some of the gap left by decriminalization and by increasing dissidence about the sinful nature of self-destruction. The popularity of a psychiatrically oriented view of human nature over the past several decades has been used for this purpose, just as Darwinism made do for earlier generations. To say that a person committed suicide because he was not in his right mind has the obvious effect of setting him apart from the rest of us. It is his problem, not ours, and is the outcome of a flawed, deviant mind. The protective function of this cultural attitude— protection, that is, against any fear that suicide might be intimately related to our own life- style—suggests that we might think twice before endorsing it.[16]

Suicide is "The Great Death"

The Buddhist tradition in China and Japan includes the image of *daishi*, which translates roughly as "The Great Death." Through their own example, Zen masters have shown how a person might pass admirably from this life. While the Zen master typically exhibited a serene life-style, his influence was also felt by those who led more action-oriented existences. The discipline and devotion of the master appealed to the warrior, for example. The *samurai* would seek *daishi* on the battlefield. This influence remained strong enough over the centuries to enlist the self-sacrifices of *kamikaze* pilots in World War II (although at least some of these young men still had their doubts about carrying through missions that meant almost certain death). The quasi-suicidal aspects of The Great Death are evident in both the ancient and the more contemporary commitments.

But direct suicide itself has been honored as a form of *daishi*. *Seppuku* is a traditional form of suicide in Japan, better known in the West as *hara-kiri*. The act itself consists of disembowelment, usually with a sword. In some situations this form of death has served as an honorable alternative to execution. A person condemned to death would be given the privilege of becoming his own executioner. Voluntary *seppuku*, by contrast, might flow from a number of different motives on the part of the individual, for example, to follow a master into the great beyond or to protest an injustice. Placing one's entire life at the disposal of an honorable or noble motive was a much-admired action. In our own time, the self-immolation of Buddhist monks in Southeast Asia to emphasize their religious and political protests has also made a deep impression on observers.

Ritualized, honorable suicide of this type seems to integrate various levels of existence. By opening his abdomen, the individual is showing the world that his center of being (thought to be located there) is pure and undefiled. The act therefore involves a network of physiological, individual, social, and religious referents. Specifically, the individual puts the sword to his *hara*, the (imagined) locus of breath control—and breath is regarded in many cultures as closely akin to both life itself and divinity.[17]

Fascination with "The Great Death" theme remains potent today despite the many changes that have been taking place in tradition-oriented cultures such as China and Japan. Yet the precise significance of this theme must be understood in terms of the total life situation of the individual. This has been shown, for example, in the suicides of two celebrated Japanese writers, Yasunari Kawabata and Mukio Mishima. Kawabata, the 1968 Nobel Prize winner for literature in 1968, killed himself in 1972 at the age of 72 (by inhalation of gas). The 45-year-old Mishima, who had been a leading candidate for the Nobel Prize, delivered an impassioned speech to his followers on a political cause, then performed a traditional *samurai* ritual and, along with one of his admirers, committed *hara-kiri* (in 1970). The lives and deaths of these two men have been carefully analyzed by Mamoru Iga.[18] He finds that although both writers drew on the same tradition and both ended their lives with self-murder, there were sharp differences between them in the motivations and contexts of their deaths and the specific meaning death held for them. Iga, along with many other contemporary suicidologists, emphasizes that both individual and cultural factors must be considered in trying to understand why a particular person chooses suicide. The allure of "The Great Death" theme must be taken into account in some suicides, but this does not by itself adequately explain the individual's actions nor provide a sufficient basis for preventing suicide.

Notice that this painful, bloody, violent, dramatic action is *not* regarded as sinful, criminal, weak, or mad when it occurs within a viable traditional context. By contrast, the person in our own society who quietly ingests an overdose of medication still runs the risk of being considered any or all of the above. Culture obviously has its say, although the voice of the individual must also be heard and understood.

The association of suicide with desirable death has not been limited to the Orient. It was one of the characteristic themes of the world of the ancient Greeks and Romans. As Alvarez comments, "the Romans looked on suicide with neither fear nor revulsion, but as a carefully considered and chosen validation of the way they had lived and the principles they had lived by."[9,p.64] Suicide as an alternative to capture, defeat, and disgrace was considered laudable; it may even have been the expected course of action by a person of character.

Suicide is a rational alternative

The belief that suicide can bring a glorious death has a more subdued echo in another cultural tradition, also dating from ancient times. This is the attitude that suicide is an acceptable, rational alternative to continued existence. It is a view often conditioned by adverse circumstances. "Life is not always preferable to death" is the thought here. The individual does not destroy himself in hope of thereby achieving a noble postmortem reputation or a place among the eternally blessed. Instead he wishes to subtract himself from a life whose quality seems a worse evil than death.

While there are individuals today who have this outlook, it is the long-standing cultural tradition that we wish to emphasize at the moment. It can be found in Renaissance thinking where death often is praised as the place of refuge from the cruelties and disappointments of life. Erasmus[19] is but one of the eminent humanists who observed what a distance there is between our aspirations for the human race and the failings discovered on every side in daily life. The newly awakened spirit of hope and progress soon became shadowed by a sense of disappointment and resignation that, it sometimes seemed, only death could swallow.

Much earlier in history there is also evidence that the harshness of life made suicide an appealing option to many. Alvarez contends that stoicism, a philosophical position that was enunciated in ancient Athens and Rome and has since become virtually a synonym for rational control, was in actuality a last defense against the murderous squalor of Rome itself. When those calm heroes looked around them they saw a life so unspeakable, cruel, wanton, corrupt, and apparently unvalued that they clung to their ideas of reason much as the Christian poor used to cling to their belief in Paradise and the goodness of God despite, or because of, this misery of their lives on this earth. Stoicism, in short, was a philosophy of despair; it was not a coincidence that Seneca, who was its most powerful and influential spokesman, was also the teacher of the most vicious of all Roman emperors, Nero.[9, p. 66]

Seneca himself died as an "honorable suicide." Maurice Faber[20] has analyzed Seneca's death in much the same vein as Iga examined the deaths of Kawabata and Mishima. What made Seneca's suicide appear "rational" in its own context included his entire psychosexual developmental history and the nature of the specific circumstances of the time, not simply an abstract philosophical belief.

From ancient philosophers to contemporary existentialists, from victims of human cruelty and injustice to people whose lives just didn't seem to work out, there has been maintained a tradition in which suicide is regarded as an option available to the reasonable person. Choron speaks of a German psychiatrist, Alfred Hoche, who proposed in 1919

the term *"Bilanz-Selbtsmord"*—"balance-sheet suicide"—to designate instances where supposedly mentally normal persons dispassionately take stock of their life situation, and, having found it unacceptable, if not intolerable, and not anticipating any change for the better, decide to put an end to their lives.[8, p. 96]

This term has not caught on as such in psychiatric circles, but the concept is still with us. When it is a particular individual who is contemplating suicide because life no longer appears preferable to death, then we are likely to find his motives and circumstances of prime interest. But there have been many times in human history when misery was so general and

the outlook so grim that it did not require any distinctive individual dynamics to think seriously of suicide. The horrors of the plague years, for example, intensified by warfare and generalized social disorganization, led many to question the value of continued life. "It's a sin!" "It's a crime!" "It's weakness!" "It's madness!" All these protests and admonitions can seem at times to be ways of discouraging a rational, balance-sheet view of life and death.

The Judeo-Christian tradition has in general advocated life. There is intrinsic value in life. One should not dispose of life, no matter what the temptations. This message has been imperfectly delivered. At times it has been contradicted by the actions of the true believers themselves. Nevertheless, enough of this spirit has come across to establish a most challenging issue for all of us: Is life to be valued and fostered under all conditions because it has primary and intrinsic value? Or is the value of life relative to the circumstances? This issue is confronted in many life-and-death situations today beyond the problem of suicide. We will be looking at it again in the next chapter.

A SOCIOLOGICAL THEORY OF SUICIDE

We have been considering some of the meanings that various cultures have given to suicide. More than one meaning may exist in the same culture at a particular time, as is the case with us. But is it possible to discover an overall relationship between culture and the individual? Emile Durkheim proposed a comprehensive sociological theory of self-destruction in 1897. *Le Suicide*[21] became a cornerstone for the then new science of sociology in general and remains one of the most influential theories of suicide in particular. Durkheim realized that the study of an act so extreme as suicide was likely to reveal much about the general structure and function of society. His work fulfilled the earlier observations of M. A. Quetelet, who suggested in 1842:

It would appear . . . that moral phenomena, when observed on a great scale, are found to resemble physical phenomena; and thus we arrive, in inquiries of this kind, at the fundamental principle, the greater the number of individuals observed, the more do individual peculiarities, whether physical or moral, become effaced, and leave in a prominent point of view the general facts, by virtue of which society exists and is preserved. [cited in 7,p.6]

The Quetelet-Durkheim approach was audacious for its time. Suicide was not essentially a matter of intimate concern between the individual and God. Moral values were not the primary focus. Instead, suicide could be regarded best at a distance and by a cool observer who was more interested in the overall pattern of self-destruction than in any particular life and death. The sociologist, then, was much like an astronomer or physicist. This approach incurred the disfavor both of those who emphasized moral issues and those who emphasized individuality. Opposition of this type remains today, but Durkheim gained an important beachhead for the objective scientific study of human society.

Rich and complex in its details, Durkheim's theory nevertheless can be reduced to several major propositions and a four-part classification of suicide "types." Why do people kill themselves? If we insisted on a simple answer to this question, Durkheim would point toward society. Large-scale social dynamics determine the probability of individual self-destruction. The concept of *social integration* is important here. Every individual is more or less integrated into the structure of his or her culture. The suicide risk depends much on the extent of social integration *between* individual and society. The culture itself shows more or less *social solidarity*, or cohesiveness within itself. Social life may be stable, consistent, and supportive, or it may be falling apart under stress. *The individual, then, may be weakly or strongly integrated into a high- or a low-solidarity culture.*

The crucial index for suicide can be found in the interaction between integration and solidarity: How much does the culture *control* the individual? Both the weakly integrated person in a solid social structure and the person caught in a disorganized culture are apt to be deprived of sufficient group control. Either of these circumstances might increase the probability of suicide. However, suicide can also result from either not enough or too much control by society. And the judgment that suicide is an undesirable outcome itself depends on the specific cultural dynamics at work, as we shall continue to see.

At least one other Durkheimian concept should be considered, even though he presents it rather vaguely in *Le Suicide*. Every culture is said to have its *collective representations*. These represent the spirit or personality of the culture as a whole, the guiding themes, moods, or emotional climate. Under certain circumstances this group spirit can turn morose and self-destructive. This means that the individual who is well integrated into the culture may be especially vulnerable. He somehow absorbs the dysphoric mood of the larger society and may act it out with fatal results. This aspect of Durkheim's theory is especially difficult to test out with the available methodology of the social and behavioral sciences. But it is much more important than the attention it has received in recent years would indicate. It suggests that the very forces that should hold a society together can take on the opposite character and lead to what we might call "*sociocide.*" At this point in the first edition of this volume, I followed introduction of the sociocide concept with the following passage: "No, the culture is not likely to destroy itself in one conclusive action as obvious as simultaneous suicide of all members. But the sociocidic mood can increase the probability of individual self-destruction not only through suicide per se but also through a variety of other modalities as well (e.g., homicide, 'accidents,' loss of will to live in illness, alcohol and drug abuse, etc.)." That was before Guyana and the mass suicide and homicide which resulted in the eradication of a unique community and more than 900 lives. Perhaps this catastrophe will at least provide a perspective from which less extreme forms of incipient sociocide can be identified.

Most of the attention to Durkheim today focuses on the four types of suicide he delineated. Each is thought to represent one particular relationship between individual and society.

The *egoistic* suicide is committed by people who do not have enough involvement with society. They are not under sufficient cultural control. The executive who literally fell from on high is one probable example. The individual whose talents, inclinations, or station in life place him in a special category, relatively immune from ordinary social restrictions, is especially vulnerable to egoistic suicide. The celebrity in the entertainment field, the creative artist who follows his own star, the person in a relatively distinct or unique role—all may go their own personal ways until they can no longer be reached effectively by cultural constraints. Intellectuals are common in this category. They are more likely than others to pick up those collective representations that we have described as sociocidic. Sensitive to underlying currents of melancholy and despair in the culture and, in a sense, lost in their own thoughts, they have little outside themselves to grasp when the suicide impulse arises.

Very different indeed is the *altruistic* suicide. We have already mentioned such examples as the *seppukuo* tradition and the *kamikaze* type of combat death. *Suttee*, the now discouraged practice in India of a widow giving her life at her husband's funeral, is another dramatic example. According to Durkheim, the altruistic suicide occurs when the individual has an exaggerated or excessive concern for the community. This is usually the strongly integrated person in a high-solidarity culture. Altruistic suicides tend to be less common in Western societies but often are admired when they do occur.

Social breakdown is reflected most directly in the *anomic* suicide. Here it is less a question of the individual's integration with society and more a question of society's ability to function as it should. People are let down, cast adrift by the failure of social institutions. Unemployment is one pertinent example. The person thrown out of work has lost a significant tie to society, and through society's doing, not his or her own. Bad times—unemployment—suicide: a predictable sequence. Similarly, a person who is forced to leave an occupation because of age may enter an anomic condition that leads to suicide. When the rupture between individual and society is sudden and unexpected, then the probability of suicide is thought to be especially high. This situation arises, for example, when death of an important person drastically reduces the survivor's place in society.

For many years it was this set of three suicide types that dominated the picture. Recently, however, more attention has been given to a fourth type that Durkheim introduced but treated more as a curiosity. A person may experience too much control by society, he suggested. A culture that stifles and oppresses some of its members may thereby encourage *fatalistic* suicide. The individual sees all opportunities and prospects blocked. Durkheim spoke of slavery as a condition that engenders fatalistic suicide but thought that civilization had put this kind of oppression well into the past. Oppression and subjugation have not disappeared from the human condition, however, as totalitarian regimes continue to manifest themselves throughout the twentieth century. Both the *altruistic* and the *fatalistic* suicide involve excessive control of the individual by society. In the former case, the individual appears to share wholeheartedly in the collective representations. He dies *for* his people. In the latter case he dies in despair of ever being able to actualize himself in a culture that affords little opportunity for self-esteem and satisfaction. (We have had to import some psychologically oriented concepts into the sociological framework here to help with the distinction.)

One very recent study has taken an interesting new approach to Durkheim's concept of fatalistic suicide. Stack[23] examined official suicide data from 45 nations, the best information available (he was well aware that even the best data are not entirely dependable). To this information he applied a measure of *political totalitarianism* previously developed by Taylor and Hudson.[24] These include such sanctions against individual freedom as banning political rallies, exile, deportation, or arrest of those expressing opposition to the regime, censorship of the media, etc. His study included other variables as well, but the relationship between suicide and totalitarian overregulation of the individual is of most relevance here. A positive and statistically significant relationship was found between degree of totalitarian overregulation of the individual and suicide. This result was seen as consistent with Durkheim's observations on fatalistic suicide, although Stack notes that the complete explanation is likely to be more complex. In my view, the data do not clearly support the conclusion that too much social control has in fact led to higher rates of fatalistic suicide. The methodology is not perfect for this purpose, and alternative explanations are possible. Nevertheless, we see here at least a promising attempt to test one of Durkheim's most challenging theses on a grand scale in our own times.

Sociological approaches to suicide have attracted their share of criticism over the years with Durkheim's theory, as the leading contender, receiving the sternest reexaminations. Clinicians complain that Durkheim's theoretical distinctions are so difficult to apply in practice that they are all but useless. Research psychologists complain that the neglect of individual dynamics leaves Durkheim's theory too incomplete to foster either understanding or prevention. Nevertheless, Durkheim's contribution is of more than historical interest. Another recent study,[25] for example, finds that sophisticated methods of data analysis available now but not in Durkheim's time support many of that pioneer's specific conclusions. This useful contribution by Nick Dangelis and Whitney Pope helps to distinguish between the more and the less accurate of Durkheim's propositions and to guide future research.

Durkheim and a number of sociologists after him have made a strong case for an intimate relationship between suicide and the social structure. Let us now see what kind of case can be made for the individual's own thoughts, motives, and life-style as factors in suicide.

SOME INDIVIDUAL MEANINGS OF SUICIDE

Just as the earlier discussion did not exhaust all the cultural meanings of suicide, so this section can only sample some of the individual meanings. There is no intention to offer a typology here. Instead, the intent is to convey something of the various states of mind with which people approach a suicidal action. Cultural influences will be acknowledged throughout, but emphasis is on the way in which the individual thinks and feels.

Suicide is reunion

Loss of a loved one can be experienced as so unbearable that the survivor is tempted to "join" the deceased. It has already been observed (Chapter 14) that recently bereaved people often experience the "presence" of the dead. Perhaps this helps mitigate the sense of abandonment. But desperate longing may impel a person to follow the dead all the way "to the other side" if the relationship has been marked by extreme dependency. "I can't go on without him." "I am not complete without her." "What's to become of me? I can't manage by myself." Many people have feelings of this kind; sometimes these feelings are accompanied by suicidal thoughts. Reunion fantasies may have some temporary value while such bereaved individuals reconstruct their lives—or they may conclude that nothing short of a hoped-for reunion through death could solve their problems.

Some components in our cultural tradition encourage suicidal fantasies and actions of this kind. Heaven is such a delightful place—and it is so miserable here. Death is not real; it is only a portal to eternal life. There is an insurance advertisement that depicts a dead husband gazing down with approval from the clouds. Messages of this type encourage a blurring of the distinction between the living and the dead. The recent upsurge of interest in near-death experiences and "life after life" could also contribute to suicide (Chapter 17).

Children are particularly vulnerable to reunion fantasies. They do not yet have a firm cognitive grasp of life and death (although more advanced in this respect than many adults believe). The child is still in the process of attempting to establish identity as an individual. The parent or older sibling who has "gone off to heaven" has left the survivor with painful feelings of incompleteness and yearning. Some adults remain relatively childlike in their dependence on others and feel very much the same way when separated from those others by death. Suicide to achieve reunion seems most likely when the person lacks a fully developed sense of selfhood, whether because of developmental level or personality constellation, when death has removed a significant source of support, and when there are salient cultural messages that make death appear unreal and the afterlife inviting.

Suicide is rest and refuge

Worn down by tribulations, a person may long for a "good rest" or a "secure harbor." This motivation can have many outcomes other than suicide. A vacation far away from the grinding routine may restore energy and confidence. Somebody else may appear on the scene to share the load. Or the vexed and fatigued person may simply drop his responsibilities for awhile. Alternatives such as these may not work out, however. Life may be experienced as too unrelenting and burdensome. The miracle of an ordinary good night's sleep may seem out of reach as depression deepens. Under such circumstances the fantasy of a prolonged, uninterrupted sleep may take on a heightened allure. The sleep-death analogy is readily available in our own as in most other cultures (Chapter 4). It is tempting to take a few more pills than usual and just drift away.

This orientation toward suicide is also encouraged by individual and cultural tendencies to blur the distinctions between life and death. It falls well within the established cultural style of solving problems by taking something into our mouths (puffing on a cigarette; sucking on a pipe; swallowing pills for headaches, indigestion, any form of distress).

Both the sleep and the reunion meanings of suicide stand in contrast to the position that self-destruction represents a revolt of pride against the establishment, whether sin or crime. Rather, these are pathways of escape made attractive and accessible by cultural tradition itself. People with oral or escapist tendencies dominant in their personalities might be expected to be especially vulnerable to these lures of suicide.

Suicide is getting back

The lover is rejected. The employee is passed over for promotion. Another child is preferred and pampered. The particular situation is not so important as is the feeling of burning resentment and hurt left inside. And it may not have been the first time. Some people repeatedly feel that they are treated unfairly. Their achievements never seem to be recognized. No matter how hard they try, love and appreciation are withheld. Others may not recognize the state of mind with which such a person approaches a situation—how intensely hope and doubt, anger and longing are intermingled.

❖ "I felt crushed. Absolutely *crushed*. It was my first really good semester. No incompletes. No withdrawals. All As and Bs. And no 'episodes.' I kept myself going all semester. I really felt strong and independent. I knew I shouldn't expect too much when I went home, but I guess . . . I mean I *know* I expected a little appreciation. You know, like maybe Mother just smiling and saying, 'Had a good semester, didn't you? I'm happy for you' or 'I'm proud of you,' though she would never say *that*."

This young woman instead felt that her achievement passed without notice, that, in fact, the family hardly noticed that she had come back home. Hurt and angry, she decided to get back by making a suicide attempt. If her family would not pay attention when she did something right, maybe they would when she did something wrong. "I wanted to hurt them—and hurt me—just enough." She slashed away at her wrist and arm. The self-wounding seemed to release some of her despair. She had not injured herself seriously, so she wrapped the wounded area in a bulky bandage. Nobody seemed to notice. A few days later she removed the bandage, exposing the patchwork of fresh scars. There still was no obvious response from the family. Instead, they were enthusing about the graduation and upcoming marriage of one of her cousins. She felt even more "crushed" and "low" when she was passed over in the wedding arrangements as well. "I couldn't even be part of somebody else's happiness."

❖ "I knew that revenge was stupid. But I *felt* like doing something stupid. Listen everybody: you're 100 percent right! I *am* a stupid person. And here is something *really* stupid to prove it!"

She hurled herself from a rooftop.

❖ "I wanted to kill myself then. I *think* I did. But I also wanted to see the look on their faces when they saw that bloody mess on the sidewalk. I could see myself standing alongside the rest of them, looking at that bloody mess of myself on the sidewalk, and looking at their shocked looks . . . I *didn't* think what it would be like if I half-killed myself and had to live with a crushed body. Maybe that was the really stupid part of it."

This woman survived a suicide attempt that might have proved fatal. She was also fortunate in that her injuries did not prove permanently crippling, although she was disabled for months. The physical pain and trauma relieved some of her emotional tension—for awhile. Yet she felt that she might "have to" do it again, perhaps "next time for keeps." She did not need a psychologist to suggest that her suicide attempts were efforts to punish others by punishing herself. She was also perfectly capable of pointing out that both attempts had been aimed at forcing either love or remorse from the people who had been letting her down for so long.

Revenge fantasies and their association with suicide are well known to people who give ear to those in emotional distress. The particular example given here illustrates several other characteristics often shown by the person who is on a self-destructive footing. This woman's fantasy included witnessing the impact of her suicide. She had divided herself into murderer and victim. The revenge fantasy would have lost much of its appeal had she recognized that she would never be able to confirm or appreciate the hoped-for impact. People who attempt suicide for reasons other than revenge may also act on the assumption that, in a sense, they will survive the death to benefit by its effect.

She also experienced some tension release through the self-destructive action itself. It is not unusual for the sight of one's own blood to relieve built-up emotional pressures, if only for a while. Another woman who had slashed her wrists on several occasions told me, "I felt as if I had done something finally. I wasn't paralyzed anymore. I wasn't suffering helplessly. I took action into my own hands, and that felt good." Perhaps the experience of surviving this type of suicide attempt encourages the fantasy that one would still be around to feel better after a fatal attempt as well.

The low self-esteem of many suicide attempters is also evident in the instance given here. Having a very unfavorable opinion of oneself may be linked with a variety of other motivations in addition to the fantasy of revenge. The combination of the revenge fantasy and low self-esteem appears to be a particularly dangerous one, however.

Suicide is the penalty for failure

The victim of suicide may also be the victim of self-expectations that have not been fulfilled. The sense of disappointment and frustration may have much in common with that experienced by the person who seeks revenge through suicide. But we are speaking now of the person who essentially holds himself or herself to blame. The judgment, "I have failed," is followed by the decision to enact a most severe penalty, one that will make further failures impossible. It is as though the person has been tried and found guilty of a capital offense in his or her own personal court. A completely unacceptable gap is felt between expectations and accomplishment. One person might take the alternative of lowering expectations to close the gap. Another person might give a

more flattering, benefit-of-the-doubt interpretation of accomplishments. And somebody else might keep trying to bring performance up to self-expectations. However, for some people a critical moment arrives when the discrepancy is experienced as too glaring and painful to be tolerated. If something has to go it may be the person himself, not the perhaps excessively high standards by which the judgment has been made.

Warren Breed and his colleagues found that a sense of failure is prominent among many people who take their own lives.[26] Their research approach is notable for considering both individual and social factors and for its concentration on those who actually kill themselves as distinguished from the larger number of people who threaten or attempt to do so. The conclusions are based on intensive case studies of suicide in New Orleans and appear to be consistent with findings of other investigators as well.[27]

The significance of a failure experience first came to Breed's attention when he reviewed the cases of 103 white males, "many of whom had taken their lives after being fired, demoted, or passed over for promotion, or had suffered business reverses."[26,p.6] He increased the size and variety of his study population and added interviews of people who had known the deceased. It was learned that suicidal women also failed, "but in a different domain—that of the family. Young female suiciders had endless troubles with men, not many became successful mothers, and older women fell into a general role atrophy."[26] For women less than 50 years old, work failure did not seem to be nearly as common or important a background to suicide as it did for men. The realms of experienced failure were different, then: work for men, family for women. Yet "very often there is multiple failure—for example, the unemployed man whose wife leaves him."

Fortunately, not every person who experiences failure commits suicide. Breed and his colleagues have discovered other factors that so intensified the failure experience as to produce a lethal suicide attempt. This has led to the concept of a *basic suicidal syndrome*. Failure plays a critical role, but takes on more lethal potential because of its association with the other factors.

The syndrome includes *rigidity, commitment, shame,* and *isolation,* as well as *failure* itself. The individual tends to be *rigid,* in that he cannot shift from one role or goal to another, nor shift level of aspiration. There is only one goal, one level of expectation, and only one way to achieve it. There is a strong *commitment,* that is, an intense desire to succeed. The sense of *failure* involves more than having performed less adequately than the person had demanded of himself; it also includes a sense of culpability, of self-blame. The feeling is likely to go beyond guilt. A person who has failed or erred still might have a chance to redeem himself. The suicidal syndrome is characterized by a generalized sense of *shame.* It is not just that the individual has failed at something—he or she feels totally worthless. "I am no good. Never will be. I am nothing." From all these interacting factors, the individual may develop a sense of *isolation.* "In his state of despair he is all too prone to believe that the others, too, are evaluating him negatively . . . a process of withdrawal often follows and the person becomes more and more isolated from other people."[28,p.117]

This syndrome has been found by Breed and his colleagues most conspicuously in white, middle-class adults, both male or female. It does not seem to hold for lower-class black men who kill themselves. They had little opportunity for occupational success, Breed suggests, and therefore little occasion either to have developed high aspirations in that sphere or to feel shamed because of their menial employment.

The intense desire for the achievement of occupational prestige is an aspiration confined, for all practical purposes, to whites and the relatively small number of middle- and upper-class blacks [in the population studied]. The proposition here is that to commit suicide one must be blocked in his aspirations; he must want to achieve very badly but cannot, or, having once made it, slips in prestige. For males in white America achievement almost always indicates occupational success.[28,p.118]

Perhaps it is going too far to speak of this as *the* basic suicidal syndrome. Breed himself readily acknowledges that there are other patterns associated with suicide. Several have already been sketched here. But the high-aspiration, shame-of-failure dynamic revealed by his research does come close to the meaning of suicide for many in our society today. It does not tell us, however, why one person with a "basic suicidal syndrome" commits suicide while another finds a different solution to his problems, nor does it explain how the syndrome develops in the first place. A sequence is at least suggested, though. An individual may not become suicidal all at once, but may start leaning toward an eventual act of self-destruction from an initial rigid setting of high aspirations. This would be followed by failure, perhaps repeated failures, leading to a shamed and despondent pattern of isolating himself from others. Further understanding of this sequence could prove helpful in identifying people who are at particular suicidal risk and providing timely assistance to them.

The failure theme can also put us on notice about our own relationship to self-destruction. The person who takes his life because he is convinced he is a shameful failure is only one of the more dramatic or extreme victims. How many of us labor under unrelenting pressure for achievement, as though our very lives depended on it? And how many of us drive others to do the same? Competitive pressure in the classroom—from nursery school through advanced graduate work—follows us throughout our educational careers. College counselors are not surprised to find suicidal thoughts in the minds of some students, especially around final exam time. But high-school and even grade-school students also are vulnerable. Children may be made to feel that they are only as good as their most recent report card. The drive to win, to be number one, is dominant in sports as well, and not limited to the professional domain. Bob Cousy, the former Boston Celtic basketball star, is among those who have expressed alarm about "the killer instinct"[29] that has come to the fore in sporting competition. He is one of an increasing number of observers who have been trying to tell us that a person's intrinsic worth should not be identified with victory in competition, promotion at work, or some form of "super performance." We may not kill ourselves because of our real or imagined failures. But many of us are pressured and harassed ourselves and transmit this pressure to others. We have some sense, then, of how the suicidal person feels even if we do not take this route. We may, however, be taking some other, more indirect route to self-destruction because of meanings associated with the shame or dread of failure. And we are all part of the cultural constellation that makes suicide appear to be the appropriate penalty for those who are not "winning the game."

Suicide is a mistake

Death may be the intended outcome of an overdose or other self-destructive action. This does not guarantee that the person will in fact die. A serious attempt may fall short of its objective for a number of reasons. An unexpected rescuer may appear on the scene, a determined self-mutilation may happen to miss a vital spot, the overdose may induce vomiting instead of coma, a loaded gun may even fail to fire. The victim may "betray" himself, as in the case of the bridge-jumper who survives the often-

deadly fall and then swims desperately for life. Shneidman[30] gives two particularly vivid examples of people who survived suicide attempts that ordinarily would have been lethal in his fascinating collection of personal documents, *Voices of Death*.

There is discrepancy between intention and outcome in the other direction as well, and that is what chiefly concerns us here. Some people kill themselves even though there is good reason to believe that they had not meant to do so. The attempt did have a meaning, but it was not to end life. The victim had counted on being rescued. The overdose was not supposed to be lethal. Some kind of control or precaution had been exercised to limit the effect—and yet the outcome was death.

We cannot automatically conclude that the death outcome was the intention any more than we can insist that a person did not intend to kill himself because the attempt happened to abort. In suicide, as in most other actions, we do not always achieve the outcome we had in mind.

Some unknown proportion of those who kill themselves each year are dead by mistake. What was their actual intention, if the death outcome itself was not absolutely fixed in mind as the desired result? Pioneering suicidologists Norman L. Farberow and Edwin S. Shneidman may have suggested the gist of the answer in the title of their book, *The Cry for Help*.[31] They call attention to "the messages of suffering and anguish and the pleas for response that are expressed by and contained within suicidal behaviors."[31,p.xi] Many have learned to agree with this view. Whatever else a suicide attempt might be, it is also a form of communication. Sometimes, unfortunately, this tortured way of reaching out for human response misses the mark. People do not respond in a helpful way to the attempt, leaving the individual as despondent as before—or the attempt may prove fatal before help can arrive. The person may have wanted much to live, but a mood, a desperate maneuver, and a misjudgment brought life to a sudden close.

People who work often with the suicidal recognize that the individual contemplating a self-destructive act is frequently of two minds. This is the impression, for example, of volunteers who pick up the phone when a call is made to a suicide-prevention hot line. The very fact that a person would reach out for human contact in this way suggests some continuing advocacy for life. We have no way of knowing if all people in a suicidal state of mind experience strong ambivalence. There do seem to be certain moments when some individuals believe suicide is the only answer, period. The feeling that there is "only one way out" is one of the most important warnings of incipient suicide and deserves immediate and careful attention. However, many people with suicide on their minds go back and forth about it, experiencing conflicting life and death tugs, even at the same time. A life-threatening act that emerges from a wavering or conflicted intention may itself show some apparent contradictions. Why would she have taken the overdose just a few minutes before her husband was due home if she was entirely of a mind to take her life? And yet, she did ingest those pills—and if her husband happens to be delayed in coming home this day, will this gesture have become indeed her final gesture?

Helping people to survive their own mistakes is an important part not only of suicide prevention but of public health and safety in general. Access to lethal means of self-destruction could be made more difficult, for example, thereby placing some time and distance between a momentary intention and a permanent error. Seiden[32] observes that suicide rates dropped significantly in England when coke gas no longer was widely available as an easily available mode of suicide in the home, or when its toxicity was reduced. He has persistently advocated the construction of a lower-span sidewalk for the Golden Gate Bridge, a place that has become known widely as a "suicide shrine." Seiden followed up on more than 700 people who had approached either the Golden Gate or Bay bridges with suicidal intentions who were intercepted by alert citizens or police before completing the action. Most of these people (96%) did not make subsequent fatal attempts—and all the survivors favored construction of a barrier. "If there had been a barrier every one of them reports they would have reconsidered."[32,p.274] The suicidal intention had been strong but ambivalent. The attempters had given society a chance to catch them before making a fatal mistake. Seiden adds that, "considering the transitory nature of suicidal crises, the presence of a highly lethal and easily available means such as the bridge must be regarded as equivalent to a loaded gun around the house ready to be used in an impulsive outburst." The implication is that society might take a more active role in protecting people from those critical moments when the possibility of making a fatal mistake is on the horizon.

A psychoanalytical approach to suicide

Durkheim was the obvious choice to illustrate a sociological approach to suicide, although there are alternative conceptions that are also worth attentions.[e.g. 33,34] Similarly, the psychoanalytical view is the most obvious choice to illustrate individual-oriented theories. However, there is no simple, neatly packaged psychoanalytical theory of self-destruction. Freud and other psychoanalysts have dealt with suicide in many contexts, from the philosophical to the clinical. It is more useful to consider the entire body of psychoanalytical writings as a resource for consultation on suicide rather than to attempt to reduce it to a few summarizing propositions. There is a richness and complexity to the psychoanalytical approach that each reader can draw on his or her own way. Nevertheless, it is useful to consider a few of the more distinctive ideas that are part of the psychoanalytical view of self-destruction.

As Robert Litman notes, Freud waited many years before attempting to explain suicide.[35] He recognized not only the complexity of suicidal phenomena but also the challenge posed to a general understanding of the human condition. *Since life seeks to preserve itself, how could a being actively pursue its own destruction?* Freud's first explanation was rather different from those that had been previously offered by others. It centered around the concept of the internalization of the wish to kill somebody else. The individual turns a murderous wish against himself.[36] By destroying himself, then, he symbolically destroys the other person. The suicide victim behaves as though he is rooting out the inner representations of another person, a representation that might derive from early childhood when the distinction between self and other is incomplete.

You will notice that this explanation has at least one major advantage. It does not require us to conclude that a person really intends to destroy himself per se, and therefore it does not go against the assumed law of nature that self-preservation is a fundamental instinct. It also suggests that in seeking the cause of suicide we should give attention to problems in early development as well as to stresses and pressures in the immediate situation.

Freud did not remain satisfied with this theory. Later he offered a more philosophical conception.[37] We do not have just one basic instinctual drive. Each of us possesses a pair of drives that have different goals. These are a life instinct—*Eros*—and a death instinct—*Thanatos*. These drives constantly interact over our lives. When Thanatos gains the upper hand, we may engage in a self-destructive action. One of the main departures from the earlier theory is that self-destructive behavior no longer seems especially remarkable. Society

has a way of frustrating all of us. We cannot pursue our personal pleasures unmindful of social demands and restrictions, nor can we express our antagonisms directly without incurring serious consequences. This, of course, is part of the id/ego/superego "myth" (Freud's own word for it) that has become so familiar a part of the psychoanalytical repertoire. Vulnerability to suicide exists for all humans because there are so many obstacles on our pathway to gratification and because much of our aggression is forced inward. Furthermore, "the extreme helplessness of the human ego in infancy is never completely overcome so that there is always a readiness under conditions of great stress and conflict to regress back to more primitive ego states."[35,p.75] The regressed ego may simply let itself die because it feels helpless and abandoned, or the suicidal action may represent a desperate last stand against the sense of impending helplessness and abandonment.

This twin-instinct theory may be of more interest as a broad, philosophical interpretation of the human condition than as a specific, applicable, and testable contribution to the understanding of suicidal behavior in particular. It does not seem to have found much application in day-by-day interactions with people at suicidal risk, and researchers have yet to come up with convincing ways of testing the theory for its fit with the facts.

However, the psychoanalytical approach does alert us to the long developmental career that precedes a self-destructive action. The young child, for example, may take into himself the negative attitudes conveyed by cruel or thoughtless parents. This burdens him with a superego that is excessively oriented toward criticism and self-destruction. Chaotic and inadequate parenting may also jeopardize the child by leaving him with a brittle ego that fragments and shatters under pressures that most people are able to withstand.

Many psychoanalytical insights (only a few of

which have been sketched here) fit in well with the meanings of suicide that have been described both in the social and individual frameworks. Many present-day clinicians and researchers have modified the early psychoanalytical approach to take sociocultural factors more into account. It has been repeatedly observed, for example, that some native Americans are at exceptionally high risk for suicide and other self-destructive actions. Research suggests that this seems to involve a sense of low self-esteem that is fostered by the subgroup's deprivation and discrimination in our society in general.[38] The native American child is in danger of growing up with a severe lack of confidence in his own identity and worth as well as with a tendency to keep aggressive impulses locked up under high pressure until efforts at control fail. This contrasts with the pride and satisfaction a child would have taken in being, say, a Cheyenne, in preceding generations when the people were independent and possessed a favorable group self-image. These dynamics of low self-esteem and self-directed aggression can lead to fatal outcomes other than suicide, as witnessed by the high alcohol-related mortality among older adults on the same reservation. The psychoanalytical approach, then, remains useful today, but it is not necessary to accept every interpretation nor to ignore other relevant data.

FACTS, MYTHS, AND GUIDELINES

Some of the major social and individual meanings of suicide have been considered. We are now ready for a brief review of established *facts*, which need to be distinguished clearly from *myths* that have grown up around the subject over the years. It will then be possible to propose a few *guidelines* for our own relationship to self-destructive behaviors.

Popular myths about suicide

Perhaps the quickest way to arrive at the facts is to identify and dismiss assumptions that have become so powerful and widespread that they have been categorized by suicidologists as myths. Alex D. Pokorny[39] has summarized the most prevalent misconceptions. This summary provides the basis for the following discussion, which also includes some additional considerations.

1. *A person who talks about suicide will not actually take his own life.* There is abundant evidence to show that this statement is not true. Approximately three out of every four people who eventually kill themselves give some detectable hint ahead of time, whether by less serious attempts or by verbal statements (the latter are sometimes as direct as can be, e.g., "I'm going to blow my head off," "If things don't get better in a hurry, you'll be reading about me in the papers."). This is one of the most dangerous myths because it encourages us to ignore communications that compose a cry for help. The rejection of the communication itself can become "the last straw."

2. *Only a specific class of people commit suicide.* It is sometimes held that suicide is a particular risk of either the poor or the rich. The poor are supposed to feel helpless and deprived, the rich to be bored and aimless. These simplifications fail to consider the complexity of the individual's relationship to society. People in all income and social-echelon brackets commit suicide. An explanation limited to economic or class distinctions alone is not adequate and contributes to our blind spots in the identification of individuals at risk.

3. *Suicide has simple causes that are easily established.* It would be closer to the truth to say that many of us are easily satisfied with hasty and superficial explanations.

As one goes more deeply into the individual case . . . each "cause" is found to be preceded by another "cause." It appears, then, that the person who ultimately commits suicide has embarked on a self-destructive course long before the final and fatal act. Thus what initially appeared as a simple "cause" of the suicide now becomes one of the last steps in a lengthy and complex situation, many motives of which are obscure and difficult to establish.[39,p.62]

The emphasis in this chapter on *meanings* rather than *causes* of suicide reflects an agreement with Pokorny's observations. Often we can gain a sense of the entire context of the individual's life and its significations to him through detailed and patient study, but this is not the same as coming up with a straightforward explanation of suicide.

4. *Only depressed people commit suicide.* This misconception is held by some professionals as well as members of the lay public. People with a psychiatric diagnosis of depression do have a higher suicide rate than those with other psychiatric syndromes or those without known syndromes. But suicide may occur in any type of psychiatric disorder. The person may not even seem to be especially unhappy immediately prior to the fatal action. It is dangerous, then, to overlook suicidal potential on the basis of the assumption that this is a risk only with the depressed person.

5. *Only crazy or insane people commit suicide.* This mistaken proposition is related to the one just described. It remains difficult for some people to believe that a person in his right mind could kill himself, but we have already acknowledged a cultural tradition of rational suicide. Psychiatrists disagree on how many suicides are associated with obvious mental disorder, but some of the most qualified researchers and clinicians find that suicide is not invariably related to psychosis.

6. *Suicide is inherited.* It is true that more than one person in the same family may commit suicide. But there is no evidence for a hereditary basis, even in special studies made of identical twins. The explanation for suicide has to be sought elsewhere.

7. *When a suicidal person shows improvement, the danger is over.* Experienced clinicians have learned that the period following an apparent improvement in overall condition is actually one of special danger. Sometimes this is because it is a client who has improved enough to be discharged from a mental hospital and therefore has more opportunity to commit suicide. At other times, it seems related to a recovery of enough energy and volition to take action. Sensitivity and interpersonal support are especially needed when the person seems to be pulling out of a suicidal crisis.

8. *People who are under a physician's care or who are hospitalized are not suicidal risks.* This is wishful thinking. Many people who commit suicide have received some form of medical or psychiatric attention within 6 months preceding the act. Suicides can and do occur in the hospital situation itself. Henry Davidson[40] has detailed from case histories some of the ways in which hospitalization has failed to deter individuals from suicide and also notes that the dynamics of the institutional situation itself can at times contribute to anxiety, low self-esteem, and other conditions conducive to suicide. Even in the most protective circumstances, Davidson notes, the suicidal individual's ingenuity or a split-second decision by a staff member that happens to be wrong can have fatal consequences. A close and extended look at how a hospital environment functions for a person at suicidal risk was obtained by David K. Reynolds. Working in collaboration with Norman L. Farberow, a pioneer suicidologist, Reynolds gained admittance to the locked ward of a Veterans Administration Hospital as a supposedly depressed and suicidal young veteran. The resulting book, *Suicide, Inside and Out*,[41] will be of interest to many readers. Most relevant here was Reynold's discovery that there were ample opportunities to kill himself, were that his actual and intense desire, even within this special and protective environment. One of the practical outcomes was a list of simple protective actions

that might reduce suicidal attempts within the hospital environment.[40,pp.191-193] Reynolds' experience was not entirely negative by any means; there was much to appreciate in what staff and environment offered. But it was once again made clear that one cannot assume a hospital, even a locked ward, guarantees 100% protection against suicide.

9. *Suicide can be prevented only by a psychiatrist or mental hospital.* Some of the most successful suicide-prevention efforts are being made by a variety of people in the community who bring concern, stamina, and sensitivity to the task. The human resources of the entire community may hold more hope than the limited cadres of professionals or the institutionalization solution. It is neither necessary nor realistic to pass all the responsibility on to a few.

The suicide rate and what it tells us

Who commits suicide? We already know the answer in a general way. It is the rich, the poor, and the in-between; the youthful, the middle-aged, and the elderly; male and female; and people representing every ethnic and racial group. Keeping mindful of the obvious is a safeguard against exaggerating the importance of statistical differences that compare various subpopulations. Yet it is worth becoming acquainted with the main features of suicide statistics and what they have to tell us.

There is a set of categories known collectively as the International Classification of Diseases, Injuries, and Causes of Death (ICD). There have been two revisions of the ICD that affect suicide statistics. In 1958 it was decided that all deaths associated with a self-inflicted injury would be classified as suicides unless there was a specific statement attesting to accidental factors. This resulted in an increase in the percentage of reported suicides. To someone who was not familiar with this change of procedure, it would look as though there had been about a 3% rise in suicide. A decade

later, in 1968, this procedure was again revised. It was decided that death associated with self-inflicted injury would not be classified as suicide unless the *intentionality* of the act was specified. Accordingly, there was a drop in the percentage of official suicides, this time about 6%.[42] These shifts in classification procedure increase the difficulty of comparing suicide rates over time. Furthermore, it is by no means easy to determine intentionality in many instances.[43,44] This is but one of the problems encountered in making use of suicide statistics.

One of the other problems becomes evident when we examine the technique used to calculate suicide rate. It is based on the following formula:

$$\text{Suicide rate} = \frac{\text{Number of suicides}}{\text{Population}} \times 100,000$$

A suicide rate of 15, for example, means that during a particular period of time, usually a calendar year, there were 15 suicidal deaths for every 100,000 people in the population. Since the size of the population is important in this formula, the accuracy of the reported rate depends on the care with which the population size has been estimated as well as on the certification of suicides per se. Some people tend to be "undercounted" in our own society and probably in other societies as well. Nonwhites and the young are often underrepresented,[45] and this may be true of some other subgroups as well. Here, then, is one more source of possible error and confusion—one more reason not to jump at conclusions based on the available statistics.

Even more patience is required if suicide statistics are to be used appropriately. The suicide rate must be distinguished from the total number of suicides in a population. Consider the fact that the population of the United States has increased throughout the twentieth century. With more people there is the likelihood of more deaths by suicide, even if the *rate* holds steady or declines somewhat. This logic can be applied to smaller geographical regions as well. Has the development of a suicide-prevention service actually reduced the rate in a particular city? The shifting population in the city (plus transients, minus young men on military duty, etc.) can make it very difficult to answer this question. If all relevant information were available over a reasonable period of time, it might be found that the true rate has declined—but, even so, the actual number of suicides might not be appreciably lower. This is one of the reasons it is difficult to come up with definitive data on the effectiveness of suicide-prevention services, a reason that has nothing directly to do with the effectiveness as such.

Furthermore, the importance of suicide as a cause of death in a particular population cannot be judged solely on the basis of rate. It must be compared with all other causes of death. In the years 1969-1971, for example, white males in the United States between the ages of 15 and 24 had a suicide rate of 13.8. This is much lower than the rate for white males between the ages of 75 and 84, which was 47.2. Yet there are relatively few high risks to life for the young men (and the number one risk also involves human agency: accidents). By contrast, old men are in jeopardy from many causes in addition to suicide. Relatively speaking, then, suicide must still be considered a significant problem for white male youths even though the rate is appreciably lower for them than for their elders.

This background might be helpful when encountering suicide statistics in the future. For the moment, let us concentrate on two general questions: (1) What type of people are most likely to commit suicide, based on the available data? (2) Is suicide on the increase?

Age has already been mentioned. The suicide rate increases with age[46] for both men and women, although the rate for women reaches its peak before age 65 and then declines a little. The rate for men continues to rise into the seventh decade.

There are also important *sex* differences in completed suicides. In the United States, as in most other nations, appreciably higher suicide rates are found for males at almost every age level. White males are almost two and a half times more likely to commit suicide than white females. This is the ratio averaged across the adult years. In the later decades of life the discrepancy becomes much greater. The suicide rate among men 85 years old and above is more than 10 times higher than that among women of comparable age. The average ratio is not much different when nonwhite males and females are compared: 2:8. The very high suicide rate of old white men is not approached by old black men, while old black women have virtually the same rate as their white counterparts.

Race is more difficult to analyze as a variable in suicide. It is subject to more differences in classification and interpretation than age or sex. The problem is heightened by the tradition of collapsing all nonwhites into a single category instead of respecting the differences within this group. Nevertheless, the overall picture shows nonwhite suicide rates to be less than half that of whites.

The interaction of age, sex, and race is more informative than any one of these variables taken separately. The big difference in suicide rates between whites and nonwhites, for example, shows up in the second half of the life span. White and nonwhite males have fairly similar rates until their middle 30s. The 2:1 ratio is established and exceeded by the middle 40s. From that point onward, the gap continues to widen: nonwhite male suicide does not change very much, while the rate for white males continues to rise. Women show a different pattern. White and nonwhite females have very similar rates through their middle 20s.

But in the next decade of life, something happens that has yet to be explained satisfactorily. The white woman between the ages of 25 and 34 is more than twice as likely to kill herself than she was a decade earlier. The increase for nonwhite women between these decades is smaller, about a 25% higher probability of suicide. Yet this represents the peak self-destructive decade for nonwhite women. The rate drops in the next decade, and never again approaches what it is between 25 and 34. The suicide rate for white women rises again appreciably in the next decade and stays near that level for another 20 years or so.

Marital status is another variable that seems to be associated with suicide rate. Most analyses find that married people have the lowest rates. Those who have never married tend to have a lower rate than those whose marriages have been dissolved by death or divorce. There are some indications that the suicide rate for widows is highest fairly soon after bereavement and then levels off and perhaps decreases.[46] Many other demographic variables have been studied (e.g., religious affiliation, occupation, place of residence), but these would require more extended discussion than is feasible here.

Familiarity with the complexities of suicide rate analysis helps prepare us for the kind of answer that must be given at present to the second question: *Is suicide on the increase?* It is often assumed that the suicide rate is definitely increasing; sometimes it is even maintained that we are suffering an "epidemic" (this latter expression is intrinsically misleading because suicide is not usefully thought of as a disease). Statistical analyses based on the dependable data available do not support these assumptions.[46,47] James Diggory concludes that:

As long as there have been any true total US mortality data, the general trend of suicide rates for the total population and for its white, male, and female components has been downward. . . . The total nonwhite population component shows no trend either for increase or decrease in suicide rates for the whole . . . period.[47,p.38]

The general suicide *rate* in our population was at its peak in the 1930s. This was also the time of "The Great Depression," when many lives were disrupted by economic catastrophe. There have been rises and falls since, but the overall rate has not changed very much in recent years. It has already been mentioned that a rise in the *number* of suicides over time would not be surprising because the size of our population continues to increase. The rate of suicide, however, does not seem to be rising appreciably.

Nevertheless, the overall stability of the suicide rate conceals important trends in both directions. In other words, some types of people are experiencing a higher rate, while others are showing a lower rate. Older men, for example, are still the highest suicide risk group, but their rate has been declining. Meanwhile, the rate among young adults of either sex, white or nonwhite, has been increasing. These opposite trends, and many of the other points that have been made here, can be seen in Table 3. (When 1980 census data have been certified and made available to statisticians around the nation, new tables of suicide rates can be prepared. Up-to-date census data are needed to provide a firm population estimate for calculating the rates.) The rates, as seen over time, do not support claims of a suicide "epidemic" on our hands, but rather a shift in probabilities for specific subgroups of the population. Continued attention to the suicide rate (for all the ambiguities and frustrations involved in interpreting them) will at least keep our speculations within limits. The rates themselves should be supplemented by attention to findings from whatever research and dependable clinical observations are available, for example, Marv Miller's review of *Suicide After Sixty*[48] and the

TABLE 3. Suicide rates in the United States over four decades: 1940-1970*

Race and sex	5-14	15-24	25-34	35-44	45-54	55-64	65-74	75-84	85+	All ages
White males										
1940	0.4	8.4	19.3	28.6	41.6	55.4	57.9	67.3	60.0	22.6
1950	0.3	6.7	13.2	22.3	32.8	44.1	51.9	58.5	69.8	18.5
1960	0.4	8.2	14.6	21.9	33.1	40.7	42.2	55.6	62.4	17.5
1970	0.5	13.8	19.3	23.0	29.0	34.9	37.9	47.2	47.1	17.8
White females										
1940	0.0	4.0	8.1	10.9	13.7	13.1	12.0	8.3	6.3	7.1
1950	0.1	2.6	5.1	8.0	10.2	10.5	10.0	8.2	7.4	5.3
1960	0.1	2.3	5.8	8.0	10.4	10.6	9.2	8.2	4.9	5.2
1970	0.2	4.2	8.7	12.9	13.8	12.2	9.8	7.4	4.4	7.1
Nonwhite males										
1940	0.2	4.7	10.6	11.0	13.5	12.1	11.4	11.8	6.8	6.8
1950	0.2	5.0	10.3	11.2	11.7	15.9	12.7	12.9	12.5	6.9
1960	0.1	6.5	14.4	12.1	13.6	15.8	13.6	17.6	12.8	7.5
1970	0.3	11.0	18.1	14.2	12.1	10.8	12.4	12.4	13.8	8.4
Nonwhite females										
1940	0.1	2.8	3.1	2.4	3.3	1.8	2.2	3.1	3.3	1.9
1950	0.1	1.9	2.6	2.5	2.8	2.3	2.0	2.3	0	1.6
1960	0.1	1.9	3.6	3.5	2.9	3.6	2.9	3.0	4.1	1.9
1970	0.3	4.5	6.1	4.9	4.1	2.5	2.7	3.5	4.2	3.0

*Rates per 100,000. Based on data collected from various sources by Linden and Breed[46]; slightly adapted for presentation here.

exploration by J. L. McIntosh and J. F. Santos of suicide among native Americans.[49]

A few guidelines

Many suicides can be prevented. Perhaps you have already played a role in preventing suicide without realizing it. The companionship you offered a person during a crucial period of time or the confidence you displayed in him after he suffered a failure experience might have provided just enough support to dissolve a self-destructive pattern in the making. Whenever we bring sensitivity and a genuinely caring attitude to our relationship with other people, we may be decisively strengthening their life-affirming spirit.

When the suicide flag is up, there is a tendency among many of us to back off. Unfortunately, this includes some professional people as well as the general public. Pretending that we haven't heard suicidal messages or distancing ourselves from a person who is contemplating self-destruction can hardly be recommended as helpful approaches.

A "formula" approach to helping the suicidal person would be of limited value. How we are best to proceed depends on precisely who the suicidal person is, who we are, and what kind of relationship we have to go on together. A few general guidelines can be offered, however.

Take the suicidal concern seriously. This does not mean panic or an exaggerated, unnatural response. Knowing as you do that thoughts, musings, and threats sometimes do eventuate in fatal attempts, you will have good reason to respect the concern.

Do not issue a provocation to suicide.

Strange though it may seem, people sometimes react to the suicidal person in such a way as to provoke or intensify the attempt. You will not be one of those "friends" who dares him to make good his threat or who intimates that he is too "chicken" to do so. On a more subtle level, you will not belittle his concern or his troubled state of mind. A belittling response can intensify the need to do something separate so that others will appreciate how bad he really feels.

Go easy on value judgments. "You can't do that—it's wrong!" This is sometimes the exclamation that would come most readily to our lips—but it is seldom a useful one. In most situations it is not very helpful to inject value judgments when a troubled person is starting to confide self-destructive thoughts. Perhaps applying value judgments is our need, but receiving them at this moment is not likely to be perceived by the troubled one as helpful.

Do not get carried away by the "good reasons" a person has for suicide. The interpersonal response to a suicidal individual sometimes involves much reading of our own thoughts and feelings into the other person's head. We may think, "If all of that was going wrong with *my* life, I'd want to kill myself too!" This conclusion might be attributed to the other person all to hastily. As you reflect on it, you recognize that the objective and the subjective sides of life are far from identical. For every person who commits suicide when faced with realistically difficult problems, there are many others who find alternative solutions. It is possible to respect the reality factors in the suicidal individual's situation without lining up on the side of self-murder. This respectful, nonevaluative approach is taken by many of the people who pick up the phone when a crisis hot-line call is put through.

Know what resources are available in the community. Who else can help this person? What kind of help might this person find most acceptable? What services are available through local schools, religious groups, mental health centers? Does your community have a crisis-intervention service? How does it operate? Learn about and, if possible, participate in your community's efforts to help those who are in periods of special vulnerability.

Listen. This is the advice you will hear again and again from people who have devoted themselves to suicide prevention. It is good advice. Listening is not the passive activity it might seem to be. It is an intent, self-giving action that shows the troubled person that you are there with him. And it is an opportunity for him to discharge at least some of the tensions that have brought him to a certain point of self-destructive intent and to sort out other possibilities for himself.

Know your own attitudes toward life, death, and suicide. Should you be interested in scanning some of your attitudes—and behaviors—right now, you might proceed to the questionnaire on pp. 264-266.

SUICIDE AND OTHER RISK-TAKING BEHAVIORS

People who attempt suicide are taking risks in both directions—a self-destructive act intended to fall short of the mark may in fact result in death, while a determined effort to end one's life may result in painful and disabling injury instead. While the intensity of the suicidal intention and the outcome of the action are often related, there are "errors" in both directions. But what about situations in which people place their lives in jeopardy and yet are not clearly suicidal? The possibility that some deaths are "subintentioned"[50] has been much discussed and investigated by suicidologists in recent years. The individual does not have a focused, explicit orientation toward suicide, but creates or places himself in situations that markedly increase risk to life. If the risk does prove fatal, the official cause may be listed as

A SELECTIVE SELF-ASSESSMENT OF
RISK-TAKING AND RISK-MINIMIZING BEHAVIORS

1. When you are driving, you use the seat belts:

   ☐ Never ☐ Rarely ☐ Usually ☐ Always

2. When you are driving, you try to have your front-seat passenger use the seat belts:

   ☐ Never ☐ Rarely ☐ Usually ☐ Always

3. What are the established facts, as you understand them, about the effect of using seat belts on the occurrence of serious injury and death in accidents? _____

   _____

   _____

   _____

   _____

4. If you do use seat belts at all, why do you? _____

   _____

   _____

   _____

5. If you don't use seat belts, why don't you? _____

   _____

   _____

   _____

6. As a driver, how many accidents have you had?

   ☐ None ☐ One ☐ Two ☐ More than two

7. As a driver, how many *near*-accidents have you had?

   ☐ None ☐ One ☐ Two ☐ More than two

8. How safe a driver do you consider yourself to be?

   ☐ Exceptionally safe ☐ Safer than average ☐ About average ☐ Not as safe as average ☐ Exceptionally unsafe

9. You smoke cigarettes?

   ☐ Not at all ☐ Just a few a day ☐ Up to half a pack a day ☐ A pack a day ☐ More

10. What are the established facts about the effects of cigarette smoking on health and longevity, as you understand these facts? Be as specific as you can. _____

    _____

    _____

    _____

    _____

11. If you smoke cigarettes at all, why do you? _____

    _____

    _____

    _____

12. If you don't smoke cigarettes at all, why don't you? _____
_____
_____
_____

13. In general, how "accident-prone" do you consider yourself to be as compared to others?
    ☐ Not at all ☐ Somewhat less than average ☐ About average ☐ Somewhat more than average
    ☐ Very much so

14. In general, to what extent do you feel events in your life are under your control or are the result of fate?
    ☐ Completely the result of fate ☐ Mostly the result of fate ☐ Somewhat the result of fate
    ☐ Somewhat more in my control ☐ Completely in my control

15. "I want to die." How often have you felt this way?
    ☐ Never ☐ Rarely ☐ Occasionally ☐ Frequently

16. You have thought about taking your own life:
    ☐ Never ☐ Yes, but not seriously ☐ Yes, and fairly seriously ☐ Yes, and very seriously

17. You have made a suicidal attempt:
    ☐ Never ☐ Yes, but not seriously ☐ Yes, and fairly seriously ☐ Yes, and very seriously

18. In an average week, how much of the time do you consider your life to be in jeopardy? Express this in terms of % of time through the 7-day week: _____%

19. Would you classify yourself as a person who increases (+), decreases (−), or has no appreciable influence one way or the other (0) on your own susceptibility to life-threatening risk?
    ☐ 0   (Your life-style neither increases nor decreases your vulnerability to life-threatening risk.)
    ☐ +   (Your life-style increases your vulnerability.)
    ☐ −   (Your life-style decreases your vulnerability.)

20. What is the riskiest thing you do with your life on a more or less regular basis and over which you have some control? _____
_____
_____
_____

21. What is the most effective thing you do with your life on a more or less regular basis that reduces your jeopardy? _____
_____
_____
_____

22. To what age do you *expect* to live? (circle nearest number)
    20   25   30   35   40   45   50   55   60   65   70   75   80   85   90   95   100

Continued.

A SELECTIVE SELF-ASSESSMENT OF
RISK-TAKING AND RISK-MINIMIZING BEHAVIORS—cont'd

23. What is the basis for this expectation or guess? _____

_____

_____

_____

24. To what age do you *want* to live? (This is a hard question for many people, but try to answer it specifically.)

    20 25 30 35 40 45 50 55 60 65 70 75 80 85 90 95 100

25. What is the basis for your preference as expressed above? _____

_____

_____

_____

_____

---

homicide, accident, or illness (and in wartime as "action of the enemy"), when in actuality the victim contributed something significant to the probability of death.

It is difficult to keep a balanced view of risk-taking behavior. One could see subintentioned suicidal impulses in a hundred daily actions ("Yes, I want whipped cream and nuts on my hot fudge sundae"—an example of eating one's self to death?). This usage could overextend the concept so much that it would lose its credibility and become useless. Or one could work hard on not noticing the possible semi-intentioned components in single-car accidents, especially when the driver had been moody, angry, despondent. It makes sense to be *aware of the possibility* that some of our actions that increase risk to life may have a motivational component.

The attitudes we hold toward life, death, suicide are not identical with our behaviors, however. While it is reasonable to attempt to "read" attitude from behavior or to predict action on the basis of attitude, there is considerable error variance involved. This, of course, is true in general of the relationship between attitude and behavior. This distinction has been reinforced recently by a study in which Herman Feifel and Vivian Tong Nagy[51] found that a history of life-threatening behaviors had little relationship to the individual's specific attitudes toward death. This finding does not completely settle the question (other populations need to be studied and other measures used to follow up the Feifel-Nagy study), but it does suggest that if we are interested in both attitudes and behaviors, we should study both attitudes and behaviors, not assume that one is equivalent to the other.

The accompanying questionnaire encompasses some of the behaviors and some of the attitudes involved in establishing the risk factor in our own lives. It is one version of an instrument that various colleagues and myself have used both for research and educational purposes. Perhaps you would like to try it out on yourself.

Some of these questions focus on behaviors, some on attitudes, still others on knowledge. In reflecting on your own answers and their implications, you might take the following considerations into account:

1. It is possible that an individual's orientation toward life risk is general, pervading many realms of functioning. But it is also possible that the orientation is specific to type of activity and situation. If the latter case applies, then it would be a mistake to emphasize a high— or low—risk-taking trait, but rather one should consider each specific context carefully. Research on this question is still fragmentary. Look over your own pattern of answers. What pattern do you see? Are you consistent or "situationalized" in your risk taking? Do you understand this pattern? Is it acceptable to you?

2. Are you consistent in your actions that affect chiefly your own risk and those that affect others? There is only one clear example on this questionnaire (the first two seat-belt items). Can you identify and explore other examples in your own life? *Should* a person be consistent in risks taken for self and risk-taking behaviors that affect others?

3. In general, do you see yourself as behaving in accordance with your knowledge? The examples surveyed here concern seat belts and cigarette smoking. Some people know one thing and do the opposite; others strive to be consistent. Are you satisfied with (a) the depth and accuracy of knowledge you have on a variety of life-risk factors, such as seat-belt usage and smoking, and (b) the way in which your knowledge is related to what you do?

4. The responses I have collected indicate that people who hold a fatalistic orientation report more accidents and more near-accidents as operators of motor vehicles. Why do you suppose this might be the case? Does this finding apply to you in some way?

5. The relationship between risk-taking behavior and outright suicidality is not clear in general. What is the situation for you personally? Does it seem to you that your thoughts and feelings about suicide show up in some way in things you do routinely (e.g., driving a car), or do these seem to be separate spheres of attitude and behavior?

6. Do you find your current life-style acceptable with respect to its implications for lethal risks (e.g., questions 18 and 19), or is there reason to rethink how and why you do what you do from the standpoint of the life hazards involved?

7. You offered your "subjective life expectancy" in response to question 22 and added your preference in response to question 24. Is your expectation and preference in line with the overall pattern of risks you take with your life? Or are you perhaps a person who desires a long life and yet engages in unnecessarily risky behaviors?

8. If an individual does not want to live as long as he or she expects to live, should this be considered as something of a suicidal orientation? Are people who "want" less than they "expect" likely to place themselves at unusual risk in order to foreshorten their lives? Is it "normal" to want to live as long as possible? If your "expect"/"want" answers are the same, is this because you thought and felt your way through life-and-death issues? Or is it because you believe it wrong to do anything that might significantly affect the length of your life?

There are many other considerations that could be raised by the items on this questionaire and many other questions that could have been included. The major point is that suicide—in the sense of a self-aware, deliberate action intended to end one's life—is but one of the ways in which we do in fact influence our own longevity and that of other people. (See, for example, Farberow's recent collection of informative essays on this topic.[52]) Important as suicide is from both a humanistic and a theoretical standpoint, it does not represent our only behavioral influence on how long we survive and how we meet our death.

SUMMARY

The search for a single and simple "cause" is less useful than a consideration of the meanings and contexts associated with suicide. Several major cultural meanings of suicide are described. These are summarized by the statements: "Suicide is *sinful*"; "Suicide is *criminal*"; "Suicide is *weakness* or *madness*"; "Suicide is *The Great Death*"; "Suicide is a *rational alternative*." Each of these represents interpretations that cultures have made of suicidal actions. The sinful and criminal interpretations see self-destruction as an act of defiance against the established order. Along with the weakness-madness interpretation that has been stimulated by a survival-of-the-fittest model of human interaction and the rise of psychiatric models, these views locate the fatal flaw within the individual. The other two views regard suicide more favorably. Death by suicide can fulfill cultural ideals rather than flaunt them in the *dashei*, or Great Death tradition, while the rational suicide is a culturally endorsed no-fault attitude that often has been conditioned by circumstances that make life seem unpalatable to society itself.

A pioneering theory emphasizing the sociocultural forces in suicide was offered by Durkheim in 1897 and has remained influential. The crucial index for suicide was the degree of control society exerted over the individual. Among Durkheim's key concepts were those of *social integration, social solidarity*, and *collective representations*. Durkheim distinguished four types of suicide based on the linkage between individual and society. The *egoistic* suicide results from a deficit of social control over the individual. The *altruistic* suicide results from excessive integration into society. The *anomic* suicide occurs when the individual suffers

a rupture in his relationship with society. *Fatalistic* suicide occurs when society oppresses and blocks individual fulfillment.

Some major meanings of suicide from the individual's standpoint were also explored. These include the orientations that "Suicide is *reunion*"; "Suicide is *rest and refuge*"; "Suicide is *getting back*"; "Suicide is the *penalty for failure*"; and "Suicide is a *mistake*." Circumstances in which each of these new orientations is likely to prevail are described. Particular attention is given to the combination of individual and social circumstances that make suicide appear to be the appropriate penalty for failure. The illusion that one would still be around to witness the results of one's suicide is common in several of these orientations. The *psychoanalytical theory* of suicide was taken as an example of attempts to explain self-destruction from an individual-oriented standpoint. In one of its formulations, this theory centers around a pair of instinctual drives: *Eros*, promoting life-sustaining actions, and *Thanatos*, urging the individual toward death. Another aspect of the psychoanalytical approach emphasizes the individual's early developmental career, particularly those experiences that might lead to ego weakness in the face of subsequent stress.

Many *erroneous assumptions* about suicide have gained currency. Several of these myths are described and rejected (e.g., the mistaken assumptions that a person who talks about suicide might not actually take his life or that only depressed people commit suicide).

Attention is given to *suicide rates* and what they can tell us. Some of the complexities in establishing and interpreting suicide rates are explored. A few *guidelines* are offered for our relationship with people in our own lives who are troubled by suicidal concerns. The chapter concludes with a questionnaire that enables a person to assess his or her own risk-taking behavior in a variety of situations and some reflections based on this exercise.

REFERENCES

1. Frazer, J. G. *The fear of the dead in primitive religion.* (3 vols). London: Macmillan & Co., 1933.
2. St. Augustine. *The city of God* (426 B.C.). (Available in many reprint editions.)
3. St. Thomas Aquinas. *Summa theologia* (1259). (Available in many reprint editions.)
4. Locke, J. Concerning the true original extent and end of civil government. In *Great books,* Vol. 35. Chicago: Encyclopedia Britannica, Inc., 1971.
5. Bakan, D. *Disease, pain, and sacrifice.* Chicago: University of Chicago Press, 1969.
6. Curphey, T. J. The role of the social scientists in the medicolegal certification of death from suicide. In N. L. Farberow & E. S. Shneidman (Eds.), *The cry for help.* New York: McGraw-Hill Book Co., 1965.
7. Douglas, J. D. *The social meanings of suicide.* Princeton, N.J.: Princeton University Press, 1967.
8. Choron, J. *Suicide.* New York: Charles Scribner's Sons, 1972.
9. Alvarez, A. *The savage god.* New York: Random House, Inc., 1970.
10. Donne, John. *Biathanatos* (1646). New York: Arno Press, 1977.
11. Shneidman, E. S. Current over-view of suicide. In E. S. Shneidman (Ed.), *Suicidology: contemporary developments.* New York: Grune & Stratton, Inc., 1976.
12. Landsberg, P. L. *The experience of death.* New York: Arno Press, 1977. (Originally published, 1953.)
13. Lester, D. *Why people kill themselves.* Springfield, Ill.: Charles C Thomas, 1972.
14. Darwin, C. *Origin of the species* (1859).
15. Tabachnick, N. (Ed.). *Accident or suicide?* Springfield, Ill.: Charles C Thomas, 1973.
16. Kastenbaum, R., & Aisenberg, R. B. *The psychology of death.* New York: Springer Publishing Co., Inc., 1972.
17. LaFleur, W. R. Japan. In F. H. Holck (Ed.), *Death and Eastern thought.* Nashville, Tenn.: Abingdon Press, 1974.
18. Iga, M. Personal situation as a factor in suicide with reference to Yasunari Kawabata and Yukio Mishima. In B. B. Wolman (Ed.), *Between survival and suicide.* New York: Gardner Press, Inc., 1976.
19. Erasmus. *The praise of folly* (1509).
20. Faber, M. D. Seneca, self-destruction, and the creative act. *Omega,* 1978, *9,* 149-166.
21. Durkheim, E. *Le Suicide* (J. A. Spaulding & G. Simpson, trans.). New York: The Free Press, 1951. (Originally published, 1897.)
22. Reference deleted in proofs.
23. Stack, S. Durkheim's theory of fatalistic suicide: a cross-national approach. *Journal of Social Psychology,* 1979, *107,* 161-168.
24. Taylor, C., & Hudson, M. C. *World handbook of political and social indicators.* New Haven, Conn.: Yale University Press, 1972.
25. Dangelis, N., & Pope, W. Durkheim's theory of suicide as applied to the family: an empirical test. *Social Forces,* 1979, *57,* 1081-1106.
26. Breed, W. Five components of a basic suicide syndrome. *Life-Threatening Behavior,* 1972, *3,* 3-18.
27. Miller, D. H. Suicidal careers: toward a symbolic interaction theory of suicide. Unpublished doctoral dissertation, School of Social Welfare, University of California at Berkeley, 1967.
28. Swanson, W. C., & Breed, W. Black suicide in New Orleans. In E. S. Shneidman (Ed.), *Suicidology: contemporary developments.* New York: Grune & Stratton, Inc., 1976.
29. Cousy, R. *The killer instinct.* New York: Random House, Inc., 1976.
30. Shneidman, E. S. *Voices of death.* New York: Harper & Row, Publishers, 1980.
31. Farberow, N. L., & Shneidman, E. S. (Eds.), *The cry for help.* New York: McGraw-Hill Book Co., 1965.
32. Seiden, R. H. Suicide prevention: a public health/public policy approach. *Omega,* 1977, *8,* 267-276.
33. Farber, M. L. *Theory of suicide.* New York: Arno Press, 1977. (Originally published, 1968.)
34. Henry, A. F., & Short, J. F. *Suicide and homicide.* New York: Arno Press, 1977. (Originally published, 1954.)
35. Litman, R. Sigmund Freud on suicide. In E. S. Shneidman (Ed.), *Essays in self-destruction.* New York: Science House, 1967.
36. Freud, S. Mourning and melancholia. In *Collected papers,* Vol. 4. New York: Basic Books, Inc., 1959.
37. Freud, S. The ego and the id (1923). *Collected psychological papers of Sigmund Freud,* Vol. 4. London: The Hogarth Press, Ltd., 1961.
38. Curlee, W. V. Suicide and self-destructive behavior on the Cheyenne Rivers Reservation. In B. Q. Hafen & E. J. Faux (Eds.), *Self-destructive behavior.* Minneapolis, Minn.: Burgess Publishing Co., 1972.
39. Pokorny, A. D. Myths about suicide. In H. L. P. Resnik (Ed.), *Suicidal behaviors.* Boston: Little, Brown & Co., 1968.
40. Davidson, H. Suicide in the hospital. *Hospitals,* 1969, *43,* 55-59.
41. Reynolds, D. K., & Farberow, N. L. *Suicide, inside and out.* Berkeley, Los Angeles, & London: University of California Press, 1976.
42. National Center for Health Statistics. *Monthly Vital*

Statistics Report, 1968, *17,* no. 8, Washington, D.C.

43. Shneidman, E. S. *Deaths of man.* New York: Quadrangle/The New York Times Book Co., 1973.

44. Picton, B. *Murder, suicide or accident. The forensic pathologist at work.* New York: St. Martin's Press, 1971.

45. Dublin, L. I. *Suicide: a sociological and statistical study.* New York: The Ronald Press Co., 1963.

46. Linden, L. L., & Breed, W. The demographic epidemiology of suicide. In E. S. Shneidman (Ed.), *Suicidology: contemporary developments.* New York: Grune & Stratton, Inc., 1976.

47. Diggory, J. C. United States suicide rates, 1933-1968: an analysis of some trends. In E. S. Shneidman (Ed.),

Suicidology: contemporary developments. New York: Grune & Stratton, Inc., 1976.

48. Miller, M. *Suicide after sixty.* New York: Springer Publishing Co., Inc., 1979.

49. McIntosh, J. L., & Santos, J. F. Suicide among Native Americans. *Omega* (in press).

50. Shneidman, E. S. Orientations toward death. In R. White (Ed.), *The study of lives.* New York: Atherton Press, 1963.

51. Feifel, H., & Nagy, V. T. Death orientation and life-threatening behavior. *Journal of Abnormal Psychology* (in press).

52. Farberow, N. L. (Ed.). *The many faces of suicide.* New York: McGraw-Hill Book Co., 1980.

CHAPTER 16

❖ BETWEEN LIFE AND DEATH

Precisely where do we stand between life and death? This question raises many images.

❖ A person is on the verge of attempting suicide. He hesitates, his life in the balance.

❖ The daredevil is ready to test his luck and skill. He will cross the ocean in a balloon, leap a canyon on a motor cycle, walk a tightrope over a waterfall—or perhaps die trying.

❖ In the private chambers of a high court, judges continue to review differing versions of capital punishment legislation. Pending the final decision, hundreds of condemned prisoners wait between life and death.

❖ A group of intense partisans are engaged in deciding whether their next action will involve violence and, if so, who are to be their targets. Unaware of what is being discussed, people go about their business. Tomorrow some of these may be described as innocent victims of terrorist attack.

❖ The report from a government regulatory agency reaches the desk of a high-ranking official. Will it be decided that the hazard to public health and safety is significant and clearly enough established to warrant government intervention? Will political and economic considerations lead to a rejection of the report and, eventually, the premature death of some citizens?

❖ The parent whose child has died so suddenly is stunned and anguished. Death has unexpectedly sealed off so much of the future. How difficult it is to think about going on with life after this death.

These are some of the images that remind us of our positions between life and death. Different from each other, as each of these images are, they all have something of a special, external, or accidental character. They supplement but do not replace the basic image of our own personal life-death trajectories. How far along life's road have we come? How far have we to go? The image of the suicide or the daredevil may not fit us, and we may not fall victim to somebody else's violence or negligence, but at each moment we do occupy a position somewhere between life and death.

TWO NEW IMAGES

Two new images of the between-life-and-death relationship have come to public attention within the past few years. More accurately, it might be said that the images have newly come to general attention: the phenomena themselves have occurred at least occasionally in the past. These phenomena seem to exist on—or perhaps beyond—the fringe of ordinary "rules" that govern how we experience and explain life. As such, the phenomena are not only challenging in their own right, but also as test cases of our ability to cope with the unknown and unprepared-for in general. This is true on both the individual and social levels. Furthermore, our core assumptions about what death "means" and life "is" may have to be reexamined with these phenomena in mind.

This chapter focuses on what some people now call the "Karen Quinlan condition," for obvious reasons. The defining characteristic of this condition is the precarious continuation of a life that is so impaired and limited that one might question whether it is life at all in the everyday sense of the term. The following chapter takes up an even more recent "discovery"—the return of some individuals from a near-death experience. This latter phenomenon is placed within the broader context of the general question: Is there survival of death?

THE SLEEPING BEAUTY SYNDROME

On the evening of April 14, 1975, several friends were celebrating a birthday at a local tavern. Early the next morning one of the celebrants lay comatose in a hospital, her breathing maintained by a respirator. The public life of Karen Ann Quinlan had begun, precisely at that moment when her personal life appeared to slip away from her. In the following months this young woman's situation became a focus of national attention. She became the best known, most widely discussed representative of those who seem to have moved beyond the ordinary bounds of life but perhaps not yet to the innermost chambers of death. Karen Ann Quinlan is no longer page-one news, but her situation and society's response to it have become part of the history and dynamics of our time, with the complete story still in the making.

The following review of pertinent facts is especially indebted to the careful and sensitive journalistic coverage provided as the events first unfolded by Joan Kron[1,2] who kindly shared her background as well as published materials with me. It was also Kron who first likened Quinlan's predicament to the sleeping beauty image. Numerous other accounts have appeared in the intervening years, among which should be especially noted a book prepared in close collaboration with Ms. Quinlan's parents.[3]

Karen Ann Quinlan: a chronology

As a 4-week-old baby, Karen Ann was adopted by Joseph and Julia Quinlan. This was at a time when the medical opinion had been that the Quinlans were unlikely to have a child of their own. Mrs. Quinlan had experienced several miscarriages and a full-term stillbirth. Two years later, however, the Quinlans did produce a daughter, Mary Ellen, and 16 months after that, a son, John.

Karen Ann reportedly had a normal childhood in an affectionate family atmosphere. The Quinlans told her that she was an adopted child. She was curious about "her other mother," but seemed to feel very much a part of the family. Karen Ann was an active, adventuresome youngster who enjoyed what in our culture at that time were called "tomboy pursuits."

She remained an active person as an adolescent, described as a "spunky," "creative," "happy-go-lucky" teen-ager whom "many people cared about." She liked to pull practical jokes and pranks, act on the spur of the moment, and be something of a daredevil. Karen Ann was described by her teachers as a bright student who did well enough in school but could have received straight As had she wanted to expend the effort. She was respected for having strong convictions that she would not hesitate to express. Karen Ann also blossomed into a beautiful young woman. The later description of "sleeping beauty" is not an overstatement. Her abundant life-style included singing in church (well enough to be paid for it), camp counseling, lifeguarding, and working as an assistant mechanic at a gas station. ("She was an expert on her Volkswagen, and she'd never ask a boy for help.")

Karen Ann's life seems to have taken a different direction for the several months preceding her sudden transition from health to coma. Differing versions have been given. The most secure facts seem to be that she was laid off from her job because of a company cutback, and then she moved out of her parents' home. Her mood near the evening of April 14 was described as depressed by some of her friends, but she was also said to be looking forward to a Florida trip with one of her girlfriends. She had kept in touch with her family. During a long telephone conversation she had invited her mother to visit at the cottage she was sharing with friends.

Several newspaper stories later alleged that she had been making frequent use of drugs. This was denied by close friends. Her roommate declared that it was "blown all out of proportion. Karen wasn't into drugs . . . . She might have taken a few pills for a high, but she wasn't that impulsive. She looked before she leaped."[2, p. 62] Karen and her friends had a pattern of drinking together, but she was not said to have any problem with alcohol.

After the birthday celebration, Karen Ann was brought home by a friend who judged that she had had one too many of her favorite drink, gin and quinine. The friend checked on her condition a little later and noticed that she was not breathing. One friend applied mouth-to-mouth resuscitation while another called the police, who also attempted resuscitation, and brought her to a hospital. The resuscitation efforts restored her breathing, but Karen Ann did not return to consciousness.

Traces of Valium, a widely used tranquilizer, and quinine were found in Karen Ann's blood. The admitting diagnosis was drug-induced coma. There has been some question, controversy, and speculation about this diagnosis. Details of her condition around the time of admission and since then have not been readily forthcoming. Apparently, the most critical physiological factor was the period of oxygen deprivation to the brain. How long the presumed oxygen-deprivation state existed has not been established, but the lapse into unconsciousness and her failure to revive seemed to be linked most significantly to this problem. Physicians who gave testimony at a later time declared they could not be sure of the cause of Karen Ann's coma, but that the lack of oxygen had resulted in severe and irreversible brain damage.

Weeks and then months passed. Karen Ann remained in the hospital, her body maintained by a respirator and other components of a life-support system in a modern intensive-care unit. She did not regain consciousness. Her body gradually wasted away to about 60 pounds. The few direct reports of her physical condition pictured her as shriveled, scarcely human, grotesque, curled up in a fetal position. Although a lovely young woman a few months previously, she could no longer be called a sleeping beauty. Hospital expenses, estimated at $450 per day, most reportedly covered by Medicaid, continued to mount. There had been talk of hope, of recovery, of a miracle return to life. Such talk became less frequent as time went by.

Mrs. Quinlan eventually came to the conclusion that Karen Ann would never recover. The Karen Ann she knew was dead. Soon after, the other two children came to the same conclusion. Joseph Quinlan maintained hope for about 5 months. His priest felt that Mr. Quinlan's reality appraisal was being blurred by his hope. Father Thomas Trapasso told him that "extraordinary means are not morally required to prolong life." Father Herbert Tillyer, vice-chancellor of his diocese, agreed: "There is a profound difference between killing someone and allowing a person to spend his or her last days free from the maze of machinery that is beautiful only so long as there is hope for some recovery."[4,p.58] Mr. Quinlan later testified that he reached his personal decision through prayer "and I . . . placed Karen's body and soul into the gentle, loving hands of the Lord . . . . It was resolved that we would turn the machine off."[4,p.58]

The legal, ethical, religious, and medical issues came into sharper focus when the Quinlans requested two physicians to turn off the respirator. The physicians declined to do so. They were not sure of the moral and legal implications of such an action, nor did they wish to expose themselves to possible charges of malpractice.

The Quinlans pursued their request through the courts. Mr. Quinlan asked to be named guardian of Karen Ann so that he would have the legal right to authorize her removal from the machine.

The time-consuming legal process provided opportunity for many opinions to be aired, in the media and in professional circles as well as in the court. We will consider some of these views after completing the basic chronology. But it is relevant here to note her physical condition around the time that the judicial process was coming to its conclusion.

Karen Ann was not dead. The EEG tracings still showed some electrical activity in the brain, although very weak. A neurologist described her condition as "a persistent vegetative state."[4] An attorney for the State of New Jersey described a brief visit to her room:

Her face is all distorted and she is sweating. Her eyes are open and blinking about twice a minute. She's sort of gasping. I'd never seen anything like that, and I'm not accustomed to death. I have no hang-ups about looking at corpses . . . [But] I was there for seven minutes and it seemed like seven hours.[1,p.35]

Medical testimony was given to the effect that Karen Ann would die within a short time if removed from the respirator.

The court ruled against the Quinlans' request. New Jersey Supreme Court Judge Robert Muir, Jr., declared that "there is a duty to continue the life-assisting apparatus if, within the treating physician's opinion, it should be done. . . . This court will not authorize that life be taken from her." Judge Muir's decision rested chiefly on the medical specifics of the case. He appeared to be saying that the decision was neither for the courts nor the church to make. (The Quinlans had based some of their case on a religious-freedom argument.) It was up to the medical people.

This decision was appealed to the New Jersey Supreme Court, which made a ruling favorable to the Quinlans' request: the respirator could be turned off. One condition was imposed: physicians must agree that Karen Ann had no reasonable chance of regaining conscious existence.[5] The New Jersey attorney general decided not to challenge this decision. This meant that the United States Supreme Court was not asked to make a decision that might have set a binding precedent for the entire nation.

Although finally given permission to discontinue use of the respirator and thereby presumably release Karen Ann to "death with dignity," the Quinlans did not immediately take this action. Instead, discussion followed within the Quinlan family and with physicians and lawyers. There was a return to Judge Muir's court to discuss developments and questions that have not been made public. It may be that some ambiguities remained in the higher court's ruling (e.g., did permission to remove the respirator mean that other elements of the total life-support system could be discontinued as well?). Newspaper reports indicated that Karen Ann's condition had changed to some extent, that in fact she had been off the respirator at times and perhaps could now breathe without machine assistance.[6] Whatever the circumstances involved, the Quinlan family did not move immediately to exercise the option granted by the courts.

Fourteen months after she lapsed into coma, Karen Ann was removed from the respirator. But this was not the end of her life. She was transferred to a nursing home with skilled-care capabilities. In preparing the first edition of this book in 1977, I reported, "At the time of this writing, Ms. Quinlan was still in the nursing home." This statement remains true at this moment in 1980 as I complete the revised edition.

Views, issues, and contentions

Karen Ann Quinlan is not the first person who has fallen into extended coma. Such instances have been reported on occasion over the centuries and there were many well-documented cases in our own times prior to Ms. Quinlan. Futhermore, she is certainly not the only person today whose existence hovers somewhere along the border between life and death. But it is her story that originally focused much of the ongoing concern about life at the borderline of death. Advances in life-sustaining technology have resulted in more instances of this kind; what had been a rare occurrence now can be regarded as one of the alternative pathways out of life—an alternative that some fear may become commonplace in the future unless there is social, medical, and legal resolve to discourage the "lingering one." Let us stay with the Quinlan situation a while longer because it did generate views, issues, and contentions that have implications for "between-life-and-death" problems in general.

Much sentiment developed for the discontinuation of life-support systems for Ms. Quinlan. Phrases often used included "death with dignity," "merciful release," and "die with grace." Some people also saw a possible relationship between her situation and that of other humans for whom life-and-death decisions are made. A high-school student combined both of these concerns in a letter to her local newspaper:

My question is regarding the life of an unborn baby. Is it right to deliberately kill an unborn child who probably has more control over, and experiences more of the bodily functions at most any stage of fetal development than Karen does? An unborn child breathes on his own—he is not plugged into a respirator within his mother.

It puzzles me that, while the courts will allow an unborn baby to be killed, it will not allow Karen Quinlan to die in peace and spare her family and loved ones the extreme mental anguish and suffering that they have encountered and endured these past several months.

Their religious beliefs support their decision to let Karen die with dignity and if they have acted in accordance with God—who, then, has the right to say no?[7]

This statement concisely expresses several of the major concerns heightened by Karen Ann Quinlan's situation. Its author, Maureen Stein, just a few years younger than Karen Ann, seems to be asking for breadth and consistency in society's actions. Abortion and euthanasia decisions should reflect a core philosophy, she implies, even though the particulars might be much different. Whatever precedents may have been established in the Quinlan case will continue to be examined for their broad implications. This has increased the burden on physicians, judges, and others with decision-making responsibilities. Nobody can be certain how far the decisions and policies formulated about Karen Ann Quinlan may be generalized to other life-death situations. Many courts throughout the United States have since been called on to consider "Quinlan-type" situations, and the decisions have not resulted in any simple and fixed outcome. Each case has its own particulars, and one has a choice of precedents and circumstances to consider.

Ms. Stein also raises questions about the psychobiological facts. To what extent can the situation of a fetus and a severely impaired adult be compared? Those who are familiar with the abortion controversy know that both moral positions and legal opinions have involved the specific facts of fetal development. What kind of being is that at 1 week after conception? Three months? Six months? Now there is a demand for similar specificity regarding the condition of people who seem to be in persistent vegetative states. A difference of opinion on the medical facts or the discovery of new information might affect social policy— which is to say, life or death. Once hard questions are asked about the status of people hovering between life and death, it is difficult to predict the final outcome. Actually, since it is in the nature of the sciences to change if not evolve in their understanding of a problem, it could be that there will be no final outcome. In other words, as knowledge of the psychobiology of "in-between" states changes, our social and legal institutions may be put in the position of continual change as well, or face the prospect of clinging to outmoded practices. This possibility—that the very definition of life and death might remain in flux indefinitely— has not yet been generally appreciated. It is my impression that most people still expect that a solid and stable set of guidelines will soon come into existence based on instances such as Ms. Quinlan's. These anticipated guidelines presumably would indicate what should and should not be done in the way of life-sustaining activities, who should make the decisions and by what process—all based on a (still presumed) conception of what life and death "really" are. Perhaps this situation actually will come about, but I continue to have my doubts.

Further complexities can be seen even within the same brief letter to the newspaper quoted earlier. This letter suggests that response must take more into account than the psychobiological status of the individual. Ms. Stein implicitly is arguing for clear recognition or legitimization of the family's needs and rights, a position also advocated in the standards of care proposed for hospices (Chapter 13). Yet it is not easy to achieve a balance between the status and needs of the victim and those of others in the situation. The Quinlans themselves have been quoted as requesting that Karen Ann die with grace and dignity, that her suffering be eased.[8] This is an understandable and compassionate attitude. But is it realistic to speak of grace, dignity, and suffering in this situation? Physicians described Karen Ann as having fallen into a "persistent vegetative state." Let us assume the accuracy of this statement, at least for the moment. Can an individual trapped in a persistent vegetative state experience either a sense of dignity or its opposite? Can she be said to suffer when blunt physicians have characterized her as a "heart-and-lung preparation," a decorticate preparation? The term "grace" is even more ambiguous. It is meant that removal of life-support systems would result in a more exalted style of dying, a more refined exit? This can scarcely be in Karen Ann's mind if the physicians are correct. Or does grace refer instead to a state of blessedness? And, if so, why would the Lord bestow more or less blessing on a stricken person depending on the type of medical or nursing care received? The phenomenology and theology behind the "grace" interpretation is unclear, to say the least. It is likely, of course, that we are not supposed to take so seriously the words uttered about Karen Ann Quinlan and others along the life-death borderline. But people do persuade and gain support for their views, and views do lead to actions of one type or another based in part on the choice of words. "Dignity" and "grace" are splendid terms, but they are often used in what careful analysis would prove to be a vague, loose, misleading manner.

One side of the logical bind has been touched on. If Ms. Quinlan has lost her ability to experience, to know, to judge, to value, then the terms that are most frequently employed to advocate life termination are not applicable to her. But if she could still have distinctively human experiences, then much of the basis for advocating life termination would be undermined. It would mean taking life away from a person rather than a nonperson. This is the other side of the bind. Let us say it again in a slightly different way. Withdrawing life-support services has been proposed largely as an action in Karen Ann's own interests. This argument has been emphasized by such terms as "death with dignity" and "release from suffering." But if she has, in effect, already died as a person or as an integrated organism, then these phrases are empty. And if the medical judgments have underestimated her functional level, then withdrawal of support might be considered the taking of a human life.

I suggest that "death with dignity" and other such terms applied to this situation reflect more the feelings of society than of Karen Ann Quinlan (and that similar dynamics prevail in many of the other instances that have come to notice since Quinlan's). The family suffered. The physicians and nurses suffered. The attorneys who looked on her suffered, no matter which side they were representing. Many who had never known Karen Ann projected themselves into her situation, or what they imagined her situation to be. This vicarious suffering can be intolerable. We want our anguish to end. By attributing some of our own distress to her, we can suppose that she is the one who is suffering and should be released by death. Furthermore, whatever most of us might mean by "death with dignity," it is often hard to find anything in the ICU situation that fulfills this phrase. It looks as though something essential to being a human is taken away by the life-support system and the hospital environment. But if the physicians were substantially correct, then we are the only ones who are in a position to be dismayed by the sight. Ms. Quinlan is beyond death and dignity from her own stand-

point. (Or, said differently, she no longer has a standpoint.) It is *our* need. We do not want such a distressful-looking situation to continue.

The anguish of the family and the discomfort of society in a Quinlan-type situation is part of reality. It merits respect. Perhaps action *should* be taken after all in such situations because it hurts and offends us to have somebody else, one of our kind, perpetuated in this condition. But if this is chiefly our own need and intention, should it not be properly identified as such? We mislead ourselves and others if we insist we are doing it for the victim's good. There is enough sorrow, anxiety, and ambiguity in the situation already without continuing to blur the distinction between how we think and feel and what we attribute to one who cannot speak for herself.

The decision to continue or terminate life-support systems requires a judgment about the prospect for recovery. One person's version of reality may rule out hope; another person may go so far as to make hope his basic reality. We have seen in previous chapters that differing perceptions and interpretations are common throughout the dying process. Differences persist when there is lingering between life and death as well. At any given moment one can assemble observations either to fan the embers of hope or to encourage acceptance of unalterable fate. Both hope and reality, though, are interpretations we make based on selected observations and our own need states. Those who are not intimately familiar with the medical situation are probably more likely to be swayed by their feelings and by their general life-style. But even the experts disagree at times—or reach consensus, only to be proven fallible by later developments.

Ms. Quinlan's situation brought to the surface numerous reports of people who had recovered after lapsing into a comatose state and being considered all but dead. A 16-year-old boy, for example, was severely injured in an automobile accident. Bruce McBlain remained in a comatose state for almost 4 months, connected, like Karen Ann, to a battery of life-sustaining devices. Prevailing opinion at the hospital was that the youth was too critically impaired to recover. Despite his unresponsiveness, however, the family continued to treat him as though he were an intact person. His parents massaged his shrunken legs and talked to him about his motorcycle, his friends in high school, and the future. Although doubting that continued treatment would be effective, the physician did take advantage of every possibility, including the installation of a shunt to carry off fluid that had accumulated in the brain. "Now, instead of tubes and wires running to respirators and monitors, the youth's bed is decorated with a trapeze that he uses to exercise his deteriorated arm and chest muscles."[9]

Another example is particularly interesting because it includes a 9-year follow-up. Carold Dusald Rogman suffered injuries to her brain stem in an automobile accident when she was 19 years old. Like Bruce McBlain, she also remained comatose for 4 months. Her mother was told by a physician that Carold was "a medical vegetable."[10] The physician recommended that the intravenous tube be removed so her daughter could perish of starvation. The mother refused, although she said she did not resent the physician's advice. By this time, Carold has wasted away to 65 pounds, very similar to Karen Ann's situation. Her body was locked into a grotesque position. She no longer resembled the Dundee Community High School Homecoming Queen she had been only a short time before.

Now recovered, married, and the mother of a baby boy, Carold remembers that her mother "kept telling me, 'You're going to make it.' . . . I realize now how much she must have loved me and cared for me"[10] She credits her mother's determination with encouraging her to pull through and believes that both of them were sustained by religious faith as well.

The occasional recovery of a person who appears to be suspended indefinitely between life and death provides a basis for hope. However, this also means that expectations sometimes will be maintained when no recovery will in fact occur. What happens then? The family cannot place the death and loss behind them. Daily life continues to be influenced by a hope that is also a burden. It is a difficult situation for physicians and nurses as well. The physician may have reason to believe that the particular case at hand differs significantly from any that have shown recovery, and, of course, he may be either correct or mistaken in that judgment. He may not want to assault the family's hope with this opinion, yet he may also feel a responsibility to offer what he sees as a more realistic assessment. One of the nurse's problems here is the question of where to align her own attitudes when there are marked differences, say, between physician and family. It is the nurse who has much of the steady contact with the patient. Her attitude toward the depth of impairment and the prospect of recovery is likely to influence her caring behavior in subtle ways. Almost nothing is known about the personal responses of physicians and nurses in the Karen Ann Quinlan situation. We have seen, however, that medical opinion was not entirely confirmed by the course of events. Ms. Quinlan has survived the removal of the respirator by about 3 years. On the other hand, she does not appear to have shown any signs of recovery.

A distinction should be made between *viability* and *recovery*. The emphasis in the Quinlan situation, as in many others, has been on the prospects for the person herself to emerge from the comatose state. At the furthest extreme is the possibility that she might die even while receiving all the life-support services available to modern medicine. It might be helpful to outline the range of alternative outcomes:

1. The individual dies while receiving inten-

sive life-support services. He is *not viable,* then, even under highly specialized circumstances.

2. The individual continues to live in the sense that vegetative functioning is maintained, but this seems to require the constant provision of intensive life-support services. This might be called *conditional viability.*

3. Bodily functions become sufficiently strengthened and stabilized for life to continue without a massive support system. This is *physiological viability.* Vulnerability remains high (e.g., to infection and a variety of biological "accidents"). But a degree of viability has been achieved, provided that the environment continues to shelter and nourish. There is, however, no appreciable psychosocial functioning. The body is viable; the person appears to remain unavailable to himself or others.

4. There is *recovery with significant impairment.* The individual is no longer unresponsive and comatose. Fragments of communication and behavior are noticed. There are indications, in short, that the body belongs to somebody, but integration and control of psychosocial functioning have not returned. Within this general classification many degrees of significant impairment can be found.

5. There is *recovery with minimal impairment.* The person resumes life as a person. Some impairments may be permanent (e.g., a limp, limited use of one hand); other impairments may be remedied by rehabilitative efforts (e.g., slurred speech, muscular weakness). Nevertheless, the individual clearly has regained a sense of selfhood, can think, experience, and pursue a reasonably full life.

It is also possible that significant recovery might be made, but for viability to remain low. The person snaps out of it, in other words, yet does not have the strength or capacity for prolonged survival. This situation has been known to occur, although it is seldom discussed. What people do continue to discuss is the type of situation that has developed around Karen Ann

Quinlan: what we might call indefinitely maintained conditional viability. This is the fate that Joseph and Julia Quinlan asked first the physicians and then the courts to spare their daughter.

Life as such is not invariably seen as a supreme value. This is evident in the Quinlan situation as well as some others we have seen (e.g., suicide, public execution, continuation of occupation health hazards for financial reasons). How important is viability, "raw survival," regardless of the quality of life? And how important is quality of life, regardless of the amount of time remaining? How much impairment is "acceptable"? And to whom?

In attempting to answer these questions we may find ourselves stymied by other issues we have not thought our way through. Religious faith, for example, does not necessarily tip the scales in one particular direction. Joseph Quinlan felt strongly that God favored the termination of life-support services to Karen Ann. Carold's mother was determined to do God's will by drawing her daughter back to life. These two people may have been equally devout, yet they came to opposite conclusions about what should be done. The significance of one's religious orientation to life and death decisions seems beyond doubt. But pious individuals have differed among themselves for centuries, sometimes violently so. Within the Catholic faith alone there was marked criticism expressed of the opinions and advice given to Joseph Quinlan by his priest. Perhaps this is one of the reasons Judge Muir tried to set aside arguments based on religious beliefs. We can respect the deep feelings involved without having to agree that a particular individual in the situation knows precisely what God wants done.

What would Karen Ann herself want done? Statements have been attributed to her. Apparently she said once that she would not want to be maintained in an intensive-care unit if something happened to her. This attributed statement was used as part of the argument in court. It was advanced as though it were a sort of informal living will.

Yet there is much that is unclear about this statement. What was the context? Was this a tryout kind of statement to test her own thinking? To nudge a response from somebody? An impulsive statement related to a specific situation? Or a firmly conceived proposition that represented her philosophy of life? We do not know. Other retrospective interpretations could also be made. Karen Ann was described as being in a depressed mood. Some of her acquaintances pictured her as self-destructive. The admission diagnosis was said to be drug-induced coma. These allegations and facts were widely circulated, although in print people have stopped short of drawing the conclusion that Karen Ann was suicidal. This possibility might just as well be stated directly rather than left to innuendo. There is no evidence we know of to indicate that Karen Ann intended to kill herself. The circumstances are consistent with a subintentional orientation.[11] Perhaps in a troubled state of mind, she tempted fate and lost. This is only a possibility. It would not be responsible to draw any firm conclusion.

But let us take a step back from the real Karen Ann Quinlan, whose actual motives and intentions we do not know. Put in her place a young woman who does have some suicidal thoughts and who is going through a difficult transitional phase in her life. This is the kind of person, young and female, who the statistics tell us has an unusually high probability of making suicidal threats and attempts, although the ratio between attempt and completion is not as high a for, say, old men. Suppose that this person imperiled her life with a dangerous mix of drugs and alcohol. She lapses into coma. Her statement about not wanting to have her life maintained by a machine is now recalled. Wouldn't this statement now take on a different meaning? Instead of being seen as a per-

sonal and permanent statement of philosophical values (e.g., "Better a quick death than a prolonged useless existence"), it might be regarded as just one more component of a self-destructive orientation. And the entire self-destructive orientation might have been potentially a passing mood. The individual who is protected from a surge of suicidality may go on to a long, active, and rewarding life. One might have taken the young woman's statement quite seriously, but more as an expression of her momentary sense of anxiety, frustration, and anger than as an immutable mandate that she be delivered over to death.

The use of attributed statements must be very cautious in any circumstances, but especially so when life and death literally hinge on them. Even if such a statement was actually made, the context and meaning must be understood. Those who advocate the living will as a formal document often hear the objection that people might change their minds after signing the form. When we actually find ourselves in a life-and-death situation we might develop a different orientation than we thought we would have when we looked at the prospect of our own death from afar. Shifts in orientation toward personal death have been noted even among people who might be said to dwell constantly within "the valley of the shadow" because of a combination of advanced age and multiple life-threatening illnesses.[12] We would often be mistaken if we simply assumed that a person's most heartfelt orientation toward life and death today can be taken as his or her final and immutable disposition. The living will can, of course, be revoked or altered so long as the individual is in a position to express preferences. For Karen Ann, there did not seem to be any opportunity to determine whether a statement made in a time of health should be binding in a time of peril.

Other people have had more advanced warning of peril. A popular congressman asked his physicians to turn off his life-support systems when he recognized he had no reasonable chance for recovery. Representative Torbert H. MacDonald's wishes were respected. He had the time he wanted to be with his family at the hospital for mutual leave-taking without the isolating effect of tubes and other life-support devices.[13] His request was considered appropriate and understandable. Because of the respect he had commanded prior to his illness and the time available to him, there was no question about his competency to decide how he wanted his life to end. People who have lived for awhile with expectations of death can develop an orientation that in turn provides guidelines for family and caregivers. This is quite different from the situation of Karen Ann Quinlan and others who have moved suddenly from the midst of life to the borderline with death.

Some neglected dimensions

For all that has been said about Ms. Quinlan's situation, there have also been many things left unsaid, perhaps unnoticed. A few of these are important enough to bring up here.

If Karen Ann Quinlan remains hovering somewhere between life and death, what is the emotional status of those who were deeply involved with her? Specifically, are they grieving? Can they grieve—and continue to grieve—for a loved one who is not quite dead if also not quite alive as a person? We have seen something of the impact and ordeal of bereavement (Chapter 14). There is a special poignancy when the deceased is a person one would have expected to survive those who are now the survivors. Yet the process of grief and reconstitution does gradually enable the bereaved person to continue with life in most instances. This "release to grieve" may not be available to the Quinlan family and to others in similar situations. The ambiguity of the situation exposes friends and families to both the anxieties of relating to a dying person and the sorrows of bidding farewell to the dead. Grief and mourning may be powerful forces welling up inside the family. But so long as the "dead" are not dead, how can an open, direct process of grief and mourning begin? A similar situation is faced by those who have a relative in cryogenic interment, maintained at low temperature in hopes of eventual resuscitation and cure.[14,15] Whether or not the body in the capsule is in a state of "suspended animation," the survivor himself may be experiencing a conflicted and suspended state. It is difficult to proceed as though Karen Ann is dead when, in fact, she is still in a nursing home bed and maintaining the rudiments of life. And yet it is difficult to relate to her as a living person.

There is reason to be concerned, then, that people such as the Quinlans have not had the opportunity to experience a "normal" grief and reconstitution process (we would not want to overemphasize the idea that there is any single process of grief that should be considered "normal," especially in light of Sanders' recent studies, Chapter 14). It would be understandable under such strained and ambiguous circumstances for pressures to develop aimed at resolving the dilemma. The decision to terminate life-support services, then, might well have been intensified by the anguish of long-delayed grief. Unfortunately, none of the reports suggest that sensitive attention was given to the problem of unfulfilled grief and mourning. It does seem important for all individuals involved in such a situation to be sensitive to the possibility that their own anxieties might influence the actions advocated presumably in the best interests of the patient. There is now even a bit of research evidence[16] suggesting a relationship between the individual's personal orientation toward death and dying attitudes held toward euthanasia and related topics.

The question of unfulfilled grief is related to the perception of Karen Ann as alive or dead.

It is possible, indeed likely, that Karen Ann has been alive to some people and dead to others at almost every point in her illness. Whether a person is alive or dead is a judgment made within a particular frame of reference.[17] This is especially evident when we concentrate on psychosocial definitions, although not limited to this framework. You are more likely to see me as dead, for example, if there are no actions or interactions you can make on my behalf. If you are a physician, you may sense me as dead fairly early, because your interest in me is mediated largely by treatment modalities that now appear useless. If you are a nurse, you may not come to this subjective conclusion quite so soon, for there are more interactions you are required to perform so long as my body is in a bed for which you have responsibility. If you are a family member or intimate friend, you may sense me as alive much longer. Your relationship to me has consisted in part of feelings and thoughts, and these have a life of their own, thereby conferring a kind of life on me.

Yet even among friends and family there are apt to be personality differences that are represented in perceptions of aliveness or deadness. Some people find it necessary to bury the dead quickly in their feelings or at least to try to do so. Others will not let go. They need to see the person as alive and viable and will keep this perception so long as it has any basis at all.

Add to this situation the fact that *communication* is often inadequate and distorted around the terminally ill person.[18] This suggests that the physicians, nurses, family, and others around Karen Ann Quinlan have been carrying around rather private psychological definitions of her status. Their attitudes and decisions may be closely related to perceptions of Ms. Quinlan as alive or dead but never be communicated or discussed. The possibility for misunderstandings and actions at cross-purposes is evident. We have often observed extreme differences in behavior among staff members caring for the same patient, some treating her as though still intact as a person while others speak and act around her as though she were completely devoid of comprehension and experimental potential.[e.g.,12] Furthermore, some people function within specialized frameworks that imply still other definitions of life and death. The attorney or judge and the medical insurance official are likely to have different perspectives than the physician, nurse, or family member.

This is one of the reasons I doubt that a purely legal or a purely medical definition of death can prove satisfactory. The Quinlan case aroused pressure for speedy enaction of legislation and for court rulings to cover such situations. Actually, this process had started before Karen Ann Quinlan's dilemma, but was much intensified as a result. I am pessimistic about the long-term adequacy of any hastily made decisions of this kind. It seems premature to allow our anxieties to pressure us into quick definitions of death and then use these as a basis for legal, medical, and social practice. Many of us have not consulted our own thoughts and feelings thoroughly, still less have we shared our views with others. The people who frame laws and carve definitions may not be in sufficient touch with the personal orientations toward dying and death that make so much difference in the actual situation. I am concerned, then, about the movement to objectify or codify death before we have opened ourselves fully to the diversity of meanings that actually exist.

Some factors involved in modifying the definition of death

It definitely is worthwhile, however, to become better acquainted with the positions that have been taken to construct some kind of legalistic framework around the nature of death and the status of the person who inhabits the borderline region. Those who are inclined to stretch their minds to encompass an historical perspective will find some fascinating material available.[e.g.,19,20,21] Among writings that focus on ethical, legalistic, and biomedical aspects of the current scene, there are also many choices.[e.g.,22,23,24] One issue of particular concern is the relationship between *brain death* and the death of the person. This is not entirely the open-and-shut case that might be supposed, especially on the basis of the widely disseminated and influential Harvard Medical School attempt to equate irreversible coma, as determined by specified medical observations, with death of the person.[25] It makes sense to keep in mind that the definition of death is vulnerable to a variety of social and economic as well as personal pressures, just as in earlier chapters it was seen that definitions and meanings have emerged from the total pattern of dynamics in a culture's death system in the past. We would be naive to think, for example, that all the motives and needs of daily life, both those of the individual and of the various competing establishments, are suspended when we are concerned with the between-life-and-death situation. We have seen that such factors as the profit motive, convenience (inertia), and the need to appear competent and secure in one's own eyes can influence all manner of death-related phenomena, whether on the level of mass catastrophe or that of the individual dying process. This happens with the medicolegal proceedings around the definition of death as well.

Pressure for organ donations, for example, can polarize a medical staff between those who are trying to keep a person alive and those seeking vitally needed transplants to save the lives of other individuals. Those concerned chiefly about the expense of maintaining "unproductive" individuals in hospital or nursing home beds also represent vested interests, as do family members who may have strong needs either to keep a person alive in any shape at all

as long as possible or to have the final curtain come down without delay.

Two rather different sets of issues are also being confronted. One is concerned with the specific relationship between the organic changes that have taken place on the life-death borderlines for a particular individual. The concept of brain death requires intensive exploration and is not synonymous with the "flat EEG" profile, although this is obviously a highly significant aspect of assessment. Another set of issues centers around the ethical implications. How should we think of the individual who is neither wholly alive nor wholly dead? And what are the implications for ethical theory in general?

It is difficult to write the "human factor" into any of the equations worked out by legislators, judges, or those who generalize about moral philosophy. Consider, for example, caregivers whose approach to the comatose patient has been coming under increasing regulation by legislative or court action. In some jurisdictions, rulings have been made that seem to require "heroic" resuscitation actions which physicians and nurses on the scene may feel to be inappropriate. This type of ruling has already been undermined at times by informal agreements among staff members that they will not "notice" or communicate signs of impending death. The patient will be allowed to die ("passive euthanasia") despite what the law appears to insist on. Informal as well as formal components in the death system continue to influence what takes place on the life-death borderlines, a pattern that may be with us indefinitely and which also may have a constructive, check-and-balance function to serve.

MOVING FROM LIFE TO DEATH: DID HE SLIP OR WAS HE PUSHED?

One more concern. Suppose Karen Ann Quinlan were a 92-year-old widow. Would we know her name now? Who would have cared?

Our culture's death concern is highly selective. We have seen this in many forms throughout the book, and once again when we examine the between-life-and-death situation. The young and beautiful are not supposed to die. Karen Ann was given extensive life-support services even though she was quoted (accurately or not) as being against such treatment and even though the likelihood of recovery has long been considered remote if not impossible. She has been given most if not every possible chance. Compare her situation with that of the elderly man or woman who *wants* to live—what begrudgings, rationalizations, and half-hearted measures we tend to offer! Ms. Quinlan became an Interesting Case. Yet thousands of other people were at peril at the same time, including many children as well as many aged. For various reasons they were less successful in capturing our interest.

Fortunately, there now seems to be some heightening of professional and public awareness in this area. Five years after Karen Ann's plight engaged widespread attention, one can find increasing concern for people who would have remained nearly invisible along the life-death borderline.

Consider one such example that is current at the moment of this writing. Earle N. Spring, described as an "active and robust outdoorsman,"[26] suffered a serious infection in November 1977. He was given a continuing thrice-weekly series of kidney dialysis treatments that have kept him going when he might otherwise have died. About 2 years later, Spring's wife and son asked the court to discontinue these treatments. By this time, Spring was resident of a geriatric facility. The family was reported as declaring that if Mr. Spring were still mentally competent, he would want the treatments stopped at this time.[27] The judge of the Franklin County Probate Court did in fact order the cessation of further treatment.

At this point a series of counterforces started to make an impact, setting the Spring case apart from many previous situations around the nation where life-sustaining efforts for the disabled elderly have been discontinued without significant protest: "At the nursing home where Spring is a patient, licensed practical nurse Kathy McEvady said the entire 3 to 11 p.m. shift . . . was torn by frustration and sorrow when two nurses asked Spring, 'Do you want to die?' and he replied, 'No.' " McEvady and five of her colleagues published a letter in a local newspaper, including excerpts of a recent conversation with Spring in which he appeared to comprehend and reply to their questions. They expressed a sense of helplessness and distress about the court's decision, adding that "We are the ones who are going to watch Earle deteriorate and die. It saddens us to think that a life can be snuffed out so easily."[28]

A group of right-to-life advocates filed affidavits with the cooperation of the nursing home administrative and nursing staff, but without prior knowledge of the family. Litigation continued, and the legal system responded to this pressure. It came to light that there had been no recent mental status examination by a psychiatrically trained individual. The process whereby it was judged or assumed that Spring was incompetent to make his own decision was called into serious question. A follow-up ruling gave permission, on a temporary basis, for the dialysis treatments to continue. Arrangements were made for a three-person team of qualified physicians and gerontologists to interview Spring and bring in a more adequate assessment of his mental status.[29] It is worth noting that about a month had passed at the time of this writing since the new mental examination, and the court has not yet rendered its next, if not its final judgment. This time period is one in which the individual's mental state could very well have changed for either the better or the worse; therefore, the court ruling could possibly be out of date with the present facts by the time it comes through—a critical factor in cases of this kind.

Another important counterforce asserted it-self. The Massachusetts Association of Older Americans (MAOA) entered the picture. This is an organization of and for the elderly that had already proved itself effective as an educational and political force in Massachusetts. MAOA now approached the court with an official complaint about the manner in which the Spring case was being handled. The organization sought permission to intervene to protect two critical rights of older persons who might be adjudicated as incompetent and for whom decisions concerning life-supporting or life-prolonging medical treatment may be required:

first, to have determination about such persons' competence to make these types of decisions based on adequate and current medical and psychological assessments; and second, to ensure that if such persons are found incompetent, decisions regarding life-prolonging medical treatment for them will reflect as much as possible their own preferences, wants, and needs, and will not be based on the judgments of others about the value of their current lives.[30]

MAOA's position especially emphasizes the distinction between "mental competence," as such, and quality of life. The organization—at this moment—is standing by to take such action as it can to see that the Spring case heightens our sensitivity to the rights of older people to high-level care and the opportunity to continue lives that may be impaired in many ways but are still, after all, their lives.

What we are starting to see, then, is a more widespread awareness that age and impairment need not signify that a person is "as good as dead," and that others, even those with close kinship ties or legal authority, must exercise the greatest sensitivity in taking the side of life termination. The nursing staff of the particular geriatric facility involved in this case apparently found a continuation of human value in this man despite—or perhaps in part because of—the suffering and limitations he had had to endure. Perhaps they have also had opportu-nity to observe, as have my colleagues and myself[31] and others around the nation, that the apparently confused, demented, and altogether "hopeless" geriatric patient often does comprehend more than he or she is given credit for and also may respond very well to loving, holistic care.

Our knowledge of the actual psychobiological status of individuals caught in between-life-and-death states may improve considerably in the years ahead. It seems clear enough that our attitudes and the sociophysical contexts in which these attitudes develop will continue to shift. And what we learn from the legal actions, social responses, and individual orientations toward Karen Ann Quinlan, Earle Spring, and others may have as yet unsuspected implications for the quality of life closer to home.

SUMMARY

When a young woman suddenly fell into a comatose state and hovered there indefinitely, the nation just as suddenly had its first compelling encounter with the between-life-and-death state. Karen Ann Quinlan's plight focused many of the questions and concerns current in our society.

After a chronological account of Ms. Quinlan's life, we explored some of the issues, views, and contentions raised by her situation. These included the *death-with-dignity* issue, the *psychobiological facts* that are in question, the possible outcomes of *viability* and *recovery*, including the awareness of medical fallibility, and the relationship between moral and religious *values* and our orientation toward the in-between states. The individual's own *preferences and intentions* were considered. The ambiguity of statements made before a life-and-death crisis develops was noted—for example, was Karen Ann philosophically opposed to life-sustaining efforts, was this instead an expression of a self-destructive tendency, or did she simply make a casual, spontaneous statement that was not intended to bear any weight?

Despite all the media and professional discussion generated by Ms. Quinlan's situation, several dimensions were substantially neglected. These include the *unfulfilled grief and mourning* of those close to her; the *differing perceptions* of Karen Ann as living or dead, with associated problems in *communication;* and the pressure to establish new *legislative rulings and precedents* before we have examined our own basic perceptions of the situation.

Characteristically, our culture has given *selective attention* to death. Our imagination is especially captured by life-and-death drama that centers around the young and attractive. There are now indications, however, that sensitivity and advocacy is maturing and that key clinical and ethical issues are being raised for elderly as well as younger people who seem to be caught in a between-life-and-death situation. An example was given of an ongoing situation (the Earle Spring case) in which a man alert enough to say that he did not want to die was to have had life-sustaining treatments discontinued—in contrast to the months of extensive life-support care given to the young Ms. Quinlan who has not able to communicate at all, so far as all reports indicate.

REFERENCES

1. Kron, J. The girl in the coma. *New York,* October 6, 1973.
2. Kron, J. Did the girl in the coma want "death with "dignity"? *New York,* October 27, 1975.
3. Quinlan, J., & Quinlan, J. *Karen Ann, the Quinlans tell their story.* New York: Bantam Books, 1978.
4. A life in the balance. *Time,* November 3, 1975.
5. "Death with dignity" asked for Karen after court ok. *Boston Globe,* April 1, 1976.
6. O'Brien, T. Weaning Quinlan from respirator puts fate in doubt. *Boston Globe,* May 25, 1976.
7. Stein, M. Let Karen die a merciful death. *The Cleveland Press,* November 12, 1975.
8. Court to hear parents of girl in coma. *Boston Globe,* October 21, 1975.
9. Montgomery, L. "Get out," coma boy tells mother—but words bring tears of joy. *Boston Globe,* April 16, 1976.
10. Former "medical vegetable" is now a mother. *Boston Globe,* December 1, 1975.
11. Shneidman, E. S. Orientations toward death. In R. W. White (Ed.), *The study of lives.* New York: Atherton Press, 1963.
12. Brustman, B., & Kastenbaum, R. *Condemned to life.* Cambridge, Mass.: Ballinger Publications (in press).
13. Torbert Macdonald dies, 21 years in Congress. *Boston Globe,* June 7, 1976.
14. Ettinger, R. C. W. *The prospect of immortality.* New York: McFadden-Bartell, 1966.
15. Ettinger, R. C. W. *Man into superman.* New York: St. Martin's Press, 1972.
16. Hart, E. J. The effects of death anxiety and mode of "case study" presentation on shifts of attitude toward euthanasia. *Omega,* 1978, 9, 239-244.
17. Kastenbaum, R., & Aisenberg, R. B. *The psychology of death.* New York: Springer Publishing Co., Inc., 1972.
18. Glaser, B. G., & Strauss, A. L. *Awareness of dying.* Chicago: Aldine Publishing Co., 1965.
19. Whiter, R. *A dissertation on the disorder of death.* New York: Arno Press, 1977. (Originally published, 1819.)
20. Gruman, G. J. Ethics of death and dying: historical perspective. *Omega,* 1978, 9, 203-238.
21. Gruman, G. J. An historical introduction to ideas about voluntary euthanasia. *Omega,* 1973, 4, 87-138.
22. Horan, D. J., & Mall, D. (Eds.). *Death, dying and euthanasia.* Washington, D.C.: University Publications of America, 1977.
23. Veatch, R. M. *Death, dying, and the biological revolution.* New Haven, Conn.: Yale University Press, 1976.
24. Wilson, J. B. *Death by decision.* Philadelphia: The Westminster Press, 1975.
25. Ad Hoc Committee of the Harvard School to Examine the Definition of Brain Death. A definition of irreversible coma. *Journal of the American Medical Association,* 1968, 205, 337-340.
26. Harvey, J. M. Tests foreseen in Spring case. *Boston Globe,* January 25, 1980.
27. Caldwell, J. Spring's nurses say he doesn't want to die. *Boston Globe,* January 22, 1980.
28. Knox, R. A. Spring's guardian asks new hearings. *Boston Globe,* January 23, 1980.
29. Spring in serious condition. *Boston Globe,* March 13, 1980.
30. Massachusetts Association of Older Americans. In the matter of the guardianship of Earle N. Spring. Complaint in intervention. Boston, Mass., February 4, 1980.
31. Kastenbaum, R., Barber, T. X., Wilson, C., Ryder, B., & Hathaway, L. *Old, sick, and helpless—where therapy begins.* Cambridge, Mass.: Ballinger Publications (in press).

CHAPTER 17

❖ DO WE SURVIVE DEATH?

We are sometimes asked to believe that this question has had a simple history. Once upon a time practically everybody assumed some form of life after death. Evidence from funeral practices and "books of the dead" is usually marshalled for this viewpoint. Enter science and skepticism: the belief shrivels into a relic of naive hope and superstition. The operative verb appears to be "cling to." Belief in survival persists chiefly among people who do not have well-developed powers of critical thinking or who need assurance that all does not end with death.

Acceptance of this simplified view of our historical relationship to the survival question would be prejudicial. It would become that much more difficult for us to examine freshly what is by any standard a most difficult topic. Yes, there is abundant evidence that through the centuries there have been flourishing thought systems, folkways, and funeral practices that assume the existence of an afterlife. The elaborate Tibetan[1] and Egyptian[2] treatises on death and the afterlife are merely the more conspicuous outcroppings of a diverse set of descriptions and prescriptions. "Cults of the dead" have been observed repeatedly by anthropologists and reconstructed by historians.[e.g.,3,4] Extraordinary monuments have been raised not only to honor but to placate and continue a relationship with the dead.[e.g.,5] Most of the world's great religions have generated images of an afterlife, images powerful enough to exert palpable influence over individual and social behavior. One can say that much of humanity has lived with the sense that the dead and the living retain some form of relationship, as well as with the prospect that one's own death represents a passage to another form of existence. Nevertheless, there have always been skeptics. Some people have remained stubbornly impressed with the apparent finality of death, preferring the evidence of their personal and pragmatic observations to the stories and rituals. Furthermore, being of two minds about the afterlife is not exclusively a modern orientation. Shamans, priests, and kings have used the cultural paraphernalia associated with the afterlife to maintain and expand their power. The tribal healer, for example, may conjure the dead because he knows this is an impressive and at times beneficial "treatment"—yet he also may know very well that what he is doing is at least in part an "act."[6] The new king may set up his throne over the grave of the deceased monarch to dramatize his right to reign.[7] He would like the royal subjects to believe that the strength of the former ruler is flowing through him: whether or not this is in fact the case is a separate question. There have also been those who have rejected the doctrine of an afterlife for emotional reasons. Conceptions of the hereafter have not always been of the beatific variety. Faced with the prospect of unlimited terror and despair, some have denied any survival at all (the "opposite-and-equal reaction" to those who have accepted survival doctrines largely for emotional reasons).

The impact of science on belief in an afterlife is real enough. Few would deny that faith has been shaken for many and lost by some. It has been fashionable for at least a century to express alarm about a "crisis of faith and values." The old rules for thinking and behaving have become more difficult to maintain in a universe rewritten by science. And yet the impact of science on belief in afterlife was never simple and has changed with time. Many scientists have themselves attempted to "rescue" human survival either through alternative conceptualizations or through scientific research itself. Some of these efforts will be examined later. We must also examine—and quite seriously—a crucial difference of opinion within the scientific community. It has already been noted that some scientists have acted as though research methodology might be able to confirm the existence of an afterlife. However, there are philosophers of science who maintain that the survival question is not amenable to empirical study. On this view, we can neither prove nor disprove survival through scientific research. "Do we survive death?" is seen as a nonquestion from the scientific standpoint no matter how much it may seem like a legitimate question on superficial acquaintance.

What can be said with some assurance at this point in the discussion is that acceptance or rejection of belief in an afterlife is a rather different proposition today than it was in prescientific times. It also appears to be a somewhat different proposition today than it was, say, in 1977 when the first edition of this book appeared. We will first examine two very recent developments that bear on the survival question. The development that has received most attention in both the popular media and the

clinical sciences concerns *near-death experiences* (NDEs). The interest aroused in this topic has spread to some extent to the ancient conception of *reincarnation,* which also has something relatively new to offer. After this critical review of recent developments, we will try to join the current wave of information and speculation to the larger body of material that has developed over the centuries.

NEAR-DEATH EXPERIENCES

The term *near-death experience* is a deliberately neutral way of referring to phenomena that have led to a wide variety of different interpretations. The most extreme of these interpretations is that a person has "returned from the dead"—and with an experience to share. When behavioral scientists and health-care professionals examine these phenomena they generally prefer to use more cautious language, hence NDE.

Human experience in the borderlands between life and death seems to have become more frequent in recent years (e.g., Chapter 16), although the phenomenon was not unknown in the past. The definition of death itself has come into question, generating medical, legal, and social concern. Within this context the NDE has emerged as a phenomenon that some people believe holds the answer to the related questions: What is death? Is there survival?

What precisely is an NDE? A person must have been in a state close to death by some reasonable standard. Unresponsiveness to external stimulation and inability to observe pulse or respiration are common criteria. The presence of cardiac arrest has given additional credibility in some instances ("They told me my heart stopped beating"). Absence of electrical activity in the brain of the type associated with life (the "flat EEG") is an even more compelling indication that a person is somewhere in the life-death borderlands. The pronouncement of death by a physician has been the essential criterion in many instances. In some cases the investigators have access to objective information. In other cases it has been the individual's self-report that furnishes all the available information. One can see, then, that there will be differences among NDE reports with respect to their apparent "closeness" to death (as well as the length of time the state persisted) and with respect to the adequacy of documentation.

The other obvious requirement of an NDE is that it be shared. This means that a person must both have had an experience and be willing and able to convey it. At present we have no way of determining how many people may have had experiences in a near-death state but have "forgotten" them. (The "forgetting" could be a function of having had an experience in a state of consciousness that does not "communicate" well with the ordinary waking state, or it could be a function of "repression" because of its emotional content.)

Theoretically an NDE could have many different characteristics, just as do our experiences in general. However, it is one particular kind of experience that has come to the fore. What might be called the primary form of the NDE quickly received widespread attention when reported by Raymond A. Moody, Jr., in *Life After Life*.[8] Moody selected 50 cases from a larger number of reports that had come to him about NDEs. Some of these people had been pronounced dead by a physician; all appeared to have been close to the end. Examining his interview notes with these people, Moody found 15 frequently occuring elements (all these elements did not necessarily appear in each interview). A typical experience would be one such as the following:

"I was hospitalized for a severe kidney condition, and I was in a coma for approximately a week. My doctors were extremely uncertain as to whether I would live. During this period when I was uncon-

scious, I felt as though I were lifted right up, just as though I didn't have a physical body at all. A brilliant white light appeared to me. The light was so bright that I could not see through it, but going into its presence was so calming and so wonderful. There is just no experience on earth like it. In the presence of the light, the thoughts or words came into my mind: 'Do you want to die?' And I replied that I didn't know since I knew nothing about death. Then the white light said, 'Come over this line and you will learn.' I felt that I knew where the line was in front of me, although I could not actually see it. As I went across the line, the most wonderful feelings came over me—feelings of peace, tranquility, a vanishing of all worries."[8,p.56]

This report illustrates some of the major features of the primary NDE. Perhaps the key or defining characteristic is the sense of serenity and well-being. Rising and floating are also common experiences reported, as well as a journey, a going-toward. "Brilliant white light" is another part of the experience that is often reported. Furthermore, there is often a turning-point encounter. The individual reports feeling as though he or she had a choice about death at this time. Moody comments that "the most common feelings reported in the first few moments following death are a desperate desire to get back into the body and an intense regret over one's demise. However, once the dying person reaches a certain depth in his experience, he does not want to come back, and he may even resist the return to the body. This is especially the case for those who have gotten so far as to encounter the being of light. As one man put it most emphatically, "I *never* wanted to leave the presence of this being."

It is the attempt to explain NDEs with these characteristics that has become the focus of controversy and the stimulus of new research. Does the primary NDE constitute proof for survival of death? This is the core question, although it is not the only one. Before examining research and theory on the NDE let us reflect on the kind of evidence that might help to settle the question:

1. If *all* people returning from a close encounter with death had experiences of the primary NDE type, this would argue for the universality of the experience and, by a speculative leap, for the likelihood that they had actually been in death's domain.

2. If experiences of the primary NDE type were associated *only* with death encounters, then the possible link between these experiences and death would be further strengthened.

3. If no alternative explanations requiring less radical assumptions were available—the conclusion that NDE's prove survival would be extreme if more parsimonious explanations could be advanced.

Additionally, one could question the authenticity of the primary NDE reports themselves. If these reports were not to be trusted for any reason, then the difficult task of interpreting them could be set aside. It does seem clear, however, that the reports are to be taken seriously. Experiential reports quite typical of those cited by Moody have been noted for many years and in many parts of the world. There have been detailed accounts of primary-type NDE experiences in our own society dating back well before the Moody book appeared.[e.g.,9] Holck[10] has pointed out examples scattered through ancient religious writings and a number of tribal societies. As will be seen later, independent researchers have come up with new cases of primary NDE since Moody's influential book. Moody did not claim that his observations constituted research findings in the technical sense of the term, but subsequent researchers have verified that reports of this kind can be obtained without much difficulty in the course of a formal investigation.

We examine the available research and theoretical literature now, primarily to see what it has to tell us about the survivel question and several related issues.

Garfield[11] has worked closely with patients who suffer from life-threatening illnesses. In one clinical study he conducted in-depth interviews with 36 patients who had had NDEs on intensive-care units. He was usually the first person to have a substantial interaction with the patient after the death encounter, placing him in a good position to learn what the patient had experienced while it was still fresh. We quote:

Eighteen patients reported no memory of the event at all. Their last memory before losing consciousness was of being in their hospital room and when they awoke they were either in the ICU or CCU (coronary care unit) "hooked up" to the hardware. Seven reported experiences similar to those collected by Moody, Kubler-Ross, and Osis, including seeing a bright light, hearing "celestial" music, and meeting religious figures or deceased relatives. Four reported lucid visions of a demonic or nightmarish nature. Four reported having dreamlike images; in two instances entirely positive and the other two alternating between positive and negative. Three patients reported drifting endlessly in outer space among the planets, but loose as if thrown from a space ship. No significant changes in content were expressed by any of the patients in three interviews conducted at weekly intervals following the event.[11,p.55]

Studies of this kind suggest that the primary NDE is not universal. Many people have close encounters with death and return with no experience at all to share (as was the case with half of the sample studied by Garfield). Additionally, there are some people who experience "bad trips." This has also been observed contemporaneously by Schnaper.[12] One might note here that there is an extensive literature, mostly forgotten, on the terror associated with NDEs. Kastenbaum and Aisenberg[13] point out that fear of premature burial was salient through much of the nineteenth century, with the near-death state characterized as frightening to the extreme. (The fiction of Edgar Allen Poe was modeled on events that many level-headed people believed to be true.) Garfield's study indicates, then, that there is more than one type of NDE and that some people appear to have no experience even though they appeared to have been just as far along the road to death.

Sabom and Kreutziger[14] studied approximately 50 patients who had suffered a documented near-fatal crisis. These were men and women in about equal number and distributed throughout the age range from 19 to 76 years. Great care was taken to avoid the use of leading questions; the patient was asked to reconstruct the situation in his or her own words. "Most of them remembered nothing during their period of unconsciousness. Eleven patients, however, had definite recollections, while unconscious, either of viewing their body from a detached position of height several feet above the ground (autoscopy) or of 'traveling' into another region."[14,p.196] Those who did have such recollections were reluctant to talk about them for fear of ridicule and also appeared not to have been familiar with the new "life-after-life" topic. Sabom and Kreutziger found that none of the usual demographic variables helped to separate out those who did and those who did not have a primary NDE (e.g., age, sex, religious affiliation, education, social background, psychiatric history—all failing to discriminate within the sample). Within the small group of patients who did have experiences to share, there was again the kind of detail available that had been noted by Moody. This is another study, then, that confirms that the primary NDE does occur, and adds the perhaps puzzling finding that conventional personal and demographic information does not appear related to occurrence or nonoccurrence of this phenomenon. But the study also is consistent with Garfield's finding that primary NDE is

found with only a minority of those who have returned from close encounters.

One of the most prolific researchers has been Kenneth Ring. Early in his work, Ring constructed an NDE Index to assess the depth of the experience. The higher the score on this index, the more the individual's report includes the elements described by Moody. This index was applied first to a sample of 102 people who had been close to death because of illness, accident, or suicide attempt.[15] Almost half of these people (48%) reported experiences that conformed at least partially to what we have since called the primary NDE. An appreciably smaller percentage (26%) had what Ring considered to be "deep" experiences. Because some of his respondents were volunteers who responded to advertisements and others were referred by physicians, it was possible to look for differences in their relative frequency of the primary NDE. The people who came in off the street were about half again as likely to report the primary NDE in comparison with those referred by health professionals. No sex differences were found with respect to NDE (a "nonfinding finding" consistent with the results of Sabom and Kreutziger). The Ring study included some data suggesting the possibility that some of the primary NDE elements occur more frequently than others. The feeling of peace and contentment seems to be the first dimension of the experience in sequence of occurrence and also the dimension that is most often reported. Elements that occur later in the sequence for experiences that go all the way (e.g., the summary from Moody quoted earlier) were also reported less frequently.

Ring later devised an index of individual religiousness for people in this sample. He reasoned that if the most religious people also were the ones with the most complete and vivid primary NDEs, then this would provide some evidence in favor of a religious hallucination interpretation of the experience—one of the alternative explanations proposed to counter the return-from-the-dead assumption. As it turned out, there was no relationship between the NDE Index and the index of religiosity. Ring concluded that "neither the likelihood nor the depth of a near-death experience was systematically related to individual religiousness. Nonreligious people—including self-professed atheists—were *just* as likely to have Moody-type experiences as were the conventionally devout."[16] As Ring notes, a cross-cultural study in the United States and India failed to find a clear relationship between religiousness and deathbed visions.[17] It should be kept in mind, however, that the relationship between what are called deathbed visions and the type of NDE being considered here has itself not been clarified. It seems premature to treat both phenomena as identical or as subject to the same principles.

In still another analysis, Ring focused on those whose brushes with death had been occasioned by suicide attempts.[18] Seventeen of the 36 people in this sample reported experiences of the primary NDE type. In general these experiences resembled those reported by people who had undergone crises related to accident or illness (and the proportion of those reporting NDEs was itself similar). Ring observes that "not one suicide survivor reported an experience that was predominately unpleasant. No one felt that he either was in or was bound for hell." In short, there was no evidence that self-destructive intent had introduced negative elements into the NDE itself when NDEs were reported.

An inquiry into the relationship between NDE and intense spiral experience has been carried out by Thomas and Cooper.[19] Their methodology differs from those of the other studies mentioned here. A questionnaire was administered to 305 persons obtained through various means and representing an age range from 17 through 85. The basis for classifying a person as having had an NDE was a positive response to the question, "Have you yourself ever had an experience during which you strongly felt you were going to die?" An experience of intense spirituality was defined by a positive answer to the question: "Have you ever had the feeling of being close to a powerful spiritual force or the feeling of being lifted out of yourself?" It should be noted that an experience of immediate and intense spirituality is not necessarily identical with conventional measures of religiousity. A person could participate in religious ceremonies throughout life and never have such an experience, while a person without formal religious affiliation could have such an experience. It should also be kept in mind that the criterion for accepting a person as having been in the position to have a NDE was considerably less rigorous in this study as compared with, for example, Garfield's work. Furthermore, a strong feeling that one is going to die can be experienced even when a person is in little objective danger. Methodological considerations such as these should never be disregarded because research quickly loses its value (and can even become dangerously misleading) when the findings are detached from their operational context. Having noted these problems, we can turn to the results of the Thomas-Cooper study. NDEs were reported by 28% of the sample and intense spiritual experiences by 34%. Those who reported NDEs were significantly more likely to have had intense spiritual experiences at some point in their lives as well. This at least suggests that there may be personality or life-style differences involved in the differential occurrence of NDEs or in the willingness to acknowledge *any* experience as "intense." Both are possibilities that require additional research. There was also a suggestion of age differences in this study, with the middle-aged group having the strongest association between NDE and intense spiritual experiences (as defined). Clearly, there is much yet to be learned about characteristics of the person (as well as the situation) that favor the occurrence of NDEs. What do studies such as these suggest about the primary ("Moody-type") NDE? There is little reason to doubt that some people do have experiences of this type when they are in an altered state of consciousness associated with a biological crisis. It is also reasonably clear that there are some recurring details in these reports. There is the further possibility that the primary NDE involves a sequence that some but not all individuals complete. In short, "there is something there" that invites continued observation and analysis.

The overall pattern of data, however, does not do much to encourage the hypothesis that the primary NDE represents an experience of death. All studies find that many people who have come close to death do not have any experiences to report, while there are also some reports of "bad trips." Even if all people with close encounters did report the primary NDE, this would not permit us to conclude that they had in fact been dead, but such a pattern would at least by consistent with the hypothesis. Why would a universal report of primary NDE *not* demonstrate the validity of the survival hypothesis? "We hear only from those who return to our midst. . . . Even if everybody who returned from such an extreme experience had the same basic story to tell, this would not prove that dying is a pleasure and death a state of bliss. We would still have a firm 'no comment' from those who stayed dead. The close call or the temporary death may be quite distinct from the one-way passage."[20,p.23] Additionally, the obvious fact should be noted that those who returned had not been "dead" very long and still had bodies sufficiently intact to permit this return.

A further *caveat* should be introduced. Survival of death is not equivalent to immortality. This distinction has been recognized by many tribal peoples who believed in an afterworld that had its own hazards, which included the possibility of a death-after-death. Those who are disinclined to entertain any possibility of survival may not be interested in this distinction, but it is a relevant if usually overlooked consideration for those who do believe. The hypothesis of a *temporary* survival was advanced many years ago by F. W. H. Myers,[21] an extraordinary scholar who pioneered the application of modern concepts and methodology in this area. The most relevant aspect of Myers' hypothesis is its implication for the kind of inferences we are entitled to draw from evidence suggestive of survival. Earlier in this book a distinction was made between death as event and as state. Evidence suggesting continued existence after death-as-event does not necessarily settle all questions about death-as-state. Reviewing an array of historical, anecdotal, and survey material, Myers and his colleagues noted that reported *contacts* with the dead followed a clear-cut temporal course.[22] In general, the longer the individual had been dead, the less was heard from him. Myers' hypothesis involved a sort of personal energy field that persisted for a while after death, then gradually dissipated (this itself was but one of numerous hypotheses he advanced for consideration).

Myers and his colleagues were trying to evaluate a type of material (communications with the dead) that is different from the NDEs being considered here. The basic logic, however, applies to both types. Even if one is persuaded by evidence suggesting some kind of survival, it may well require quite another type of evidence to draw the inference that the survival is "permanent." There is nothing in the primary NDE literature that bears on the question of extended or permanent survival.

Another criterion for evaluation of NDEs was raised earlier in this chapter: Do such experiences occur *only* in association with life-threatening crises? The answer appears to be in the negative. The "out-of-the-body" experience (OBE) that is intrinsic to many primary NDEs has often been reported in contexts that seem to have nothing to do with death[e.g.,23,24] At least one professor has been inducing OBEs in college classrooms for years an experiential device to further understanding of basic principles of perception,[25] quite innocent of the NDE. Those familiar with the literature on "mystical experiences" have no difficulty in recognizing familiar elements. Both the "mystical experience" and the NDE seem to occur during altered states of consciousness. Improved understanding of either experience might be expected to improve our understanding of the other as well.

We have seen that: (1) Not all people with close encounters have a primary NDE to report and (2) experiences similar to if not identical with the NDE have been reported in situations that do not involve life jeopardy. When we add the other logical and methodological considerations noted earlier, there appears little reason to accept the current spate of NDEs as demonstrating anything about the death state per se or about the possibility of survival.

But how are NDEs to be explained if they do not constitute evidence for survival? Alternative explanations have not been lacking. One of the most interesting conceptualizations has been provided by psychiatrist Russell Noyes, Jr., and his colleagues. In conducting his own series of studies,[e.g.,26-28] Noyes has obtained phenomenological reports from many people who have survived a variety of life-threatening crises. He and his colleagues have found a set of common features in these reports. These common features were further delineated through the statistical procedure known as factor analysis. Three major factors emerged: mystical consciousness, depersonalization, and

hyperalertness. It is worth becoming acquainted with the components of each of these factors.

The *mystical* consciousness dimension of experiences close to death includes:

Feeling of great understanding
Images sharp or vivid
Revival of memories
Sense of harmony, unity
Feeling of joy
Revelation
Sense of being controlled by outside force
Colors or visions
Strange body sensations

The *depersonalization* dimension includes:

Loss of emotion
Body apart from self
Self strange or unreal
Objects small, far away
Detachment from body
World strange or unreal
Wall between self and emotions
Detachment from world
Body changed in shape or size
Strange sounds
Altered passage of time

The *hyperalertness* dimension includes:

Thoughts sharp or vivid
Thoughts speeded
Vision, hearing sharper
Thoughts blurred or dull
Altered passage of time
Thoughts, movements mechanical

Methodologically, the work of Noyes and his colleagues is of the highest level available. Based on these findings, how does he attempt to explain the nature—and *function*—of the primary NDE? He believes it is important to consider both physiological and psychological levels. Hyperalertness and depersonalization are interpreted as part of the same neural mechanism. The function of this hypothetical mechanism is to help the human organism react to dangerous circumstances. Drawing on earlier observations of Roth and Harper,[29] Noyes suggests that this is an adaptive mechanism that combines opposing reaction tendencies, "the one serving to intensify alertness and the other to dampen potentially disorganizing emotion."[28,p.78] When this mechanism is working properly, a person is able to cope exceptionally well (cooly, calmly, objectively) in the midst of a crisis situation.

Noyes writes:

On a *psychological* level, depersonalization may be interpreted as a defense against the threat of death. Not only did people in the studies . . . find themselves calm in otherwise frightening situations but they also felt detached from what was happening. . . . *The depersonalized state is one that mimics death* [italics added]. In it a person experiences himself as empty, lifeless, and unfamiliar. In a sense he creates psychologically the very situation that environmental circumstances threaten to impose. In so doing he escapes death, for what has already happened cannot happen again; he cannot die, because he is already dead.[28,p.79]

This is a cogent and powerful line of explanation because it is in contact both with NDE data and with the broader realm of psychobiological dynamics. The dimension of mystical consciousness is seen by Noyes as being somewhat apart from the depersonalization-hyperalertness mechanism. This feature occurs most often with people who are dying from physical disease. Noyes suggests that the physiological changes associated with terminal illness may induce altered states of consciousness in which experiences of a mystical type are more likely to appear. Noyes' theoretical analysis, with many points of reference to clinical data, is richer than what can be presented here. The reader with a serious interest in this topic should certainly become familiar with Noyes' work in more detail.

Another line of explanation (not necessarily inconsistent with Noyes) has recently been elaborated by psychologist Ronald K. Siegel. In his erudite (and entertaining) survey of "The Psychology of Life After Death,"[30] Siegel critically reviews many types of evidence purporting to demonstrate survival. With respect to NDEs and deathbed visions in particular, Siegel emphasizes their hallucinatory aspect. This means he has to explain both the occurrence of the hallucinations in the first place and their specific content and features. In developing his argument on the latter point, Siegel draws in particular on the work of Grof and Halifax[31]:

The specific content of complex hallucinatory imagery is determined largely by set (expectations and attitudes) and setting (physical and psychological environments). For many dying and near-death experiences, the sets (fear of approaching death, changes in body and mental functioning, etc.) and settings (hospital wards, accident scenes, etc.) can influence specific eschatological thoughts and images. Grof and Halifax (1977) suggest that the universal themes of this imagery may be related to stored memories of biological events which are activated in the brain. Accordingly . . . the feelings of peace and quiet may be related to the original state of intrauterine existence when there is complete biological equilibrium with the environment. The experience of moving down a dark tunnel may be associated with the clinical stage of delivery in which the cervix is open and there is a gradual propulsion through the birth canal . . . the dying or near-death experience triggers a flashback or retrieval of an equally dramatic and emotional memory of the birth experience. . . . To the extent that this reasoning is correct, the experience of dying and rebirth in the afterlife may be a special case of state-dependent recall of birth itself.[30]

Why the hallucinations in the first place? Siegel suggests (as others have) that the sensory world of the terminally ill person is likely to be drastically reduced. The relative lack of sensory input from the outside encourages the release or escape of stored memories. These memories reenter conscious awareness as though they were perceptions. The result is that experiential state known as the hallucination.

Explanations of the Noyes and Siegel types require much additional research if they are to be fully confirmed. It is also possible that because of the nature of their assumptions (especially the death-as-rebirth vein of speculation), it may be exceedingly difficult ever to test the hypotheses directly. Nevertheless the assumption that NDEs prove survival must contend with a pair of formidable alternatives. Other alternative explanations can be offered as well, but enough has been presented here to give a fair view of the current state of knowledge and theory.

Reincarnation

The ancient belief in reincarnation until recently had little place in the "death-awareness movement." It was not a topic that seemed relevant to clinical practice, nor did it command the attention of researchers. In fact, one could hardly imagine a death-related topic that seemed more remote from the modern view. This situation is starting to change. Attention to NDEs has encouraged—perhaps "licensed"—renewed attention to phenomena suggestive of reincarnation. This phrase itself, "suggestive of reincarnation," has been made familiar by the systematic research of psychiatrist Ian Stevenson. His work in this area started well before the current increase of interest, and provides the most substantial and systematic body of information from a clinical research standpoint. His *Twenty Cases Suggestive of Reincarnation*[32] is perhaps the classic book in this field, but he has contributed many other articles and books.[e.g.,33-36]

A hallmark of Stevenson's approach is intensive case-by-case analysis. These case histories often are presented in considerable detail, so there is little mystery about what information was obtained and by what means. Readers are left with their own conclusions to draw. It is a method that combines some of the art of the researcher and some of the detective. The easiest way to dispose of this material would be to categorize the methodology as slipshod, the observations as naive or fraudulent. This "easy way out" is not available. Stevenson's work is lucid, systematic, and detailed. His series of case histories are a model of their kind. The reader, therefore, has no easy way out. One can simply refuse to examine evidence "suggestive of reincarnation" because the idea itself appears incredible. If one does examine the evidence, however, it becomes difficult to make a quick and decisive judgment.

Stevenson characterizes the typical case as one that starts early in childhood, usually between ages 2 and 4. The child starts to describe details of a previous life.

The child often begins talking about this previous life as soon as he gains any ability to speak, and sometimes before his capacity for verbal expression matches his need to communicate. . . . The subjects . . . vary greatly both in the quantity of their utterances and in the richness of the memories. . . . Some children make only three or four different statements about a previous life, but others may be credited with 60 or 70 separate items pertaining to different details in the life remembered. . . . In most cases the volume and clarity of the child's statements increase until at the age of between 5 and 6 [when] he usually starts to forget the memories; or, if he does not forget them, he begins to talk about them less. Spontaneous remarks about the previous life have usually ceased by the time the child has reached the age of 8 and often before. Unexpected behavior . . . nearly always accompanies the statements the child makes about the previous life he claims to remember, or occurs contemporaneously with them. This behavior is unusual for a child of the subject's family, but concordant with what he says concerning the previous life, and in most instances it is found to correspond with what other informants say concerning the behavior of the deceased person about whom the subject has been talking, if such a person is traced.[36]

Attention has been given here to only a few characteristics of the "suggestive" cases; many other characteristics are described by Stevenson.

The possibility of fraud is considered highly unlikely by Stevenson because of the large number of witnesses in many of the cases and the lack of opportunity or motivation for deception. Suppose for sake of further discussion that fraud could be ruled out decisively. Are there alternative explanations of these phenomena that require assumptions less radical than reincarnation? Perhaps the most obvious alternative is what has become known as the "Super-ESP hypothesis."[37] The child who acts as though he were a reincarnated spirit may instead be an exceptionally adept recipient of psychic communications from others. One might well protest that this alternative does not have much advantage over the reincarnation thesis. Many remain skeptical of "ordinary" ESP and are even less inclined to accept the "super" variety. This alternative, although itself quite controversial, does seem a shade more parsimonious. The "messages" are thought to be some form of communication from one living being to another. On this view, it is not necessary to assume any direct connection between a deceased and a living person. The "Super-ESP" hypothesis has problems of its own and, though more conservative than the reincarnation interpretation, can offer little positive evidence in its favor. The patterns of thought and action reported in reincarnation-type cases have not yet proved amenable to solid explanation.

Additional questions rather than answers come forth when evidence for reincarnation is sought through hypnosis. This approach has the advantage of introducing an experimental condition under circumstances that are more or less within the researcher's control. One can go "reincarnation hunting" with specified respondents and standard procedures instead of waiting for spontaneous cases to appear wherever and whenever they choose. Helen Wambach has prepared a nontechnical report of her explorations with hypnosis. *Life Before Life*[38] offers statistical information and brief case examples from her work with 750 people. The material obtained from her respondents often dealt with experiences they believed were associated with birth. Some of the recollections elicited in the hypnotic state, however, concerned supposed previous existences—including one or more death experiences. These cases, as presented, do not include the extensive detectivelike verification process that characterizes Stevenson's work. One has less reason, then, to accept these reincarnation accounts as having strong ties with objective reality. There is also the question of how we are inclined to interpret the hypnotic state. Commercial hypnotists have encouraged a mystique that portrays this as a very special state of the organism in which almost anything can happen. Leading researchers, however, tend to favor a different conception.[e.g.,39] *Hypnosis* is seen to be more of an interactive process, a collaborative effort—not the passive response of one person to the influence of the other. It is reasonably clear that the hypnotic process can help some individuals recall events that do not seem to have been available to them under ordinary circumstances. The limits of this recollection have not been definitively established. The claim for recalling actual birth or reincarnation experiences is an extreme one.

Of the many questions that might be asked about available data suggestive of reincarnation, there is one that appears especially salient to this writer. How could *anybody* be reincarnated unless *everybody* is reincarnated? The test of universality was applied earlier in this chapter to NDEs, which were found clearly lacking in this respect. The true incidence of reincarnation experiences is not known. From the voluminous files of Stevenson and from other cases that have been described, it would seem that this is not so rare a phenomenon as was once believed. Yet these cases do remain unusual—which is one of the reasons they have generated such interest. One might argue that everybody does become reincarnated, but that only a few have conscious awareness. This possible explanation would be difficult to put to the test, although refinements of the Wambach approach might be useful. There is an even more radical possibility: *death may not be the same for everybody.* Of all the possibilities considered in this chapter, the prospect of *pluralistic death* might well be the most extreme. It could be the possibility that would most challenge our basic assumptions about the nature of life and the universe. There is survival of death—or there is not survival. The rational mind may find either of these alternatives more acceptable, more probable than the possibility that death may be not an immutable certainty, but itself a variable. It may be important to recognize this possibility, since conventional views of death do not seem quite able to encompass all the phenomena that have been described in this book.

Is the medium the message?

We have reviewed recent observations on NDEs and cases suggestive of reincarnation. There is a sizable older literature that explores the survival hypothesis through a different approach. The *medium* is a person who is thought to have an unusual sensitivity to communications from the deceased. Interest in "spiritism" ran high from the middle of the nineteenth century onward. Although in decline during recent decades, interest in reputed communications with the dead has not completely disappeared. Neglect of this topic would leave us with a very incomplete picture of attempts to prove the survival hypothesis. Because more detailed accounts of mediumship and its vicissitudes are readily available,[e.g.,40-42] we will con-

centrate here on a few points of particular relevance.

First, it is important to distinguish between a "high road" and a "low road." There have been repeated exposures of bogus mediums; indeed, "spook sleuths" have enjoyed themselves mightily in uncovering both the out-and-out frauds and the self-deceived.[e.g.,43] The stereotype of the charlatan has gained wide distribution: the unprincipled phony who preys on the sorrows and hopes of the bereaved and the uncritical innocence of the curious. This stereotype is well justified. It does not encompass all the phenomena in this area, however. We will focus, if briefly, on the "high road"—efforts made by people who appeared to have both integrity and critical intelligence.

Earlier it was mentioned that science was viewed with alarm by many of those who cherished traditional values. God's universe with the human's place secure was giving way to an alien, mechanistic conception. The doctrine of an afterlife seemed in particular jeopardy. Some people fought against the inroads of science with the weapons of emotion and scripture. Others decided to bend science's methods to their own use. People of both types joined in the establishment of the British Society for Psychical Research (SPR) in 1882 (still quite alive). Our interest centers on the scholars and scientists in this group. Myers has already been mentioned, a man of prodigious learning in the classics and right up to date in his comprehension of the very new depth-psychology movement. A number of others in the SPR charter group were also learned people with rigorous criteria for evidence. These people differed among themselves in their attitude toward survival, but all were keenly interested in trying to come up with a conclusive answer.

They tried every method that came to mind. A "Census of Hallucinations" was taken (one of the first major public surveys). Personal observations suggestive of communications with the deceased were critically examined, and most were discarded. This left a core of incidents that they believed deserved to be taken more seriously. Myers presented and discussed many of these in his monumental two-volume work, *Human Personality and Its Survival of Bodily Death.*[21] In attempting to explain these phenomena, Myers weighed many alternative possibilities. The books are still a treasure trove for those who seek a starting point in this area. A "spirit photography" approach became popular for a while, but was rather quickly deflated by the prick of multiple criticisms. Of more promise were the relatively new phenomena of automatic writing and trance reception. Automatic writing seemed to be a dissociative state. A person would write rapidly— sometimes amazingly so—and scarcely be aware of this activity either then or later. More interestingly, the writings sometimes seemed to be unrelated to the individual's personality and experience. The thoughts seemed to write themselves down, as messages from some other person, whether living or deceased. A little later more phenomena of the trance type appeared. The individual would appear to go into what these days would be called an altered state of consciousness. In this state there were sometimes the intrusion of thoughts and personalities that appeared alien to the individual.

Serious investigators into the survival hypothesis were fascinated with these phenomena. Here was an improved opportunity to check out possible cases of communication. Automatic writing provided a written text that could be examined at leisure and checked against external data. Trance states could be witnessed and monitored. One could—and did—devise strategies to detect fraud, self-deceit, and other possible influences. The "sensitive" or "medium" became the star—and, in a real sense, the defendant—in survival research proceedings. The life of more than one impressive medium was made miserable by the controls and invasions of privacy demanded by skeptical investigators. A very few of these mediums seemed to survive continuous scrutiny, although criticism was not lacking even in these instances. (The names of Mrs. Leonard and Mrs. Piper are among those that most often are mentioned when one looks for the strongest exemplars of the mediumistic tradition.) Even in the best investigations there is room for question, a situation that has not changed much up to the present. One could choose to be persuaded by the evidence or reject it on the basis either of flaws actually noted or of flaws that might have thus far escaped detection.

There was a particularly interesting variation or intensification of the medium studies that still has not been satisfactorily resolved. Soon after the death of Myers there appeared a series of "communications" that had special characteristics. These communications did not come intact and coherent to any one individual. Instead, they seemed to come in the form of scattered and coded messages—sense could be made only when the various part-messages were collated. Furthermore, the messages seemed to be highly distinctive and specialized. The impression grew that Myers had himself made a postmortem innovation: a research method that would make it clear beyond reasonable doubt that he had communicated to the living. The "cross-correspondences" started in this manner, but became even more complex as various people tried to "interview" Myers, and as the range of both "transmitters" and "receivers" increased somewhat over the years. Saltmarsh[41] has given a fascinating account of cross-correspondence phenomena up to about half a century ago. The phenomena require even more intensive and extensive consideration for thorough evaluation (if only computer technology had been available around the turn of the century!). Lacking a definitive evaluation of cross-correspondence material, other investigators have been suggesting methodologies that embody a similar logic (e.g., a lock whose combination can be solved only through communications from the dead to the living[42]).

The central question—is there survival of death?—was not decisively answered by the first generation of "professional" researchers, nor by their successors. The material they have gathered has enriched our general understanding of psychosocial dynamics, and some of their side observations (e.g., the sensing of "presences" soon after bereavement) have become part of established knowledge. Can the central question *ever* be answered? *Ever* is a long time. The inability to answer the question definitely today on the basis of available knowledge and methodology tells us little about the prospects tomorrow.

Perhaps this is the perfect chapter to conclude with a question: Can we ever stop *asking* the survival question?

SUMMARY

There has been renewed interest lately in the question of survival. This interest has focused around the report of near-death experiences (NDEs) and, to a lesser extent, of cases "suggestive of reincarnation." Reports of both kinds have been interpreted by some people as indicating that there is, in effect, no death. It has been proposed that the NDE represents a transition from life as we know it into another realm of existence. The experiential state is characterized by an unusual sense of well-being. For some people, this experience is assumed to be not just a transition, but an actual "taste" of death.

Recent research into NDEs cautions against accepting such an extreme interpretation. What is termed here the *primary NDE* has a configuration of characteristics that includes the positive emotional state but also such details as the sense of rising, floating, journeying,

and encountering a source of brilliant light. Studies show that primary NDEs are reported with some frequency, but that many people who have close brushes with death do not have such experiences to report. Along with the "non-experiences" there are some people who return as though from a "bad trip." The variability in reports from close encounters does not favor the assumption that these people had indeed been dead. Furthermore, there is no known way to determine what experiences, if any, were had by people who did *not* return. Ten thousand cases of people returning from biological crises with a primary NDE would tell us nothing trustworthy about the experiences of the person who died. Alternative explanations of the primary NDE have been offered. One of these lines of explanation emphasizes the dynamics of depersonalization and hyperalertness, another emphasizes the dynamics of sensory deficit and the release into consciousness of long-submerged memories. It has also been noted that experiences virtually identical to NDEs have occurred to people in circumstances that do not involve any threat to life. These are among the reasons for exercising great caution in reasoning from the NDE to the concepts of death and survival.

There has been much misunderstanding and overinterpretation of the NDE material ever since its introduction by Raymond A. Moody, Jr., in his *Life After Life*. But who recently wrote the following statement?

"In my opinion anyone who claims that near death experiences prove or give scientific evidence of an afterlife is only betraying his ignorance of what terms like evidence or proof mean."[44]

These words were written by Raymond A. Moody, Jr.!

Reincarnation—a doctrine that assumes a radical dualism of body and mind—has long had many adherents around the world. Renewed attention has been given to reincarnation lately, partly as a spread of interest from

NDEs, but partly because of the extensive series of case analyses developed by Ian Stevenson. Typical features of cases "suggestive of reincarnation" are reviewed. It is always possible to suspect fraud or error when confronted with data that have such incredible implications. Stevenson's work, however, is a model of the case-analysis method. It may be in the nature of the material that many people will remain in doubt about the reincarnation hypothesis no matter how carefully such cases are prepared and checked. Nevertheless, the possibility of reincarnation has probably never before been presented so well. Stevenson at least has many of us thinking about this topic more seriously than before. Alternative explanations to phenomena suggesting reincarnation are themselves rather shaky, requiring more assumptions than many researchers are likely to endorse.

In a speculative vein, I have raised the possibility that death might be plural. This notion seems to run counter to our most entrenched assumptions. It is possible, however, that a conception of *pluralistic death* would accommodate available information, with all its apparent diversities and contradictions, better than the usual assumption that death must be the same state (or nonstate) under all circumstances.

Very briefly, we also reviewed an older tradition of research into the survival question. Late in the nineteenth century a number of scientists and scholars attempted to settle the survival question "once and for all" in the face of a mechanistic brand of science that threatened cherished values and concepts. This responsible research effort was distinguished from the rampant commercial quackery that flourished for many years and from the self-deceptions of uncritical dabblers. Particular attention was given to the phenomena of automatic writing and trance states. Much of this material was rejected as nonevidential. There remains, how-

ever, a core of observations that have stood up fairly well to critical scrutiny. Some of these phenomena (such as the "cross-correspondences") have yet to be analyzed fully. Those interested in further studies of the survival question would be well advised to familiarize themselves intensively with this literature, notwithstanding the fact that it has been unfashionable for a long time and is just the sort of thing that induces some people to laughter and scorn at its very mention.

The survival question has not been answered satisfactorily, but there is now an increasing willingness at least to put the question to ourselves.

REFERENCES

1. Evans-Wentz, W. Y. (Ed. & Trans.). *Bardo Thodol, the Tibetan book of the dead.* Oxford England: Oxford University Press, 1960.
2. Gardiner, A. *The attitude of ancient Egyptians to death and the dead.* Cambridge, England: Cambridge University Press, 1935.
3. La Barre, W. *The ghost dance. The origins of religion.* New York: Dell Publishers, 1972.
4. Frazer, J. G. *The fear of the dead in primitive religion.* New York: Arno Press, 1977. (Originally published in 3 volumes, 1933.)
5. Wunderlich, H. G. *The secret of Crete.* New York: Macmillan, Inc., 1974.
6. Reichbart, R. Magic and ESP, *Journal of the American Association for Psychic Research*, 72, 1978.
7. Ellis, H. R. *The Road to Hel.* Westport, Conn.: Greenwood Press, 1968.
8. Moody, R. A., Jr. *Life after life.* Atlanta, Ga.: Mockingbird Press, 1975.
9. Ruderman, S. A personal encounter with death and some consequences. In R. Kastenbaum (Ed.), *Between life and death.* New York: Springer Publishing Co., Inc., 1979, pp. 1-14.
10. Holck, F. H. Life revisited (parallels in death experiences). *Omega*, 1978, 9, 1-12.
11. Garfield, C. A. The dying patient's concern with "life after death." In R. Kastenbaum (Ed.), *Between life and death.* New York: Springer Publishing Co., Inc., 1979, pp. 45-60.
12. Schnaper, N. Comments germane to the paper entitled "the reality of death experiences" by Ernst Rodin. *Journal of Nervous and Mental Disease*, 1980, *168*, 268-270.

13. Kastenbaum, R., & Aisenberg, R. B. *The psychology of death.* New York: Springer Publishing Co., Inc., 1972. (Concise edition published, 1976.)

14. Sabom, M. B., & Kreutziger, S. The experience of near death. *Death Education,* 1977, *2,* 195-204.

15. Ring, K. Some determinants of the prototypic near death experience. Presented at annual meetings of the American Psychological Association, 1978.

16. Ring, K. Religiousness and near-death experiences. Presented at annual meetings of the American Psychological Association, 1979,

17. Osis, K., & Haraldsson, E. *At the hour of death.* New York: Avon Press, 1977.

18. Ring, K. Do suicide survivors report near-death experiences? *Omega* (in press).

19. Thomas, L. E., & Cooper, P. E. Incidence of near-death and intense spiritual experiences in an intergenerational sample: an interpretation. *Omega* (in press).

20. Kastenbaum, R. Happily ever after. In R. Kastenbaum (Ed.), *Between life and death.* New York: Springer Publishing Co., Inc., 1979, pp. 15-29.

21. Myers, F. W. H. *Human personality and its survival of bodily death* (2 vols.). New York: Arno Press, 1975. (Originally published, 1903.)

22. Gurney, E., Podmore, F., & Myers, F. W. H. *Phantasms of the living.* London: Trubner, 1886.

23. Clark, W. H. *Chemical ecstasy: psychedelic drugs and religion.* New York: Sheed & Ward, 1969.

24. LeShan, L. *The medium, the mystic, and the physicist.* New York: Viking Press, 1974.

25. Brent, S. Deliberately induced, premortem out-of-body experiences: an experimental and theoretical approach. In R. Kastenbaum (Ed.), *Between life and death.* New York: Springer Publishing Co., Inc., 1979, pp. 89-123.

26. Noyes, R., Jr., & Kletti, R. Depersonalization in the face of life-threatening danger: a description. *Psychiatry,* 1976, *39,* 19-27.

27. Noyes, R., Jr., & Kletti, R. Depersonalization in the face of life-threatening danger: an interpretation. *Omega,* 1976, *7,* 103-114.

28. Noyes, R., Jr. Near-death experiences: their interpretation. In R. Kastenbaum (Ed.), *Between life and death.* New York: Springer Publishing Co., Inc., 1979, pp. 73-88.

29. Roth, M., & Harper, M. Temporal lobe epilepsy and the phobic anxiety-depersonalization syndrome. Part II: Practical and theoretical considerations. *Comprehensive Psychiatry,* 1962, *3,* 215-226.

30. Siegel, R. K. The psychology of life after death. *American Psychologist,* 1980, *35,* 911-931.

31. Grof, S., & Halifax, J. *The human encounter with death.* New York: Dutton, 1977.

32. Stevenson, I. *Twenty cases suggestive of reincarnation* (rev. ed.). Charlottesville, Va.: University Press of Virginia, 1974.

33. Stevenson, I. *Cases of the reincarnation type. Vol. 1. Ten cases in India.* Charlottesville, Va.: University Press of Virginia, 1975.

34. Stevenson, I. *Cases of the reincarnation type. Vol. 2. Ten cases in Sri Lanka.* Charlottesville, Va.: University Press of Virginia, 1978.

35. Stevenson, I. The "perfect" reincarnation case. In W. G. Roll, R. L. Morris, & J. D. Morris (Eds.), *Research in parapsychology.* Methuchen, N.Y.: Scarecrow Press, 1973, pp. 185-187.

36. Stevenson, I. Reincarnation: field studies and theoretical issues. In B. B. Wolman (Ed.), *Handbook of parapsychology.* New York: Van Nostrand Reinhold Co., 1977, pp. 631-666.

37. Gauld, A. The "Super-ESP" hypothesis. *Proceedings of the Society for Psychical Research,* 1961, *53,* 226-246.

38. Wambach, H. *Life before life.* New York: Bantam Books, 1979.

39. Barber, T. X. *Hypnosis: a scientific approach.* New York: Van Nostrand Reinhold Co., 1969.

40. Douglas, A. *Extra-sensory powers. A century of psychical research.* Woodstock, N.Y.: The Overlook Press, 1977.

41. Saltmarsh, H. F. *Evidence of personal survival from cross correspondences.* New York: Arno Press, 1975. (Originally published, 1938.)

42. Stevenson, I. The combination lock test for survival. *Journal of the American Society for Psychical Research,* 1968, *62,* 246-254.

43. Proskauer, J. *Spook crooks.* London: Selwyn and Blount, 1928.

44. Moody, R. A., Jr. Commentary on "the reality of death experiences: a personal perspective" by Ernst Rodin. *Journal of Nervous and Mental Disease,* 1980, *168,* 265.

CHAPTER 18

❖ DEATH WILL BE

We started this book by drifting in and out of a variety of situations in which our relationship to death had prominence. Let us also conclude in an easy, drifting sort of way. There is no intention here to insist on a fixed set of rules and principles. You will take what you can use from what has been offered.

Since it is the future we will all inhabit, let us impart a little forward motion to our thoughts. The method is simple. We look around and sample some of the phenomena taking place in our own lives and those of our neighbors. What might these phenomena be telling us about our future relationship to death?

HEAT KILLS HENS

As many as one million of the estimated fifteen million egg-laying chickens in New England may have died as a result of last weekend's head wave, according to industry and government spokesmen.[1]

What is interesting about this news item? Big numbers are interesting in themselves. One million . . . have died. The death of two or three chickens would not command notice. Often the death of two or three humans does not command much notice either. Even violent and unexpected deaths are not necessarily considered newsworthy in major metropolitan areas. We do respond to *number*, however. Mass death seems to justify attention. A multiple death by murder or accident will arouse some interest in the media. But if the victims are remote from our own psychosocial worlds, we require more fatalities before attention is given. When thousands die in a natural catastrophe in a distant part of the world, there may be fleeting headlines on page one. The follow-up accounts shrink in size and position in the newspaper, seemingly justified for inclusion at all because there is remaining uncertainty about how many have perished—again, the fascination with numbers.

Really big numbers tend to have a numbing effect though, don't they? Can we truly grasp the millions and billions of dollars spent for armaments? Can we comprehend the millions of civilians systematically killed by Nazi Germany? Both dollars and deaths run into the millions in our own times. The relationship between dollars and deaths often is more intimate than a shared proclivity for magnitude. Come back to the chickens for a moment. What did the newspaper consider interesting or important about one million deaths?

Retail egg prices of $1 a dozen or more for the three largest sizes may be expected throughout the region within two weeks as a result of what were termed unprecedented losses when 100-degree temperatures were recorded, particularly on Saturday.[1]

Our answer is clear. The deaths are important because of the dollars. Notice also that the losses do not pertain to the chickens' loss of their own lives. A chicken's life may not mean very much in the infinite scheme of things, but it is the only life that chicken has. *We,* the buyers, sellers, and egg consumers, take the loss. Perhaps your mind will also drift to the animals who are "sacrificed" by researchers. It is the animal's life; it is the researcher's "sacrifice." This, by the way, is not necessarily an antivivisectionist comment; it is a reaction to the readiness with which some of us translate death of the other into terms of our private interests.

Within the same news item there is additional evidence of the prevailing attitude toward life in our culture's death system. Numbers are consistently important. The temperature was 100 degrees, and, of course, it was *recorded,* as all numbers should be. Many other chickens died as well. These are described as broilers. We do not bat an eye that a living creature is characterized specifically for its function in our death system. It exists to be broiled (a proposition that Descartes might have rendered more elegantly). To be sure, chicken and men are quite different, although both are bipeds with limited life expectancies at best. Yet the culture that brands some chickens broilers and suffers when they perish by the wrong modality also has branded some men cannon fodder in times of war. It is the same mind that interprets both chickens and people, so we should not be terribly surprised if some common attitudes are noted.

The death of chickens is not so trivial an event that it escapes the larger network of social institutions. It energizes a political and economic strategy. "I've hired extra workers to dig pits and bury the dead birds." Obviously, somebody must pay for this expense and for others incurred by the poultry raisers. There was talk of "producers asking for emergency Federal aid, probably in the form of loans at favorable interest rates." In other words, forces

have been set in motion that will affect decisions and policies at several levels within our culture. Whatever else death may be, it is a strong factor in political and economic decisions, most of which are at long remove from the particular deaths themselves.

The future of death in general will have something to do with our ability to comprehend big numbers. Can we relate cognitively and emotionally to large-scale death? Does the threat of nuclear holocaust that could destroy, say, a thousand million people, arouse a response in us that is a thousand million times greater than the prospect of the death of a particular individual? How do we understand and cope with the sheer magnitude of death?

And how do we at the same time relate to the death of an individual as an individual? If a thousand million are to perish, does it matter whether we are talking of chickens or humans? If we cannot *realize* the significance of death with a core of thought, feeling, and value, then are we not at the mercy of the numbers? *What death will be* depends to some extent on our ability to rise to the challenge of comprehending both the universal and the individual aspects of death. This is apt to require a heightened sense of relatedness to deaths that are outside our immediate orbits. In turn, sensitivity to the deaths of others seems to demand a basic recognition that others truly exist. It has been frequently remarked that when a person settles behind the wheel of his automobile, those in other cars are seen as something less than humans—Fords, VWs, Buicks, Datsuns, not people. The bombardier's perspective does not face him with the sight of living men, women, and children who may presently be slaughtered by his action.

How deep can our sense of affinity with other humans go? How broadly can it be cast? The answers to questions such as these will do much to determine the future of death.

CAR HIT BY STOLEN VEHICLE, DRIVER DIES

One man was killed shortly after 1:15 this morning when his car crashed into a pole beside Rte. 9 in Newton after being rammed by a stolen car Needham police had chased unsuccessfully a few minutes earlier.[2]

This event's implication for our death system is self-interpreting when a few follow-up statements are added.

YOUNG VICTIM'S FRIENDS BITTER AT CAR CHASE DEATH

The friends of Bruce Randall, 25, of Jamaica Plain are sad they have lost him, but, more than that, they are angry—angry at the senseless way he died.

"I'd like to see an issue made out of that chase," Debora Booth, 27, his girl friend of the last three years, declared. "The police have no business chasing anyone at 100 m.p.h. to get back a stolen car. It's not worth it."[3]

Ironically, Randall had been out late because his car had accidentally struck a cat in the road. He had stopped to pick up the cat and bring it to a veterinarian, thereby delaying him enroute to a friend's house.

POLICE OFFICIALS QUESTION HIGH-SPEED AUTO CHASE POLICIES

To chase or not to chase—that has become an increasingly difficult question for Greater Boston police departments in the wake of at least four accidents involving high-speed pursuit of cars by police cruisers during the last 10 days.[4]

The article revealed concern about where to draw the line between essential and nonessential high-speed pursuit. This may be the same line that has to be drawn between property and human life. I have seen a security officer stand with a pistol in his hand on a crowded city street because an armored car was transferring funds—an invitation to accident or incident.

You have seen in your own life many examples of conflicts between priorities. *What death will be* depends on our priorities for life and what we are willing to do in support of these priorities.

TOWN GIVES PROPER BURIAL TO A 16TH CENTURY INDIAN

Wellfleet—An increasing concern for the traditions and feelings of native Americans led yesterday to the reburying of the remains of a Wampanoag woman discovered during a house excavation in Wellfleet in 1953.

The remains had been on display at the Wellfleet Historical Society.[5]

The meaning of death is not easily separated from the meaning of the dead. The news item reports a reconsideration of the social meaning of a long-deceased person. In the meantime our culture is in process of making changes in its practices and attitudes toward the dead, toward funerals, and toward memorialization in general. It is possible that decades or centuries from now somebody will rectify errors that we make in the process. That would of course be too late for those who had been affected by insensitive dealings with the dead. *What death will be* depends to some extent on our success in discovering what we really think, feel, and need today. Yesterday's orientation toward the dead may no longer meet our needs—but are we developing a new orientation from secure contact with our feelings or from external pressures and expediencies?

BUS CRASH VICTIM'S HEART BEATS—IN ANOTHER PERSON

Concord, Calif.—One of the young victims of last week's school bus tragedy has—in death—given life to another person.

The heart of 15-year-old Donald Wright has been transplanted in a 33-year-old man at Stanford University Medical Center.[6]

HOSPITAL SOLD INFANT ORGANS TO FIRMS WITHOUT
PARENTS' CONSENT

Washington—For the past decade, the D.C.
General Hospital pathology department here has received payments from private firms for supplying
them with organs removed from stillborn and dead
premature babies after autopsy, a *Washington Post*
investigation has revealed. . . .

. . . District law, which forbids the sale or traf-
ficking of whole human bodies, is vague about the
sale of individual organs removed from bodies.[7]

The future is already here in one sense. The
recycling of human anatomy may have its star-
tling and widespread implications yet to come,
but organ transplants have already entered our
death system at many levels. The two news
items just cited suggest two sides to the picture. Which side will dominate in the future?

Do we have the wisdom to use organ transplants—and whatever technologic innovations
may be made in the future—in the service of
life and our higher values? Or will new developments quickly be warped to fit into already
existing patterns of thought and behavior?
What death will be depends much on our ability to escape the habitual and the petty in our
culture.

It is possible that we will be overwhelmed
by dramatic innovations and advances at the
frontiers of dying and death. It is also possible
that we will be slowly but insistently transformed by small changes. In either case, we
may fail to exercise options that remain to us
between "now" and "then." Awareness and
concern at the present moment come none too
soon.

And yet it is also possible that death will be
in the future essentially what it is now, that
each individual will still have to come to terms
with personal and universal mortality. Expecting the ancient human concerns with death to
disappear miraculously because of break-
throughs in science or technology may be an
exercise in naivete. Today's life is preparation
for tomorrow's death, as so many have recognized throughout the centuries. We are in
rather good company, you know.

REFERENCES

1. Heat kills hens. *Boston Globe*, August 5, 1975.
2. Martin, Richard. Car hit by stolen vehicle, driver dies.
   Boston Globe, June 22, 1976.
3. Longcope, Kay. Young victim's friends bitter at car
   chase death. *Boston Globe*, June 24, 1976.
4. Pilati, Joe. Police officials question high-speed auto
   chase policies. *Boston Globe*, November 18, 1975.
5. Town gives proper burial to a 16th century Indian. *Boston Globe*, May 31, 1976.
6. Bus crash victim's heart beats—in another person. *Boston Globe*, May 29, 1976.
7. Colen, B. D. Hospital sold infant organs to firms without parents' consent. *Boston Globe*, February 15, 1976.

❖ SUGGESTED READINGS

This list of suggested readings includes a number of useful books that were not cited in the text, as well as some previously mentioned.

Additionally, current research, theory and practice are reported in *Omega, Journal of Dying and Death* (Baywood Publishing Co., 120 Marine Street, Farmingdale, N.Y. 11735). Material relevant to self-destructive behavior and suicide prevention is reported in *Suicide,* the official publication of the American Association of Suicidology (Behavioral Publications, Inc., 2852 Broadway–Morningside Heights, New York, N.Y. 10025).

Alsop, S. *Stay of execution.* Philadelphia: J. B. Lippincott Co., 1973.

Alvarez, A. *The savage god.* New York: Random House, Inc., 1972.

Anthony, S. *The discovery of death in childhood and after.* New York: Basic Books, Inc., 1972.

Aries, P. *Western attitudes toward death.* Baltimore: The Johns Hopkins University Press, 1974.

Becker, E. *The denial of death.* New York: The Free Press, 1973.

Brim, et al. (Eds.). *The dying patient.* New York: Russell Sage Foundation, 1970.

Burton, L. (Ed.). *Care of the child facing death.* London: Routledge & Kegal Paul, 1974.

Cartwright, A., Hockey, L., & Anderson, J. L. *Life before death.* London: Routledge & Kegan Paul, 1973.

Choron, J. *Death and Western thought.* New York: Collier Books, 1963.

Choron, J. *Suicide.* New York: Charles Scribner's Sons, 1972.

Crane, D. *The sanctity of social life: physicians' treatment of critically ill patients.* New York: Russell Sage Foundation, 1975.

Des Pres, T. *The survivor.* New York: Pocketbooks, 1977.

Eliade, M. *Death, afterlife and eschatology.* New York: Harper & Row, Publishers, 1967.

Farberow, N. L. (Ed.). *The many faces of suicide.* New York: McGraw-Hill Book Co., 1980.

Farberow, N. L., & Shneidman, E. S. (Eds.). *The cry for help.* New York: McGraw-Hill Book Co., 1965.

Feifel, H. (Ed.). *The meaning of death.* New York: McGraw-Hill Book Co., 1959.

Feifel, H. (Ed.). *New meanings of death.* New York: McGraw-Hill Book Co., 1977.

Feigenberg, L. *Terminal care: friendship contracts with dying cancer patients.* New York: Brunner/Mazel, 1980.

Furman, E. *A child's parent dies: studies in childhood bereavement.* New Haven, Conn.: Yale University Press, 1974.

Garfield, C. A. (Ed.). *Psychosocial care of the dying patient.* New York: McGraw-Hill Book Co., 1978.

Glaser, B., & Strauss, A. L. *Awareness of dying.* Chicago: Aldine Publishing Co., 1966.

Glaser, B. & Strauss, A. L. *Time for dying.* Chicago: Aldine Publishing Co., 1967.

Grof, S., & Halifax, J. *The human encounter with death.* New York: Dutton, 1977.

Grollman, E. (Ed.). *Explaining death to children.* Boston: Beacon Press, 1967.

Gruman, G. J. *A history of ideas about the prolongation of life.* New York: Arno Press, 1977. (Originally published, 1963.)

Gunther, J. *Death be not proud.* New York: Harper & Row, Publishers, 1965.

Hagglund, T-B. *Dying. A psychoanalytic study with special reference to individual creativity and defensive organization.* New York: International Universities Press, 1978.

Harrington, A. *The immortalist.* New York: Random House, Inc., 1969.

Hinton, J. *Dying.* Penguin Books, 1967.

Hocking, W. E. *The meaning of immortality in human experience.* New York: Harper & Brothers, 1957.

Irion, P. *Cremation.* Philadelphia: Fortress Press, 1968.

Irion, P. *The funeral: vestige or value?* Nashville, Tenn.: Abingdon Press, 1966.

Kastenbaum, R. (Ed.). *Between life and death*. New York: Springer Publishing Co., Inc., 1979.

Kastenbaum, R., & Aisenberg, R. B. *The psychology of death*. New York: Springer Publishing Co., Inc., 1972.

Kubler-Ross, E. *On death and dying*. New York: Macmillan, Inc., 1969.

Lamm, M. *The Jewish way in death & mourning*. New York: Jonathan David Publishers, Inc., 1969.

Lamont, C. *The illusion of immortality*. New York: Philosophical Library, Inc., 1950.

LaPlanche, J. *Life and death in psychoanalysis*. Baltimore: Johns Hopkins University Press, 1976.

Lee, J. Y. *Death and beyond in the Eastern perspective*. New York: Gorden & Breach, Science Publishers, Inc., 1974.

Levy, N. B. *Living or dying: adaptation to hemodialysis*. Springfield, Ill.: Charles C Thomas, 1974.

Lifton, R. L. *Death in life: survivors of Hiroshima*. New York: Random House, Inc., 1974.

Mack, A. (Ed.). *Death in American experience*. New York: Schocken Books, Inc., 1973.

Maguire, D. *Death by choice*. New York: Doubleday and Co., Inc., 1974.

Parkes, C. M. *Bereavement: studies of grief in adult life*. New York: International Universities Press, 1973.

Pearson, L. S. (Ed.). *Death and dying: current issues in the treatment of the dying person*. Cleveland: Case Western Reserve University Press, 1969.

Pincus, L. *Death and the family*. New York: Pantheon Books, Inc., 1974.

Pine, V. *Caretaker of the dead*. New York: Irvington Publishers, Inc., 1975.

Rahner, K. *On the theology of death*. New York: Herder & Herder, 1961.

Ring, K. *Life at death*. New York: Coward, McCann & Geoghegan, Inc., 1980.

Schoenberg, B., et al. (Eds.). *Loss and grief*. New York: Columbia University Press, 1970.

Shneidman, E. S. *Voices of death*. New York: Harper & Row, Publishers, 1980.

Shneidman, E. S. *The deaths of man*. New York: Quadrangle/The New York Times Book Co., 1973.

Shneidman, E. S. (Ed.). *Suicidology: current developments*. New York: Grune & Stratton, Inc., 1976.

Switzer, D. K. *Dynamics of grief: its sources, pain and healing*. Nashville, Tenn.: Abingdon Press, 1970.

Tolstoy, L. *The death of Ivan Ilych*. New York: The New American Library, Inc., 1960. (Originally published, 1886.)

Toynbee, A. (Ed.). *Man's concern with death*. New York: McGraw-Hill Book Co., 1968.

Troup, S. B., & Greene, W. A. *The patient, death and the family*. New York: Charles Scribner's Sons, 1974.

Wallis, C. L. *Stories on stone*. London: Oxford University Press, 1954.

Weisman, A. D. *Death and denial*. New York: Behavioral Publications, Inc., 1972.

Weisman, A. D., & Kastenbaum, R. *The psychological autopsy: a study of the terminal phase of life*. New York: Behavioral Publications, Inc., 1968.

Wertenbaker, L. T. *Death of a man*. New York: Random House, Inc., 1957.

❖ INDEX